Bonefishing!

Bonefishing!

By Randall Kaufmann

Photography—Brian O'Keefe

Illustrations—Mike Stidham

Western Fisherman's Press
2000

Books By
Randall Kaufmann

American Nymph Fly Tying Manual
Lake Fishing With a Fly
The Fly Tyers Nymph Manual
Tying Dry Flies
Bonefishing With a Fly
Tying Nymphs
Tying Dry Flies, Revised Edition
Fly Patterns Of Umpqua Feather Merchants
Fly Patterns Of Umpqua Feather Merchants, Second Edition
Tying Nymphs, Second Edition
Tying Dry Flies, Third Edition
Tying Nymphs, Third Edition
Fly Fishing Made Easy For Beginners
Fly Fishing Made Easy

Library of Congress Catalog Card Number: 98-060933

International Standard Book Number: 1-885212-13-5

Printed in Thailand
10 9 8 7 6 5 4 3 2

Published by
Western Fisherman's Press
P.O. Box 357
Moose, Wyoming 83012
E-Mail: westernfishermanspress@comcast.net
www.westernfishermanspress.com
Phone: 971-235-8390
Fax: 866-859-9592

Cover photos by Brian O'Keefe
Page i: Randall Kaufmann, North Andros, Bahamas.
Page ii-iii: Randall Kaufmann, North Abaco, Bahamas
All photos by Brian O'Keefe unless otherwise credited.
Artwork photography by Tony Capone.
Studio photography by Randall Kaufmann.
Editors: Bob Rector, Ian Templeton.
Typesetting, copy editing, and design by Joyce Sherman, River Graphics.

Contributors

Randall Kaufmann is an international expert on flies, fly tying, and fly fishing and is the author of several books on the subject, incuding *Tying Dry Flies* and *Tying Nymphs*. His book, *Bonefishing with a Fly*, published in 1992, was the first book on the subject. Randall has been fishing the flats for bonefish, designing bonefish flies, and researching the world of bonefish for 30 years. He is a founder and past co-owner of Kaufmanns' Streamborn, Inc. Randall lives in Jackson Hole, Wyoming, with his wife Mary, where he continues his writing, research, music, photography, backpacking, fly tying, fly fishing, and outdoor adventures. Randall can be reached at randall.kaufmann@comcast.net or via www.randallkaufmann.com.

Brian O'Keefe is a free-lance adventure photographer and fishing tackle manufacturers' representative living in Powell Butte, Oregon. Brian has traveled from Africa to Alaska and throughout the Pacific, Atlantic, Indian, and Caribbean oceans exploring off-the-beaten-track angling locations with fly rod and camera. He has pioneered more bonefish waters than most anglers have fished. Brian put some areas of Belize on the fly fishing map and was one of the first to photograph and report on Los Roques, Yucatan, Tonga, Seychelles, and the Marshall Islands. He has explored most places in the Bahamas. Brian's work has appeared in books, calendars, catalogs, and all major outdoor magazines. His fly fishing slide show-lectures are legendary. Brian can be reached via www.brianokeefephotos.com.

Photography Notes: Brian's images were exposed using Velvia film, polarizing filters, and Canon and Nikonos cameras. Photos are unaltered and all are accurately identified. Every effort has been made to handle and photograph fish properly. Some of the fish photos are hero shots, anglers posing with fish. Most are held low over the water or at water level. Fish should never be brought into the boat or held in an unnatural manner. Remember, you don't need a photo of every fish. When photographing fish, set up everything in advance. When displaying fish at or above the water's surface, support them underneath with one hand and hold their tail with the other. *Keep them in or close to the water!* In the water and underwater photos are best.

Mike Stidham is one of the world's pre-eminent angler-artists, specializing in oils but equally comfortable with watercolor and pencil. His commissioned oils are highly prized by collectors, and his work appears in exclusive western galleries. His favorite subjects are bonefish, permit, and tarpon. Mike has illustrated several books. He has guided and fished throughout North America and the Pacific and Caribbean oceans. Mike lives in Sandy, Utah, and can be reached at (801) 942-0758.

For Mary, with love

Contents

Acknowledgements

Brian O'Keefe for the hundreds of stunningly beautiful photographs that made this book possible. Sorting through Brian's one-of-a-kind collection was as exciting as spotting tailing bonefish...well, almost! Hundreds of his images begged, "Pick me!" I couldn't decide so I picked them all. In addition, thank you for the adventures, for pioneering far-off destinations, and for bringing the beauty and thrill of bonefishing to so many anglers.

Mike Stidham for the fabulous acrylics and illustrations.

Joyce Sherman for typesetting, layout, design, editing, advice, and encouragement. Barry Garriety for typesetting and for scanning hundreds of photos.

Bob Rector and Ian Templeton for editing and attention to detail.

Contributing writers: Tim Borski, Paul Bruun, Buck Buchenroth, Yvon Chouinard, Jon Covich, Ralph Cutter, John Ecklund, Kevin Erickson, Doug Jorgensen, Lance Kaufmann, Gordon Nash, Brian O'Keefe, Ed Opler, John Randolph, and Jerry Swanson. Special thanks to R. Valentine Atkinson for the piece on Kanton Island and to Buck Buchenroth for the concise analysis of Little Cayman.

Contributing photographers: Bernie Baker, Paul Bruun, Jon Covich, Ralph and Lisa Cutter, Steve DeMoulin, John Ecklund, Mary Kaufmann, John Hull, Richard Humphrey, Lance Kaufmann, Bill Klyne, Captain Tom Rowland, Jerry Swanson, and Rick Williams. Special thanks to R.Valentine Atkinson for the beautiful Kanton Island photos.

The guides and lodge owners who provided information and insight, and helped make our visits successful, including: Alaska Sea Coast Adventures, Andros Island Bonefish Club, Belize River Lodge, Cargill Creek, Carlos Vega Guide Service, Casa Blanca, Cuzan Guest House, Deep Water Cay Club, El Pescador, Fernandez Bay Village, Frontiers International, Peace and Plenty, Pelican Bay, Pete and Gay Guest House, Robert Reimer's Enterprises, Southern Cross Club, Stella Maris Inn, Tortuga Lodge, and Turneffe Flats Lodge.

Tony Capone for studio photography. Jack Dennis for ideas and encouragement. Jim Kenyon for fly line specifics. Bill Klyne for Cuba insights. Craig Mathews for fly pattern and Belize fishing insight. For reviewing the manuscript: Kevin Erickson, Gordon Nash, Brian O'Keefe, David J. Pokorny, M.D., and Jerry Swanson.

Ken Mitchell for printing, press check, and design advice.

My brother, Lance and mother, Oda Kaufmann for keeping our business running smoothly during my absence.

The many authors, writers, biologists, and fly innovators whose works I have drawn upon.

Most important of all, you the angling reader, who ultimately makes it possible for Brian, Mike, and myself to delve into the wonderfully fascinating and magical world of bonefishing. May you receive as much pleasure and enjoyment from reading this book as we did assembling it. Thank you, everyone, very much.

Introduction

Calf deep in 80-degree water, I scan the tropical sand flat intently for signs of bonefish: a glistening tail or any slight surface disturbance or underwater movement. Moving cautiously, I become attuned to my remote surroundings. Powdery sand swirls and slowly drifts toward shore, indicating an incoming tide. Frequent pauses allow me to savor the watery wilderness, which seems to extend to infinity. Vivid tropical colors that, depending on water depth, range from misty tan to indigo blue dazzle my senses. A slight breeze sways the coconut palms that line the deserted beach, and no one else is within sight. Paradise? Perhaps.

Within a few minutes the mid-morning sun reflects metallic silver off the unmistakable upended tails of three feeding bonefish. In the shimmering light they look like transparent 3-D holograms suspended in air. They are 100 feet away, moving steadily in my direction. Quickly assessing the situation, I position myself for the best presentation. When they are within 40 feet, I cast to the lead fish, wait for the fly to settle to the bottom, and give it a slight twitch. The bonefish rushes to the offering, tips down, and inhales the fly. I tighten up on the fish.

Upon feeling resistance, the bonefish panics. It bolts in terror, instantly peeling most of the backing from my reel. I am amazed at its strength and quickness. After a 100-yard straight-away run, it suddenly turns and rushes directly toward me. I frantically strip in fly line, letting it fall about my feet. As the fish nears my position, it zooms away, literally tearing line through the guides.

I chuckle, point the rod tip at the fish, clear the line, and continue the battle.

Fish should be landed quickly before they become exhausted, so I apply maximum pressure on the 8-weight tackle and 01X tippet. Soon the beautiful silvery "ghost" fish is at my feet. Keeping the bonefish in the water and not handling it, I gently back out the barbless fly. The bonefish is in good shape, and it swims away. Following its movement, I make a mental note of its color pattern. The next fish will be easier to spot.

I check my leader, knot, and fly. All is well. I glance back at the untrodden beach and the beautiful clear water about my feet and s-l-o-w d-o-w-n. A frigate bird soars effortlessly and quietly overhead. The sound of the surf crashing on the distant reef is barely audible. The surf is visible only as an indefinite white line on the horizon. The 80-degree surroundings send forth a feeling of tranquillity, yet there is the unmistakable aura of excitement and danger. I scan the water's surface and suddenly see more bonefish at two o'clock, coming my way!

Bonefish are not the only quarry. Startling situations and angling opportunities can appear, disappear, and reappear before you comprehend what is happening. An unseen barracuda rushes from a depression and instantly slices your bonefish in half at your

Few places on earth are as intoxicating as bonefish flats. The surreal landscape consists of layer upon layer of unimaginable colors, textures, and life forms. All the precious colors are represented—amethyst, turquoise, emerald, and opal. Textures range between razor sharp coral and slippery water. Life is bizarre—flying fish and sea horses. The tropics have captured the imagination of countless authors, scientists, naturalists, painters, photographers, and anglers. Experience the dream.

feet! Before you can gather your wits, the 'cuda has circled, finished off the second half, and settled into a pool of aqua water. You contemplate the basic ocean rule—if you slow down, something bigger and faster eats you. Indeed, bonefish have only two concerns when on the flats—eating and not being eaten.

A school of 10,000, perhaps 50,000, tiny baitfish explodes into the air, wheeling like birds in perfect synchronization, reflecting a million iridescent silver-green sunbeams. You are mesmerized by the blinding aerial display and are held hostage in a time-lapse hallucination of motion and color. Before you can toss a fly into their frantic midst, the petrified fish have somersaulted out of sight and raced on to invisibility. What caused such panic? Was it an unseen school of rampaging trevally or marauding jacks or a pair of 80-pound tarpon?

When fishing saltwater flats, you experience a heightened awareness of yourself and your surroundings. The seemingly casual yet dangerous pace of life is a puzzling paradox. The vastness and power of nature forces you to contemplate your insignificance.

Bonefish are splendidly designed to feed on bottom organisms in extremely shallow saltwater environs. Remarkable eyesight, acute sense of hearing and smell, and hyper speed are their main survival mechanisms. Bonefish are also masters at disguise and blend amazingly well into their transparent, skinny water habitat. Their

mysterious unseen presence constantly befuddles anglers. A bonefish mirage can suddenly transform into reality and just as quickly dissolve into illusion. Bonefish are indeed phantoms of the flats.

Bonefish have congenial personalities. Unless you are an organism selected for a meal, you would describe bonefish as playful yet serious, suspicious yet trustful, cautious yet curious, aggressive yet gentle. There are bigger, meaner, and more exotic fish in the sea, but the magnificent and elegant bonefish has captured the imagination of anglers everywhere, amassing converts with every fly rod they bend.

Bonefish are plentiful and readily engage anglers in matchless sport, but they are not so easily duped as to cause boredom. Quite the contrary: unskilled anglers could stumble over a school and not see them or present their fly improperly and go fishless. Bonefish are, however, usually cooperative and provide anglers with the most thrilling shallow-water fly fishing to be found.

When hooked, their attempts to escape are awesome. First-time bonefish anglers have difficulty comprehending what a medium-sized five-pound bonefish can do to them and their tackle. Even veteran anglers are continually astonished at the strength and speed at which bonefish move. Every fish commands awe and respect.

Fly fishing for bonefish is not difficult. It does not require mythical prowess or exceptional angling skills. Bonefishing often reminds anglers of lake, river, spring creek, and surf fishing. In lakes, fish move, and water does not. In streams, water moves, and fish do not. On saltwater flats, both fish *and* water move. It is much less complicated and technical than fly fishing for trout.

Lake anglers relate to the broad expanse of shallow water. Presenting a fly to tailing bonefish is similar to presenting a fly to a trout patrolling a particular "beat." When bonefish flats are glassy calm and bonefish are spooky and selective, the toughest spring creek conditions come to mind. Sometimes tidal flux creates the sensation of rivers with the addition of line-cutting coral and sharks! At other places, surf pounds the reef and waves wash past (sometimes nearly over!) you, much like striper fishing. Like trout fishing in New Zealand, bonefishing is as much hunting and stalking as fishing. You see it all happen—the presentation, the take or refusal, the hookup, and the exit run.

Bonefishing offers everything freshwater fishing does plus the added dimension and extremes found in saltwater environments, including the bonus of other species that feed with and on bonefish!

Everything in bonefish country bombards the senses, and you become completely mesmerized by the intensity of life and surreal colors. Experiencing the expansive flats wilderness is like living behind a fish-eye lens. One's view of the world is enhanced, yet distance and possibility are distorted. Anglers soon dissolve into both water and air and forget that they cannot fly or swim in this environment. Bonefishing heightens the imagination, alters the senses, and enthralls the spirit.

Bonefishing is a game of stealth and unrivaled visuals. Indeed, *visuals are the single most captivating aspect of bonefishing.* Anglers who have yet to experience the hunt, stalk, and electrifying pull of a bonefish still have the best to look forward to.

Distribution

Bonefish inhabit some of the most beautiful ocean waters on Earth. They are present in all tropical and semitropical waters between, roughly, 30 degrees north and 30 degrees south of the equator. In the Pacific, they are found from Mazatlan and Acapulco, Mexico, south to Panama and west to Australia. In the Atlantic, they exist from Bermuda south to Brazil and east to Africa. Bonefish are also known throughout the Indian Ocean and have been documented in the Red Sea.

In the Pacific, the most developed and consistent bonefishing is at Christmas Island, about 1,200 miles south of Hawaii. Bonefish can be found throughout the Cook and Caroline islands and French Polynesia. I have observed them for sale in fish markets throughout Tahiti. Occasionally, anglers fly fish for them on the outer reefs and remote sand flats. Visitors to the Tahiti atolls should consider packing a fly rod. Classic flats habitat is almost nonexistent there, but reef fishing is easily accessed. Hire a boat to reach the reef and begin your search. If bonefish are scarce, a multitude of other species is available. These islands are some of the most beautiful on earth.

The Marshall Islands, including remote Bikini Atoll, offer bonefish plus myriad other species that were heretofore mostly unknown to fly rodders. Bonefish are not abundant everywhere in the South Pacific; they are uncommon in Fiji.

Anglers in search of remote South Sea bonefish waters can go by sailboat or book passage on any number of freighters or barges traveling remote waters. Such trips, by the way, are not for the

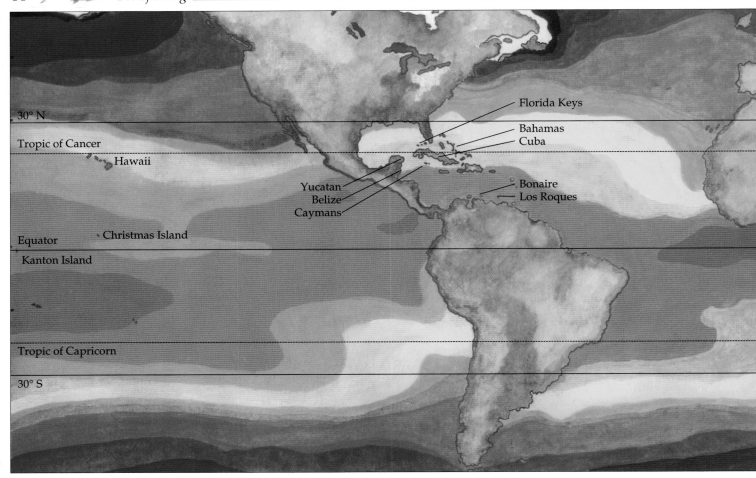

30° N

Tropic of Cancer

Hawaii

Florida Keys

Bahamas
Cuba

Yucatan
Belize
Caymans

Bonaire
Los Roques

Equator　Christmas Island

Kanton Island

Tropic of Capricorn

30° S

Bonefish anglers have increased dramatically in number during the past decade. Today, anglers seek bonefish in the Atlantic, Caribbean, Indian, and Pacific oceans. Boats are usually used to access flats. Anglers either fish from a poled boat or on foot. John Hull found this bonefish in shallow water wading near Honolulu, Hawaii.

Rick Williams

faint-hearted, queasy, or modest. You often eat and sleep on an open deck never far from diesel fumes and saltwater spray.

Bonefish are common in the Hawaiian Islands, but shallow-water habitat is scarce. An occasional fish is hooked in shallow areas near Honolulu, Oahu; Hana, Maui; Kaunakakai, Molokai; Kona, Hawaii; Princeville, Kauai; and off the north coast of Lanai. I recently heard of an 11 pounder landed on Molokai and of several five and six pounders from the waters near Honolulu. Lucky and clever anglers have success in Hawaii, but there is a far better chance of success casting poppers for trevally that cruise the rocky shoreline. Nevertheless, pack a picnic, snorkel, camera, and fly rod and do some scouting. A good time is guaranteed.

In Australia, bonefish range the length of the Queensland coastline and out to the Barrier Reef. Most bonefish in Australia are taken incidentally by bait and commercial fishermen. Fly fishing the shallow areas in Australia is mostly an unknown sport. There is plenty of water to explore!

The Indian Ocean offers a scattering of bonefishing. Bonefish are present at Christmas Island (there are two) and at the Cocos Islands off the southwest coast of Indonesia. The Maldives offer beautiful flats habitat, and bonefish are said to be present, but my scouts were unable to locate any. The Seychelles seem to offer the best bonefishing in the Indian Ocean.

In the western North Atlantic, bonefish are common in the Florida Keys, mostly from Key Biscayne south. The Bahamas offer excellent bonefish grounds. Bonefish are available in Bermuda

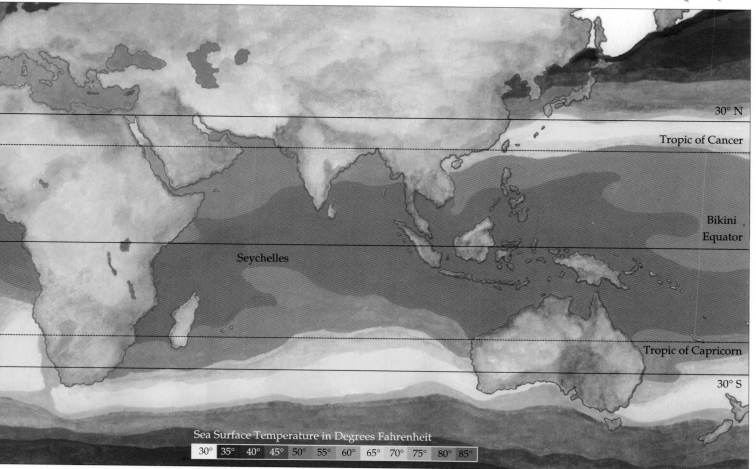

30° N

Tropic of Cancer

Bikini
Equator

Seychelles

Tropic of Capricorn

30° S

Sea Surface Temperature in Degrees Fahrenheit

| 30° | 35° | 40° | 45° | 50° | 55° | 60° | 65° | 70° | 75° | 80° | 85° |

during the warm summer months. Anglers are again enjoying excellent sport in Cuba after being restricted from this island since the 1950s. Bonefish are also common from the Yucatan, Mexico, south to Belize and Honduras, where many flats and reefs offer excellent sport.

While bonefish probably inhabit most of the Caribbean, limited shallow water makes them much less visible and available to fly anglers. Puerto Rico and the West Indies south and east to the Lesser Antilles support bonefish populations in selected areas. They are common at Little Cayman, Turks and Caicos Islands, Anegada in the British Virgin Islands, Aruba, Bonaire, and Los Roques, Venezuela. They are uncommon in Jamaica, Haiti, and Barbados.

Bonefish probably have been consumed since early tropical man first appeared. Natives of the Caribbean captured them during Columbus' time. Today, natives still consume bonefish, and they are considered a prized delicacy in many locations.

A few countries have recognized the recreational value of bonefish and have banned netting, but locals often poach them whenever they can. Belize has a netting ban on bonefish, but piracy stories abound in the out islands and cays (pronounced "keys").

The Bahamas government recognizes the value bonefish bring to the islands and has made netting a crime. Reportedly, offenders are sentenced to six months in jail. A bonefish is worth $10 to $30 on the local black market and is considered a delicacy. Fish can be consumed legally if caught with a hand line or with a rod and reel,

The bonefish "zone" encircles the earth and is roughly between 30 degrees north and 30 degrees south of the equator. Bonefish are common throughout this zone and inhabit both shallow and deep water. Fly anglers require shallow water habitat to spot and present their fly to bonefish. The popular bonefish areas frequented by anglers are shown on this map, but anglers may encounter bonefish anywhere that suitable conditions and shallow-water habitat is found.
Ocean currents and water temperatures vary according to seasons.

but not by net. Anglers are often requested by locals, especially ladies, to bring them a bonefish. Poaching is common at undeveloped locations. Anglers visiting the Bahamas may be interested in the 10-cent coin that pictures a bonefish.

Because bonefish travel shallow contour lines, they are easy to net in large quantities. A single net can wipe out an entire school. A thousand dead bonefish bring a few dollars into the local economy once. A thousand live bonefish bring thousands of dollars into the local economy week after week, month after month, year after year. It doesn't take a master's degree in economics to pencil it out. With the growing popularity of bonefishing, several countries are sitting on an unrecognized treasure. Accommodations and access are all that is necessary.

Bonefish live in some of the most beautiful waters on Earth. Walking through the liquid colors is reason enough for being there. This enchanting scene is in the Bahamas.

Chapter 2

Angling History

George Sand, author of *Saltwater Fly Fishing,* reports that British anglers were hooking "bony" fish weighing up to 15 pounds in the Indian Ocean along the coast of Africa around 1900. Stanley Babson, author of the book *Bonefishing,* published in 1965, wrote that the first bonefish to be landed with rod and reel in America was caught in the Florida Keys in 1891 by J. P. McFerran of Louisville, Kentucky. The account was published in "Where, When and How To Catch Fish On the East Coast of Florida" in 1902. McFerran, writing to the author of the article, W. H. Gregg, closed his letter with these words: "I verily believe that, pound for pound, the Bonefish is, far and away, the King of all swimmers and the only objection I can urge against him is that an experience with him disqualifies one for all other fishing." Babson also reported that the first bonefish taken on a fly was by accident in 1924 when Holmes Allen of Miami accidentally landed one while fly fishing for snapper in the Florida Keys.

In 1926, Colonel L. S. Thompson of Red Bank, New Jersey, was fishing in Florida at the Long Key Fishing Club with veteran bonefish guide T. J. Harrod. They were fishing with bait in the orthodox manner. When the bonefishing fell off, Thompson got out his fly rod, put on a size 6 Royal Coachman, and cast for baby tarpon. He caught some bonefish but considered it an accident. Florida guide Captain Bill Smith is credited with intentionally hooking and landing the first bonefish on a fly near Islamorada in 1939. The legendary Joe Brooks believed he was the first angler to *deliberately*

hook a *tailing* bonefish with a fly, which he did while guided by Captain Jimmy Albright at Islamorada in June 1947. Bonefishing with a fly was born.

The all-tackle world record bonefish weighed 19 pounds and was inadvertently caught in Zululand, South Africa, by Brian W. Batchelor on May 26, 1962. Bonefish over 20 pounds sometimes enter the commercial markets in Mozambique. An 18-pound 2-ounce specimen was landed at Kauai, Hawaii, on October 14, 1954, and a 17-pound 8-ounce fish was caught at Oahu, Hawaii, on August 23, 1952. On the average, bonefish run three to seven pounds. This size range is found at most locations. Larger bonefish are common to 10 pounds, and 15-pound fish are occasionally hooked but seldom landed.

During the last 80 years, bonefishing has captured the imagination of many famous anglers. Zane Grey, who was president of the Long Key Fishing Club in Florida (built in 1906 and demolished by the hurricane of 1935), became so addicted to bonefishing that in his story, "The Bonefish Brigade," the skillful storyteller was at a loss to describe bonefishing. He wrote, "I have never been able to tell why it seems the fullest, the most difficult, the strangest and most thrilling, the most lonesome and most satisfying of all kinds of angling."

After joining the Long Key Fishing Club, George LaBranche, author of dry fly classics *The Dry Fly In Fast Water* (1914) and *The Salmon and the Dry Fly* (1924), abandoned his rivers to pursue bonefish exclusively. President Herbert Hoover, humorist Irvin S. Cobb, and fishing experts Van Campen Heilner, John Alden Knight, and Joe Brooks found bonefish an obsession, dictating a lifestyle that included buying second homes in the Florida Keys and Bahamas.

Fly fishermen who have not hooked bonefish cannot understand how a five-pound fish can cause so much excitement. A five-pound bonefish will act like nothing you have ever caught in fresh water. Don't underestimate the speed and power of these fish. Pound for pound, few fish can compare. A rainbow or brown trout attains a burst speed of up to about five miles per hour, steelhead and Atlantic salmon about twice that. Bonefish clock in between 20 and 30 miles per hour, and they keep going long after the competition has quit. They do it in *15 inches of calm water.* If they swam in rivers, we would never land them!

Today there are tens of thousands of bonefish anglers and dozens of specialized fishing lodges catering to bonefishermen. The list of famous bonefish aficionados who frequent bonefish flats includes Tom Brokaw, Jimmy Buffett, Yvon Chouinard, Thomas McGuane, and Jack Nicklaus. Describing the thrills associated with bonefishing is still difficult. They must be experienced first hand.

Angler and guide ply a flat at Andros Island in the Bahamas much like they did when the sport was in its infancy. Note the handmade wooden push pole.

Chapter 3

Natural History

Bonefish, *Albula vulpes*, have many names, including ghost of the flats, white fox, fox of the flats, grubber, banana fish, and Houdini fins. The family Albulidae (order Elopiformes) is ancient and considered one of the most primitive families of living teleostean (bony skeleton) fish. Bonefish fossils dating back 50 million years to the Eocene period are known throughout the world. An extinct species, *Albula antiqua*, dates back 125 million years to the Cretaceous period of Florida.

Albula vulpes is the present representation of the genus. Other species have been identified recently, and still others probably exist. *Albula nemoptera* is found on the Atlantic and Pacific coasts of the Americas. *Albula neoguinaica* and *Albula glossodonta* occur in Hawaii and the Indo-West Pacific region. Taxonomic differences are so slight that to most anglers the fish are indistinguishable from each other. The most obvious differences between Atlantic *Albula vulpes* and Pacific *Albula nemoptera* are that Pacific bonefish have a slightly larger mouth and slightly longer dorsal and anal fins. Other slight differences include certain proportions, dentition, and color markings. Fossil material suggests the two should not be considered as representing separate monotypic genera. As far as anglers are concerned, a bonefish is a bonefish regardless of where it is found.

Although bonefish are widely dispersed and highly prized as game and food fish in many parts of the world, little is known of their early life cycle. The actual spawning and egg hatching of bonefish have not been documented. Studies done in the Gulf of

Approximate Size and Weight Table for Bonefish			
18"	3.5 lbs.	28"	8.6 lbs.
19"	3.8 lbs.	29"	9.6 lbs.
20"	4.1 lbs.	30"	10.8 lbs.
21"	4.6 lbs.	31"	11.9 lbs.
22"	5.1 lbs.	32"	13.0 lbs.
23"	5.5 lbs.	33"	14.4 lbs.
24"	6.0 lbs.	34"	15.6 lbs.
25"	6.5 lbs.	35"	16.8 lbs.
26"	7.2 lbs.	36"	18.0 lbs.
27"	7.7 lbs.	37"	19.2 lbs.

Bonefish mirror their environment and are perfectly adapted to their unique, skinny water world. They are a fascinating study in color, texture, and form.

California near Guaymas, Sonora, Mexico, suggest that spawning occurs between mid-May and mid-October. This interval corresponds to a period of increased sea surface temperatures. In contrast to this, a study in the West Indies region of the Caribbean concluded that spawning occurs throughout the year. This conclusion is supported by the observation that ripe and near-ripe adults are found throughout the year in southern Florida. Locals at Christmas Island say that fish spawn whenever the moon is full.

A study recently completed at Lee Stocking Island in the Bahamas indicates that limited spawning occurs on a continuing basis. Fish probably spawn between October and May with peak spawning activity occurring between mid-October and early January. There is a strong correlation between peak spawning times and when the dark flood tide is at its maximum level for the month. Dark flood tide is a measure of the total hours of flood tide that occur between sunrise and sunset under moonless conditions. When the moon is full, there might not be any period of darkness. During the week after the full moon, moonrise becomes progressively later each night and the amount of flood tide occurring between sunset and moonrise increases dramatically. This window of opportunity minimizes the bonefish's vulnerability to visual predators.

It is highly probable that bonefish spawn at different times in different geographical locations and that subspecies may spawn at different times in the same geographic location. It is likely that bonefish do not spawn on flats where fishing takes place but, rather, offshore or in areas where currents are likely to carry the eggs offshore. As both angling and food harvesting pressures on bonefish increase, we must have a precise understanding of these remarkable fish so they can be protected.

Early life history from egg to larva is poorly understood. The larva is known as the leptocephalus and in no way resembles a bonefish. This stage is elongated, thin, and, except for the head, almost completely transparent. These characteristics are similar to other primitive teleost fish, including tarpon, *Megalops atlanticus*, and true eels (order Anguilliformes). The metamorphic period in leptocephalus larvae of the bonefish is characterized by a rapid and pronounced decrease in body length accompanied by other morphological and biochemical changes. These radical changes are involved in the transformation of the thin larva into a juvenile fish resembling the shape familiar to anglers. The fish actually grows by shrinking. Evidently, the larvae are dispersed by oceanic currents as they have been collected as far north as Great South Bay, New York, and San Francisco, California.

Larval development is divided into three stages. The first is an initial growth stage, followed by the amazing shrinking phase, and ending with another growth stage. Metamorphosis in leptocephalus has been observed under laboratory conditions as occurring within a period of eight to 12 days. Recent field studies in the Bahamas have suggested times between 41 and 71 days. After hatching, leptocephali remained in the pelagic environment of Exuma Sound an average of 56 days. This helps support the contention of some researchers that some fish species can actively control their onshore movements in certain environments, perhaps by delaying their metamorphosis until suitable environmental

conditions or opportunities develop. Little is known of their habits between the juvenile and adult stages.

Characteristics

Shape and Color: The color of a large bonefish is bluish green above and bright silvery on the sides and below. There are dark longitudinal streaks between the rows of scales, at least on the dorsal half of each side, and the dorsal and caudal fins have dusky margins. Very young adults have a double series of dark spots on the back. These spots unite to form about nine dark bands across the back that extend nearly to the lateral line. Another band crosses the back at the origin of the dorsal fin. The next two are situated posteriorly under the base of the dorsal fin. The bands persist until the fish reaches a length of about three inches. The dark longitudinal streaks of the adult appear shortly before the cross bands become obscure. Bonefish seem to shimmer like a hologram.

Other distinguishing features are a slender body, which is rounder and less compressed in large specimens than in young adults. Scales are firm with crenelated membranous edges. The head is low, especially in larger specimens. Flat above, the head's depth exceeds its width at mid-eye by about the diameter of the pupil. The snout is long and conical, projecting about a third of its length beyond the lower jaw. The eye is moderately small, its center nearer to the margin of the operculum than to the tip of the snout. The maxillary does not reach to the eye in larger specimens but extends to, or slightly beyond, the anterior margin of the eye in young specimens.

The dorsal fin is somewhat elevated anteriorly, its origin a little nearer to the tip of the snout than to the base of the caudal fin. The caudal fin is deeply forked, the upper lobe somewhat longer than the lower. The anal fin is very small, its origin notably nearer to the base of the caudal than to the base of the pelvic. The pelvic fin is somewhat smaller than the pectoral, inserted under or slightly behind the middle of the dorsal fin. The pectoral fin has a rounded margin that reaches less than halfway to the pelvic fin. The axillary

A bonefish could be one of nature's perfect creations. It has speed, which it needs to elude both shallow- and deep-water predators. Its mirrored scales reflect its surroundings, allowing it to disguise itself much like a chameleon. Its sense of hearing and smell are acute, and its eyesight is a wondrous marvel.

Bonefish have an amiable personality, and they are a creature you could become friends with. There are, undoubtedly, many secret aspects of bonefish that we have yet to discover...secrets that may aid our own evolution.

Bonefish are built for speed. Their deeply forked tail and hydrodynamic shape help make them the undisputed speed holder in shallow water and the fastest fish that is readily caught by light-tackle anglers.

Randall Kaufmann

scale of the pectoral is about half as long as the fin, adherent to the body.

Speed: Bonefish are built for speed. Their deeply forked tail and hydrodynamic shape help make them the undisputed speed holder in shallow water and the fastest fish that is readily caught by light tackle anglers. Billfish, wahoo, and tuna are faster, but you don't catch them in 10 inches of water! Estimates of bonefish burst speed is from 20 to 30 miles per hour. In contrast, trout clock in at a top speed of five miles per hour. Larger bonefish are the fastest, but many variables enter into the equation, such as where and how fish are hooked, water temperature and depth, individual metabolism, angler resistance, and tidal flows.

A bonefish free of the hook can outrun a shark or barracuda in a straightaway race, and it can maintain top speed longer than these species. When bonefish are restrained by rod and reel, many species can catch them. Suppose a bonefish is sprinting away with your fly at 25 mph. This translates to 36.67 feet per second! The first run might be 25 yards (2.04 seconds), 50 yards (4.09 seconds), or 100 yards, possibly in 8.18 seconds, although fish usually slow down over this distance. Besides speed, there are other features unique to bonefish.

Mouth and Tongue: The tongue and roof of the mouth are covered with hundreds of tiny armored beads called pharyngeal teeth. At the back of the tongue on both sides are powerful crushers that compress prey and allow bonefish to disintegrate the toughest clam shell much like a rock crusher in a quarry. The mouth area contains the bonefish's lateral line sensory system. Skin is stretched across hollow cavities. It is believed these drum-like transmitters relay vibrations of prey.

A bonefish normally breathes by drawing water into its mouth, then closing it while contracting the gill arches and raising the rear edge of its gill cover, which forces water through slits between the oxygen-absorbing gill filaments. When a bonefish suspects the presence of prey hidden in the substrata, it instantly reverses the flow by a powerful adduction of its gill covers and jets a stream of water from its mouth, exposing the prey.

Age: The age of bonefish can only be estimated by reading their scales, especially on bonefish over six to nine years old. This method is not reliable for aging long-lived fish. Estimates derived from scales are typically lower than validated estimates derived from sectional otoliths, a tiny bone-like structure in the inner ear.

Bonefish inhabit a psychedelic world of fluid colors. They swim through and become rainbows of light. This bonefish wanders through a forest of pneumatophores, breathing tubes of the black mangrove, Avicennia germinans, *at Andros Island in the Bahamas.*

Bonefish live in an ever-changing and dangerous environment. Their amazing sensory perception, endurance, and voracious appetite are legendary. Bonefish are a favorite with all who visit their strange and beautiful world.

Researchers in the Florida Keys have documented two bonefish (one male, one female) of 19 years. Ages to nine years are common. Small numbers of bonefish were present in each age class from 10 to 19 years. In one Florida Keys study, fish growth was rapid for the first six years, then slowed considerably. The length of females was greater than males in one-year and older fish. Females were found to be more abundant. In this particular study, most fish were caught with hook and line and were from three to 10 years old. On average a 20-inch bonefish is four to five years old, a 23- to 24-inch, seven years old. One 12-year-old female weighed 9.25 pounds and measured 24.4 inches.

Sight: A unique and little understood physical feature of the highly specialized bonefish (and perhaps a key factor in explaining some of its behavior) is its adipose eyelid. Unlike most other fish, which have unprotected eyes, the eyes of bonefish are protected behind a smooth, transparent sheath much like goggles or a face mask. A tiny opening is centered over the pupil, which allows bonefish to see well even when their faces are pushed into the mud or sand and surrounded by thick sediment. Hydrodynamically, the sheath reduces water turbulence around the eyes when fish swim at maximum speed. Some scientists have suggested that this tough covering somehow polarizes light, accounting for the keen color vision of the bonefish. Other species that have similar eye coverings include mullet (another mudding fish) and the fast-swimming wahoo and jack crevalle. The convex eyes of bonefish allow them a wide-angle, if not a fisheye, view of its skinny underwater world and the world above. On land, visibility may be several miles. Underwater, 50 feet is a great distance. To function in such a muted environment, fish rely on other senses.

Hearing: Bonefish have acute hearing, especially in the range of 300 hertz, which includes anglers' feet shuffling along the bottom, the noise of a boat motor, or a heavy fly hitting the water. Water amplifies and transmits sound much better than air. Even above-water noise, such as shouting, can put bonefish on alert. Remember, bonefish easily detect all but the stealthiest intruders.

Smell: While bonefish feed by sight, they also detect hidden and buried prey by smell. Nostrils, called nares, in front of the eyes and nasal sac sensing devices send signals through the olfactory nerve to the brain, giving bonefish an amazing sense of smell. For fish to smell, water must move quickly over these sensor cells. This fact may help explain why bonefish usually feed into the tide or move about quickly.

We know dogs smell 10, sometimes 100, times better than we do. It is believed that some fish can detect odors a million times better than we can. There have been many studies on how important the sense of smell is in helping fish locate food, avoid predators, communicate between themselves, and navigate great distances. To my knowledge, no specific human odor studies have been conducted in relation to bonefish, but studies with other species have shown an aversion to L-serine, a chemical found in the oils of human skin. Other common disliked chemicals include lotions, insect repellent, sunscreen, diesel, gasoline, and nicotine. Washing your hands in seawater helps eliminate offensive odors. Apply lotions with the back or palm of your hand, keeping your fingers clean.

Chapter 4

Types of Flats—Habitat

A saltwater flat is any area of relatively even shallow depth. Some flats are continuously covered with water, while others are completely exposed during low tide. Water depth can range from a couple of inches to several feet, but anglers usually fish in water less than two or three feet deep.

Flats range in size from tiny shallow shoals to broad expanses covering a thousand acres or more. Some are adjacent to land masses and may be narrow, extending only a few yards from shore. Others might extend for miles or might be surrounded by deep water.

For our discussion, a reef is any coral mass lying at or near the water's surface that causes surf to form. All other shallow coral areas are considered flats.

Flats are feeding and nursery areas for countless species that swim, cling, drift, crawl, burrow, and crowd into every possible crevice, soft spot, and depression. This high-density living attracts a multitude of predators, including bonefish. For bonefish, flats are the promised land.

Strong winds and tides keep flats in a constant state of flux. Sometimes they are barely submerged, even completely exposed to air, but they are always exposed to intense sunlight and temperature variations. It is a precarious world of harsh contrasts and harsher realities in which the predators might become the prey. Mere survival is an ongoing quest. All these factors combine to make this skinny water environment one of the most exciting places on earth.

This aerial view of Aitutaki Lagoon in the Cook Islands shows a microcosm of bonefish habitat and illustrates the various types and geography of flats. Visible are reef, outside, transition, and inside flats that consist of mud, coral, and sand. Also visible are channels, cuts, drop-offs, points, edges, and depressions, all of which are discussed in the following chapter. Can you locate them all?

Flats are obviously a dangerous zone for bonefish, but so is deep water. They are drawn to flats by the abundant and relatively accessible food supply. Their favorite feeding zones can sometimes be reached only briefly during high tide. When bonefish enter such marginal survival zones, their dorsal fins may be out of the water. They do not linger long, and every sensory device is on full alert. Anglers hoping to deceive such bonefish must be extremely cautious, for bonefish often sense an angler long before the angler sees the bonefish.

Bonefish, like lake-dwelling trout, often frequent specific areas at specific times. This chapter explains how to recognize and locate such areas and how to read the water. An understanding of the favorite haunts and habitats of bonefish also helps you select the proper imitation and present it effectively. Much like a country or city, each flat has its own "food print," culture, and idiosyncrasies.

It is a good idea to carry a small notebook in your shirt pocket in which to keep a journal and prepare a map of where you are fishing. Make note of any pertinent information about tides, feeding zones, migration routes—anything that might help you at a later date. This not only makes for interesting reading but enables

Flats are easily spotted from space photos or from an airplane. During interisland flights in the Bahamas, anglers press their noses against the windows, enchanted by the pristine flats that beckon from below. Nowhere is this more exemplified than between Nassau and Great Exuma. The ocean is a liquid mosaic of partly exposed sand and every tropical water color imaginable. This hypnotic seascape is indeed captivating.

you to remember subtle ideas and techniques that you would otherwise forget.

Locating Flats

Flats are easy to locate. During low tide they have very little or no water on them. They usually extend from the leeward side of low-lying islands or atolls or are found in the immediate vicinity. Flats that can be reached and waded from highways are few in number; anglers on foot are restricted to relatively small areas and short periods of fishing. Mobility is the key to locating fish. While many flats are wadeable, a boat is needed for transportation to and from fishing areas.

Most of the world's bonefish flats remain a mystery because they are not accessible to the average angler. The only way to reach them is by yacht with a shallow-water skiff or inflatable in tow, or by float plane. A lifetime of adventure in the world's most exquisite and sublime saltwater destinations lies in silent seclusion just beyond the horizon. Many such areas exist in the Caribbean and the fabled South Pacific seas.

Besides locating flats visually, adept map readers can often deduce the possibility of ocean flats by studying land masses. Most flat land masses, especially coral atolls, have flats or coral reefs nearby. Steeper volcanic land masses, like the U.S. Virgin Islands and Hawaii, have few flats or shallow water suitable for bonefishing with a fly. Navigational charts can provide clues as to the location of reefs and flats that might offer bonefish. If you are fishing from an established lodge, you do not have to worry about finding flats, just about hooking bonefish.

Flats are classified by their physical characteristics and location. There are reef (usually mostly coral), outside, beach, transition, and inside flats. Some are isolated (pancake flats); others are connected to or adjacent to land (edges, extension flats). Flats may consist of mud, sand, grass, coral, or a combination of all. Mangroves may be present.

Mud Flats

Mud flats are usually protected from excessive wave action and collect sediment much like a backwater in a river. Some mud flats are endless mounds of muck and deep goo. They remind me of quicksand fairy tales. Don't stand in the same spot too long. When wading such areas, you get your aerobic workout. Anglers should remember to shuffle their feet when wading mud, sand, and grass flats. This flushes out rays and helps detect other hidden dangers that might be submerged in the bottom strata.

Mud is an excellent habitat for a multitude of organisms and, when interspersed with grass, can create quite a dining experience for bonefish. The best mud flats I have seen are in the Bahamas, especially in the North and Middle bights at Andros Island. These areas are protected from excessive wind and wave action, and there are hundreds of places to fish. Most of these flats are marginally wadeable, but it is best to stay in the boat. You can cover much more water and explore some very spectacular back country.

Mud flats are also referred to as marl, muck, and ooze. As the name implies, mud flats can be gooey places. Mud flats often have uneven bottoms. Many mud flats are wadeable, and, while you might settle a few inches, they present no problems other than sticky footgear and suction-cup walking. Others are so soft and deep that they are dangerous. It is possible to sink out of sight and join the countless other organisms that compose the near-prehistoric mixture of sediment that has built up on the coral floor. Do not jump out of the boat without first ascertaining that it is safe to do so. Do not continue walking in soft muck. Turn around!

Clear sand flats are often described as snow white, but they are usually more tannish to cream or ivory in color. Sand flats are everyone's favorite. They are smooth and reflect brilliant colors. They are easy to wade, and fish are easy targets. They are one of the most beautiful places to hunt bonefish. Long Island, Bahamas.

Pancake flats are surrounded by water on all sides. Inside the lagoon at Christmas Island.

If conditions are right, you might experience versicolor, the blending of many colors. Like a snowstorm whiteout or flying through clouds, it is sometimes difficult to determine up from down and sky from water. Jamie Lyle and Kristen Munger, Berry Islands, Bahamas.

Sand Flats

Most sand flats are intermixed with other substrata and can vary in color from rust to white, but flats that consist solely of pure white sand are the rarest and visually the most stunning. The white sand reflects light like snow. Colors and contrasts are accentuated. Blues become electric, white turns into neon, and you can spot a bonefish tipping down to capture a crab at 100 yards. You can almost see the crab! Isolated sand, or pancake, flats (those surrounded by deep water on all sides) are my favorite. Because there are no reference points on the horizon, you seem to be looking at the world through a fisheye lens. It is difficult to determine where the sky ends and the water begins. If conditions are right, you might experience *versicolor,* the blending of many colors. The effect is surreal, and you really do not care if you hook any fish. The light show is reward enough.

When bonefish are over white sand, they are extremely wary, using their Ph.D. in survival. You need a graduate course in stalking and presentation. Once hooked, bonefish race at hyperspeed toward deeper water, which might be a half mile or more away. Don't worry—the smooth bottom is easy on fly lines and leaders; eventually the well-muscled dynamo is closely circling your position, soon to be within your grasp. You feel as if the halo of the sun is just for you when you release your silvery prize back into its transparent world. Most bonefish locations have some pure sand flats, but some of the most extensive and visually stimulating are at Christmas Island, Cuba, Venezuela, Seychelles, and the Bahamas. One area in the Bahamas is particularly special:

As I walked through the shallow water, I splashed clear droplets into the calm tropical air. The tide, pushed along by unseen forces, slowly and silently spread along the beach, being careful, it seemed, not to disturb the perfectly contoured sand. Ah, yes, the sand! The tiny particles were chalky white and nearly perfectly round, like miniature marbles. I marveled at their feel, color,

and extraordinary texture. The sand created the most dazzling flat I had ever seen.

Called ooids, the individual sand particles are concentric layers of calcium carbonate, or limestone, and they are found on only a few beaches on earth. They are probably formed either by ocean currents or by tidal action. No one is certain, and no one has been able to reproduce such particles in the laboratory.

I forgot about the cruising bonefish and knelt down amid the overwhelming splendor. I ran my hands through the strange particles and tried to find some misfits intermingled with the perfect forms. I could not. I rolled the tiny spheres in the palm of my hand and guessed at their mysterious origin. What magical process created these beautiful treasures, and how did they end up here? What unseen power and force of nature was unique to this particular location? Why? How?

A bonefish tail flashed like a mirror, reminding me why I was there. I knew if I were going to hook any bonefish in this hyaline environment I must fish like a ghost. I watched the movement of fish for a few minutes, then the surrounding sand bottom. Tiny whitish crabs about the size of a nickel seemed to be the object of the fish's attentions.

I remained motionless for several minutes. The bonefish did not detect me, and one swam within a rod length. The solution was simple. Stay quiet in a kneeling position and place the crab imitation in advance of where bonefish were likely to approach. I cast and waited for a good fish to cruise within attack range of my waiting crab. As one approached, I imparted one short pull to the crab and let it lie. The first fish pounced on the fake crab. As I tightened up on the fish, it spat out the crab faster than fast and shot off into distant shadows. I had removed the hook point so I didn't have to blow my cover.

As I sat motionless waiting for my next opportunity, I savored the overpowering scene, realizing that it doesn't get any better than this. As I reveled in the enjoyment of the moment, I wondered aloud how I could ever convey this magical interlude to friends. Words fail, time fails, and I dread when I no longer will be able to return to the ooids, but for now I know where to find them and the beautiful bonefish that feed among them.

If you pause from fishing and act like a heron, it is possible to get close-up views of bonefish. This solitary hunter flashed electric blue-green colors as it casually worked this shallow sand flat. It is usually more rewarding to observe than to disturb. Abaco, Bahamas.

This fisheye view of Brian O'Keefe, a priceless bonefish, and the pristine landscape is always worth the price of admission. Bonefish should be handled gently. If a photo must be taken, set up everything in advance and support the fish in the water or only inches above the water. Acklins Island, Bahamas.

Plants constitute the basic link in the food chain. Freshwater anglers are well aware of the correlation between weed beds and healthy, well-fed trout. Weeds shelter large populations of most food sources, and, as a result, trout are attracted to them. Shallow saltwater flats that support luxuriant grass growth are nursery and feeding areas for a multitude of small marine animals, shrimp, crab, bonefish, shark, and man. From a distance, grass flats appear dark. Pictured is wilderness bonefish habitat in the Seychelles.

Grass Flats

Grass flats consist mostly of turtle grass, *Thalassia testudinum.* Turtle grass is a common sight throughout Florida and the Caribbean but is absent at Christmas Island and some other Pacific locations. Its leaves are rigid, about a half-inch to three-quarters-inch wide, usually four to 12 inches long, and arise from a dense rhizome system. It flowers with curved whitish pistils or stamens low on the stalk. Usually only five to 10 percent of the plants flower at one time in the spring and summer. It is medium olive to dark green and sometimes mottled tan or brown, especially along the edges. It will stand up and move in tidal currents but usually lies flat like a lawn that has been soaked with a hose. As water becomes six inches deep or less, the leaves project out of the water. This exposure, even though slight in many cases, results in desiccation and leaf kill. This may explain the absence of turtle grass in may areas where tidal flats become completely exposed during low tidal periods.

Turtle grass can grow in tropical and subtropical water with temperatures between 68 and 86 degrees Fahrenheit wherever there is protection from wind-driven surf and strong currents. Its broad leaves reduce the velocity of slower currents and act as huge filters, removing particles from the water and depositing them as fine sediments. Snorkeling through grass is a marvelous experience. These sea meadows support many interesting and usually unseen plants and animals. The most luxuriant turtle grass flats are found in sheltered areas, especially Florida's back country, but there are some good grass banks intermixed with coral and sand just inside the reef in Belize and at other Caribbean locations. Florida flats contain a heavy sedimentation of very fine, loose grayish calcium carbonate, which evidently favors growth of turtle grass. A combination of coral and grass might harbor the greatest concentration of foods for bonefish.

Anglers should note that fire worms, *Hermodice carunculata*, inhabit turtle grass beds. They are greenish to chocolate brown and grow up to 12 inches long. If touched, their bristles cause a burning sensation that may last several days. Removing the bristles reduces the pain. Cortisone cream helps relieve the inflammation. Be careful what you touch; don't put your hand where you cannot see; and wear *good* footgear.

Vegetation might also include ripweed; Merman's shaving brushes; sea lettuce; common disk, or segmented, algae; Laurence's weeds; shoal grass; and manatee grass. From a distance, grass flats and grass patches on flats appear dark. They are usually firm and easy to wade. When walking flats with numerous grass patches, I like to walk a path that connects as many grassy spots as possible. Grass helps muffle your approach, but walk slowly and slide your feet along the bottom in such a manner that you do not create too much noise or vibration yet you flush out any hidden rays and other dangers. If you are stalking spooky fish, incorporate the lift-and-point walking technique; otherwise, shuffle your feet slowly and carefully.

When bonefish are tailing in grass, their vision is somewhat obscured, allowing you to get a bit closer and perhaps get away with a less-than-perfect fly presentation. This is especially true in tall grass, which is common in Florida but uncommon elsewhere. The disadvantage is that the cast must be right on target, or the bonefish might not see your offering. Imagine yourself feeding in a field of corn, poking your head up for a look around. Your fly must also be the proper weight. A fly that is too heavy will tangle in the grass; you can imagine what bonefish think about a cockeyed shrimp towing grass! This is one of the biggest challenges in the Florida Keys: making your fly look alive and showing it to fish before it snags grass.

Turtle grass, Thalassia testudinum, *leaves are rigid, about a half-inch to three-quarters inch wide and up to 12 inches long. It sometimes stands up and moves with tidal currents but usually lies flat like a lawn that has been soaked with a hose. Turneffe Island, Belize.*

The proper weight fly and accurate casts are essential when fishing in grass beds. Note how the bonefish blends into its surroundings and the reflection at the water surface. Los Roques, Venezuela.

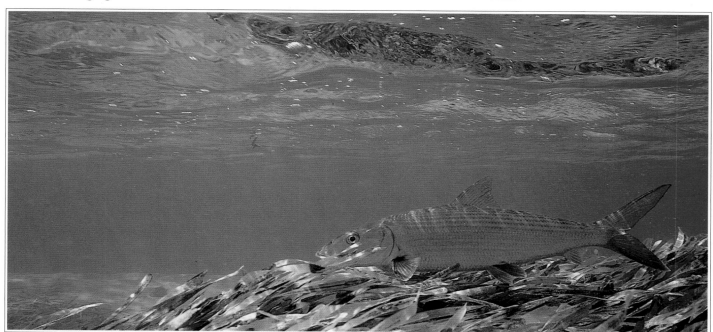

Coral heads and sand on an outside flat present a challenge to anglers, but so what if you lose a few bonefish and flies? Who cares? Bikini Atoll, Marshall Islands.

Perfectly formed coral heads in a surreal landscape of water, land, and sky. Snorkeling over and around these living mounds of coral is a fascinating study in color, architecture, and evolution. The out islands, Seychelles.

This scene could be from a different planet, and it might as well be because it is at Bikini Atoll in the Marshall Islands. Species are yet to be discovered in high density coral communities like this. Hard, dense coral can rip your gear and your body. Once fish swim into a coral hole the game is over. Bring plenty of flies!

Jerry Swanson

Coral Flats

Corals are unique limestone formations that have been formed by multiple tiny carnivorous polyps that feed on minute organisms. Corals, called polyps, sometimes exist in huge dense colonies called reefs. Their limestone skeletons are formed by extracting calcium from sea water and depositing calcium carbonate around the lower half of their bodies. One end of the polyp is attached to a secure surface (ocean bottom, submerged volcano rim, or the reef itself). They build on one another, slowly rising toward the surface. One small piece of coral represents millions of individuals and years of growth. Coral grows in many shapes (tree-like branches, lace, fans, antlers, domes, stalks, "heads") and in myriad colors.

Some coral is very sharp and potentially dangerous. *Most are alive;* some are dead. Some are extremely delicate and brittle. If you feel coral crunching beneath your feet, you should not walk on it because thousands of the tiny creatures are being destroyed with every step. It might take a human lifetime or more to regenerate. Anglers should fish from a boat or move to another area. Some coral flats are interspersed with grass and sand, and careful, conscientious anglers can avoid stepping on the coral. *Anglers should not fish fragile areas on foot.*

When wading in areas of coral, wear sturdy footgear. Coral poisoning (blood poisoning) is nothing to trifle with, especially when you are a long way from medical help. Cuts, or even scratches, from coral can become infected. Remove all coral and wash all cuts and scratches *immediately* and *thoroughly.* Apply an antibiotic cream. If coral breaks off in a deep cut or puncture, even a tiny piece can cause a serious blood infection. If infection occurs, see a doctor *immediately.*

Coral flats are a challenge to anglers. A speeding bonefish can easily slice your fly line on coral; you should *always carry a spare.* When you hook a fish around coral, raise your rod as high as possible. If it runs toward the drop-off, so should you. Position yourself near the edge and keep your line and leader high so they cannot abrade on the edge of the drop-off. Coral is found at every bonefish destination and is most evident on outside flats and reefs, which are mostly coral, but it can be encountered anywhere.

Outside Flats

Because of their close proximity to the open ocean, outside flats are often called ocean flats. They are exposed to strong wave and tidal action and are buffeted by nearly constant winds.

Most outside flats have dark coral sediment-free bottoms and harbor an abundance of marine organisms. Outside flats that front deep water but not pounding surf might consist of hard-packed sand interspersed with coral, sea fans, and some vegetation. Outside flats are almost always wadeable.

Larger bonefish are usually associated with outside flats. Their above-average size helps them survive in this dangerous location at the edge of deep water. Anglers fishing the deep-water edge might also see many other species of fish. Even when bonefish are feeding in skinny water, they are seldom more than a flip of the tail away from deeper water. Examples of outside flats include much of the west coast of Andros Island and other west-facing locations throughout the Bahamas and the rest of the Caribbean.

Transition Flats

Also known as *in-between flats*, transition flats are usually located behind coral reefs. The reefs protect the flats from excessive winds and waves, but there is not enough seclusion from the elements to form true inside flats. Transition flats generally consist of a combination of coral, grass, and sand. Their proximity to the usually noisy reef makes them an interesting place to fish. Transition flats are often surrounded by tiny cays and intoxicating blue-green pools. Because of their location, they have many divergent currents and are frequented by species normally relegated to the reef. I have seen larger-than-normal sharks patrolling the fringes of these flats, and big rays are also a common sight.

The most beautiful transition flats are found at the Seychelles and the offshore islands of Belize, especially Turneffe Island. Anglers can spend an entire tide cycle on such flats because so many habitats and physical characteristics are crowded into a relatively small area. I like to follow the tide back from the reef to the highest ground near the brush-choked cays, meander through the scattered pot holes and grass banks, and then walk out with the tide to the reef and perhaps fish the outside margin for the big boys. Anglers appreciate the variety of food sources and angling situations that transition flats offer.

Some outside flats gradually slope toward deeper water, like those on the west coast off Andros Island. Others, like at Turneffe Island (above) and Seychelles (below), are somewhat protected from surging surf by reefs. Distance and time tend to moderate normal tidal flux except when a major storm is brewing. Wave action is gentler and seldom breaks on the beach.

Transition flats are often surrounded by tiny cays and intoxicating blue-green pools. They are enchanting places to stalk bonefish and to lose one's self in nature's mysteries. Dale Kremer exploring unknown waters in the Seychelles.

Randall Kaufmann

Coral reef areas are the most stimulating and exciting areas for anglers to pursue bonefish. They are also the most dangerous. Depending on tides, anglers fish the edge of the actual reef or the area between the reef and shoreline. The most aggressive and rambunctious bonefish can be found here. Fish routinely steal flies, coral slices fly lines, and sharks munch your fish. Be prepared. Christmas Island.

Coral Reefs

Coral reefs have been compared to tropical rain forests because they, too, are centers of diversity. The richest tropical reefs in the Indo-Pacific are home to more than 700 species of coral, 5,000 species of mollusks, 2,000 species of fish, and numerous species of crabs, worms, stars, cucumbers, and the like. Undoubtedly, many species remain undiscovered, along with their secrets.

There are three types of reefs: barrier, fringing, and atoll.

A *barrier reef* runs offshore and parallel to the coast. It can be completely submerged or partly exposed above high tide. In Atlantic-Caribbean waters, barrier reefs are usually divided into clearly marked zones—the outer reef, main ridge, reef platform, and inner reef. There are also so-called bank reefs, ranging in depth from 35 feet to those that barely break the surface, several miles out from the islands. A long barrier reef is usually a series of parallel reefs broken by deep-water channels. The longest barrier reefs that I have been able to locate are:

1. Great Barrier Reef, Australia—1,250 miles
2. Southwest Barrier Reef, New Caledonia—373 miles
3. Papua Barrier Reef, New Guinea—348 miles
4. Northeast Barrier Reef, New Caledonia—335 miles
5. Great Sea Reef, Fiji—162 miles
6. Belize Reef, Belize—155 miles

A *fringing reef* extends outward as platforms from shore. Anglers will notice many such small reefs, some of which will be overlaid with patches of grass or sand.

An *atoll* is commonly formed when polyps begin building their colonies around the edge of the crater of a submerged volcano. Many atolls exist in the world's tropical waters, especially throughout the South Pacific seas. Bonefishermen know that lagoon flats encircled by atolls are some of the most beautiful and productive waters.

Exposed reefs bear the brunt of the ocean's relentless power, and heavy surf often rolls nearly unimpeded over the tops of such reefs. When surf and tides are low, reef tops may be exposed and gentle swells lift and lazily roll over the lowest points. Examples include Belize, Bikini Atoll, Kanton Island, and the entire outer reef at Christmas Island.

For many anglers, coral reefs are the most exhilarating habitat in which to pursue bonefish. Sights and sounds are amplified, and abundant reef life is constantly in evidence, either scurrying away from your feet, swimming closer for a look, or soaring above your head. The diversity of living organisms found on the reef is, perhaps, unmatched elsewhere in the world.

Imagine yourself in this place and time. Life is 3-D, with real-time surround sound. The fragrance and expanse of the open ocean, wilderness at its wildest, is in your face. You are certain you are fishing where no one has fished before. It is only you and bonefish, trevally, emperor, and shark. This could be the beginning of geologic time. Bikini Atoll, Marshall Islands, South Pacific.

When the surf is up, powerful waves scatter electric ions and fluorescent white spray into the air. The thundering, sometimes deafening, noise charges your senses, and you have a heightened awareness of the power of nature and your insignificance. The flattened surf rolls toward the beach, seductively tugging at your legs on its round trip from sea to shore to sea. The swirling waters seem to be teasing and urging you to join the melee involving land, water, and gravity.

The myriad colors create a kaleidoscope of tropical sensations, and you may find yourself mesmerized, or even held hostage, by the untamed yet soothing milieu. Don't daydream too long in never-never land; reefs are a potentially dangerous area. When surf is strong, you must be constantly alert for rogue sneaker waves that can upend and tumble you like a plastic beach ball. *Do not turn your back to the surf or wade too deep.* Reef areas have uneven bottoms and demand constant wading attention. It is easy to trip and stumble into a hole. Leave your camera on the beach with anything else you don't want to get wet.

During periods of diminished surf and at low tide, you might be able to walk near the outer edge of the reef and look into blue water that abruptly drops hundreds of feet. Hard, irregular coral can make this area difficult to reach on foot. Be careful not to venture too close to the edge. Bonefish can be big, rough customers in these areas, and one never knows what else might swim by only a rod's length away.

Bonefish may be spotted anywhere in the subtropics and tropics. Many bonefish destinations offer beach fishing out your front door. Bruce Richards fishes a beautiful shoreline fringed with rock, sand, and Australian pines on Abaco, Bahamas.

Beach Flats

Most sunny tropical and subtropical vacation resorts are located on a beach. There may or may not be surf. It doesn't matter; there are fish somewhere nearby.

Like lakes, a beach may stretch out of sight and appear featureless. Also like lakes, fish may not be found everywhere. How do you find fish along a beach? Just like you would in a lake—by reading the bottom structure and understanding where the concentration of food is.

Hard-packed sand beaches often look sterile and void of food, but a close inspection may reveal various crabs, small fish, clams, and worms. During high tides, worms exit or protrude from their protective burrows to feed and are easy prey for bonefish. Crabs are also relatively easy prey when caught in the open over hard sand. Sand is ideal habitat for clams and minnows seeking shelter in shallow water.

Water movement creates shorelines. A rough and irregular shoreline is caused by fast, irregular currents, which, in turn, are created by bottom structure. Look for protruding or slightly submerged coral. Bottom color variations often signal more or less concentrated food organisms. Look for rip tides, areas of deeper water close to shore, concentrations of grass, and the like. Look for areas on the beach of different composition, such as coral or coarse sand, anything that breaks the local pattern.

Some areas have a relatively consistent water depth and structure and are not prime bonefish habitat. Never mind; if you are out for an evening or afternoon stroll, take your rod. Occasional bonefish are spotted almost everywhere throughout the tropics, from Australia to Hawaii, Cancun to Aruba, and from Africa to Indonesia. More than one honeymoon has been interrupted by bonefish fever. If bonefish are scarce, there are always other species. Rule number one: if you are at the ocean, there are fish to be caught on the fly. Never leave home without your gear. You can't catch 'em with your hands!

Sandy beaches can be considered either inside or outside flats. These may be protected from heavy surf by an offshore reef, but small rollers often reach the shoreline. They may also be adjacent to interisland ocean channels or on the leeward side of islands; surf is usually calm.

Wading is easy and fish are usually easy to spot on sandy beaches. They are fun to fish. If the beach has immediate access to deeper water, large fish can sometimes be found. The best time to fish is during incoming tides as bonefish drift into shallow water to feed and then drift back to the safety of deeper water on the outgoing tide.

Brian O'Keefe, the photographer for this book, and I fished a sandy beach off Andros Island that proved productive. The beach flat looked like an underwater sand dune, but some very large fish were known to frequent the area. Both fishing and casting conditions were poor. Taking our time, we walked the transition zone between shallow and slightly deeper water, stopping often to look for any sign of bonefish. Large crabs raised their legs in protest when startled, and we surmised that bonefish were having their way with them. We changed to a size 1 crab, fished until dark, and released some decent fish.

Another time I was lazing away a sunny afternoon at a tourist resort in the Yucatan when I spotted two bonefish cruising along the beach. The next day I was ready for them. Bonefish are where and when you find them. Be prepared and keep fishing.

Randall Kaufmann

Bonefish can be found prowling the beach inside the surf, especially in secluded coves on a rising tide. Even if you don't find bonefish, it shouldn't be too difficult to amuse yourself. I went for a memorable swim in this idyllic Jacuzzi-like pool on the east coast of Long Island in the Bahamas.

It doesn't take much imagination to immerse yourself in this nirvana. What would you do first? To find out, fly Air Seychelles to where even the palm trees look relaxed.

The author stalks bonefish on a rising tide at an inside flat. Follow creeks and channels into mangrove country; then explore tiny openings. You might discover secret "isolated" inside flats completely surrounded by mangroves. Long Island, Bahamas.

Harmony and tranquility usually prevail on inside flats. It is where nature seems to calm herself, even relax, and let the rhythm of tides dictate the schedule and daily outcome of evolution. Because they are at the highest point of the water's reach, inside flats often collect sediment and may be vegetated and soft. They are often ringed by mangroves and exposed at low tide. Jardines, Cuba.

Inside Flats

Reefs, islands, and bays protect inside flats from excessive wind and water movement. Inside flats offer a much more gentle environment than transition flats and can provide anglers with classic flats fishing at its best. The substrata of inside flats consists of mud, sand, and grass, or a combination of two or more of these characteristics. Mud flats can be very soft, making wading impossible.

The general nature of inside flats usually makes for easier angling conditions, but fish can be more wary. Deep water is not always readily accessible, and this, coupled with the absence of sharp coral, makes landing fish easier. However, inside flats can have mangrove snags that help fish escape. Food sources on inside flats are plentiful but not as abundant as those of the outside flats and reefs.

Sounds are geographical ocean areas that are surrounded on three sides by land. These areas are often protected by an offshore reef but can have strong ocean currents. The inside centers of sounds are often relatively deep with flats along the margins and at the far inside reaches. Inside flats in these areas can be formed of sand, muck, marl, grass, and coral toward the outside and mangrove on the inside margin. Sounds can be very good bonefish habitat. Some of the best examples are at Andros Island in the Bahamas.

The most beautiful classic inside flats are located inside lagoons at Los Roques, Christmas Island, Ascension Bay, and the bights at Andros Island. Others are found throughout the South Pacific inside fringing reefs such as at Bikini and Mili Atolls in the Marshall Islands. Some are wadeable; others are not.

In addition to the classic inside sand flats, creeks and channels often open up to inside flats. These are usually small openings that lead into protected backcountry. Some of the backcountry flats are small, but others are vast and are comparatively insulated from high winds. These quiet places can offer all types of flats, everything from sand, muck, marl, and grass to mangrove. Andros Island has the most extensive system of creeks.

Jon Covich

Chapter 5

Mangroves

Not a riffle disrupted the smooth surface of the water as our boat raced toward The Bight off Sandy Point, Abaco. Long before reaching this remote settlement, our guide, Ricardo, cut the engine. The only noise was the gentle rhythmic splash of water against the hull and the occasional surface commotion of a needlefish or a diving bird. Mutton snapper (a real prize for anglers) scooted away at our quiet approach. The occasional putt-putt of a small motor radiated out from the dock, and the chitchat of shore birds materialized as we neared the shoreline.

As we neared the dock, huge piles of conch shells stood like ragged pyramids on the shore, and the laughter of happy children wafted across the quiet water. The lackadaisical morning lulled me into far-off thought. Before I knew it, Brian O'Keefe had made a 10-foot cast off the bow and hooked a seven-pound bonefish. It quickly released itself, and Brian made a 15-foot cast. Another seven-pound bonefish grabbed the fly as it sank. It streaked off toward the dense mangroves that lined the shoreline.

I couldn't help laughing as Brian tried to finesse the bonefish and his fly line through an impossible maze of mangroves. Ricardo frantically poled the boat this way, then that way, never giving up hope of landing the fish. If I had been giving odds, I would have made it 10 to 1 in favor of the fish. Seeing there was nothing I could contribute, I relaxed in the boat and sang, "I caught a big one, it looked like it could run, off to the mangroves it quickly did run." The entertainment was grand, and the fish zigzagged through 150 yards of mangroves. Brian jumped from the boat into waist-deep

This stand of red mangroves creates a sheltered wind shadow where anglers can avoid the wind and spot bonefish easily. Jon Covich in Cuba.

Randall Kaufmann

A bonefish leads Ricardo and Brian into dense red mangroves. They follow the trail of fly line, hoping the bonefish is still attached. After carefully untangling line and leader, their persistence paid off.

They find their prize—a beautiful strong fish patiently awaiting release.

Randall Kaufmann

goo to untangle his line from a serious mangrove root and became the muck man of the bight. To my amazement and delight, eventually the fish was landed, photographed, and released. I was impressed.

The trick to increasing your odds when battling a bonefish in mangrove country is to release almost all drag, keep the line high, and follow the fish as quickly as possible until it is mostly clear of mangroves. If there is any tension on the line when it goes around a mangrove root, a sharp barnacle is likely to cut it. I always carry a spare line just in case.

A gutsy, sometimes reckless, trick is to throw your rod in the water. This eliminates all drag except the resistance of the rod being towed through the water. This often slows fish and buys you time to untangle line, whether it be from mangroves, coral, or an overrun on your reel.

One ploy is to position yourself between bonefish and mangroves. When hooked, bonefish sense the boat and your presence and flee away from the root systems.

Bonefish relish feeding around and under mangrove roots. It can be difficult to make an accurate cast. Often there isn't a second chance. Unlike casting hoppers onto shoreline grass for trout, you can seldom pull a fly free from a mangrove. Often the path of retrieve is littered with mangrove shoots. Look for a clear path. If you hang up, be careful not to make a commotion that alerts bonefish to your presence.

Mangroves grow in the intertidal zone in subtropical and tropical seas where the water temperature averages at least 73 degrees Fahrenheit. Where land and sea mesh together, mangroves inhabit both worlds. The word *mangrove* applies to vascular plants that are able to live in shallow seawater. They are able either to prevent entry of salt into or to expel it from their tissues.

Defiant colonizers, mangroves grow most densely at the edge of the highest tides. They seem to always be attempting to extend their range beyond their ability to survive. Seedpods drift with the tide and eventually tip over and attempt to take root. Anglers may see newly migrated "shoots" attempting to root far from their nearest neighbor, and seedpods are often observed drifting like the proverbial message-carrying bottle.

Mangroves can be found throughout the world where conditions are right but are noticeably absent from the central Pacific. It is theorized that the floating seeds from these trees cannot reach such locations. Christmas Island anglers will not encounter any mangroves.

In the Western Hemisphere three types of mangroves are common—red, black, and white. Red mangroves are by far the most common. The red mangrove, *Rhizophora mangle*, is unique in that it can survive and even thrive with its roots exposed to saltwater. Red mangroves are recognized by their red-colored roots that form arched tepee-like skeletons. In addition to providing support, these aerial roots bear superficial cells and internal tissues specialized for gaseous exchange, a distinct advantage in a species that resides in poorly aerated muds. Red mangroves thrive at the lowest limits of the intertidal zone because of their stilt-like roots and the ability of young shoots to colonize these areas. Some grow to heights of 15 feet or more.

Black mangrove, *Avicennia germinans*, can be recognized by its dark, grayish-black trunks. Its leaf is the most elongated and has a sharp tip. Salt crystals are often found on the leaf surface, evidence of their unique ability to secrete excess salt. Black mangroves have the highest tolerance for salt and cold and are found in the upper reaches of the tidal zone. Their roots grow subsurface. "Peg roots," or structures known as pneumatophores, poke up three to seven inches from the sand to breathe. Shoots are often observed as dense mats at low tide. This breathing adaptation allows the trees to survive despite being rooted in oxygen-deprived intertidal soils. Be careful not to trample them—black mangroves grow very slowly.

White mangroves, *Laguncularia racemosa*, have light-colored trunks, and their leaves are much thicker than other mangrove leaves, with a fleshy, succulent appearance. They have the least tolerance for salt and are the least hardy. They are restricted to the highest ground and are the least common. The accessory root system of the white mangrove is much like that of the black, except its pneumatophores (peg roots) arise from the subsurface root system and are usually not detectable above ground. I mention this as a reminder that nature operates in subtle, mysterious ways and that there is much for us to observe and learn. Tread lightly; you never know what life form you may be injuring, or what you are really observing. All these species overlap and I have seen them all in a 50-foot radius.

Groves can be young, short, and spaced apart, or they can be old, tall, and dense. The most productive groves are a combination

This mangrove shoot is encrusted with barnacles, waiting to break leaders and fly lines.

Red mangrove, Rhizophora mangle, *is a constant companion throughout Caribbean waters. When high tide floods their roots, mangroves afford bonefish food and shelter.*

Black mangrove, Avicennia germinans, *is easily recognized by its breathing tubes, which surround the plants. Be careful not to walk on the tubes.*

of the two. Mangroves specialize in land reclamation and are of great ecological importance. Once established, the maze of roots slows down the currents and causes tiny suspended particles to drop to the bottom. The sandy sediment evolves to muddy sand. Eventually a fertile environment develops.

Mangroves provide unique shelter for a rich and diverse colony of creatures. Several environs are stacked upon one another, from muck to water to air. These mangrove condominiums may provide habitat for more species than any other habitat in bonefish country, with the possible exception of reefs.

Inhabitants include polychaete worms, sponges, anemones, jellyfish, octopus, crustaceans, barnacles, oysters, crabs, and *many* species of fish (including juvenile deep-water fish), all of which are preyed on by bonefish. Studies have shown that many rare and unusual species inhabit mangroves. One such inhabitant in Belize at Twin Cays is *Rivulus marmoratus.* This small hermaphroditic fish is one of nature's rare examples of a vertebrate that can clone itself.

Anglers can judge the stage of the tide by looking at mangroves. If all the roots are exposed to bare ground, the tide is most likely at its lowest level. If water covers the roots and reaches to the green branches, it is near its highest level.

The Bahamas offer excellent mangrove fishing. I had an advanced class on mangrove fishing from Wellington Taylor on Long Island in the Bahamas. This particular stretch of shoreline had mature mangroves spaced 10 to 20 feet apart with younger plants scattered about. Against the shoreline, head-high mangroves grew shoulder to shoulder. The tide was full, and we walked 200 yards without seeing any fish. I was beginning to doubt there were bonefish around. Welly said the fish were in the mangroves where we couldn't get to them. He was waiting to locate one on the fringe of the grove. We relaxed, waited for the tide to turn, and talked about bonefish feeding in the mangroves on snails that cling to mangrove roots. As the tide rises, snails climb up the roots. Bonefish move in and either pick them off the

Mangroves shelter a diverse assortment of foods. Bonefish regularly visit this contorted environment to search out prey. It is easy to envision a bonefish swimming through this maze with, then without, your fly!

roots or "blat" them, knock them off with their tails or body, and then grab them. Bonefish also root crabs under the tepee root system.

We soon spotted a bonefish leaving the shoreline mangroves. Its swimming signature was so subtle that it looked like an insect trailing its legs across the surface. I waited until the bonefish was on the outward side of a mangrove before presenting the fly. Once hooked, I let the fish run with minimum resistance until it was in open water.

This particular shoreline stretched for a few miles. You never know where they are going to be. Welly's advice was, "Keep moving; hunting them is the main sport. Hunting, always hunting. Keep moving." He was right. When we found one, there were others. The morning provided some high-tech angling for wary fish in skinny water. Occasionally, narrow openings large enough to get a boat through appeared in an otherwise closely guarded shoreline. Sometimes these slots opened into a secret lagoon or a sparsely populated mangrove plantation—young shoots attempting to colonize shallow water. I like to explore such places because they often hold bonefish.

While poling along a mangrove shoreline at Grand Bahama Island with Mary Kaufmann, we were invited into just such a place for a look around. Our guide poled stealthily, and, rounding the first corner, we were suddenly face-to-tail with a dozen bonefish in water no more than 10 inches deep. No one uttered a sound or made the slightest move for fear of spooking them. If one bonefish sensed our presence, they would all panic. We were close enough to hear their tails lift out of the water and see bottom debris disturbed by their rooting. This would be a one-fish affair and, if hooked, it would almost certainly be lost to the many mangroves.

Bonefish enter mangroves on a rising tide and exit them on a falling tide. Working the edges can be productive. Cat Island, Bahamas.

Bonefish love to eat snails, and mangroves offer the best source. Bonefish either pick them off the roots or knock them off with their tail or body. Hors d'oeuvres, escargot!

Crab holes and mounds at the base of a mangrove, favorite feeding locations of bonefish. Once bonefish enter dense mangroves, anglers have a difficult time reaching them. Wait until they enter more open areas or exit the groves on a falling tide.

Fumbling with my tippet, I lengthened my leader and tied on a sparse size 8 Mini Shrimp without eyes. Mary made the cast to the nearest bonefish, and the fish pounced on the fly before she could gain control of the fly line. Recovering quickly, she managed to tighten the line, and the fish, feeling the resistance, bolted under the boat intent on breaking my rod! In the confusion I grabbed the rod, somehow cleared it from the prop, and handed it back to Mary, laughing as the fish wove a mindless course through the mangroves toward open water. I figured there was no chance of her getting this baby in. I put my camera down and awaited the inevitable. It didn't happen. Somehow the boat, the line, and the fish made it through the maze together, and Mary was soon backing out the barbless hook and setting the bonefish free.

Mangroves add excitement and refinement to your fishing. The roots and the barnacles that attach themselves to mangroves can slice waders and fly lines. When bonefish wrap you around a major root, the best you can usually hope for is to retrieve your fly. So what if you lose it? The excitement is worth it!

If possible, position yourself between mangroves and bonefish. When one is hooked, it is likely that the bonefish may swim away from you into more open water. Mangroves, however, do not move at all, and the angler let this bonefish find sanctuary among the roots. Jardines, Cuba.

Jon Covich

Chapter 6

Geography of Flats

The geography of flats reveals both obvious and subtle indications of how to best approach and fish a particular flat. Basic physical characteristics to consider include contours, or elevation variations; channels; cuts; depressions; drop-offs; points; and edges.

Contours

Bonefish navigate by sight, smell, and, possibly, electromagnetic waves bouncing from and emitted by the earth. Anglers can only relate to sight navigation. Contours denote and define the water depth and bottom characteristics of flats. An understanding of these physical characteristics allows you to better understand the movements and feeding habits of bonefish.

To bonefish, flats are anything but flat. Water depth is one of the critical factors that determine where bonefish feed. Numerous elevation changes, no matter how subtle they appear to us, create travel lanes leading to quiet, out-of-the-way gourmet restaurants. If undisturbed, bonefish often explore the limits of their existence. Water six to eight inches deep is about their shallow-water limit, but smaller bonefish can feed in water four or five inches deep.

Generally, the average flats feeding depth is between 10 and 18 inches. Bonefish feeding on incoming and outgoing tides often follow and feed at a specific water depth, referred to as the "comfort zone," moving higher up or lower down on the flat as the tide and bottom contours fluctuate. Walking the zone is an effective method of staying with fish or locating fish as they move about. Veteran

Seasoned flats anglers know that bonefish follow specific waterways on a rising tide, and that they prefer a specific water depth at certain places and times. Waiting for and hunting them at this depth usually pays off.

This aerial view of Crooked Island in the Bahamas reveals possible travel routes and shallow-water feeding areas. The most productive area may be the shallow sand flat behind the cay in the lower right corner or either the inside or beach flat left of center.

bonefish anglers wade mid-calf deep, which is the best general zone, until a more specific zone can be determined.

Underwater changes, however slight, can have a profound impact on the entire underwater community. Bonefish respond dramatically to changes in water depth and weather that affect their eating habits, safety, and navigation.

If water depth is not to their liking, bonefish sometimes gather in schools just off a flat at a drop-off, channel, or creek. They wait to enter the flat when conditions are right; then they break up into smaller pods and begin feeding. Allow fish to enter the flat, break up, and begin a steady feeding rhythm before approaching them. By doing this you can have an hour of fishing instead of five minutes.

As with any fishing, a few extra minutes spent observing usually pays big dividends. Allow common sense to prevail. Remember to look, think, look again, and move slowly. It is usually more fun and enlightening to quietly observe than to intrude and disrupt. Create a few words in your notebook or an image on film.

The area southwest of San Pedro, Belize, offers some refined contour fishing. Numerous small cuts lead to shallow grass flats ringed by mangroves. The boatman needs to read the contours carefully, as all the surrounding flats are usually too shallow for the boat, and they are too soft to wade. Nearly all fish are tailers and can be seen for some distance. The trick is to approach close enough in the boat to make a cast without spooking the wary feeders.

Bonefish shelter in this channel until a rising tide floods the surrounding flats. Then, they swim in with the current, feed, and swim out with the current. It is orderly and predictable. Two "cuts" entering the channel can be seen below the wing struts. Note the depressions at the lower left. Andros Island, Bahamas.

It is low tide and these anglers are plying the shoreline edge of a channel. Possible hookups include snapper, jacks, barracuda, shark, and bonefish. Note the flat in the background. Long Island, Bahamas.

Channels

In bonefish country, the word *channel* is often interchangeable with *cut*. Generally, channels are longer and deeper than cuts, and provide access to deep water. Channels almost always have water in them, cuts often become dry during low tide. Channels may parallel shallow areas and provide direct access to flats.

Anglers fishing channels never know what might jump their offering, but barracuda, trevally, snapper, jacks, and sharks are all possibilities. It is possible to fish bonefish in the shallows or along the drop-off from one side of the boat and deepwater species from the other side of the boat. Wading anglers often fish the drop-off or edge of channels from flats. Channel water may be 10 or more feet deep, and offer access to many species. Casting baitfish imitations or poppers can pay exciting dividends.

Cuts are often the first areas bonefish enter on a rising tide. If you are positioned along an access route bonefish may come to you. There is little reason to move. Andros Island, Bahamas.

Cuts

Cuts are routes or highways that lead fish to and from feeding areas. Cuts usually divide or fragment flats, offering bonefish ease of entry to feeding grounds, much like a driveway offers easy and gradual access to supermarket parking. Cuts may be only inches or a foot or two deeper than the flats they feed water to and from. Shallow cuts show green, and deeper cuts look darker green-blue, contrasting vividly with the lighter-colored shallow-water flats.

This cut or mini channel leads bonefish to inside flats and mangroves. When the tide is low, the cut contains schools of bonefish. Long Island, Bahamas.

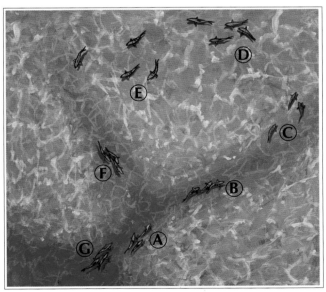

Bonefish following flats contours according to depth on a rising tide:
A Fish holding in channel before entering flat.
B Fish entering flats along channels.
C As tide floods, fish scatter.
D Fish at top of flat at top of tide.
E As tide ebbs, fish work toward edge of flat.
F Fish concentrate in channels as tide ebbs further.
G Fish holding at channel to collect food flushing from flat.

Cuts are often the first areas of a flat that bonefish enter during an incoming tide and the last areas they leave on an outgoing tide. As the tide rises, bonefish fan out and dine on the highest, most productive areas of the flat, areas that are not always accessible. As the tide drops, bonefish congregate and mill about in cuts. Guides often station clients near cuts that abut deeper areas, knowing that bonefish will probably come to them.

During moving tides, a strategic cut that allows quick and direct access to and from flats is a prime location, one where you might position yourself.

During an incoming tide you have an opportunity to cast to rambunctious fish eager to feed. They must feel like youngsters scurrying down Main Street Disneyland as the park opens and spreading out for their favorite attractions. Cast only to the best fish entering through the cut, allowing the others to swim onto the flat unaware of your presence. Make note of their travel direction so you have a general idea of where to find them during high tide. When fish movement slows on the incoming tide, it is time to work the high ground of the flat.

Cuts are also excellent places to station yourself during an outgoing tide. Bonefish sometimes exit a flat by the same route they entered. Cuts provide wonderful pass casting for singles, doubles, and larger pods. Should you find such a location, remember that bonefish seldom tolerate repeated harassment. It is best to rest small flats at least a day between visits because bonefish might alter their migration habits or become unreasonably picky.

Cuts act as funnels for many helpless organisms that are swept around by the tide. As a result, bonefish are often eagerly awaiting their catered meal. I once had some excellent action at a cut inlet to a flat. After action slowed, I decided to circumnavigate the flat and work the highest ground. I was too late, wasted an hour, and found no fish up high. The tide had already turned, and, disappointed, I began the long trek back to the boat at the inlet area. When I arrived, I found the inlet had turned into the outlet, and every fish on the flat must have been facing into the out-pouring water gobbling everything the tide drained from the flat. I had misread the flat and mistimed the outward migration, losing two hours of the best angling. There is a good deal of truth to the old adage about being in the right place at the right time.

During my first visit to Christmas Island, in 1986, my guide, Moana T. Kofe, told me, "Stand here. You'll see plenty of bonefish when the tide turns." The area was a classic cut about a foot deeper than the flat that fed into a channel. Sure enough, within 30 minutes a continuous stream of bonefish was cruising the drop-off. They wanted to enter the flat, but their survival instincts urged caution. They seemed to be sniffing the water much like a dog on a hot trail. Perhaps they sensed food or predators or were making certain there was enough water on the flat. They soon tested the entrance, and the first wave of scouts entered without incident.

I was fascinated by their behavior and did not cast for quite awhile. The technique was much like fishing a lake inlet. You could not crowd the inlet area or no fish would show. By standing back 30 feet and keeping a low profile, I could cast to and hook a specific fish on every cast. When one was hooked, new arrivals were clearly concerned. I moved away from the inlet to battle fish, and new fish continued to enter the cut. After several fish, I became bored and moved onto the flat in search of individual tailers.

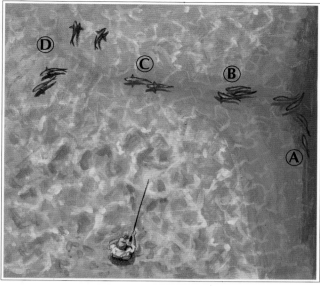

A Deep-water drop-off.
B "Cut"—transition zone or mouth of shallow channel draining flat.
C Shallow channel—lowest contour of channel—first area to be flooded by tide.
D Actual "flat" area—bonefish spread out to feed once water depth is to their liking.

Various water depths provide ribbons of color and are a blueprint for finding bonefish. Like bonefish, anglers should follow the tide. The author casts to channel cruisers near Cape Santa Maria on Long Island in the Bahamas.

Depressions can be two to several feet deeper than surrounding waters. All are worth investigating. Bonefish, jacks, trevally, etc. often cruise the edge of larger depressions. Christmas Island.

Bonefish often cruise in and out of the transition zone between shallow and deeper water, or between sand and coral and grass. As to an oasis in the desert, fish are attracted to food, shelter, and the different water temperatures that depressions offer. Anglers, too, are irresistibly drawn to their emerald waters. Acklins Island, Bahamas.

Depressions

At Los Roques, Venezuela, I was walking a two-mile-long flat adjacent to a coral reef. Back from the reef about 200 yards was a beautifully colored depression 150 feet across. I was irresistibly drawn toward its inviting shoreline and would have considered a swim, but it was inhabited by bonefish! It was three to five feet deep with a sand and grass bottom. I surmised that tidal hydraulics kept it fed with cooler water and that numerous crustaceans crept into its seductive environs—two very good reasons for the presence of bonefish. It was a beautiful place to relax and observe, but eventually I had to make a cast.

Often "aqua holes," small shallow depressions in flats, may be only a few feet in diameter and a foot or two deeper than surrounding waters. This is enough depth to change the water color, making depressions easy to locate. Many times I have blindly thrown a fly into just such places, and from out of nowhere a bonefish has appeared. Even if you can't see any fish, make the cast.

Any obstruction to tidal movement, such as a mangrove, conch shell pile, exposed coral, wrecked boat, and the like, creates water turbulence, which in turn creates mini whirlpools, sand bars, sink holes, depressions, pot holes, and uneven bottoms. Depressions range in size from a couple of feet to hundreds of feet. Depth can be from one foot to over 20, but three to six feet seems to be most productive.

Incoming tides usually stir up depressions and entrap small fish and crustaceans. Look for fish facing the current when tides are in flux, and do not approach too closely. Bonefish can be difficult to see; make a cast even if you do not see any. Do not overlook depressions on reefs, especially those with grass or sand in them. Uneven or slightly deeper areas can act like magnets for bonefish and their prey.

As you make your way across flats, include depressions on your route. You won't have much trouble doing this because their turquoise color attracts you like a rainbow in the desert. Sometimes you find a treasure of bonefish.

Drop-Offs

Drop-offs are deep-water areas adjacent to shallow flats and reefs. These areas offer bonefish the best of both underwater worlds. Deep water provides variations in water temperatures, specialized food sources, and shelter from shallow-water predators. Shallow water provides the best feeding areas and protection from deep-water predators.

Learn to recognize the difference between drop-off "feeders" and drop-off "cruisers." Feeders usually patrol the bottom at a particular depth, rooting out and pursuing fleeing prey. Present your fly on the bottom, calculating time and distance plus the sink rate of your fly. Cruisers can be suspended above the bottom but adhering to a specific contour along the drop-off, aimlessly wandering or patrolling a particular area. Such fish are more susceptible to a mid-water food source such as a small fish. Note the depth of such fish and present your imitation accordingly. Pursuing drop-off cruisers or feeders on foot usually pushes them offshore into deeper water, and out of reach.

When bonefish are spotted in deeper water (over four feet), it may be advantageous for the angler to wait until the fish enters shallower water before making a presentation. Always note the direction bonefish are swimming and look for others to be moving in the same direction. Stalk fish with the wind and sun at your back if possible.

Bonefish come up over the drop-off to feed on flats during incoming tides. Drop-offs are excellent places to locate resident or schooling fish during low tide. Their "beat" might include various water depths and habitats within a specific area. Once you have established the feeding area, take up the most advantageous casting position and wait for the fish to reappear. Usually you do not have to wait long.

I like to employ the "cast and wait" technique in which the fly is cast and positioned on the bottom in a strategic position. As the fish approaches, give the imitation a short pull and let it lie. You will, in all probability, soon be fast to a confused bonefish. This technique is nearly fool-proof, as there is no cast to spook the fish or sink-rate time to consider. Make the cast a little longer so the fly can be repositioned to coincide with the path of approaching fish or to compensate for current speed.

Anglers stalking drop-off cruisers and feeders are wading the flats yet concentrating on the transition zone, water three to 10 feet deep. Anglers should maintain a safe distance from the drop-off and stay out of sight of fish.

Larger fish seem to be more comfortable in deeper water than their smaller brethren and are most often sighted drifting in and out of the transition zone between deep and shallow water, just a tail flip away from either environment.

Large bonefish require deeper water than do their smaller brethren to swim and tip downward when feeding. Therefore, anglers desiring a shot at the largest bonefish should concentrate on deeper water. If you always fish the shallows, you seldom hook the main characters. Drop-offs are an excellent bet. Cook Islands, South Pacific.

When a bonefish is hooked at the end of a point, it usually spooks other nearby companions, especially if you are forced to follow it to the edge. Little Cayman Island.

Bonefish often gather at points, especially on rising and falling tides.

Cast slightly ahead of and beyond cruising bonefish, allowing you to reposition the fly in relation to bonefish movement. When a bonefish takes the fly, it is looking away from the boat.

Points

Points offer deep water on three sides and a gradual drop-off that allows fish to select a comfortable water depth or a specific feeding location in relation to tidal stages. Long, narrow flats usually offer the best points. Anglers approaching points on a flats drop-off should approach cautiously and pay particular attention to water two- to five-feet deep.

The point can be a turnaround or gathering position for cruising fish or for those that have been "herded" by approaching anglers. Such fish might not be spooked but have simply been moving ahead of approaching anglers and are reluctant to leave their feeding flat prematurely. Allow such fish some quiet time and do not cast before they have spread out and begun to feed. Position yourself in a favorable position and always pick off the nearest feeder. Once you know a particular flat attracts fish, it might be worthwhile to position yourself in advance of their arrival. Points can offer larger-than-average fish because they feel more secure in deeper water.

Edges

Christmas Island is shaped like a giant horseshoe and encompasses a huge lagoon. The southeast inside shoreline of the lagoon has an erratic shape and is pockmarked with many tiny coral islets that barely reach above high tide. Along these shorelines are narrow bands of shallow water that extend from a few feet to many yards offshore before dropping into deeper water. These edges offer a narrow dining room for singles and small pods of bonefish, plus milkfish.

Fishing edges is like shore fishing freshwater lakes. Anglers stalk and cast to specific cruisers. Moving slowly is important. Keep a low profile and walk toward cruising bonefish. Edge fish are often "locals" and usually live nearby. The larger fish generally feed at the drop-off, while smaller fish will sometimes be found tight against the shoreline. The edges at Christmas Island vary

This deep-water shaded shoreline in the Exuma Island chain in the Bahamas is perfect cover for snapper. Such areas may also be productive for snook, tarpon, and jacks.

from hard coral to sand and soft mud. Be careful of coral holes and soft areas. Because these edges are at the back of the lagoon and are protected by numerous flats and islets, there is little wave action and less wind. I prefer to fish the big open flats, but, when the weather is bad or for anglers who are physically unable to walk and wade, edges are an excellent alternative.

The Bahamas, Yucatan, and Turneffe Island offer some fine edge fishing. Guides select the leeward side of cays and approach with the wind and sun at their backs. At such times a wind shadow is usually available along the shoreline, which makes for enjoyable angling in an otherwise tough situation. Poling the boat quietly, the guide finds bonefish cruising the shoreline, sometimes only inches from mangroves. With the right cast, the bonefish is yours. If you cast too far, the mangrove is your prize and any nearby fish are out of there.

Edges may be shallow areas that extend only a few yards from shore, and they may disappear at low tide. Others may be drop-offs from flats as pictured here at low tide. Keep moving and looking for fish in both deep water and adjacent to the beach in only inches of water. Long Island, Bahamas.

Chapter 7

Weather and Temperature

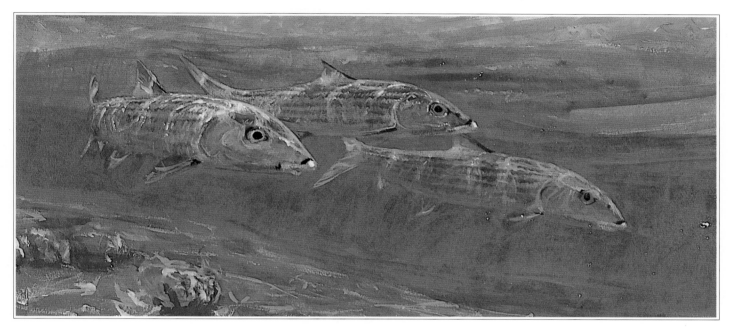

Weather affects bonefish and their feeding habits. Many of their reactions to weather are little understood, but we do have some knowledge of how wind, temperature, and barometric pressure affect bonefish.

Wind

Wind is created and influenced by water movement and air temperature variations. Because land and water are of varying temperatures and in close proximity, wind is constantly in flux around atolls, reefs, and shallow saltwater flats. You wouldn't want it any other way.

The first few days of one bonefish adventure, the wind blew 30 mph day and night, and we complained day and night. The wind gods must have heard us because it did come to a stop, a dead stop. It was so calm that birds were not flying. It was also hot, and the humidity gave us a bath every 20 minutes. We spent two days hugging the fan, playing backgammon in our beachside bungalow, and hoping the generator wouldn't break down. There were no clouds in the sky, and the sun was bright beyond belief. I won't tell you about the biting bugs or where we were because, if I did, you won't go there, and I want you to. I want you to experience the dearth of wind in the tropics so you will never again complain about too much wind.

Learn to take advantage of the wind and understand that it is your friend. Wind disturbs the water's surface, acts as a muffler of noise, movement, and light, and obscures your cast and your leader. Surface disturbance also obscures and reduces the bonefish's window to the sky, helping to hide your physical presence.

Landmasses create their own weather—wind, clouds, and rain. All affect fishing and your comfort. Don't underestimate the dangers associated with tropical weather. Be prepared every day. Exumas, Bahamas.

When a stationary cloud casts a shadow over flats it may be advisable to move toward a sunny area where bonefish are easier to spot. Sometimes anglers need to coerce their guide to crank up the motor and get moving. Christmas Island.

Windy conditions seem to calm bonefish, and they may feel a sense of security with less exposure to predators.

Wind direction affects the feeding habits and migration of bonefish. When winds blow from a constant direction, seek bonefish in sheltered areas. These may include leeward shorelines, lagoons, edges protected by shoreline vegetation, and the backcountry. Storm fronts may cause winds to blow from shifting directions. When this happens, seek bonefish on outside flats or the opposite side of normal areas. Another excellent possibility during any strong blow is backcountry mangrove areas. These groves are usually too dense to penetrate very far, so position yourself at entrance and exit areas. These may include channels, cuts, dropoffs, and where there is immediate access to deeper water. Remember that wind can have a cooling effect on water.

Consistent or excessive wind might roil, or churn, soft flats, sometimes dislodging food organisms and attracting bonefish, especially after winds abate. Compact sand flats should remain clear and little affected because heavier sand moves slowly and settles quickly. However, broad exposed sand flats are usually best avoided during extreme winds and saved for another day.

Bonefish often travel upwind. If the tide coincides with wind direction, you can virtually bet on bonefish traveling this direction. Strong winds and tides funnel bonefish to specific areas, but, once there, they usually disperse into small pods or into pairs and singles.

If possible, you should fish across and downwind, which positions you to intercept fish as they approach. This allows you to have a good angle of presentation and to cast with the wind. Such a presentation may not always be possible or desirable, which means you may have to cast into the wind. Long casts are seldom necessary, and casts should be kept low to the water where wind velocity is lower. Fly lines that are specifically designed for such conditions are a big advantage. They load the rod quickly and require very little effort to make a 30-foot cast, which is usually plenty of distance.

A five to 10 mph wind is ideal, and wind up to 20 mph may be tolerable. Winds over 20 to 25 mph create wave action, making spotting difficult. Depending on water depth and exposure, boat travel may be uncomfortable.

Properly prepared anglers can almost always experience good action in salt water. When flats are too windy, consider fishing for other species, especially those that do not require spotting and stalking techniques. Possibilities may include snook, shark, barracuda, jacks, or snapper. You might try trolling for whatever comes along. Be prepared for all options.

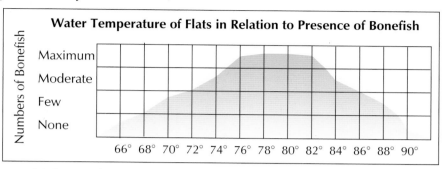

Temperature

Air temperature and wind directly affect water temperature, especially in shallow-water environs. While thermal requirements for *Albula vulpes* have not yet been experimentally determined, research scientists', anglers', and guides' observations in shallow water support the theory that bonefish are most active in water temperatures between 75 and 83 degrees Fahrenheit. They seem to tolerate water from 69 to 72 degrees Fahrenheit and from 86 to 89 degrees Fahrenheit for short periods of time. Below 68 degrees Fahrenheit (the temperature definition of a tropical sea and the temperature at which coral ceases to grow) and above 86 degrees, bonefish disappear.

Water Temperature of Flats in Relation to Presence of Bonefish

Numbers of Bonefish: Maximum, Moderate, Few, None

66° 68° 70° 72° 74° 76° 78° 80° 82° 84° 86° 88° 90°

For example, water temperatures over 90 degrees Fahrenheit are common from early summer to fall at many Caribbean locations, especially during low tides. At such times, very few fish are present. A rising tide can drop the water temperature to 84 degrees Fahrenheit, and bonefish may be everywhere. Explore all possibilities and keep moving until you locate bonefish.

Seasoned bonefish anglers realize the most consistent fishing is synonymous with a consistent water temperature. This is the reason Christmas Island is always good. It is close to the equator, hence the amount of daylight (12 hours of light, 12 hours of darkness all year) and the air temperature fluctuates very little. At Christmas Island in December/January, I monitored the air temperature at sunrise and sunset for a week, and it varied only two degrees, between 79 and 81 degrees Fahrenheit. Because of tidal

Storm fronts that approach from the open ocean like this one in the Seychelles are the most violent. Wind, rain, and electricity can be ferocious. When temperatures drop 15 degrees and you are soaking wet, it seems like you are freezing. Hypothermia is possible. Always have warm clothing and a rain parka at hand.

flow and different locations, water temperature varied slightly more (usually between 77 and 83 degrees Fahrenheit). With such stable and preferred temperatures, it is easy to understand why fishing is so consistent at Christmas Island.

Equatorial temperatures in shallow waters seem to be near ideal for bonefish. Assuming this is true, the greater the distance north or south from the equator, the less ideal the conditions. Eventually a location is reached that does not support bonefish at any water depth. For example, some bonefish are present in shallow water at Bermuda (32 degrees north latitude, the same as South Carolina) during the hottest days of summer. Somewhere around the Bahamas (26 degrees north) bonefish are comfortable all year. Cold fronts from the north can temporarily chase them into deeper, warmer water and out of sight from anglers, but they are present all year.

Latitude is not the only gauge of temperature. Longitude, ocean currents, associated landmasses, and weather patterns are also important factors. For example, fishing in January is much more consistent at Grand Bahama off Palm Beach than it is in the Florida Keys, 150 miles and two degrees farther south.

Water temperature can vary radically in bonefish country. Tidal flow, wind, air temperature, and solar radiation are the major influences. Water temperatures on an inside flat may be warmer by 10 degrees than at a nearby outside flat. It pays to carry a thermometer and to record your findings. Over a period of time and places, you can draw some remarkable conclusions, allowing you to better understand both your fishing success and the habits and preferences of bonefish.

Barometric Pressure

Some Bahamian guides claim that bonefish are sensitive to barometric pressure changes and are unusually spooky and picky prior to an incoming weather front. Others claim bonefish feed aggressively during such times. I have experienced both circumstances. My brother, Lance, was fishing off Grand Bahama Island in mid-March just prior to a late-season storm. He experienced some outrageous action 12 hours before the storm hit the island. Above-average-sized fish were plentiful and very aggressive. At Christmas Island I have witnessed the same scenario: fish feeding in an unusually aggressive manner just prior to an approaching storm front.

Bonefish feed rain or shine. Sometimes too much rainfall or runoff can dilute a shallow flat or small lagoon, and bonefish may leave. Fresh water can sometimes be seen mixing with salt water. Fresh water looks like a film of oil. While snorkeling and looking for bonefish in the Yucatan, I once noticed a slippery film intermixed throughout the water column. The water felt silky smooth to my skin, and I didn't crust up after drying off. I later learned that this particular area receives a great amount of

Rain droplets the size of silver dollars exploded on the water, but they didn't bother these bonefish near Sandy Point on Abaco Island in the Bahamas. Action was good until we couldn't take the cold any longer.

Randall Kaufmann

freshwater seepage from the vast Yucatan aquifer and was a favorite beach of Mayans. Bonefish avoid waters with too much fresh water.

If temperatures are right and winds are calm, bonefish can be very aggressive during intense squalls and storms. I have experienced such feeding binges in Florida and at Christmas Island when rain was pounding down or damp, cloudy conditions prevailed. Perhaps other factors beyond barometric pressure are involved.

Like trout, bonefish move to feed when food is available, when the water temperature either warms or cools to their liking, and when the sun is less intense (lower angle of sun, cloud cover, etc.). Tidal flow and water temperature are the two major factors that determine where and when bonefish feed. Once bonefish are located, a good rule is to go to where they are coming from. When they quit coming, go to where they are going.

Bonefish Movement

Research scientists in the Bahamas tracked bonefish using ultrasonic telemetry for 16 months. The widest range of water temperatures measured for any bonefish was no more than 15 degrees Fahrenheit, with a low of 75 and a high of 89. Water depth ranged between three inches and 13 feet. The general pattern of daily movement was to retreat to deeper water on an ebbing tide and to move into shallow water on a rising tide.

The proportion of captured large fish (over 22 inches, which

When a storm breaks, bonefish often become aggressive, especially toward dark on a rising or falling tide. Clouds create kaleidoscope sunsets, which often reflect golden off the upended tails of bonefish. The author at the south end of Abaco Island in the Bahamas.

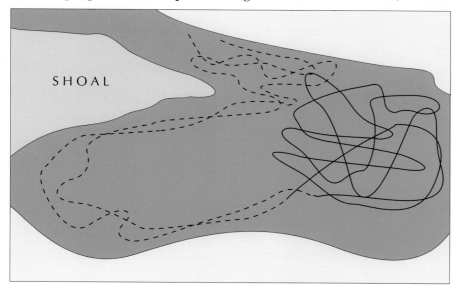

Dashed line shows movement of a 24-inch bonefish during a rising tide.
Solid line shows movement of the same fish during falling tides.
This particular fish moved into shallow water to feed during high tide and back into deeper water during low tidal periods. Note the erratic path and generally consistent direction of travel, suggesting consistent migration routes in relation to water depth.

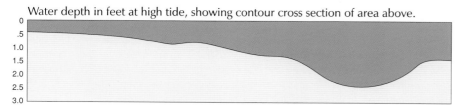

corresponds to the division between five- and six-year-olds) showed a pronounced seasonal change, which might be temperature related. Larger bonefish, while not common in winter months, are extremely rare in summer. This observed reduction in the proportion of large bonefish during warm-water periods may correspond to general offshore movement in preparation for spawning, or, perhaps, it takes advantage of a specialized feeding phenomenon.

This hypothesis is supported by local Bahamian fishermen. They believe that large individuals migrate to deeper water during the summer months and return in October or November to spawn in shallow creeks. A similar observation has been reported by commercial fishermen in Puerto Rico. At the time of this inshore movement, fish are said to be lighter in color with a silvery appearance. Angler observations of large bonefish caught at this time revealed nearly all individuals to be sexually ripe. Additional evidence of seasonal offshore movement of bonefish comes from scuba divers in the Freeport area of the Bahamas who have reported observing schools of thousands of bonefish suspended above submerged reefs. Similar sightings have been made off Tongue of the Ocean at Green Cay in the Bahamas.

Water temperatures also fluctuate daily. Light-colored sand flats reflect sunlight and heat and are cooler than dark or grass flats. During cold spells, grass flats are the places to be. Conversely, cooler sand flats may hold fish when grass flats are too warm. During warm summer conditions, bonefish might

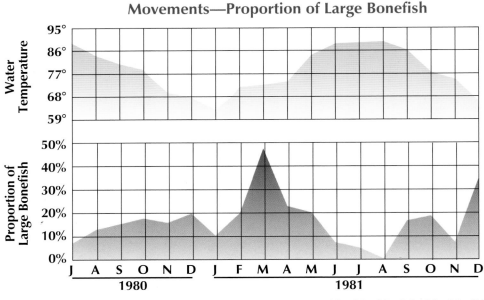

Movements—Proportion of Large Bonefish

The chart above shows the percentage of large individuals (fish exceeding 22 inches) found in monthly collections of bonefish in the waters around Deep Water Cay, Grand Bahama. Temperature is shown in the top half of the graph; the percentage of large individuals is shown in the bottom half. This data suggests that the best time to catch a large bonefish in shallow water around Deep Water Cay is March when water temperature is between 70 and 74 degrees Fahrenheit. The chart shows a small percentage of large bonefish during June, July, and August. The above information suggests that larger bonefish may tolerate cooler water better than smaller bonefish.

Every bonefish is special, but this is an extraordinary individual. Note the scale pattern, light-tipped tail and fins, and muscular shape. This is what you are fishing for! Brian O'Keefe at Long Island in the Bahamas.

avoid the flats during midday, but cooler conditions could exist early and late in the day or during an incoming tide. When temperatures are less radical, bonefish may stay on the flats whenever water conditions are suitable. Tropical flats near the equator (such as Christmas Island) have relatively consistent water temperatures and, as a result, stable bonefish populations. Semitropical areas, such as Florida, have more radical temperature fluctuations and more pronounced bonefish movements to and from the flats.

The study done at Deep Water Cay in the Bahamas revealed that the movements of bonefish on a long-term basis are highly variable and without apparent pattern. Individuals often remain at a given location for less than a week and then move to another location. In general, these bonefish can be characterized as transient wanderers.

First-time visitors to the tropics have a preconceived notion that the weather is always ideal. It usually is, but it isn't always. It can be nasty. These three anglers are experiencing a torrential downpour in the Seychelles complete with high winds, thunder, and lightning. Notice that two anglers do not have rain gear; one does. Which angler would you want to be?

Chapter 8

Tides

Tides define where and when the best fishing is found. A knowledgeable guide can supply this information. If your guide is only a boat handler or if you are fishing on your own, a basic understanding of tides is necessary.

Bonefish instinctively use tides to their advantage, following incoming tides to prime feeding areas and following outgoing tides back to deeper water. Once you correlate their movements in relation to tidal fluctuations, you have it made.

If you understand the tide cycle, it is relatively easy to figure out the basics and be able to take advantage of them and plan your fishing accordingly.

Wind speed, direction, and duration and the distance over which wind blows (fetch) have a measurable effect on tides. A strong wind blowing with an incoming tide causes it to rise faster and higher. Conversely, a strong wind blowing against an incoming tide delays it and keeps it from rising to its expected height. When barometric pressure is high, slightly less water fills the flats.

Shallow water heats and cools readily. Hot sun heats water quickly and can make the water too hot for bonefish, especially during the summer in semitropical areas. As the tide rises, it brings in cooler water and bonefish. During winter, shallow flats cool quickly at night, forcing bonefish into deeper, warmer water. As the tide rises, it brings in warmer water and, perhaps, hungry bonefish.

Every land mass, lagoon, creek, and obstruction restricts tidal movements. The tide is not the same at every location on an island or even on a particular flat. For example, the tide might be high at the entrance to the lagoon at Christmas Island at 1 p.m., but it might be 4 p.m. before the high tide reaches the back of the lagoon 15 miles away. A knowledgeable guide begins to work the flats closest to the lagoon entrance before noon, gradually moving toward the back of the lagoon, and then follows the tide back out, achieving several hours of good fishing during optimum tides. A less knowledgeable guide might begin working the flats at the back of the lagoon and find only a few fish until the tide reaches this area in midafternoon. Which guide would you rather fish with? Being at the right place at the right time (and with the right guide) can make a great deal of difference.

The best fishing might be during an incoming or an outgoing tide, but understanding tidal movements helps you determine where and when fish are likely to feed during any stage of the tide. Anglers who understand tides direct their fishing destiny. A simple and effective method of monitoring tides is to place a measuring stick at the water's edge or to make note of other stationary objects in relation to water depth.

Water clarity is seldom a problem, but wind and river drainage can cloud flats. A change of tides brings a change of water, usually for the better. High tides wash debris onto shore or back to sea.

Tidal movements are like a breath of fresh air to flats creatures. Tides bring in clear, oxygenated water and fresh nutrients. They also sweep in a multitude of small fish and other organisms that are unable to swim against the tide. Flats-dwelling animals and visitors are most active one-and-a-half hours before and one hour after high tides. The stronger (faster and higher) the tidal influx, the more bottom- and weed-dwelling organisms (crabs, shrimps, worms, etc.) are churned up. Various creatures will be observed in depressions, sink holes, coral formations, mangroves, and grass.

Bonefish often face, or feed, into a strong tide. During strong incoming (flood) tides, bonefish are aggressive and less wary. They tend to spread out and break up into smaller groups. At high tide look for them along the shoreline or the highest areas of the flat, especially during primary spring tides when there is a full moon. At this time the highest tides of the month allow access to areas that otherwise do not have enough water for bonefish. One or two inches of water might mean the difference between access and no access. As a result, bonefish might feed at specific areas during specific stages of specific tides. Such in-depth knowledge is gained slowly; a guide who understands the movements of tides and bonefish is indeed worth the price you pay.

During full and dark moon tides in mangrove areas, fish often feed beyond the reach of anglers. If you can't access other areas, wait along the edge of the mangroves until the tide ebbs and turns down, at which time fish often stream out of such areas.

As the tide ebbs and flows out, bonefish follow, sometimes loitering in deeper water adjacent to their favorite flat waiting for the next incoming tide. Sometimes they settle in deeper water out of reach or bunch up at the edge of flats along drop-offs. They can hole up in deep-water pools or lakes located on flats such as those found at Christmas Island and Los Roques. These areas are large and deep enough to provide protection for bonefish and excellent angling. Lagoons and narrow entrance and exit areas such as those

As a rising tide floods the highest flats, bonefish often move into extremely thin water as seen here in the Seychelles. Anglers fishing clean sand do not have to worry about coral and mangrove hazards.

Chasing mangrove-bound bonefish on foot through soft mud and thigh-deep water is not easy and seldom pays a reward. Be certain to wash yourself off before getting back into the boat. In the lagoon at Castaway Island in the Bahamas.

found throughout the Bahamas can be worthwhile to stake out and fish at low tide. Fish often mill around these areas, waiting for the next dinner call, knowing that an outgoing tide will funnel a multitude of baitfish and crustaceans to them. Other gamefish, such as jacks, trevally, snapper, and tarpon, also frequent such areas.

As the tide ebbs and turns downward, so do the many tiny inhabitants and temporary visitors. Nobody wants to be left high and dry except the permanent residents, and a sense of urgency is in evidence. Bonefish can still be aggressive, but they move more quickly, with a sense of necessity. They begin to funnel off the flat, merging into travel lanes and bunching up like inner-city rush-hour traffic. They follow the tide downslope, often turning into the tide to feed. Sometimes the best tailing action is available on the lower stages of an outgoing tide. Often huge schools will be seen tailing in the quickly dropping water at the edge of the flat, enjoying a last snack before abandoning the dessert tray. Bonefish tend to congregate during low tide. They can be skittish, curious, picky, or nonaggressive, and they are always unpredictable.

In stark contrast to high tide, little life stirs during dead low tide. It is siesta, even hibernation, time. Many flats are void of water, and those creatures who stayed behind are tucked snugly into their hiding places and burrows. At a glance, the once lush watery garden has turned into a desert or mucky wasteland.

Except during a low incoming tide when fish can move onto flats with incoming water, bonefish usually swim and feed against the tide and wind, sniffing out their route and prey. Guides and anglers who lay out chum know this is true. Bonefish can be seen changing direction hundreds of feet away, heading straight for chum. While this technique is successful in attracting bonefish within easy casting range, it is certainly not bonefishing in the true sense of the word. Absent is the all-consuming hunt, stalk, and presentation strategy. Bonefish attracted to chum are often less wary and less skill is required to make the cast and hook them.

The tide cycle is divided into four seven-day periods that actually total 29.5 days. This cycle continually repeats itself. The seven-day periods are a direct result of the gravitational force of the sun

High tide. Notice that the water covers the mangrove roots and the lower portion of their foliage. These anglers are waiting for the tide to turn downward and for fish to migrate out of the groves at Andros Island in the Bahamas.

These anglers are taking a fun break and watching the tide rise. Soon it will be time to fish, and, they hope, bonefish will swim over this flat.

Low tide. Both wind and water are dead calm, making fishing conditions difficult. The distant island could easily be reached at this tide level, but could you get back when the tide is high? Always a prudent question to ask, especially at unfamiliar locations like this in the Seychelles.

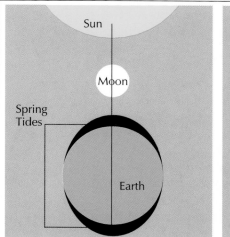
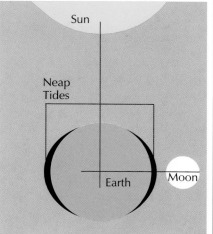

Spring and Neap Tides: When the sun and moon are in line with the earth (left), strong tides called *springs* occur. When the sun and the moon are at 90 degrees (right), the result is weaker tides called *neaps*.

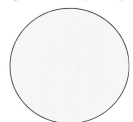

First Cycle: Full moon—primary spring tides.

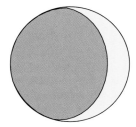

Second Cycle: Last quarter—neap tides.

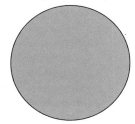

Third Cycle: Dark moon—secondary spring tides.

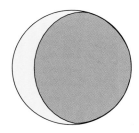

The tide charts on the following page show the daily cycle of tides over a 30-day period. The height of the tides in feet is shown at the left of the chart. Solid vertical lines indicate noon. Broken vertical lines indicate midnight. The radical fluctuations each month are when the moon is full or dark. Every location has a unique "tide print." Some areas have relatively flat tides; in other areas they are more radical.

and moon. The moon exerts nearly 2.5 times the gravitational pull of the sun. Its effect changes as it travels an elliptical path around the earth, while pulling the water toward it.

The illustrations at the left depict the relation between tidal height and the phase of the moon.

The first cycle: During the seven-day period when the moon is full, it is at its closest point to the earth. The sun and moon are in a nearly direct line with the earth. This once-a-month alignment causes tides to rise higher and drop lower than at any other time during the month. These are referred to as primary spring tides, although they have nothing to do with the seasons.

The second cycle: During the following seven-day period, the moon is in the last quarter. At this time the moon is at a right angle to the earth in relation to the sun. Tides have only minimal fluctuation. These are referred to as nip or neap tides.

The third cycle: During the next seven-day period, the moon is dark or a small sliver (new moon). The earth is now between the moon and sun. This brings a set of spring tides that are less radical than when the moon is full. These tides are often referred to as secondary spring tides.

The fourth cycle: During the next seven-day period, the moon is in its first quarter, which creates minimal water fluctuation. The moon is again at a right angle to the earth in relation to the sun. These are also referred to as nip or neap tides. The 29.5-day cycle is now complete and begins anew.

When the moon is full or dark, high tides are faster and higher, and low tides are lower. During a quarter moon, tides are slower and more even (neap tides), which allows bonefish to spend more time on the flats—and so can you. You can easily determine this in advance by looking at a calendar. You will not know at what time of day the high and low tides will occur; only on-site observation, local knowledge, or specific tide charts reveal that information.

Except for a few places that have only one low and high tide every 24 hours (large land masses slow down the flow of water), the tide reaches its high point twice every 24 hours and 50 minutes. A primary high and a lower secondary high are spread 12 hours apart. They occur 50 minutes later each day. If there is a high tide at noon today, it will occur at 12:50 p.m. tomorrow. If fishing is good at noon on a flat one day, similiar conditions might prevail the next day at 12:50 p.m.

Tides repeat themselves every two weeks. A high tide at noon on June first will repeat itself at noon on June 15. Consequently, a low tide will occur at noon June 8 and June 22.

Tides react like a seesaw. The outer ends move up and down, but the center stays at the same level. Some areas at the tidal center, such as Pensacola, Florida, hardly fluctuate at all. In the tidal flats in Alaska, the tide may fluctuate 20 feet or more! In the long and narrow Bay of Fundy in Canada, the tidal range may be 49 feet! The most spectacular tidal flows often occur during the spring and autumn equinoxes when the combined gravitational effect of the moon and sun is greatest. A sudden rush of water may create a visible wave front called a bore. At the mouth of the Amazon, this may move at over 10 miles per hour and be 15 feet high! Be careful where you wade! At Ascension Bay a two-foot variation is strong.

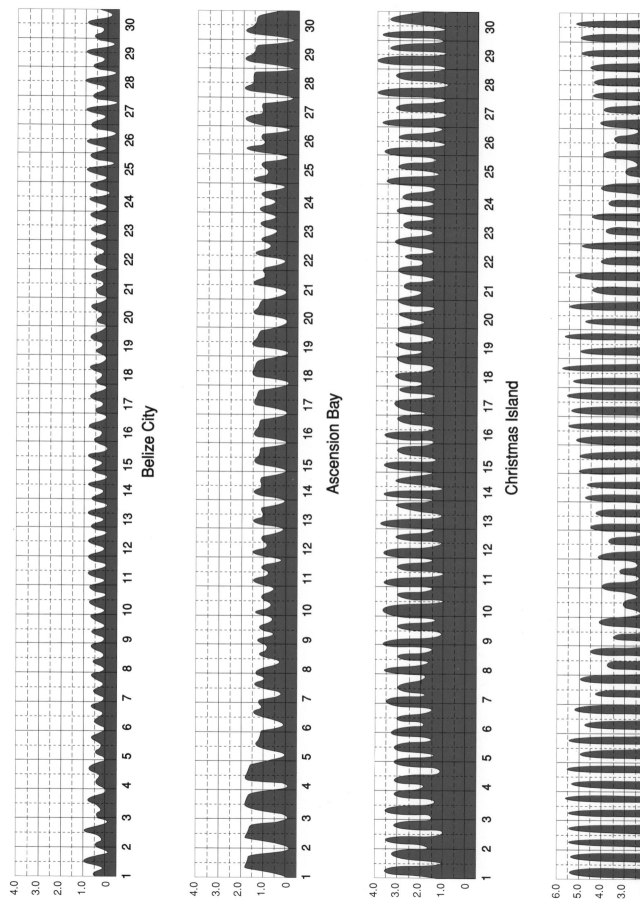

Belize City

Ascension Bay

Christmas Island

Bikini Atoll

This low tide in the Berry Islands in the Bahamas occurred during a full moon. At this time there are higher high tides and lower low tides. When there is a full moon, anglers often experience excellent fishing as fish rush onto and off flats during fast water flows. Bonefish and permit are able to feed on otherwise unreachable areas, and larger bonefish may appear on flats that otherwise are too shallow for them.

A surging tide is about to inundate the highest ground on this flat on Abaco in the Bahamas. When land disappears, you may feel marooned, but bonefish feel liberated. All but the tallest tails or those in thin water are now hidden by the tide, and fish can feed anywhere.

Hire a guide who knows the area you will be fishing and start compiling your own notebook of where, when, and how tides affect bonefishing.

Local tide charts are published in coastal newspapers. Sport shops often have pocket tide charts. The National Oceanic and Atmospheric Administration (NOAA), U.S. Department of Commerce, Washington, D.C. 20230, publishes two books that contain tide predictions, one for the east coast of North and South America and the other for the west coast of North and South America. Books are also available at marine stores. Software is available to determine the tides at most bonefish locations, and Internet sites offer information—check the NOAA site. Your booking agent can usually supply a weekly tide chart for general areas in the Bahamas, Christmas Island, and the like or advise you of tidal patterns. Remember, tide predictions are only predictions. Tides are influenced by many unforeseen and uncontrollable factors. Most published tidal information is extrapolated from a few key locations and applied to all others.

If you want accurate tidal information for a specific flat or area, you probably have to figure it yourself. Begin by observing the tide over a complete cycle, about 12 hours. Measure the tidal height against a fixed object or a stake marked in six-inch increments. Plot hourly measurements on a graph. Later, plot another cycle and compare the two; then make your prediction. Your chart should look like the tide illustrations on the previous page.

During a full moon and primary spring tides, anglers should experience at least three to four hours of excellent fishing each day, but sometimes bonefish might not seem overly aggressive. This might be explained in part because bonefish feed at night during a full moon. David Pinder, Jr., (affectionately known as David, Jr.), an excellent second-generation guide working on Grand Bahama Island, tells of fishing at night and having some outrageous action. "You cast to noisy splashing tails. You never know what size you'll hook, where it will run, or if a shark gets it. You don't land many, no, not many at all."

If you want to combine bonefish and permit or trevally, consider spring tides. Trevally and permit require eight to 14 inches deeper water than bones, and spring tides can provide these conditions.

While good sport can always be found, I like to fish the top two-thirds of an incoming tide when bonefish are aggressive, and the first third of an outgoing tide when fish demand more finesse. During these times bonefish are usually less cautious and are more likely to be broken up into singles, doubles, or small pods. Action is often continuous. Remember that specific flats fish best during specific stages of tidal fluctuations depending on their individual contours. For example, deepwater flats can be productive at low tide. A flat choked with mangroves is best avoided during a high spring tide but could be an excellent choice early or late in the tidal stage when you are able to fish the outer edges for fish entering or leaving the mangrove thickets. During neap tides (less flow, lower highs, higher lows) you may need to go to the big fish. During spring tides (higher highs, lower lows) the strong water flows may bring the "steroid" fish to you.

More important than tidal stage is tidal timing. If you can time your fishing so you have a rising tide at the time of day and specific location you prefer to fish, so much the better. A rising tide in late morning and a falling tide in the afternoon allow you to fish rising and falling water all day. A dead low at noon might mean a few hours of slow fishing during midday. However, just because a low tide is predicted at noon doesn't mean that every location in the area is experiencing a low tide at noon. This is where a knowledgeable guide is indispensable. If you are fishing in July and the weather is uncomfortable at midday, time the incoming tide for early or late in the day. Consider all the variables, but remember that any time is a good time to bonefish. They can be found at any stage of the tide.

Other Tidal Considerations

Like bonefish, other sport fish are also dependent on the tide for food. Once you learn to recognize the hangouts created by tidal movement in deeper water—channels, cuts, depressions, edges, and drop-offs—you may temporarily forget about bonefish. These areas can provide exceptional sport for saltwater boxers.

Look at the water surface for clues. Fast-moving water or hydraulic currents are a good beginning. As tidal currents enter narrow passages, they constrict, or bottleneck, then slow down, especially when flowing uphill into shallower water.

As waters flow over submerged obstructions, a surface rip may be created, possibly indicating good bottom structure. At deep-water intersections, currents collide and collect smaller organisms that large predators relish. Look for bird activity, leaping baitfish, and aggressive surface attacks by big fish.

This is a perfect place to find a big piggy wallowing at the edge of feeder channels on a dropping tide. The angler is in the ready position.

Jon Covich

Randall Kaufmann works a pod of feeders off North Abaco. Can you determine which way the tide is moving?

Tidelines, denoted by surface foam and debris that collects or travels in defined areas or lines, can also define areas where different currents, water temperatures, or salinity levels meet. Like trout in a river, larger fish often lie in slower water adjacent to fast water, conserving energy while waiting for prey to appear on the food conveyor, which, in this case, is the tide. Tidelines are an excellent place to concentrate your angling efforts for snapper, jacks, trevally, shark, etc.

The biggest fish are the most sensitive to water depth and current speed. They are most aggressive during the fastest two hours of the tide, which is during an incoming before it crests and during an outgoing after it has picked up momentum. During this time fish often school together and the competitive edge works to your advantage. Sometimes bigger fish are near the bottom, smaller fish near the surface. A sinking line is often the difference between success and failure.

A popper can be both seen and heard and is always my first choice. A white or silvery streamer with bright color highlights is another excellent choice (Combs' Sea Habit, Sea Serpent, Popovic's Epoxy Series, or tube-style 'cuda patterns). I often like flies with metal eyes because of the jig-like swimming action they offer. If brightly-colored snapper are abundant (and they often are), I like a red/yellow color combination. For deep water, a dark fly (purple, blue, black) can be effective. Smaller match-the-food translucent streamers are excellent when a feeding frenzy on like-color and like-size minnows is underway.

Vary your retrieve according to light, water depth, and water clarity. Bright light usually requires a quicker retrieve; low light and darkness, a slower retrieve. When fishing surface poppers for aggressive quick swimmers such as trevally or jacks, it is nearly impossible to make too much noise or surface commotion, or to pull the fly too quickly. Tuck the rod between your legs and pull with both hands. Get the picture? If they want it, they will have it.

Illustration depicts low and high tide cycles on a hypothetical flat for a 24-hour period. The dark shaded area is the best stage of the tide. In the top chart, the best fishing during daylight hours is from 6 a.m. until 1 p.m. In the bottom chart the best fishing is between 10 a.m. to 5 p.m. Because of the low angle of light, it is more difficult to spot fish early in the morning. Besides, who wants to get up that early? An understanding of the daily tidal stage can reveal where and when you should fish. If you have a choice, it makes a difference at the location you plan to fish, and accurate information is available. Plan your trip when there is a rising tide during midday.

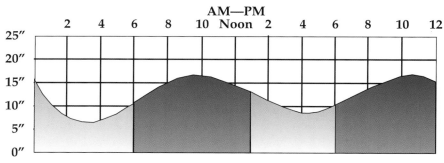

TIDE HEIGHT IN INCHES   DARK BLUE AREAS: BEST

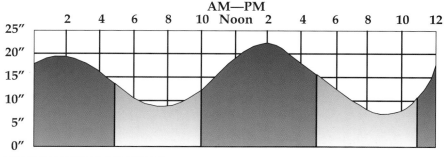

TIDE HEIGHT IN INCHES   DARK BLUE AREAS: BEST

Chapter 9

Foods

Bonefish are referred to as flats scavengers, terminators, and shallow-water pigs. They eat almost anything: fish, mussels, clams, snails, eels, conch, lobster, shrimp, squid, octopus, sea horses, sea anemones, sea urchins, sea lice, worms, crabs, and assorted bonefish flies, some of which can't possibly resemble anything alive or dead. Bonefish are opportunistic gluttons and nose into every corner of their world extracting energy-rich foods to sustain their near-frantic existence. Like sheep, their heads are usually pointed down in the grazing position. Their favorite greeting to each other must be *"Bon appétit!"* Bonefish do, however, usually concentrate on a few plentiful and available foods: clams, shrimp, crabs, and assorted small fish.

Bonefish Feeding Areas

Bonefish are grazers and feed about a flat much like sheep or cattle do on a pasture. Sometimes bonefish feed at a particular location until they have harvested their food supply, forcing them to temporarily abandon a flat and seek another area. Other bonefish populations naturally rotate between a number of feeding areas, possibly in an attempt not to diminish their foods in any one area. Populations of bonefish that are small relative to their food supply do not need to feed at several areas or change locations; they feed constantly in the same area.

These ideas help to explain why some bonefish populations seem to be local while others exhibit a wandering nature and do

Pooled Stomach Contents of 365 Bonefish Collected During 19 Months Near Deep Water Cay, Grand Bahama

Prey	Dry Weight	Frequency of Occurrence In Fish
Bivalvia (Clams, Mussels)	39.2%	66.3%
Portunidae (Crabs)	20.1%	40.5%
Xanthidae: Majidae (Crabs)	15.0%	24.8%
Gobiidae: Batrachoididae (Gobies)	4.9%	15.3%
Alphaeidae (Shrimp)	4.6%	16.2%
Squillidae (Shrimp)	3.2%	15.2%
Polychaeta (Worms)	3.2%	17.9%
Gastropoda (Snails, Squid)	2.4%	25.4%
Penaeidae (Shrimp)	1.6%	24.1%
Miscellaneous (Fish)	5.8%	

not remain in the same area for long periods of time. It might also explain their propensity for working with incoming tides and frequenting the shallowest of waters where maximum densities of prey exist. Anglers should remember that shallow-water fringes of dense crab populations can be available to bonefish during primary spring tides, creating a bonanza for both bonefish and anglers.

In the natural world everything has a cause and an effect. The more correlations you understand, the more pleasure you derive, whether it be from angling or from insights into nature's subtle complexities. The more you understand about food sources, how they become available, and the habits of bonefish, the better you are at hooking bonefish.

The following three scientific studies are from widely separated areas in the Caribbean. A brief look at the results helps anglers to better understand the feeding habits and prey of bonefish in relation to their habitat.

Deep Water Cay, Bahamas, Study

Douglas E. Colton and William S. Alevizon report that of 393 10- to 27-inch bonefish collected, 365 had food in their stomachs. Prey included only six major food sources but 60 individual species. Clams and mussels made up the bulk of the diet for these bonefish, followed by crabs and shrimp. Small fish were found to be of some importance to bonefish over 22 inches.

Grass areas represented a more complex environment than sand and had higher densities and diversities of prey. Bonefish in grassy areas seemed to feed more selectively than bonefish in sandy areas. In grassy areas bonefish were observed to pick out individual items. In comparison, bonefish feeding in sandy areas appeared to forage less discriminately, processing large amounts of substrata to acquire buried prey. However, such rooting behavior may be selective, as clams, mussels, and crabs were over-represented in stomach contents.

Utilization of Prey by Bahamian Bonefish Feeding in Seagrass and Sand
Values are Percents of Prey Numbers

	Summer		Winter	
	Seagrass	Sand	Seagrass	Sand
Prey	79 fish	40 fish	125 fish	18 fish
Gastropoda (Snails)	5	6	5	7
Alphaeidae (Shrimp)	9		19	16
Penaeidae (Shrimp)	11	20	28	1
Gobiidae: Batrachoididae (Gobies)	2	2	6	4
Xanthidae: Majidae (Crabs)	6	11	4	17
Bilvalvia (Clams)	49	44	22	43
Polychaeta (Worms)	4	6	9	
Portunidae (Crabs)	12	8	5	5
Squillidae (Shrimp)	2	3	2	7

During the winter, shrimp were heavily eaten by bonefish in grassy areas but were nearly absent from bonefish in sandy areas. Fish from sandy areas ate crabs, mussels, and clams to a greater extent than fish from grassy areas. During summer, shrimp made up 20 percent of items eaten in both habitats. The wide variety of prey eaten clearly indicates the overall generalized nature of bonefish feeding habits in this area. The table at the left breaks down the specific food sources of fish during the study in the Bahamas.

Puerto Rico Study

Germine L. Warmke and Donald S. Redman sampled 56 bonefish weighing between 0.75 and 10.25 pounds. All fish were collected at the reef areas of La Parguera on the Island of Culebra in Puerto Rico. Clams made up half of the bonefish's diet. Crabs accounted for 31 percent, shrimp 11 percent, snails five percent, and miscellaneous two percent.

Clams 51%
Snails 5%
Crabs 31%
Shrimp 11%
Others 2%

Puerto Rico Study

Florida Keys Study

Gerald E. Burger found that shrimp and crabs constitute the majority of food for Florida bonefish. Crustaceans, principally penaeid and alpheid shrimp and portunid and xanthid crabs (found in 73 percent of the stomachs), predominated as food items. Noncrustacean items, including mollusks (28 percent) and fish (15 percent) made up the other food items. The table at the right details Burger's findings.

It can be concluded that the dissimilarity in diets between bonefish of Florida, the Bahamas, and Puerto Rico is probably related to habitat and available food sources. Habitat (substrata type) exerts the strongest effect on the type of prey bonefish eat; preferred or available foods can vary from location to location. Seasonal, even monthly and weekly, changes are possible.

Bonefish generally feed on relatively slow-moving bottom dwellers, specializing in mollusks and crustaceans, but they readily accept almost anything they can get into their sucker-like mouths. This is fortunate for anglers because bonefish eagerly pounce on most offerings if they are properly presented and the fish have not been alerted to your presence.

Anglers interested in more exact imitation and presentation of bonefish foods should do some investigating where and when they fish. Each area may have a food print with one or more unique foods that bonefish may capitalize on. Obviously, anglers armed with specific information have an advantage, especially if bonefish show selectivity.

Anglers need not identify food sources down to specific genera or learn scientific names. As they do with trout food sources, anglers should recognize what the food sources are; their size, shape, and color; and how they react in their environment—in other words, how to best present them in the proper habitat.

Food sources are attracted to and held by bottom structure: depressions, sponges, coral, mangrove roots, etc. Other animals hide in cracks, crevices, and weeds, while still others burrow below the surface. An investigation of such areas will reveal the primary bonefish foods that you can imitate, including shrimp, crabs, small fish, worms, octopus, and squid. Observe their physical characteristics and movements. Remember that most food sources usually blend into the color of their surroundings. For example, grass dwellers will usually be olives, greens, browns, tans, grays, and mottled combinations thereof.

Serious anglers should take to the water with a face mask and snorkel for a close-up face-to-face view of a bonefish's world. Snorkelers should wear protective gloves and footgear and be careful of coral, sea urchins, and other underwater hazards. The variety of movement and life forms on a strong incoming tide is amazing. Use your hands to lightly stimulate the bottom strata and watch animals flee. You will exit the water with new insights and ideas for imitations and presentations.

Frequency of Occurrence of Crustacean Food Items Found in 129 Bonefish Stomachs

Food Item	No. Stomachs Containing Items	Percentage
Stomotopoda (Mantis Shrimp)	5	3.9
Penaeidae (Shrimp)	27	21.0
Palaemonidae (Grass Shrimp)	2	1.6
Alpheidae (Shrimp)	45	34.9
Brachyura (Shameface and Box Crabs)	5	3.9
Portunidae (Crabs)	40	31.0
Xanthidae (Mud and Stone Crabs)	46	35.7
Oxyrhyncha (Spider Crabs)	20	15.5

This big dog was chasing shrimp in grass patches at Abaco Island, Bahamas. One perfect cast and a short pull were all it took. Usually, the first cast is your best chance of fooling big bones. If they do not jump the fly the first time they see it, your chances are greatly diminished.

Shrimp

From a tying and angling point of view, shrimp are easiest to imitate and fish. Shrimp usually appear translucent with darker contrasting mottling and outside edges. Pinkish and orange mottling is common. Adult shrimp are often between one and two inches in length and swim backwards, or tail first, in short bursts, then remain still, relying on camouflage to protect them from predators. As a result, anglers who wish to observe them must be alert.

Snapping Shrimp: The snapping shrimp belongs to the family Alphaeidae and appears most often in the stomach contents of some Florida bonefish. It is also well documented throughout other Caribbean locations. Six of the most common snapping shrimp include the common snapping shrimp, *Alpheus heterochaelis*; red snapping shrimp, *A. armatus*; banded snapping shrimp, *A. armillatus*; long-clawed sponge shrimp, *Synalpheus longicarpus*; short-clawed sponge shrimp, *Synalpheus brevicarpus*; and the brown snapping shrimp, *A. armatus*, which is easily distinguished by its red and white banded antennae.

This burrowing crustacean looks like a tiny lobster with one large protective claw and a much smaller feeding claw. When others infringe on its territory, or if the shrimp is disturbed, a lock mechanism releases and the large claw snaps shut, making a snapping sound or a loud click that can be heard by anglers, hence its name. This noise surely attracts bonefish, which are known to locate prey by vibration. Snorklers often hear this snapping sound, and attentive anglers can also distinguish this unique noise as they walk or pole the flats.

Snapping shrimp live in coral crevices in reefs, under the ringed anemone, and in sponge chambers, especially at the edges of flats, but the young are widely dispersed by tidal currents and often take refuge in turtle grass. Adult snapping shrimp are one to two inches in length and, like many shrimp, dart in short, quick bursts and rest motionless for protection. Their colors range from whitish to brown with tan and greenish markings with a mottled tan claw, to shades of greenish to greenish yellow to chartreuse with a reddish-orange claw. Other colors include orange brown with black bands, greenish tan with alternating white bands, and brown with tan bands. Snapping shrimp have inspired several imitations. They are probably the reason why the Yucatan Special, Deep Water H_2O, and Snapping Shrimp patterns are productive.

Snapping Shrimp

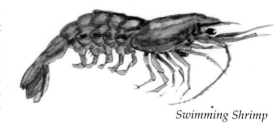

Swimming Shrimp: The swimming shrimp (commonly called commercial shrimp) of the family Penaeidae are the second most common shrimp found in stomach samples of some bonefish in Florida waters. They are also the most common shrimp found in anglers' stomachs and are usually served with a squeeze of lemon and cocktail sauce. The white shrimp, *Penaeus setiferus*, grows to seven inches. It is mostly transparent with a bluish tinge and dusky bands and black dots. The American pink shrimp, *Penaeus duorarum*, may reach eight inches, but bonefish eat juveniles when they are available. Juveniles are gray or reddish brown with a dark spot at the junction of the third and fourth abdominal segments. Brown shrimp, *Penaeus aztecus*, are brown with tan markings and are common throughout the Caribbean into Mexico and Belize. The young tolerate brackish estuaries that are not well flushed by tides, but adults like fresh marine water. Bonefish commonly ingest specimens to three inches or more.

Swimming Shrimp

Grass Shrimp: Grass shrimp, *Palaemonetes pugio*, are most common in areas with slightly higher salinity and turtle grass, especially at some locations in the Bahamas and Belize where the families Palaemonidae and Hippolytidae are abundant. Bahamian guides claim the shrimp hang around the mangrove roots and that the larger fish that cruise these areas are shrimp hunters. Their claws are located on their first and second legs, which are the largest. They are slender, delicate-looking shrimp ranging in size between one and two inches. They are commonly a translucent tannish-brown color but can also be gray and olive with a touch of lavender.

Grass Shrimp

Mantis Shrimp: The mantis shrimp is a member of the order Stomotopoda, which encompasses about 200 species. Its head is unlike that of any other crustacean because it is jointed. The finger of the second leg has strong teeth and is folded along a groove in the preceding joint. The raptorial legs are very sharp and can cut other shrimp in half. The lightning-like speed of the mantis shrimp's strike resembles that of the praying mantis, after which it is named.

Mantis Shrimp

It has a narrow body and a fan-shaped tail and looks like a cross between a shrimp and a baby lobster with small claws. It resembles freshwater crayfish. The mantis shrimp can grow to several inches and can inflict nasty bites with its serrated claws. It prefers to burrow in sand or mud but also lives in grass and dead coral. While mantis shrimp are not as abundant as snapping shrimp, they are readily taken by bonefish, which prey on one- to four-inch specimens. Bonefish often root them out of the bottom strata or find them foraging in the open along the bottom. In the Caribbean there are more than 60 species. Color varies with individual species and the habitat, but greenish or bluish green with darker ridges or margins and creamy with yellow to orange ridges are some of the more common colors.

At Christmas Island, mantis shrimp are often referred to as "manta" shrimp. It burrows into soft bottom strata and grows to about 10 inches in length. It defends itself vigorously and is considered a delicacy by both man and bonefish. Man eats the big ones; bonefish eat smaller specimens.

Christmas Island locals are adept at finding mantis shrimp. Mantis are formidable adversaries. They are agressive, quick, and mobile—much like a helicopter. Unless you know what you are doing, don't put your hand in their burrow!

Crab to bonefish—"Got something stuck in your lip? Ya, yada, ya, ya...you can't catch me, you can't catch me!"

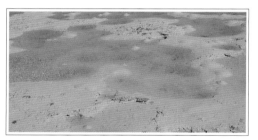

Crab mounds at low tide. Grand Bahama Island.

Crabs this size are no problem for a medium-sized bonefish. North Andros, Bahamas.

Swimming Crab

Crabs

Aside from mollusks, crabs are the most important and consistent bonefish food source and are of major importance to anglers. Crabs inhabit every shallow-water habitat and are, perhaps, one of the reasons bonefish venture into shallow water. Crabs come in assorted shapes and many sizes and colors, usually blending and burrowing into their surroundings. Like small fish, smaller crabs usually inhabit shallow shoreline areas. Crabs are usually most plentiful in muck. Some crabs follow the tidal flow in and out; others burrow downward. When water temperatures cool, crabs burrow deeper in the muck. When temperatures warm, they are seen on top of the strata, sometimes nibbling your toes if you're barefoot.

Usually, bonefish do not feed too selectively on crab species. As a result, anglers do not need to identify and exactly imitate specific species. A general knowledge of the basic species helps you select and present reasonable imitations. If your imitation is the right size and color and looks like a crab, bonefish usually eat first and ask questions when it is too late.

At More's Island off Abaco in the Bahamas, we found a small pod of bonefish trapped in a sink hole at low tide. We cast a crab fly into their midst and had an immediate hookup. This panicked the others and they raced about their confined quarters in a state of uncontrollable fear, showing no more interest in our fake. As an experiment, we found a live crab, hooked it onto the fake, and tossed it into their confused midst. One ate it even as it raced by at near full speed.

Swimming Crabs: Scientific research and reports from guides and commercial fishermen who have autopsied hundreds of bonefish confirm that swimming crabs of the family Portunidae are very important to bonefish. As their name implies, they are good swimmers and give approaching bonefish a good run, especially if they have time to burrow into the bottom strata. Tenacious bonefish, however, usually discover shallow burrows and turn the crabs into crab salad. Crabs in their permanent shelter are usually four inches deep and dislodging them requires major excavation. Bonefish seldom bother with these. They prefer to let the excitement of incoming tides and the promise of plentiful food coax crabs from their subsurface burrows.

Portunus swimming crabs are similar in shape and behavior to blue crabs. My brother, Lance, has collected many in Belize that are

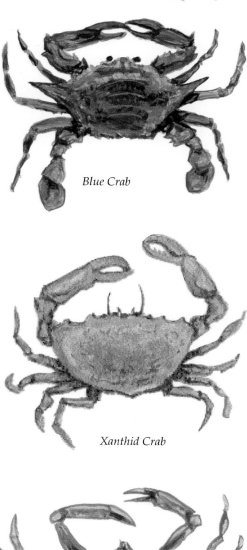

the size of a nickel or dime and colored greenish olive-brown with yellow markings fading to light olive and tan.

While we were fishing an outside hard sand flat at Staniard Creek on Andros, our guide, Prescott Smith, mentioned that blue crabs were the main prey of bonefish and that we couldn't fish too large an imitation. Big fish eat big crabs! A four-inch crab is nothing to a 30-inch bonefish. Prescott mentioned that standard-colored crab flies are good, but you have to work them to entice fish. A blue crab imitation is gobbled with no questions asked. Crab imitations are underfished by most anglers. I always have an extensive selection of sizes and colors, and so should you.

The common blue crab, _Callinectes sapidus_, is often the most abundant, and anglers can't help but notice its aggressive nature. When approached by humans, it rears up with claws poised for attack, boldly fending off any challenger with its one large blue-to-purple claw. It is white underneath with blue gray on top and shading to bright blue on the claws. Leg joints are orange. Its preferred habitat is mud and sand, but I have also observed them around grassy areas. Other species of blue crabs include ornate, _C. ornatus_, which has a greenish carapace (body) covered with brown hairs, and Dana's, _C. danae_, which has an olive carapace that becomes indigo on the edges with purple claws.

Mud and Stone Crabs: These intertidal crabs of the family Xanthidae are a favorite of bonefish. The small herbivorous xanthid crab, _Cataleptodius floridanus_, inhabits intertidal coral rubble (sand, mud, coral, grass). Populations of this prolific crab reach 100 individuals per square meter in shallow areas where bonefish cannot reach them. They are often uncommon in only slightly deeper adjacent waters because bonefish harvest them on a continual basis. These crabs range in length up to 3.5 inches and commonly take on the color of their surroundings: whites, tans, grays, olives, and browns; reds are common. Bonefish most often ingest small specimens.

Spider Crab: The spider crab, _Pitho aculeata_, family Majidae, commonly known as the gray spider crab, is about one inch long and is a favorite bonefish food. This species is mostly nocturnal and is cryptically colored with greenish hues, factors that somewhat reduce predation, but bonefish do eat them.

Hermit Crabs: There are many species of hermit crabs, family Coenobitidae. Anglers commonly see mollusk and other shells scattered about beaches, mangroves, and grass flats. A close inspection reveals that these shells are actually the home of hermit crabs. Hermit crabs can be almost any size and color. They move from shell to shell as they mature. Specific species often select specific shells. Because of their general nature and habitat, few anglers are aware of their importance to bonefish.

The best hermit crab habitat I have encountered is along the beach at Christmas Island and among mangroves in the Bahamas. Some Florida guides and anglers have recognized the value of fishing imitations of hermit crabs in the Keys. Bunches of hermit crabs can sometimes be found along the edges of turtle grass, and foraging bonefish can be downright picky, even snooty. When this is the case, near exact imitations of crabs inside their shells should be retrieved slowly or allowed to drift.

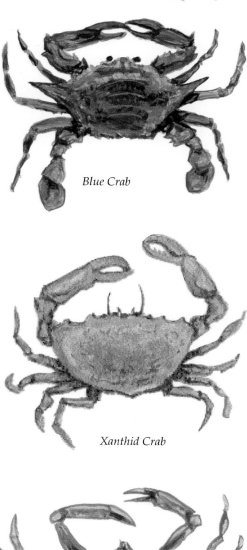

Blue Crab

Xanthid Crab

Spider Crab

Randall Kaufmann

Hermit crabs inhabit all sizes of abandoned shells. This shell is approximately three inches across.

Fish find safety in numbers. Hopefully, you survive while your neighbor doesn't. This school was surrounded by tarpon in Belize.

Goby.

Goby.

Mojarra.

Fish

Hundreds of species of small fish inhabit shallow salt water. Species that commonly become victims of bonefish, especially larger bonefish, include glass minnows, gobies, mojarras, pipefish, snapper, and toadfish. Most of these forage fish are three inches or less in length and swim in small schools. Many are relatively slow swimmers and rely on their camouflage coloration for protection. Bonefish seldom encounter small fish in open territory but usually frighten them into motion while hunting along the bottom. Gobies are the most prevalent, followed by pipefish, but the young of almost any shallow-water fish are potential prey.

Any translucent minnow is loosely referred to by anglers as a "glass" minnow. True glass minnows are thought to be anchovy or sardine that spawn and live in and around sand. Flats geography and seasonal phenomena dictate available bonefish foods. When minnows congregate at the surface, bonefish might be observed slashing and gulping them, creating a top-water frenzy. Usually, minnow feeding is less obvious and anglers all to often underestimate the importance of small fish in the diet of bonefish.

Gobies: Fish of the family Gobiidae, small bottom-dwelling sculpin-like fish that are usually one- to three-inches long. They are a very successful group that occupies a shallow-water niche throughout the world's tropical seas. They are most abundant in shallow intertidal waters, preferring sand, mud, grass, and coral bottoms. Gobies commonly rest on the bottom, sometimes propped on their pelvic fins, and they dart quickly from place to place. Some live in burrows in the sand or mud. They can be multicolored and vary in shape.

Gobies show an inclination to come out of the water; some species are able to trap air and water in their gill chambers and survive for several hours out of the water. If they are kept damp, they can live for weeks without being submerged. Perhaps some evolutionary change may be in progress, and we are witnessing another walking fish in the making.

The bases of their pelvic and ventral fins are united, forming a sucking disc with which they hold on to the bottom or any stationary object. This helps them avoid the battering they might otherwise receive in rough intertidal areas. Typical gobies have no lateral line. They have tapering tails and two dorsal fins. The second dorsal fin and the anal fin mirror each other in size and shape. Some species are brightly colored, but many blend into their surroundings and are olive, tan, brown, cream, gold, and green, sometimes with banding or mottling.

Mojarras: Like bonefish, *Gerres cinereus* feed on shrimp, crabs,

worms, and mollusks that they dig out of sandy flats with their protrusible mouths. They exhibit chameleon characteristics—they can change to a silvery color over sand and olive brown over grass. Mojarras grow to 15 inches, but two- to three-inch silvery tan juveniles are prime bonefish prey. They inhabit all Caribbean bonefish waters.

Pipefish: The family Syngnathidae of the order Solenichthys includes sea horses, needlefish, and pipefish and is common in tropical seas. A sea horse is actually a curled-up pipefish with a tilted head. Most pipefish inhabit shallow waters with grassy bottoms. All have straight segmented bodies formed by a bony armor beneath the skin. Because of the general rigidity imposed by the armor, body movement is minimal. Locomotion is made possible by means of a rapid but gentle wave-like motion of the fins. Pipefish are slow moving, adept at concealing themselves, and live a low-key existence. They can move their eyes independently, and, like chameleons, they change their color to some degree to match their surroundings. They are commonly recognized by their elongate shape, absent ventral and (sometimes) caudal fins, tubular snouts with small mouths, and characteristic tufted lobed gills. They range in color from olive, green, brown, tan, and cream to silvery or yellowish with dark, bright, or light mottling, stripes, and spots. Bonefish commonly eat pipefish that are one to three inches in length.

Snapper: A snapper is a delicacy to both angler and bonefish, and they are common in nearly all bonefish waters. There are several species in the Lutjanidae family, including cubera, red, Lane, mutton, yellowtail, schoolmaster, and mangrove. Their color is as varied as their habitat. They are found in sandy grass flats, under mangrove roots, in depressions and channels, under piers and docks, anywhere there is cover or structure. They are colored red-to-olive browns to gray and are most active at night. Pier dwelling snapper provide anglers with excellent entertainment. Just try to catch one of these wary critters on a fly. Throw out some table scraps and watch the frenzy. Next, insert a hook into a table scrap. Do you think they will eat it? Fat chance. Pier snapper have seen it all and they remember.

Toadfish: Gulf toadfish, _Opsanus beta_, live in burrows and are common in grass and coral habitat throughout Florida, the Bahamas, and the Gulf of Mexico. They grow to 10 inches, have a large flat head, large pectoral fins, and round caudal fin. They are mottled brownish tan. Larger specimens croak at divers and snap at anything that comes past their burrows. Smaller toadfish are often preyed on by bonefish.

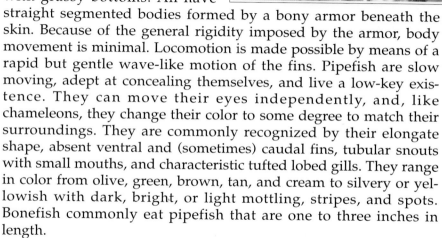

This habitat is home to a multitude of creatures, including this mangrove snapper, caught foraging on North Abaco, Bahamas.

Pipefish.

Snapper.

Toadfish.

The largest, most beautiful, and best eating snail in bonefish country is the conch, pictured here in Belize. Travelers to Caribbean waters look forward to conch fritters and conch seviche.

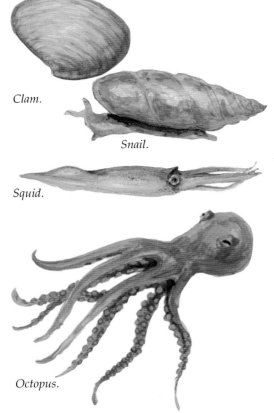

Clam.

Snail.

Squid.

Octopus.

Mollusks

Mollusks are animals possessing a shell. The phylum of the mollusks is divided into five classes, three of which are meaningful to bonefishermen. Bivalvia is the class of clams and mussels, Gastropoda is the class of snails, and the class Cephalopoda includes squid and octopus.

Bivalves (Clams, Mussels): Many of the shells we find on the beach are the products of laterally flattened mollusks that breathe through gills. The shell halves are joined at the hinge by an elastic ligament and can be closed quickly. Various species exist on bonefish flats, and bonefish readily ingest them.

Brian O'Keefe and I once encountered several permit feeding in a brackish lagoon in southern Belize. After the fish snubbed all our offerings, Brian began to investigate and discovered the muddy bottom of the lagoon was a rich clam bed. The clams were white and about the size of the buttons on his shirt. He removed two of them, lashed them over the top and bottom of a hook, and had a permit on his first cast! He dubbed the "fly" the McClam. *Pay attention and be resourceful!*

Snails: These animals glide slowly forward by using a "foot," which has a muscular interior and a rather slimy exterior. The foot glides easily over a thin layer of mucous secreted by a gland under the head. The eye stalks are well-known features. Snail shells come in a variety of colors and shapes. Bonefish generally prey on those species that are three-fourths of an inch or less. Anglers interested in particulars should look closely at the snails available in the area of intended fishing.

Octopus: Octopuses are classified as mollusks, but they have long since abandoned their protective shell, relying more on brain power than armor. The octopus has a large brain, and it needs it to control its three hearts, high blood pressure, eight legs, sometimes thousands of suckers, and amazing camouflage mechanism. When it comes to camouflage, the octopus is in a class of its own. Chromatophore cells in their skin are controlled by muscles. The walls of these cells can be altered within a fraction of a second, bringing different pigments to the surface and allowing near perfect camouflage!

Astonishingly compressible, octopuses can squeeze into nearly any crevice or abandoned shell. Their primary diet is similar to that of bonefish: shrimp, crabs, and mollusks. Like squid, they jettison purplish-black ink to disorient predators and elude capture.

Bonefish seem to relish these delicate creatures when they can find them. Perhaps some marabou patterns are suggestive of octopuses, but anglers need to refine imitations.

Worms

At Christmas Island I asked several guides what the best bonefish imitation was and received several answers, including crabs and shrimp. Moana Kofe mentioned that his white Moana's Worm is sometimes very effective. It represents a long whitish worm that lives in the mud. The Christmas Island worm needs more defining, but Moana mentioned that early winter provides the best action. Perhaps this is the time they breed and are more available to bonefish.

Palolo Worms: Eunice schemacephala are iridescent pale green worms with brownish tentacles. They are sometimes available briefly to bonefish when they emerge partially from their coral burrows while searching for food; the best opportunity presents itself when the worms breed. Segments from the posterior ends of the worm, called epitokes, twist sideways, break off, and swim to the surface where the eggs or sperm are released. In Florida this phenomenon can create a feeding frenzy even among tarpon and is thought to be partly triggered by the warming water temperatures and growing length of daylight in early summer. Surface density of epitokes can range from one per three square feet to wriggling masses that look like maggot soup. If only they could fly.

Tube Worm: Onuphis eremita oculata is sometimes abundant in turtle grass throughout the Caribbean. This worm's one- to two-inch shell- and debris-covered tube can also be found in sand. The slightest disturbance causes the worm to retreat into its tube. Worms are seldom observed by anglers, and little is known about when, where, and how bonefish feed on them. They can, however, be an important consideration.

There are many other species of worms. Some build tubes or live in burrows, others are free ranging. They vary in shape, size, and color, but tans, creams, browns, olives, and whites are the most common. Jim Kenyon, of 3M/Scientific Anglers fame, stumbled onto some selective worm fishing at Cat Island in the Bahamas and related that fish were selective to color. His white worm imitations were successful, but fish bolted at the sight of a tan imitation. Many bonefish flies could be perceived by bonefish as many types of food, including worms. Do you think that soft worm bodies might be akin to us eating a chocolate mousse? I don't know. Chocolate worms just don't appeal to me no matter how you package them.

Eels

Eels burrow into soft substrata and make their homes in coral crevices, grassy rocky areas, etc. This broad group of snake-like fish is irresistible to marauding bonefish. Sand eels, family Ophichthidae, are found in all bonefish habitats that support grass, where they like to burrow. Any wiggly eel-like imitation is likely to provoke an instant attack. Baby eels that frequent bonefish habitat are colored like their surroundings—tan, cream, brown, olive, etc.

Worm.

The conch is visible inside the shell. Before over-harvesting, conch this size were common on many bonefish flats. Today only the most remote areas harbor conch in shallow waters.

Bonefish relish clams, which are high in energy and unable to escape.

Sea urchin.

Sea Urchins

Sea urchins belong to the family Echinoidae. Echinoderms usually have a five-sided hard skelton and are often covered with spines. A vascular system circulates water to move their suction cup-like feet. Enchinodermata include brittle stars, sea cucumbers, starfish, and urchins.

Urchins are mostly algae feeders and are most often encountered by anglers wading grass flats. Every saltwater flats fisherman runs into the black sea urchin, *Diadema antillarum,* at least once. Their pointed spines easily penetrate neoprene and tennis shoe footgear. The larger, more troublesome, specimens are easy to spot and avoid. Other species are less well known but are found in many shapes, sizes, and colors. Many have less defined and rigid bristles. Many live on or just under the surface. The smaller juveniles are seldom spotted by anglers, but bonefish know where and how to find them. You can't fish imitations too slowly.

Miscellaneous

Understanding bonefish food sources is in its infancy. There are many regional and local phenomena that are little observed, even unknown. A hatch-type situation occurs in the Bahamas when jellyfish congregate to spawn in shallow water. According to ace Andros Island guides Glister Wallace and Andy Smith, the jellyfish hatch is an experience worth searching for. When jellyfish eggs hatch, there are millions of them, and they grow quickly. Bonefish relish them and feed with abandon for about two weeks in the spring. A tiny unweighted fly is necessary. Glister and Andy are quick to add that the tiny jellyfish sting. They are irritating, more so if they get in your shorts! Fly tiers should become familiar with eels, worms, fish, sea urchins, and sea lice. There is plenty of room for research and development. Specific bonefish foods in the Pacific are virtually unknown to anglers. A person could spend years just classifying and observing bonefish food sources at Christmas Island. Coupled with associated fly pattern innovation, the possibilities are nearly endless.

Anglers pursue bonefish in many types of habitat. As you select a fly, keep this thought in mind: fly selection is usually based upon prevailing conditions—bottom type and color, and water depth, which determines the needed sink rate. This bonefish swims in grass flats off Grand Bahama Island in the Bahamas. Imagine how a fly would fish in this habitat. Note how the bonefish assumes the color of its surroundings.

Chapter 10

Choosing a Fly

We live in a world in which difficult decisions are never very distant. When you are walking a bonefish flat and open your fly box to choose a fly, the decision is simple. Just pick one! Because bonefish are opportunistic feeders, if they see it and it looks edible, odds are they will eat it. This is an over simplification, but bonefish are seldom selective in the true sense of the word. Few bonefish flies have evolved into specific imitations, and fly selection is primarily based upon prevailing conditions: bottom type and color, and water depth. Aside from the rare times when you are imitating a specific food source or when bonefish are feeding selectively, the most important considerations in choosing a fly are:

1. Sink rate and associated retrieve.
2. Shape, size, and color.

Sink Rate

Bonefish are mostly bottom feeders, so flies should be presented at or below a fish's level. This is not to say bonefish do not tip up to feed, but it is not the norm.

When selecting an imitation, the sink rate is of paramount importance. Generally, the fly should reach the bottom in 2.5 seconds, or on the count of three. A fly weighted in this manner can usually be presented close to bonefish without spooking them and will reach the bottom and intersect their path before they change direction. You can usually plan on bonefish continuing on the same feeding path for 10 to 20 feet.

When bonefish are in a travel/feed mode they usually travel and feed between one and two miles per hour, which translates to between 1.5 and three feet per second. At two miles per hour, or three feet per second, the fly must be presented at *least* 7.5 feet ahead of the fish in order to have the fly resting on the bottom when the bonefish arrives. If the fly took twice the recommended time, or five seconds, to reach the bottom, you would need to present it 15 feet ahead of the fish. This considerably reduces the chances of the bonefish maintaining its course and finding the fly. Conversely, if the fly is still sinking and above the fish as it passes, it may not be noticed.

Cast as close to bonefish as conditions allow. If you can cast 18 inches in front of a fish, you know where your fly is in relation to the fish. If you cast eight feet out, it is much more difficult to determine the exact location of the fly. If fish are aggressive, make an aggressive presentation. Fast swimmers require more lead time. Tailers and slow-moving feeders require a closer presentation. As you make your presentation to moving bonefish, consider the following:

1. Speed the bonefish are traveling.
2. Water depth.
3. Sink rate of fly.
4. Speed and direction of the current.

Remember that the 2.5 second sink time is only a guideline. Specific circumstances will require a slower or faster sinking fly. An

If bonefish are traveling/feeding at two miles per hour and it takes three seconds for the fly to sink to the bottom, the fly must be presented at least 7.5 feet ahead of them so the fly is resting on the bottom when the bonefish arrive.

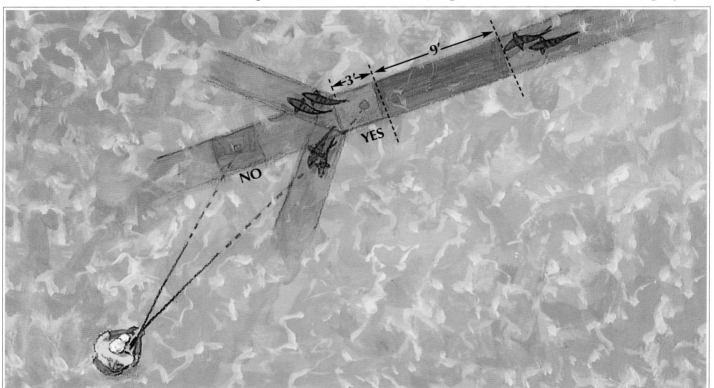

Speed of Bonefish	Distance Travelled (Feet Per Second)	Sink Rate of Fly	Lead Distance
1 mph	1.5 Feet/Second	3 Seconds	4.5 Feet
2 mph	2.9 Feet/Second	3 Seconds	9.0 Feet
3 mph	4.4 Feet/Second	3 Seconds	13.5 Feet
4 mph	5.9 Feet/Second	3 Seconds	18.0 Feet

exceptionally calm day might demand a lighter and smaller fly. A windy day might dictate a slightly larger and heavier fly. If you are fishing over a soft bottom, a heavier and larger fly might be needed to attract the fish's attention. If you are fishing off the bow of a boat and conditions are such that you can only spot fish 15 feet out, the fly should be heavy enough to sink quickly so that a retrieve can begin before the fish becomes aware of your presence. Reefs and other areas where wind and currents are strong might require a heavier fly. On the other hand, if the fly is too heavy, it may hang up on bottom debris, especially weeds, instantly spooking any bonefish. An open-ended understanding of cause and effect allows you to compute any necessary adjustments. I find the count of three sink rate is usually about right.

If the "plop" of a weighted fly sends fish running, it is too heavy or it was cast too close to the fish. Sometimes the plop of a fly, especially when cast behind fish or to their blind side, can arouse their curiosity and turn them around. It may be necessary to lighten the weight when casting close to tailers and stationary feeders. Sometimes a smaller, lighter fly is the tradeoff to the desired sink rate. The quiet "blip" of a small, light, streamlined fly when it hits the water may be more important than a faster sink rate. Shallow water requires a smaller or lighter fly so a closer presentation can be made.

Tails in the air usually denote feeding fish, but, when both tails and fins are seen in skinny water, it may be that fish are traveling. Because of their size, small fish can tail and feed in shallower water than large fish. When a tailer is observed in very shallow water, it is a small fish. When a tailer is observed in deeper water, you know it is a large fish because the tail of a small fish would not reach the surface. When a pod of tailers is observed, fish to the tallest tail, which is the largest fish.

The run-and-hide response of shrimp, and, to a lesser degree, of crabs and other foods, is one best described as a lift-off, scurry, settle, and hide movement whereby prey flees up off the bottom, then settles back down. This hopping, jigging, or rise-and-settle movement is best achieved by incorporating heavy eyes on the fly, either bead chain or various weights of metal eyes. To a small degree, hook size influences the sink rate. In lieu of metal eyes, heavy wire can be added to the top of the hook shank, which helps the hook ride up, but this does not create the hop retrieve.

Metal eyes are added to the top of the hook shank so the finished fly will fish point up. Bonefish flies are constructed to ride point up to minimize the chances of the fly hanging up on the bottom. A bonefish's mouth is designed to feed on the bottom with the upper jaw protruding out over the lower jaw. As a result, an inverted fly has more hooking power.

The sink rate, set-down splash, and swimming action can also be influenced with the amount and type of materials used in fly construction. A bulky fly might be useful when a quiet presentation and slow sink rate are desired in skinny water. Except for specialized circumstances, I usually like to fish sparse flies. These penetrate the water's surface more easily, sink faster, and, depending on the materials and rate of retrieve, they have more animation.

The heavier the fly, the harder it will land. Heavy flies need to be retrieved harder to lift them off the bottom to create the hopping effect. A heavy fly settles deeper into a soft bottom, creating a cloud of mud when it is moved. This is an excellent attraction ploy; bonefish recognize the smoke signal from a great distance. Over hard or grassy bottoms, a heavy fly might bump or momentarily snag, scattering bonefish like a lighted fuse on a firecracker scatters

When fishing over soft sediment bottoms, a heavy eyed fly creates a noticeable disturbance (mud cloud) if retrieved with a strip action. Sometimes bonefish are attracted to this smoke signal.

A bonefish's mouth is designed to feed on the bottom. Flies that fish point up are best. Note the position of the fly—it is inverted and in the front of the upper lip—the perfect hookup.

kids. When visibility is impaired, when it is windy, or when bonefish are rooting, a close presentation with a heavier fly can sometimes be made without arousing suspicion.

The lighter the fly, the slower it needs to be retrieved. With a fast retrieve, the fly will lift off the bottom and stall. Sometimes this is an effective ploy but not usually. Shallow-water feeders can be spooked by sudden quick fly movement. Slow down the retrieve. Remember, once you have the attention of bonefish, letting the fly remain motionless or giving it a slight twitch is often sufficient.

Shape

Most standard bonefish flies are reasonable imitations of shrimp, and there are also some good crab imitations available. For now, over-the-counter bonefish anglers can choose from a good selection of colors and sink rates, but specific patterns, other than crabs, are not easily located. Fortunately, these standard patterns fool most fish most of the time. Specific patterns are being designed by innovative tyers, and these are often effective on large, sophisticated bonefish. As new patterns become mainstream, they should be available at your favorite fly fishing store.

Size

Bonefish flies are usually tied on size 2 to 8 hooks, but 4 and 6 are the most popular. The overall length of a fly (not the hook size), its shape, and its color are usually about equal in importance. The length of bonefish imitations should be related to the food source you intend to imitate. Shrimp are often one to two inches long, but bonefish easily consume shrimp four inches and longer. Crabs are usually the size of a nickel, dime, or quarter, but large bonefish think nothing of chasing down a crab three inches in diameter. Sometimes a larger fly makes too much noise and commotion in shallow water. Larger flies usually should be cast farther away from bonefish. Deeper water and cloudy or windy conditions require larger flies.

Generally, clear shallow water and clear calm weather conditions demand smaller flies, perhaps even a lighter fly line, for a more delicate presentation. Smaller flies are less likely to be detected as fraudulent, especially by wiser, more careful fish. For extreme conditions and when bonefish are ultra picky, size 10 to 14 mini flies may prove invaluable. Small shrimp and worm imitations commonly used by trout fishermen can be effective. Saltwater hooks are not available this small; use strong scud-style hooks such as Tiemco 2457, sizes 6 to 14.

Be certain that hooks are sharp. I like to sharpen hooks to a diamond or triangle shape with three or four cutting edges. A sharp barbless hook easily penetrates the mouth of a bonefish. If you break off a bonefish, the fish can work out a barbless hook, or, if it is made of steel, the hook will rust away.

Color

I usually ask my guide which fly I should fish. I do this both out of respect and out of curiosity. Over the years the general response has been a shrug of the shoulders and a casual pick that would be considered a habitat matcher. However, when the fly has

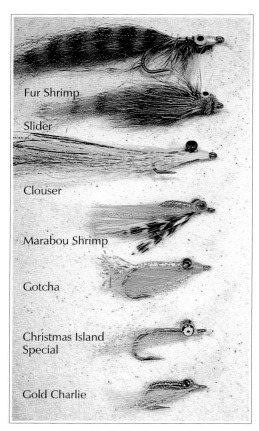

Fur Shrimp

Slider

Clouser

Marabou Shrimp

Gotcha

Christmas Island Special

Gold Charlie

The overall length of a fly is of concern to bonefish, not the hook size. Most standard bonefish flies are similar in shape. Colors range from white to neon. Tan is the most universal color.

been refused twice, most guides quickly demand a change of color, knowing that color is an important aspect of success.

Fly color makes a big difference from location to location, from flat to flat, and from hour to hour. These preferences are partly based on habitat and prevailing light conditions. There are two primary color selection strategies. Select a color that matches or complements the bottom strata on the assumption that common foods blend into their surroundings, or select a contrasting color that offers high visibility. I like to temper this process and consider the prevailing light conditions and stage of the tide.

Subtle natural colors (tans, browns, olives, golds) work best during bright light conditions and in shallow water when bonefish are more cautious. During intense sunlight, brighter colors reflect too much light, and bonefish often avoid them. Bright colors (yellows, pinks, whites, greens, and oranges) work best during darker, cloudy conditions and later in the afternoon. During muted light conditions, bright flies are less harsh, yet are seen more easily, especially from a distance. Brighter flies also produce better in deeper water and when there is a rising tide (fish are more aggressive).

Trout anglers, especially those who fish lakes, may find this dark condition-bright fly, bright condition-dark fly advice contrary to their usual tactics. Remember that bonefish usually feed in a downward position in shallow water over a bottom that often reflects a great amount of light. When sun/sky conditions are brightest, a darker fly usually shows best over a light bottom.

I once fished the Bahamas when a cold front dropped the water temperature to 69 degrees Fahrenheit and iced out most bonefish. The few chances I did have were frustrating. Bonefish passed my usual conservative flies like they were not there. That observation was my tip-off: bonefish either were not seeing the offering, or it was not interesting enough to arouse their curiosity. I switched to a long Interceptor pattern that looked like a neon marquee, and it was an instant success, even in bright light conditions. As is always the case with fishing, there are no absolutes.

Certain colors (and sizes) seem more productive in some general areas. Green (especially fluorescent green), pink, and hot orange in smaller sizes are popular in Mexico and Belize. Some guides believe pink and orange imitate baby lobsters. White, tan, and pink in medium to large sizes are favorites in the Bahamas. White, tan, and yellow in small to medium sizes have been consistent favorites with bonefish at Christmas Island. Tans in larger sizes are favorites with Florida Keys anglers. Over the years, I have had success at all locations with six basic colors: white, tan, pink, yellow, orange, and fluorescent green. I also like to fish wild-colored flashy attractor flies like the Interceptor.

Under most conditions, the single most important aspect of fly selection is sink rate. A selection of standard-style flies in assorted colors, sizes, and sink rates will prove effective. I recommend at least three sink rates for each color of the most productive flies. Anglers armed in this manner are able to fish effectively anywhere.

This selection of small, mostly tan flies is productive nearly everywhere. Note the variation in shape, sink rate, and materials used to construct them. Flies are actual size.

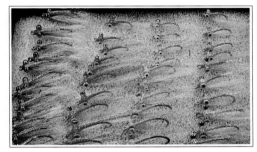

Certain colors are more productive in specific areas. This selection of tan Charlies and Christmas Island Specials is for varying water depths at Christmas Island but is productive almost anywhere.

Surface Flies

The fact that bonefish *sometimes* feed at the surface escapes most anglers. When feeding in clear water, bonefish take surface

The best-prepared anglers have the best success. If you find yourself surrounded by jacks or permit, you want to have the right fly. The only way to do that is to have lots of flies in assorted shapes, colors, and sink rates.

Flies are like film, golf balls, and ammunition: if you run out, it's over. Pictured are Marabou Shrimp tied in a varying degree of sink rates.

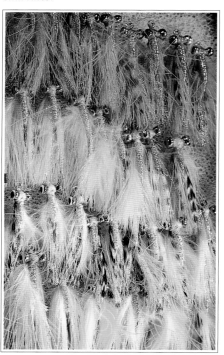

flies on rare occasions. They can sometimes be coaxed into taking a small surface popper. A good time to try is when a competitive school is feeding in shallow water with a fast-moving tide and a brisk wind. Perhaps they mistake the fly for a crab at the surface, or the fly may just be enough out of the ordinary that it attracts their attention and gets eaten—much like a maverick mullet out of sync in a school of thousands.

There are times and places when bonefish prey on schools of small fish, and action is reminiscent of smelting trout. Minnows fly everywhere as bonefish attack them at and just below the surface. There are also times when bonefish attack the fly the instant it hits the water, proving they can and do feed at and near the surface.

Since the construction of a bonefish's mouth is designed to feed on the bottom, they sometimes have trouble positioning themselves for a surface attack, pushing the offering away as they approach closely. Slow down the rate of retrieve and be patient; eventually the bonefish should get the popper!

Fly Selection

Fortunately for anglers, bonefish (except the biggest and smartest) are seldom selective. If they see a properly presented imitation, they are likely to eat it. Exact imitation is seldom necessary, and you certainly do not need to imitate all possible food sources down to exact size, shape, and color. However, I would be the last person to advise you to skimp on your fly selection. Indeed, if you have a selection of two to four standard-style patterns in five colors and three to five sink rates plus two different styles, sizes, and colors of crabs along with some forage fish, poppers, and a 'cuda or big-fish fly, you are ready to fish almost anywhere. This translates to between 40 and 80 possibilities. The critical question is how deep your selection should be. One hundred flies translate to one to three of each. How long do you think your three favorite flies will last?

Anglers are always asking me how many flies they need. This depends on how fast the fishing is, how many fish you break off, and how many flies you wear out, lose, and "loan" to your buddy. How many flies can you tie or afford to buy?

You never use everything, but you never have enough of the hot pattern. It is better to have a few of the hot patterns left over than to run out. After all, flies are a small expense compared to your overall expenses, and they will not spoil. Before you pack your flies, be certain *all barbs are smashed completely flat*. Use smooth-nosed pliers. If you tie your own, you are ahead of the game.

As is always the case, specific colors/patterns work best in different locations. Seek the advice of an angler or supplier who knows what you need. If you tie your own, take your materials with you and experiment with different patterns. You can also replenish your supply of the patterns that bonefish relish best.

Tyers constructing bonefish flies have a limited selection of reference and instructional materials. Besides reading the monthly issues of fly tying and fly fishing publications, consider viewing Jack Dennis' video, *Tying and Fishing Saltwater Flies Volumes I & II* with Jimmy Nix. Fly tying books include *Saltwater Fly Tying* by Frank Wentink and *Bonefish Fly Patterns* by Dick Brown, which is the best bonefish fly pattern/prey book currently available. Other fly pattern books include *Saltwater Fly Patterns* by Lefty Kreh and my book, *Fly Patterns of Umpqua Feather Merchants, Second Edition*.

Chapter 11

Spotting

The first bonefish flat I walked was strangely reminiscent of my first snipe hunt as a youngster. During that hunt, my brother, Lance, and I held a burlap bag over the end of a culvert on a moonless night during an Indiana thunderstorm while waiting for our cousin, Tom Fuhrman, to flush the snipe from the other side of the field into the culvert and then into our bag. We really *wanted* to believe that snipe existed and that we would catch one. After an hour we returned to the house as disbelievers, but an illustration of a snipe in the dictionary sent us back to that culvert with renewed excitement.

Dennis Black, founder of Umpqua Feather Merchants, Inc., and I were on a cross-country fishing tour in 1969, and the Florida Keys and bonefish were on our "must do" list. Neither of us had ever fished flats or seen a bonefish, and we had no idea what we were doing. Nevertheless, we rented a boat at a roadside marina and ventured out into the maze of creeks, mangroves, and flats somewhere out of Marathon. We ran the boat aground a couple of times, became completely disoriented, and finally stumbled upon what looked like a good flat.

As we trudged through calf-deep water, our belief in bonefish waned. My rod tip dropped to the water, and I no longer held my line at the ready. I believed that, if there were any bonefish around, I would certainly see them. After three hours I convinced myself there were no bonefish present, and, in retrospect, there probably were not. Even if there had been, I would have had to step on one to see it. Bonefish are not called "ghosts of the flats" for nothing!

You see them one second, then you don't. Let your eyes wander for an instant, and they vanish into a watery hallucination. There could be a dozen within casting range, but, unless you know what to look for, they may detect you and evaporate unnoticed. If spotting conditions are perfect, you can easily see fish at 100 feet. When conditions are poor, you may spook them at 15 feet and never see them.

If you don't know bonefish are present, your excitement wanes. I call this the doubt factor. It is important to see fish or at least be able to recognize bonefish signs. Then, at the very least, you know bonefish were or may be present. This keeps you fishing. Besides casting, spotting bonefish is the toughest obstacle anglers must overcome. *A flats-style hat and polarized sunglasses are a must.* See Chapter 17 for specifics.

Spotting bonefish is a skill of perception rather than acuity. A few basic spotting techniques will help unveil their secretive camouflage. To paraphrase the Buddhist, Dawa Tenzing, many people come looking; some come and *see!*

Upon arrival, quickly inventory the flat. If any fish are visible, note their direction and speed of travel. Next, note the direction of the wind, the position of the sun, and the areas of coral, sand, grass, mud, mangroves, drop-offs, depressions, and channels. Determine the tide's stage and the direction it is flowing. This information helps you decide how to proceed.

Anglers seldom *see* a well-defined bonefish. Look for anything out of the ordinary—motions, wakes, tails, color contrasts, shadows, or even vague outlines of fish themselves. Often an ill-defined shape or shadow, blurred movement, subtle surface disturbance, or your sixth sense alerts you to concentrate on a particular area. Bonefish have many disguises, and they change their wardrobe to fit the occasion. Each scale on a bonefish is a reflector pointed in a different direction. This helps break up the fish's image and contributes to its "ghost" legend. Bonefish apparitions often appear where and when you least expect them. Once you spot a fish, do not take your eyes off it! If you do, chances are good it may dissolve into invisiblity.

A school of big bonefish at Andros Island. When big bonefish swim over light-colored sand and there are this many this close, it is easy to see them. Note their shape, color, and shadow, and how they become more difficult to see at a distance. Now imagine one or two somewhere in the far distance, or in grass patches, and you may begin to understand how difficult they can be to spot.

Low, angled light makes peering below the water's surface impossible, but these are excellent conditions for spotting fins, tails, V wakes, and nervous water. Concentrate on shallow water, and move slowly. Depending on conditions, late evening can offer excellent angling.

Cloudy, flat-light, and wind-riffled surface conditions are tough for penetrating surface glare. Scan for fins and tails, and for bonefish disrupting the water surface as they move through shallows.

Average spotting conditions—good but somewhat muted light with a mottled light and dark bottom. This school of bones recently arrived from deep water so the fish have dark backs. Look for movement over light patches.

Good spotting but tough fishing conditions— overhead light is high and bright, and a mottled light and dark bottom provides good contrast. Under such conditions bonefish appear silvery and are on their guard. Casts must be gentle and on target. Leaders should be long.

Light

Light is the overriding factor in spotting fish. The more ideal the light, the easier it is to spot fish before they sense or spot you. Ideal light conditions are to have the sun overhead (11 a.m. to 1 p.m.) in a clear sky. Walking into direct sunlight makes spotting difficult. It is best to have the sun behind you.

When the sun is high in the sky, shadows, which frighten fish, are at a minimum and you can take advantage of highlights created by the sun. When the arc of the sun falls below about 25 degrees, light rays do not illuminate the bottom of the flats. Anglers arriving early and staying late cannot see the bottom and must rely on other means of locating fish.

While light is great for spotting fish, it can work to your disadvantage. Besides beating you down with its intense rays and its reflection off the water, it can also cause fish to be wary. If fish have a choice (they seldom do at Christmas Island and some Bahamian locations), they may prefer mangroves or grass beds to clear sand.

Wind

Wind is a critical factor when spotting and fishing for bonefish. When winds are dead calm and the water's surface is smooth and flat, it is easy to see the bottom. Unfortunately, such ideal spotting conditions can make fishing difficult and uncomfortable. Winds five to 10 miles per hour are perfect. This is enough wind to help disguise you and your presentation. It is also perfect for keeping bugs down and making the humidity tolerable. Excessive winds (over 20 or 25 miles per hour) disrupt the water's surface, making it difficult to spot bonefish in all but very shallow water. Seek sheltered areas.

Flats anglers usually must compromise between the angle of the sun and the direction of the wind. Keeping both behind you is ideal. If both are off to either side, you should not complain. When both are in your face, it is time to find another area to fish.

There are times when wind conditions make it nearly impossible to get a fly to fish. One such time occurred while I was fishing on Long Island in the Bahamas. The wind was sideways at 25 miles per hour, and sporadic rain was blowing in our faces. I was only there because it was early in the day and I kept thinking I would get one good wind-free shot. My guide was spotting fish angling downwind inside a 20-foot radius. It didn't take too long for complete frustration to set in, and I spent more time unraveling fly line and leader knots than I did casting. Each time I couldn't see the fish or I blew a cast, my guide just rolled his eyes, and I became more inept. Fortunately, such days are the exception and not the rule. Most days on the flats have just enough wind to keep you comfortable, and spotting conditions are good.

Clouds

Light-colored clouds make spotting bonefish difficult because clouds reflect a great deal of light, increasing glare and reflection off the water. Dark clouds reduce glare and reflection but also cut down on the available sunlight that illuminates the bottom. Sporadic clouds are typical over tropical flats, but they often move quickly. When clouds are constantly moving or building,

These are the worst possible conditions. Everything is against you. When conditions are this rough, bonefish can only be spotted in shallow water within 20 feet or less, and only by expert spotters unless the tails are very tall! Look for nervous water, vee wakes, and tails. Note the water depth.

Long narrow bands of clouds sometimes remain stationary near islands. If you find yourself under their shadow, change location.

Elevated poling platforms greatly increase visibility—and hookups. These anglers have detected feeding bonefish to the rear.

concentrate on the light holes, or sunny spots. _Look when you can see!_ You might catch a glimpse of bonefish and be able to get a quick cast off or at least determine their direction of travel and cast blind.

When clouds, or any other conditions, obscure your visibility, slow down and scan the water in close (10 to 15 feet) for color variation or movement. Concentrate on the wave window and have 15 to 20 feet of line ready to cast. If clouds appear stationary, move to another location. A short run in the boat often puts you in sunshine. If this is not possible, move into shallow water and look for tailers. To maximize your chances of success, you must take advantage of every spotting opportunity and all external forces.

Rain

Anglers with sharp acuity can use rainsqualls to their advantage. Look for nervous water, V wakes, and tails. These surface clues can show up remarkably well on a rain-ruffled surface. The sight and hearing of bonefish become somewhat muddled when large drops of water pelt shallow water. Such conditions help camouflage the boat, you, your cast, and fly definition. Remember, you cannot catch bonefish in your room or in the bar.

During unsettled conditions I once crawled within six feet of an intent tailer rooting in a crab garden. When it discovered my close-up stare, its expression was like that of a child caught with its hand in the cookie jar. Putting the sneak on this fish was more fun than catching any fish that day.

Blue sky, still water, white sand bottom, light wind, and the sun at your back (note shadow) equal excellent spotting conditions.

Flat calm conditions in shallow water over a light-colored bottom are perfect spotting conditions at over 100 yards, but bonefish can be wary. Note the V wakes.

These are the best possible spotting conditions. The sun is at your back, the sky is bright, there is a slight breeze from behind, and the flat is light colored. It doesn't get any better. Dale Kremer in the Seychelles.

Concentration and Scan Zone

Once you are fishing, light conditions dictate the concentration and scan zones. The better the spotting conditions, the further away you can see fish. The *concentration zone* is that area immediately in front of you where the bottom is clearly visible, usually out to 20 feet or, perhaps, to 50 feet. This is where you spot bonefish. If conditions are poor, the concentration zone may only extend to 15 feet. Sun and wind may alter the zone field. Look where your vision is clear. The *scan zone* extends beyond the concentration zone, perhaps out 100 yards or more.

Investigate the concentration zone slowly and carefully, systematically working a 120-degree arc from left to right, then from right to left. Walk slowly and stop often. At intervals, cover the scan zone for nervous water, V wakes, or tailing fish. To avoid eye fatigue and seeing what does not exist, keep your eyes moving. Do not look at the sun—it destroys your vision concentration for a while. Do not concentrate on one spot or particular distance. If you are not seeing fish, take a practice cast or two about your concentration zone. If I am having trouble spotting fish and I know they are around, I'll purposely try to scare some. This gives me confidence that they are present and allows me to key into their color and movement.

Scanning the *bottom* is equally important as scanning the water's surface for nervous water, V wakes, and tailers. To do this effectively, pretend the water does not exist and look *through* it.

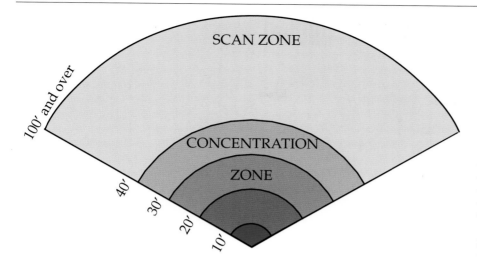

Once you are under way, it may be possible to determine the general direction bonefish are traveling. If so, adjust your concentration and scan zones to your advantage. This ploy allows you to spot more fish at a greater distance and make the optimum presentation. If you waste time looking too far to the left or right of the prime zone, any presentation to fish would be retrieved at a less-than-ideal angle.

Color variations on the bottom provide important clues. Scan for a contrasting or out of place moving color.

Your concentration and scan zones are greatest when the sun is above or behind you on a clear calm day. If it is windy, this area shrinks. If it is both windy and cloudy, these zones decrease dramatically.

Because of their height, boat anglers have an advantage in spotting fish, especially if the guide has an elevated poling platform. When fishing from a boat, divide up the water. Each person should be responsible for a specific area—except the guide, who can effectively spot 360 degrees and see nearly every fish before you do.

Fisheye view of the scan and concentration zones. Spotting, casting, and fishing conditions are ideal. The sun is behind and to the right, and wind is light from the right. Perfect for a left-handed caster. Fish on! At Long Island in the Bahamas.

When bonefish are in extremely shallow water or when they are swimming just below the water's surface, both their dorsal fin and tail may protrude. The tail and dorsal fin may create nervous or V water.

Tailing Bonefish

When bonefish tip down to root and feed along the bottom, the tilt of their bodies thrusts their tails up. Their tails may protrude from shallow water. When they stop to feed, their tails are still and nearly transparent, making them difficult to see. When they move, their wet metallic-looking tails reflect sunlight, which dazzles the eye from a great distance. When anglers spot their first tailing bonefish, they are guaranteed to contract a serious case of tail fever. My first experience with tailing bonefish involved a pod of big fish on a long Florida flat near Big Pine Key. I jumped out of the boat and literally chased my feet, splashing water and churning up the bottom. Needless to say, that was a mistake and a lesson quickly learned. Once you experience them, tailers will lure you like the Sirens.

Tailers can be difficult to find simply because conditions must be right. The determining factor is water depth. If it is too shallow, bonefish can't tip down, but you may see dorsal fins and tails exposed as they swim. If it is too deep, their tails do not protrude from the water when they tip down to feed.

Calm or light winds coupled with low-angled lighting offer the best conditions for finding tailers. Early and late in the day the sun is too low to penetrate the water and your best chance of finding bonefish is spotting tails.

Fish are often the happiest during relatively calm conditions, especially if they have worked up onto a flat into shallows without being disturbed. Their tails seem to wag like those of a dog happy to see you. The tip-off to spotting tailing bonefish is their movement and splashing and the nearly silver light reflected by their tails. Even so, tails are not always easy to see. Depending on the angle of the sun and the reflection off the water, bright glare and light reflected from tails may blur into common water reflection. In

When bonefish tip down to feed along the bottom, the tilt of their body thrusts their tail upward. Depending on water depth and the size of the bonefish, their tails may protrude above the water's surface. The taller the tail, the larger the bonefish.

order to spot tails, scan two to four inches above the water's surface while looking for any movement or reflective light above the water.

Some anglers like to search for tailers in heavy wind, believing fish are less spooky and easier to approach. Others think that bonefish do not like to stick their tails into the wind. I have seen good tailing activity during heavy wind, and I have seen no tailing during windy chop. More variables than wind probably come into play, but I would bet my fly box on calmer conditions being best. During choppy conditions, tailing activity is seldom so pronounced as to disturb the top of a heavy wind chop. During such conditions, walk and look into the wind. Walk slowly and look for nervous water and the tips of tails. Once you spot fish, work into an advantageous casting position. If there is a choice, position yourself in front of the fish so you are facing it.

The size of tailing fish is in direct proportion to water depth. In deeper water, only the tails of the largest fish can show. In medium depth water, look for the tallest tails because these are the biggest fish. In a pod or school of tailing bonefish, the largest fish may be in the lead or may be surrounded by sentry fish. Individual tailers are often the largest and most difficult to hook. Trios can be the easiest, usually because the competitive factor comes into play and three fish have a better chance of seeing your fly than does a single fish.

Bonefish tails can be differentiated from permit caudal fins by their silvery appearance. Permit have a sickle-shaped black dorsal fin and a deeply forked black tail. Unlike bonefish, permit have a deep body and seldom enter extremely shallow water where their backs would be exposed. When you happen on tailing permit, you temporarily forget bonefish!

This bonefish swims in very shallow water at Andros Island in the Bahamas. When bonefish "tail," their dorsal fin does not usually show. Tails are silvery and glisten in sunlight.

Permit fins and tails are dark, and the dorsal fin is sickle-shaped. When a permit is "tailing," both the fin and the tail often show above the water's surface.

Once you see bonefish tails, there is no mistaking them. They are semitransparent and silvery with a dark inside margin and pointed tip. Notice how the back color blends with the vegetation and the underside mirrors the sandy bottom. Also take note of the shadow, which is sometimes the first thing you see. Bonefish usually swim on the bottom; hence, their shadow is tight to their bodies. This bonefish was observed in Belize.

Can you tell the bonefish apart from the darker bottom patches?

Bonefish feeding over clear sand in bright conditions may be nearly transparent. This bonefish was spotted when it tailed only 20 feet away. Jamie Lyle at Long Island, Bahamas.

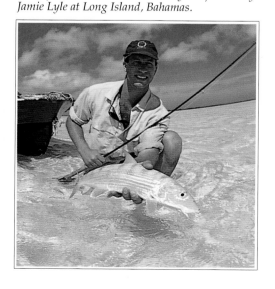

Bonefish Camouflage

Scientists have discovered that a layer of color-bearing cells lies just beneath a fish's scales. Colors include orange, yellow, red, black, and other colors that combine to make green. A crystalline tissue adds silver, white, or iridescence. Fish are believed to change colors for many reasons, including anger, fear, protection (camouflage), and sexual attraction. These color changes, along with body signals, may combine to form simple communication between individuals and species. Some fish have been found to communicate by electrical impulses and by flashing bioluminescence (cold light). This is a little-known science, and it has not been researched on bonefish. Casual observation, however, reveals both subtle and obvious changes in the color of bonefish.

When bonefish are stressed or frightened, they change color. This subtle change of color, coupled with unnatural frantic movement (body language, water vibration) may be forms of communication. Bonefish may emit a chemical odor when they are frightened or attacked. When the fish are injured, blood, damaged tissue, or cells may trigger a chemical release. All these and other factors contribute to the "fear signal." When one bonefish is frightened, all others almost instantly become aware of danger. The existence of a fear signal may explain why predators pick up the trail of distressed bonefish so readily. In the Bahamas I observed a shark working across a flat on almost exactly the same route as a bonefish I had just released. The shark followed it to the mangroves as if it were a foxhound on a fresh trail.

Like a magician's vanishing act, bonefish can disappear before your very eyes. This is possible because bonefish are covered with hundreds of tiny scales that act as mirrors. These mirrors reflect the colors around them, making bonefish all but invisible. If they didn't move, you might step on them. Bonefish look different over different bottoms and at different water depths. Bonefish in a tea-colored mangrove shoreline area might be camouflaged olive brown. Fifty yards offshore the bottom might be white sand, and bonefish might be silvery and equally difficult to spot. Bonefish that feed in smoke (mud) have light-colored backs. Those that go into mangroves are greenish across the back.

Fish arriving from deeper water have darker green backs that stand out markedly on lighter-colored flats. Within five to 15 minutes, their color lightens considerably, and they blend into their new surroundings. The darker-colored fish, or recent arrivals, are usually more aggressive. If you have a choice between casting to a dark or a light fish, pick the dark one; your chances of a hookup are much better. In deeper water, larger bonefish move faster and are more difficult to spot. When you are patrolling drop-off areas, look for larger, darker shapes.

When the tide is high and you are on the higher areas of the flat, bonefish are silvery. Silvery bonefish are more difficult to see on a light-colored bottom. When they are at a right angle, you can only see the tops of their backs. This is because their silvery sides are like mirrors and reflect concentrated light off the bottom, making them resemble the bottom. When such fish are moving directly toward or away from you, their backs do not reflect the bottom, and they are much easier to see. In shallow water, larger fish are easier to spot and often light up like a neon sign.

Locating fish in darker coral and grassy areas is a challenge. Their mottled-green backs blend into such areas amazingly well. If there are light areas mixed with dark areas, concentrate on the light areas. Again, if you are spooking fish before you see them, you are moving too fast. Slow down, reduce your noise and above-water movement, and search more carefully.

These fish have adjusted to the light and their surroundings. Their backs take on an amazingly effective camouflage pattern.

Take away the shadow, and this bonefish becomes invisible. It has assumed the color of sand, mud, coral, rock, and vegetation. This is possible because bonefish are covered with hundreds of tiny scales that act as mirrors. These mirrors reflect surrounding colors, which makes them almost invisible. Long Island, Bahamas.

Bonefish tracks. Two bonefish pushed their noses into the sand on the last rising tide. Each chased one or more crabs three times. The receding tide obliterated most of the tailings except for the largest holes. Which fish appears to be the largest?

This bonefish has been doing some serious rooting in rough country, or it tangled with a tough crab!

Mudding

Our Belizian guide steered our speeding boat through a maze of shallow coral reefs, sand flats, and outer cays somewhere near Cross Cay. Suddenly he throttled down the engine and said, "Muds." Brian O'Keefe and I scanned the flat 100 yards away and easily located the cloudy water. Beaching the boat 100 feet away, we walked to the up-tide side and pitched our flies into the watery cloud. Instantly, both of us were cranking in bonefish. The water was so cloudy we could only see about two inches into it. There were probably hundreds of bonefish in the acre-sized cloud. Brian and I hooked a fish every cast for 20 minutes before we decided it was time to move on to more challenging quarry.

Hooking mudding fish can be ridiculously easy, almost boring. Once in a while, to add extra excitement, try fishing two or more flies for mudding schools. Imagine hooking two bonefish simultaneously, each pulling in a different direction! Prepare yourself for some great laughs, and some lost flies. Don't make a glutton of yourself. A couple hookups is enough. Then, break off the hooks and feel the multiple grabs. You may be surprised at how aggressive small school fish can be. Mudding bonefish are especially appreciated by neophytes who have not hooked many bonefish or perfected the skills necessary to stalk single feeders in clear water. Mudding bonefish can also provide an action-packed diversion for accomplished anglers, but most would not want to spend too much time fishing for them.

Mudding, or muds, is the term used to describe fish that are rooting in soft bottoms for food. Mudding fish displace sediment, which becomes suspended and creates a cloud in the water. This is referred to as "smoke" or a "mud." Bonefish, milkfish, rays, sharks, permit, and mullet commonly create muds.

Unless you are intimately familiar with an area, there is no way of knowing for certain what has created a mud. Local guides will point to a large mud and say, "Not bonefish. Mullet." When asked how they know, they mutter something like, "I see them before. I know." Exceedingly large muds are seldom created by bonefish.

Muds can linger long after fish have left the area. A dense mud that you are unable to see into is probably fresh. Fish might still be feeding inside the cloudy cloak. Muds that have settled down or become partly scattered by wind and tide are probably vacant, but you cannot be certain. For this reason, all muds deserve a few casts.

While fishing off Barnes Key in Florida, we became surrounded by storms. Heavy clouds hovered low, forming a solid 360-degree circle of smoke-gray rain curtains. There was a slight riffle on the water but no glare. "Perfect for spotting muds," remarked our guide, John. I looked at the disturbed mud from the push pole, and it did indeed look like a neon sign. We located a mudding fish shortly, but, after we presented the fly and watched the fish flee, John pronounced it a chicken fin.

Mudding bonefish are usually aggressive feeders and a couple of casts into the cloud determines if fish are present. If you are stealthy, you may hook several fish before the school figures out that some devious external force is at work. Determine the direction of wind and tide and begin fishing at the upper end. Cast into the darkest part. Start at the fringe and work toward the inside. Lift the fly out of the water before it exits the mud. This will alleviate the chances of any followers sighting you. Remember, a mud obscures visibility, but not hearing. Keep it quiet.

Small muds created by single bonefish may be only a few inches across. Muds created by large schools may cover several acres. Small muds are difficult to spot by all but the most observant anglers, but large muds are easily spotted from 100 yards or more. Single mudding bonefish may root in the mud, swim a few feet, and mud again. Their trails, and sometimes their tails, are easy to spot and follow. The fewer the fish and the stronger the tide, the more difficult muds are to spot.

Bonefish usually root uptide or facing into the tide. The tide clears the cloudy water from their faces, keeping their sight and smell at optimum acuity. They use their body weight and muscles to force their nose into the substrata or a crab hole. They force a stream of water out of their mouths as they excavate edible animals. Immediately after excavating a hole, they sometimes patrol the perimeter looking for any escaping prey. If nothing flushes out, they may try again. When several fish are rooting, any escaping edible is fair game and competition can be keen. Rooting bonefish often forget their inherent caution, making them relatively easy prey for anglers.

When casting to a single mudding fish, try to keep the mud between you and the bonefish. Present your fly when the fish is tipped down rooting in the mud. Pull the fly away from the mud when the fish is not rooting.

A basic understanding of how to read bonefish muds helps anglers determine that bonefish do indeed visit a particular flat. A good flats tracker is able to spot a single mud hole long after it has settled and to determine the direction the bonefish were feeding, roughly how many there were, their size, and approximately how long ago they were there.

A crab hole has a mound with a round hole. A root hole is a depression with tailings. Root holes that are well pronounced with detailed, dramatically discolored tailings may be only a few minutes old. Scratch the sand and notice the direction of flow and the color of the disturbed area. Check the surrounding area for other nose prints and note their direction and size. When you find rooting bonefish, take the time to investigate their recent root holes and begin to pay attention to the bottom strata. There is a little detective in all of us, and mud flats offer plenty of clues to both preceding events and those yet to unfold.

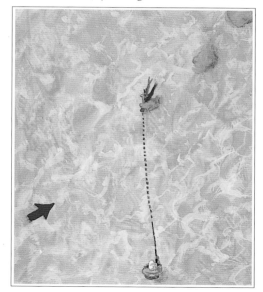

Bonefish root facing into the tide. When casting, try to keep mud between you and the bonefish.

Muds! These are relatively small and were probably made by only a few fish. Giant muds sometimes stretch for hundreds of feet and contain hundreds of fish. Muds are, of course, only possible in soft bottoms. Notice that the current is carrying the muds from left to right as fish feed right to left, or into the current.

Anglers create muds when they walk. If sharks are present, step out of the mud and land fish in clear water. Note that the author is protected from intense tropical sun with long sleeves, long pants, hat, and gloves. Long Island, Bahamas.

One of the most remote islands in the world is Bikini Atoll in the Marshall Islands. A necklace of small islands is connected by a reef that encircles a large lagoon. Surf breaks upon the reef and rolls onto outside flats. Shallow flats and drop-offs are visible on the inside of the islands. Bonefish (and every other imaginable species) are spotted throughout the shallow waters. Flats in the vicinity of channels, passages, or breaks in the reef that lead inside to the lagoon are usually the most productive areas. Most species either follow the channel currents, cruise parallel to shorelines, or cruise along drop-offs.

Reefs

Most reef fishing actually takes place inside the edge of the reef because rough surf usually makes the reef itself inaccessible. Exceptionally rough surf might preclude fishing inside the reef, but, if there is plenty of distance between the surf and shore, high surf seldom presents access problems.

The presence of bonefish in reef areas is directly related to the physical design of the environment. When inside reef access is available, there might be many bonefish. When inside access is curtailed, fewer bonefish are found. When surf is low, anglers can see channels, cuts, or breaks in the reef that allow inside access. When tide and surf are high, anglers can monitor wave characteristics as they roll toward shore and read the configuration of the bottom. Waves *break* over shallow areas and *roll* over deep areas. When you observe a relatively flat area with waves breaking to either side, you have found a deeper cut. Sometimes the face of the wave will flatten or smooth ever so slightly, but bonefish do not require much depth. Reef areas with numerous channels provide the best bonefishing.

Once inside the reef, bonefish have access to a smorgasboard of feasts, but the bottom contour still influences their movements.

Channels usually run at a right angle to the reef or angle toward the shoreline. Depressions often run parallel to the shoreline. As a result, bonefish are usually observed feeding or traveling from the surf line toward shore or parallel to the shoreline.

Inside the reef, fish usually work with the tide the same way they do on flats: feeding toward the beach on incoming water and away from the beach on outgoing water often at an angle to the tide. As long as fish follow this flow, they cannot get into trouble. Christmas Island is surrounded by a reef that is seldom more than 200 yards offshore. The area between the surf and the beach is anywhere from a few inches to several feet deep. Most fishing takes place in water less than three feet deep. Other reef areas, especially those in Belize, are sometimes backed by extensive transition flats that provide varied habitat.

Incoming rollers and swells constantly cause bonefish to disappear and reappear. Look for bonefish between the waves and rollers in the bottom of the trough. As the roller or swell bottoms out, it will clear, providing a window through which you can view the bottom. The faces of rollers also provide windows to the bottom, and rolling waves may lift fish off the bottom, making them easier to detect. Wave windows open briefly. Bonefish move quickly

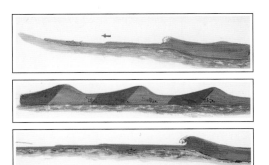

Like a slick spot moving down a stream, a wave window offers a peek below the surface. Follow the wave window as far as possible while looking for movement, shadows, and anything out of the ordinary.

Blue-fin trevally are frequent visitors to reef areas throughout Pacific waters. They are relatively easy to spot because of their size and aggressive manner. Note the combination of dead coral and sand beach. This is Bikini Atoll.

Clams and tropical fish are common reef residents.

in these areas. To project their speed and direction of travel, scan the next available window. When casting to bonefish in rolling waves, it is best to cast across the wave at an angle. This allows for better line and fly control.

Bonefish recently arrived from deeper water or from coral habitat have dark bands across their backs. They are best spotted when they cross light-colored patches and when they are in the face of a wave. Look for movement counter to the water flow. For best success, cast when they are feeding, not when they are traveling. When feeding, bonefish are less able to detect you or your cast, but they are very much aware of predators, as you should be. Be alert for any larger-than-normal sharks that are inside the reef. If you feel threatened, slowly make your way to the beach.

When entering reef areas on a high tide, some bonefish head for the highest ground or shallowest water, while others take up feeding positions only inches from the beach. For me, the most satisfying bonefishing at Christmas Island is for backwash feeders on the beach.

The first one I spotted was the most thrilling. As incoming waves washed up the steep beach, hermit crabs were displaced. As the crabs awkwardly made their way back to land, a bonefish eagerly grabbed them. The bonefish was only visible when the waves left the beach, almost stranding it in the shoreline quicksand. Its mirror-like sides, dorsal, and tail were like partly-exposed treasure. Amazed at its ingenuity and boldness, I crept on my belly to within 10 feet and watched, transfixed, as it picked up the tiny shell-armored crabs. The fish was completely oblivious to my presence. I could see its dark black eye and surrounding iridescence. It had a wild "living-on-the-edge" excitement about it, and I knew this was an explorer and adventurer out of the ordinary.

I was torn between hooking it and leaving it to its quest. I settled on a compromise. Breaking off the hook point, I dropped the fly three feet ahead on the beach and waited for the next wave to guide the fish toward it. When the time was right, I twitched the fly slightly. I saw the fish's eyes instantly fix on my offering. Simultaneously, all muscles and fins responded, and it glided over the decomposed coral and picked up my fly. When it attempted to crush the fly, it realized something was wrong. It quickly darted 10 feet into deeper water. I did not tighten up on the line, but the slight drag of the fly line across the beach caused the fish confusion, then panic, and it was gone. I wondered what strange tale it would tell its friends.

Backwash feeders should be approached from behind. Walk the beach slowly, staying on higher ground or at least 30 feet back from the water. *Cautiously* approach only when waves wash in, which helps disguise noise, vibrations, and shadows. Stay low and walk lightly, keeping your rod behind you. When you make the cast, the fly line and most of the leader should land on the beach with only the fly and perhaps two feet of leader entering the water.

Bonefish may be tailing on the outside edge of the reef. When surf and tidal conditions are low, anglers may be able to reach the outside edge of the reef. This is the area that receives the full pounding from the surf and is seldom accessible. Scan two to four inches above the water as you walk, staying at least 30 feet back from the edge. Walk slowly and, if possible, avoid stepping on brittle coral. The sound of crunching coral is like a freight train; you

How difficult can it be to see arm-long fish in 12 inches of calm, clear water? **Very difficult!** *Bonefish are easier to spook than they are to see. If they didn't move, you could stumble over them before you would see them. This amazing bonefish camouflage scene is in Cuba, but it could be anywhere in bonefish country. Walk quietly and slowly, and look for clues.*

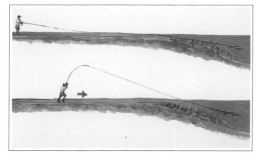

To avoid being detected by fish, stand back from dropoffs. When a fish is hooked, raise the rod tip high and move to the dropoff. This reduces the chance of fish breaking off on coral.

hear and feel it long before you see it. Besides, such coral is usually a living organism! Position your fly so incoming water rolls or carries it toward feeding bonefish. Small, unweighted flies that fish with the point up are usually required. Bonefish sometimes get right on top of the reef and their backs may be exposed as waves flatten out. They usually face the surf and must be approached cautiously from behind or slightly off to either side. The outer reefs at Belize offer some exceptional bonefishing.

Bonefish may also be beyond the reef where the outside edge often drops abruptly to deep blue. Look for bonefish cruising this edge. You might not see a lot of bonefish, but the ones you see are worth looking for. Patient and observant anglers can enjoy some exciting sport, but conditions must be right for spotting. For safety and concealment, stay at least 10 feet back from the edge. You will need a variety of fast-sinking weighted flies.

If I had to choose one location to fish bonefish at Belize and Christmas Island, I would choose the reef. At Christmas Island, the reef encircles the entire atoll. The Korean wreck area, located along the extreme southern shore, is the most popular, and anglers await their chance to fish its sometimes wild waters. The presence of the wreck used to add another dimension. Its tilted, rusted-out hull created plenty of lost-at-sea and shipwreck fantasies, but the ocean has now disintegrated most of it.

I like to fish areas of the reef that are no more than 100 yards from surf to beach. One afternoon I went to a quiet, out-of-the-way spot that is seldom fished. Although many such areas exist, this stretch of beach looked particularly wild and unvisited. Neither a parking area nor a beaten path to the beach was evident. In fact, there really wasn't much of a beach, just a steep pile of coral rubble and sand that had been deposited 10 feet up into the saltbrush and heliotrope by rough seas. I can only imagine what the ocean looks like when this building process takes place.

Our guide, Moana, related that heliotrope needs a bit more moisture to survive than saltbrush, whose roots are used as orange dye. Yellowed saltbrush leaves can be crumbled up and put on wounds to prevent infection. Many guides have extensive knowledge about their environment but need to be coaxed into sharing it. Once they know you are interested they gladly share information.

A flat area in the waves denotes a deeper area (cut or channel), that allows bonefish access inside the reef.

Top view (below), showing break in reef that allows fish easy access inside the reef.

After a brief look at the surf, depressions, and channels, we spotted a trio of bones working to our left. This was a strong indication which direction other fish would be moving, so we opted to fish right and execute a face-the-fish approach. We set up to fish 80 feet apart at a 60-degree angle from each other. Moana was between us, slightly behind, in spotting position. Such positioning allowed us to maximize bonefish contact. If one angler didn't get a shot, the other probably would. Fishing as a team, we took our time, and the reef proved to be a fascinating and productive location.

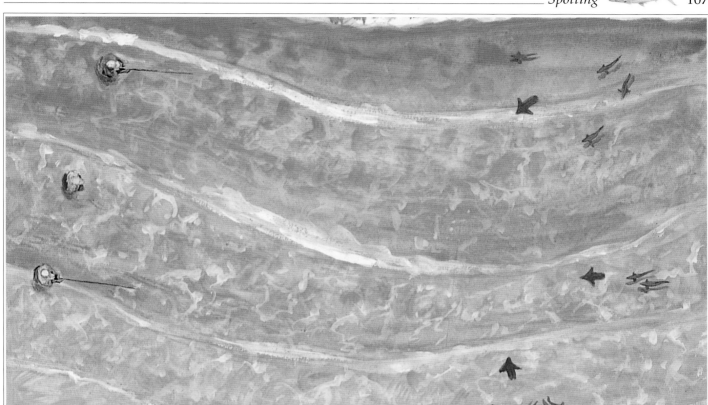

V Wakes

Water depth and visibility determine what you focus on. In shallow water (10 to 12 inches or less) you should focus on the surface. Any fish in the area will probably disturb the surface with their dorsal fins or their tails, creating V wakes as they swim. Because bonefish swim quickly, they can be two to five feet ahead of the V. When light conditions preclude looking at the bottom, you should fish shallow water and concentrate on the surface. Remember that bonefish are commonly encountered in water barely deep enough to allow them to swim. If they are moving slowly and not tailing, you might miss them on your first scan. Walk slowly and look carefully.

In slightly deeper water, larger fish push water off their noses and over their backs, parting the water as they swim. The faster they swim, the more of a V disturbance they create.

Nervous Water

Nervous water is the tip-off to underwater movement. As bonefish move, they push water that sometimes causes a surface movement. The surface is not broken, only disturbed. Look for slightly rippled water or a surface pattern that is at odds with or moving against the surrounding water. Single moving bonefish causing nervous water are difficult to spot, but a large school can be spotted from 100 yards or more, especially if the water's surface is otherwise calm. A patch of nervous water moves around, reflects light, and sometimes takes on shades of gray, brown, or green. In shallow areas, always scan as far as possible for nervous water. "High frequency" nervous water is not created by bonefish but by erratically swimming smaller fish.

Anglers should spread out at an angle and work toward feeding fish. This strategy maximizes contact, and both anglers may have a shot at fish swimming away from and toward the shoreline. This strategy can be effective when fishing any flat. The angler closest to the guide should be slightly behind so the guide can see in both directions. Let the guide set the pace.

V wake, top and side perspective.

Nervous water, top and side perspective.

Can you spot the bonefish? The shadow is the best clue and is often the first thing an angler sees.

Jailed bonefish. These thugs were jailed for harvesting crabs, snails, fish, and shrimp without a permit.

Final Notes On Spotting Bonefish

First-time bonefish anglers become adept at spotting bonefish within a few days. To better impress on your memory exactly what you are looking for, don't rush into casting position but take time to follow fish as they move in and out of sight. Look away from the fish and then attempt to spot them again. Study their color, movement, and shape. When you release bonefish, get in the habit of following them out of sight. This helps fine tune your eye over different-colored bottoms and under various conditions. Soon you will have keen spotting skills; you might even spot one before your guide does.

If you have difficulty spotting bonefish or if conditions are poor, concentrate on close-in shallow areas 12 inches or less in depth. Bonefish will be easier to see, especially if their tails protrude from the water. Remember to move very slowly because bonefish in shallow water are unsettled and wary.

If you can't immediately identify the species of a fish, make the cast! You have nothing to lose, except your fly, and everything to gain. Remember, all species are fun on the fly rod! Be prepared, expand your horizons and double your pleasure.

Some anglers are not physically able to see bonefish under normal conditions. These anglers should secure the aid of a personal guide who will point to fish and give specific casting instructions. There is no need to miss out on the wonderful world of bonefishing because of poor eyesight.

Bonefish colors are perpetually changing. Like their surroundings, their coloration is vivid yet indistinct. No two fish are exactly the same, but they all meld into their habitat like shadow into dusk. Think of a bonefish image as one piece of a puzzle in which all the pieces are colored and shaped the same. How do you tell them apart? The bonefish piece moves!

Chapter 12

Stalking

Bonefish are very alert creatures. They have been described as bundles of nerves with fins and are highly attuned to their skinny water environment. Seemingly insignificant noises, movements, light reflections, or unfamiliar objects can have a profound effect on them. Once you become familiar with bonefish, you can tell by their body language whether or not they are concerned about something. From a distance of 100 feet or more, a slight hesitation or change in their speed, direction, or attitude should alert you that they are unhappy about something. That something is probably you. When one bonefish becomes uneasy or frightened, the feeling is transmitted instantaneously throughout the entire school. Researchers believe bonefish communicate an alarm by body language, low-frequency toothy noises, and thumps that are produced by their swim bladders. Learning to recognize and avoid some of the major factors that contribute to frightening bonefish will lead you to more angling opportunities.

Bonefish are almost always on the move. Most anglers would believe it if they were told that bonefish sleep at three miles per hour! Sometimes bonefish sense your presence and tolerate you, but usually they are then in an unsettled and tempermental mood. I once chased a pod of big tails for half a mile and was never able to get close enough for a decent cast. They knew I was there and were clever at staying in their safety zone. Fish that are moving slowly, poking and probing the bottom in a relaxed mode are referred to as "happy" fish. Careful stalkers can move to within a

The author keeps a low silhouette and casts low to the water, both important stalking and presentation ploys. Bonefish usually sense you long before they see you. Move slowly, present the fly at the right place and time with minimal disturbance, and the game is won. This is especially true if your fly triggers an immediate response. Fly line color can be critical when fish are unusually pressured. Clothing color is seldom a consideration. Notice that the fly has yet to land and sink but the hands and rod tip are in position for the retrieve. Be ready!

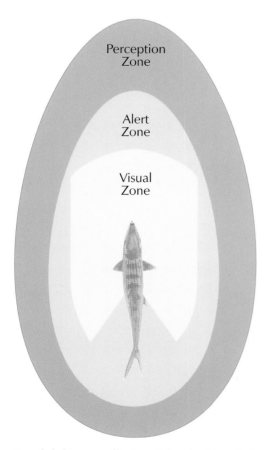

Bonefish have excellent peripheral vision, but other senses alert them to their surroundings. Their immediate visual range is determined by water depth and clarity. Beyond the visual zone, vision fades, and other senses provide data.

dozen feet of happy fish. The slower bonefish move, the easier they are to cast to and interest in a fly.

Reduce or eliminate all noise. When bonefish are in shallow water, noise originating *above* the water easily frightens them. Refrain from loud talk. Sound is magnified and travels five times faster *under* water; it is imperative that all boat noise be eliminated. Do not slam the cooler lid, drop a fly box, or stumble over the anchor. Just the sound of waves lapping against the boat or the push pole hitting coral can run bonefish off the flat. More than one angler has observed that a fly ticking coral can make bonefish disappear. I've watched a pod of tailers bolt from 200 feet away when the boat eased up onto a sandbar. Sometimes an unfamiliar sound arouses their curiosity, but usually only temporarily.

Boat motors spook fish, especially larger and wiser fish. Run boats *way* outside flats. Drift and pole in quietly. Your chances of finding large fish will be much improved.

When you are wading, learn to walk *lightly, quietly,* and *slowly.* Most anglers move too fast. Slow down. An average pace under average spotting conditions might be a step every two seconds with frequent pauses to scan the surroundings. One step per second is fast. Vary your walking rhythm. When you are pursuing bonefish, do not shuffle your feet along the bottom or push water with your legs. (Still, be careful of rays and other bottom hazards.) Lift your feet out of the water and angle them back into the water toe first (lift-and-point technique) being careful not to make the slightest sound. Walk on the sides of your feet or on your heels, reducing pressure between your feet and the ground and minimizing bottom disturbance and noise. Your pants can generate noise while you are walking. Roll them up if necessary. These ideas may sound extreme, and they usually are, but, if you hope to consistently have a shot at the big players, you must eliminate *all* noise.

Shadows and tall silhouettes are notorious for scattering bonefish—shadows from rods, fly lines, birds, push poles, anything. Sometimes bonefish are scared by their own shadows. Keep your silhouette as low as possible. When making a close-in presentation on foot or from a boat, kneel down after the cast. Do not wave your rod around in the air; keep it low. When necessary, freeze in your tracks and let bonefish pass without scaring their fins off them. I have had them swim within an arm's length, move off, resume feeding, and then be tricked by my fly.

Some anglers believe that bright colors that do not blend with shoreline vegetation or with the sky can help alert fish to your presence. It is much more likely that noise or movement will scare bonefish long before a yellow or red shirt.

Bonefish have a keen sense of smell. Do not use oils, lotions, or repellents on your fingers. Rub sunscreen on the back of one hand with the back of the other hand, keeping your fingers clean. Odors are transmitted under water, and your scents will not attract many bonefish.

Bonefishing can require a great deal of stealth. If you are spooking fish within 20 to 30 feet under average conditions, you are not paying attention and are probably walking too fast. Slow down, make frequent stops, and scan the area carefully. You should be able to see bonefish 30 feet away. If you hope to consistently approach feeders in shallow water, pretend you have feathers and stilt legs.

Make a game of creeping close to bonefish (possibly within 10 feet of rooting tailers) and dabbing the fly to them. When you hook fish this close, you can "tuna fish" them out of the water before they can bolt away. There is usually a split second after you hook them before they panic. In this split second, it is possible to lift their head up and out of the water and skim them toward you. This requires perfect timing and execution. When fish are landed this quickly, there is no survival problem, providing, of course, that you release them properly. Avoid many of the common factors that alert bonefish to your presence, and your success rate should soar.

Brian O'Keefe in stealth mode. If you think and act like a heron, your catch rate should soar.

Exceptionally spooky bonefish may require a stealthy approach. Remember, water, air, and ground vibrations are believed to be detected by bonefish. Walk lightly and slowly. Do not push water with your legs. Lift your feet out of the water and angle them back into the water toe first. Pretend you have a long bill and feathers. Brian O'Keefe in the Seychelles.

Factors That Scare Bonefish

Noise:
- Water slapping boat
- Fly hitting water or landing on water
- Fly line landing on water or lifting off water
- Boat motor running
- Push pole hitting bottom
- Boat scraping bottom of flat
- Anything banging in the boat
- Angler stepping into water, splashing, or walking (vibration)
- Loud talking
- Fly ticking bottom

Movement or Shadows:
- Line moving in air or water
- Boat
- Birds
- Any shadow or movement
- Angler's silhouette
- Rod movement
- Sudden fly movement

Light:
- Reflection off any material— rod, reel, line, clothing, fly

Vibrations:
- Any unnatural vibrations are transmitted through water and bottom strata

This placid yet exciting scene shows several nuances of bonefishing. Light conditions and the absence of wind combine to produce muted tones nearly identical in the sky and water. These conditions, plus extremely shallow water, demand a stealthy approach. Anglers must walk slowly, to avoid creating waves and vibrations. This bonefish is relatively easy to spot in ankle-deep water. Nevertheless, the fish perceived danger and moved cautiously, nervously, toward deeper water before the angler spotted it. This movement alerted the angler. Notice the wakes as the angler moved to intercept the bonefish. This alarmed the bonefish further, and the fish increased its speed. Notice the rooster tail. The water signature created by the fish is a perfect example of a V wake, although it is often more subtle. Notice the position of the bonefish in relation to the V wake. If you can't see the bonefish, always lead the surface disturbance by several feet. This bonefish is spooked! Just for fun, Bob Ezell makes a "goodbye, see-you-later" cast at Andros Island in the Bahamas.

Chapter 13

Presentation and Angling Strategies

Feeding bonefish have comical personalities and display many entertaining traits. Sometimes they look like chipmunks scurrying around, playfully stopping to investigate or to pick up an interesting morsel, pausing to socialize, and then scurrying on. At other times they appear like bird dogs tenaciously following an enticing trail. Given a chance, they are friendly and playful, but they are also shy and sly. Bonefish are more catlike than other fish.

Small school fish are often referred to as rats because they travel in packs and, when startled, they scatter like rats from garbage. Bonefish provide amusing viewing to those who can rest their rod. Their feeding *modus operandi* is as varied as their food sources and habitat. An understanding of these habits helps you choose your imitation and presentation strategy.

In streams, the water moves, but the fish do not. Stream trout anglers have plenty of time to contemplate the possibilities, change flies, and get into position while trout remain stationary and continue to feed.

In lakes, the fish move, but the water does not. Lake anglers fish a relatively stable water mass where fish cruise and feed the same "beat" or structure. When fish feed at or near the surface, anglers know where the fish are and can often predict where, even when, they will feed next.

On saltwater flats, both the fish *and* the water move. When bonefish are on the move and feeding, you must consider many variables—wind, tide direction, water speed, boat movement, visibility, depth and speed of the bonefish, and the sink rate of the fly.

Glister Wallace and Randall Kaufmann are in the crouched position while working a pod of close-in tailers in the Middle Bight at Andros Island in the Bahamas.

Every option must be computed and a cast executed within seconds before the bonefish are gone. This is opportunistic fishing at its finest.

The most successful bonefishermen have mastered quick, accurate, and strategic presentations. *If you can't present the fly to the proper spot without spooking bonefish, all other points are moot.* Neophyte bonefish anglers should be able to *cast at least 30 feet quickly and accurately in any direction.* Anglers who can single and double haul have a tremendous advantage. The hauls increase line speed and casting distance. They also help form tighter casting loops, which facilitates casting into or across the wind. If you cannot do this, *learn as soon as you can.* I recommend getting hands-on casting instruction from a friend or from your local fly fishing specialty store. There are also some excellent videos on casting. Do not worry about how your cast looks, just get the fly to the target quickly. Because bonefish change their feeding direction often, you should cast as close to them as possible without alarming them. Place targets at 30, 40, and 50 feet and practice casting one or two feet to either side and five feet ahead of them.

For some beginning anglers it may be easier to cast on foot than from a boat because the boat variables (movement and position) are removed from the presentation equation. A knowledgeable guide will, however, compute these factors and pole the boat in such a manner as to allow the best option. Wading anglers have a stealth advantage, can reach very shallow water, and have the fun and intimacy of walking the flats. A boat allows better visibility and mobility, and anglers cover a greater amount and variety of water. A boat also allows anglers to fish soft or deep flats.

When two anglers are fishing from a boat, only one angler can fish at a time. Some anglers get bored or feel shortchanged on fishing time when sharing a boat. If you are a Type A angler, book your own boat. It can, however, get tiring standing in the ready

position for long periods of time and there is no one to share ideas, take photos, or serve you a drink.

When two anglers share a boat, the routine is much like trout fishing in New Zealand. One person fishes and the other spots. The spotter also makes certain your line is neatly coiled and ready to cast, helps with any other urgent details, and takes photos. When a fish is spotted or hooked, the angler has the benefit of two different experts yelling conflicting instructions. It can be quite comical and entertaining, and I highly recommend it. The spotter is always on the fastest learning curve.

Keep a low profile when wading and in the boat. When making a presentation on foot, get in the habit of assuming the bonefish stance: bend forward at the waist and crouch low at the knees. When bonefish approach within 25 feet, assume a squatting position. Keep your rod tip low and behind you. Remain motionless. Don't worry about getting your posterior wet but do keep your flies dry.

When fishing from a boat, maintain a stable stance on the bow. Waves, poling motion, and weight shifting in the boat all contribute to your unsteadiness while positioned at the bow. It is easy to lose your balance, and you wouldn't be the first person to fall off. Many flats boats have a flat smooth bow so there is nothing for your feet to cling to. To avoid fatigue you must stay relaxed. Envision your legs as shock absorbers. Bend your knees slightly, spread your feet apart, and go with the flow. If the boat is rocking from side to side, keep your feet on an even plane. If the boat is lifting and falling in a front-to-back motion, put one foot slightly ahead of the other. If fish appear in close, crouch low or drop to your knees to lower your silhouette.

Holding the rod in the optimum ready position can be tiring. Your arms are positioned as though you are reading a book. Relax them once in awhile or invite your fishing partner to "man the bow."

Guide and angler work as a team. The guide points out tailers. Note that the angler is positioned perfectly to make the cast and that his fly has just left his hand.

The ready position in the boat—the fly is in hand, a loop of line is beyond the rod tip, and the desired length of line is stripped from the reel. Notice that it is off the deck. When it is windy, this is the best place to coil the line. Your fishing partner can also help keep it tangle free and ready to shoot. The angler's feet are spread apart and he is slightly bent at the knees for balance. When the boat rocks left to right, your feet are spread as shown. If the motion is more back to front, one foot is out in front of the other.

The Ready Position

Whether you are fishing from the boat or wading, always have your rod and line in the ready position. Strip out more line than you need; it is better to have some left over than to come up short. The time it takes to pull additional line from the reel and recast is often far more time than you have. Consider your spotting range in conjunction with your casting ability. I like to have 10 feet beyond my spotting range ready to cast. If your spotting range is 40 feet, strip off 50 feet. If 50 feet is your maximum cast, mark the fly line at the 50-foot mark. As you strip off line, you'll know when to stop and will not have excess line waiting on the deck or swirling around your feet in the water waiting to tangle or snag.

When line is stripped from a reel while you are fishing from a boat, the back is piled over the front. When a cast is made, the line must uncoil from the bottom of the pile, which often causes the line to tangle. To avoid this, either strip the coiled line again (erroneously called stretching the line), thereby reversing it, or make a quick cast, then strip the line back. By doing this, you position the line to uncoil top-to-bottom, or front-to-back, as it unfurls on the cast.

Hold the rod in your casting hand and the fly at the bend of the hook between the first finger and thumb of your other hand. At least 15 feet of fly line should be beyond the rod tip. The more you can handle the better, especially if you plan to make a long cast. This loop of fly line allows you to load the rod quickly and get a cast off. The excess fly line that has been stripped from the reel should be untangled and free of any obstructions in the boat. If it is windy, coil the line in the bottom of the boat instead of on the bow and keep it between your legs. You can also gently kneel on or step on a coil to keep it in place. Just remember to move your foot before you cast. Your angling partner can also help control coiled fly line. Sometimes keeping the fly line in the boat is difficult. If so, keep the fly line on the downwind side of the boat. Be certain the line does not extend back to where the push pole enters the water.

When wading, have the rod and fly line in the ready position. Be careful not to get your feet or clothing entangled in any excess fly line or let the tide drag it too far behind you. Both situations preclude a quick cast. If you need to strip additional fly line from the reel quickly for a longer-than-expected cast, do so by spreading both arms apart as far as possible and stripping off four-foot lengths.

When you are ready to cast, flip the loop of line forward into action. Don't release the fly immediately but hold onto it until the momentum of the line pulls the fly from your grasp. This helps the fly line load the rod. Shoot the remaining line on the back and forward casts.

Timely Presentation

Be at the ready position with the line out of your rod tip and properly coiled. Check it often. How long does it take you to strip out 40 feet of line? Try it. If you looked at your reel, you took your eyes off the fish. Did the line coil properly after your last retrieve? Did it catch on something during the cast? Did your fly get tangled around a guide or the rod tip?

Most missed opportunities occur because you can't put the fly on target quickly, often because you aren't ready. In the course of a day's fishing you can make an occasional error or many errors. Each slowdown or mistake may cost you a hookup.

If there are plenty of fish to keep you excited, it is easy to stay focused and in the ready position. After a fishless period, your enthusiasm begins to wane. Your eyes wander, your feet drag, your rod droops, and your concentration is lost. The best elixir for this situation are the words "Bonefish, 10 o'clock, 50 feet, moving our way." The second best remedy is to let your angling partner have a turn at the angling position.

The following chart underscores the need to make a timely on-target presentation. Quick and accurate casters hook the most fish because they can capitalize on almost every opportunity.

The ready position in the boat—the fly is in hand, a loop of line is beyond the rod tip, and the desired length of line is stripped on deck. Be certain the fly line is positioned so that it uncoils top to bottom when the cast is made.

Speed of Bonefish	Distance Bonefish Travel	Elapsed Presentation Time. . .Distance Traveled			
		5 seconds	10 seconds	15 seconds	20 seconds
1 mph	1.50' per second	7.5'	15'	22.5'	30'
1½ mph	2.20' per second	11'	22'	33'	44'
2 mph	2.90' per second	14.5'	29'	43.5'	58'
2½ mph	3.65' per second	18.25'	36.5'	54.75'	73'
3 mph	4.40' per second	22'	44'	66'	88'
4 mph	5.90' per second	29.5'	59'	88.5'	118'

Success depends on how far away the bonefish is spotted, the direction and speed it is traveling in relation to your position, and how long it takes for you to present the fly. Let's look at a possible scenario: You are wading and spot a bonefish at 50 feet traveling toward you at two miles per hour, or 2.9 feet per second. In 10 seconds, assuming it has not stopped to eat, it has traveled 29 feet and is within 20 feet of you. It will notice you any second and bolt. If you can strip out or ready your line, cast it, and sink the fly into fishing position within 10 seconds or less, you can hook the fish. Practice this imaginary game until you can do it.

If you are at the ready position with your fly line neatly coiled, you can be fishing in five to seven seconds. Speed greatly enhances your chances of success. If the presentation is made farther away from you, there is time to reposition the fly, finesse the fish, and perhaps cast again if the fish changes direction or slows to feed.

Beginning anglers can take heart in that bonefish often move slowly and there is ample time to move into position and make a presentation. Many first-time fly rodders hook dozens of bonefish at destinations that offer an abundance of unsophisticated bonefish.

The ready position on foot—the fly is in hand, a loop of line is beyond the rod tip, and the desired length of line is stripped from the reel. Notice that the wind and/or tide are moving right to left, and the line is carried in that direction in front of and past the angler. When the cast is made, the loose line must first break free of the water's tension and downstream drag, then clear the angler to the rod, which is in the right hand. To avoid this possible entanglement and slowdown in making the cast, some of the line can be looped in either hand. The best solution in this situation is to cast left handed.

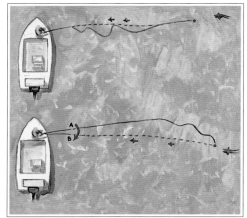

One of the most common errors anglers make is misjudging the retrieve speed in conjunction with wind, tide, and boat movement. Suppose the boat is moving with the tide at two miles per hour toward a bonefish, and a bonefish is moving toward the boat at one mile per hour. The wind is creating a belly in the fly line, which is moving the fly one mile per hour at a right angle to your cast and the fish. The cast is made, and you wait for the fly to sink to the bottom. In those few seconds the boat, fish, and fly have all moved. A sighting at 35 feet may diminish to 20 feet. Whew. . .what a mess!

What do you do? You may need to reposition, or mend, the fly line if an air mend was not made during the cast. Then make several quick long pulls on the line until there is a tight connection to the fly. Now the fly moves when you want it to, and you can fish effectively. Where is the fish? Ask your guide!

There is always more wind above the water than at its surface. It is easier to cast a tight loop low to the water (right) than high above it (left), and a low cast is less likely to be detected by fish. For these reasons, keep your cast low to the water.

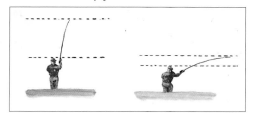

Casting

I always ask guides what the single greatest obstacle is for their clients in relation to hooking fish. The answer is universal—casting. If you were to ask me for my best pretrip advice, I would tell you to *learn to cast!*

A first-time bonefisherman spent months gathering gear, reading books, watching videos, researching destinations, and tying flies. He didn't take time to learn to cast an 8 weight 30 feet in a breeze. Your guide can pole the boat, spot the fish, and talk you through the hookup, but he cannot make the cast for you. You have to make the cast. If you can't cast, you can't fish—period!

Bonefish anglers do not have to cast far to hook fish. Neophytes and non-casters often hook bonefish the first day if fish are plentiful and eager, but, if you are a competent caster, the sport is much more enjoyable. If you can cast accurately at 30 to 40 feet, action will be good. If you can place most casts inside a Hula-Hoop in a moderate wind, you are considered expert. Casting should be automatic. If you have to fumble about or watch your line, you can't watch the fish, which is where your attention should be focused. Get some professional casting instruction and practice before you go bonefishing!

Always cast low to the water and keep your line and line shadow away from bonefish. A low cast to the side allows the fly to be dropped from a short distance above the water, which results in a softer presentation. There usually is less wind low to the water, making casting easier and more accurate. False casts should be kept to a minimum—none is best, but no more than two or three. False casting wastes time and increases the chance of entangling your fly or scaring bonefish with shadows, light reflection, movement, and noise. If you are casting from a boat, do not rock the boat as you cast.

When you lift the fly line off the water for another cast, do not create any unnecessary noise or splash. This is best accomplished by lifting as much line as possible off the water before beginning the power stroke. Begin with a tight line and with the rod tip at the water's surface. Lift the rod tip, which lifts the line, and begin to bring it toward you. This is the initial stage of the back cast. When most of the line is off the water, follow through with the back cast. When the fly line is lifted off the water, it carries water droplets with it. Deposit this excess water on the backcast with line acceleration and an abrupt halt.

If you are making a standard overhead cast, direct the fly to an imaginary spot two feet above the water's surface, and it will land gently. A soft presentation can be achieved with a heavy fly in wind by lengthening your leader tippet to five or six feet and casting with the wind. Aim the cast four feet above the water. The fly will land softly. Lighter flies obviously land more gently than heavier flies and might need to be placed well in advance of bonefish.

When you want to turn a fly over in the wind or want quick penetration of the water, drive the fly at the water's surface.

Sloppy casts are usually unforgivable on bonefish flats. When you make a cast that inadvertently hits the water or lands off target, leave it. Wait until it is safe to cast again.

If possible, cast with the wind or across the wind. Don't fight

the wind. Casting directly into it is a last resort and is very difficult to accomplish for the average caster.

Before you make your cast, be certain you see all the fish between you and your target. You might inadvertently line a fish, which could spook the others. As you move into casting position and make the cast, do not take your eyes off the fish.

Approach bonefish as closely as possible before making a cast. You have better casting accuracy and more good quick shots at various angles from short range. Making three 30-foot casts is more effective than making one 90-foot cast. When you are close in, it is easier to keep fish in sight and to observe their response and fly pick up.

Under some circumstances you may have to make a long cast. If you can cast accurately and fish well at 90 feet—make the cast. If you do not get a take, strip in—you should have time for another chance closer in. If you cannot make the cast, don't risk disturbing the water or fish. Wait for a better shot.

When bonefish are moving directly toward you, don't let them get too close before making a cast. It is often advisable to place the fly well in advance of such fish so they do not overrun your position without at least seeing the fly.

Left-handed and right-handed casters might possibly need to approach fish from different angles or from the opposite side of the

If you can cast 30 feet quickly and accurately, you can hook bonefish. With decent instruction, you should be able to cast 30 feet on target within an hour. Additional practice gets you up to speed, but learn before you get in the boat or wade the flats. The angler casts to mudding bonefish and cruising trevally at the Cook Islands in the South Pacific.

boat. If two opposite-casting anglers are walking a flat, they should be positioned accordingly. Anglers who cast with either hand have an advantage because they can make the most of bonefish entering casting range from any angle and take advantage of wind direction.

Obstructions and water depth also dictate how close you can get to fish. Mud bottoms with undulating mounds and a scattering of mangroves on a rising tide on a breezy day might allow you to gig bonefish with your rod tip. Fish feeding in grass often have limited vision, and grass helps muffle footfalls. Mud tailers engrossed with a crab colony on a windy day are much easier to approach than random coral tailers in skinny water during dead calm conditions.

When you are walking a flat, do so in a manner that allows you to intersect bonefish head-on or slightly off to one side. Be careful that they are not slipping by behind you.

I like to place the fly close enough to tantalize bonefish without revealing the fly's distinct features. Such a presentation seldom frightens fish and can excite their curiosity. If it doesn't, place the next cast closer. If bonefish turn away from you to grab the fly, so much the better. Your chances of being seen decrease and the odds of a solid hookup increase. This is especially true when bonefish are very close.

When you have a choice, place the fly between the bonefish and the sun. The fly is backlighted, and bonefish see the dark side of the fly, which is more subtle and indistinct. Movement may also appear somewhat blurred. In contrast, the sunny side of the fly is often too sharply highlighted by harsh reflective sunlight, betraying it as a fraud.

When bonefish swim in water this skinny, their dorsal fins and tails may break the water's surface, creating V wakes. Even if their fins do not break the surface, the fish's movement causes nervous water. Such skinny water conditions may require unweighted flies with a foam body so they suspend. Imagine yourself surviving in such a skinny environment surrounded by predators!

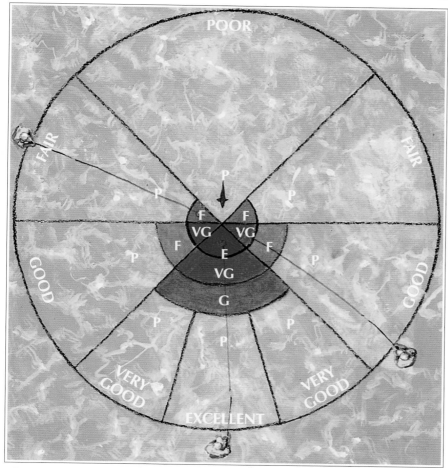

The circumference shows the angler's location and angle of presentation. The inside "wedges" depict fly placement and the angle of retrieve. The best casting position is from Very Good to Excellent, casting toward the fish to the pie-shaped "E." This allows you to retrieve the fly within a 20-degree angle in the direction the fish is traveling.

Interception Zone—Frontal Presentation

Ideally, your fly should hit the water quietly, sink to the bottom on the count of three (about 2½ seconds), and be in position within one to five feet ahead of an approaching bonefish. The closer it is to a bonefish, the better the chance that it might be discovered. This is known as the *interception zone,* and it varies according to water depth, bottom type, and the speed that bonefish are traveling. To place the fly in the optimum interception zone, anglers must estimate the speed and direction of the bonefish and allow for the fly's sink rate and for any current or wind that might also influence the fly.

The best presentation allows you to retrieve the fly within a 20-degree angle of the direction the fish is traveling. This straight-away retrieve portrays the best illusion of a fleeing animal. Bonefish do not have to change direction to accept the offering, and there is more time to entice a particular fish or to encounter another nearby fish. When fish are spooky, cast to the outer edge of their visual zone. Allow them to move within sight of your offering; then slightly twitch the fly. When the imitation is presented at a 90-degree angle, or broadside, it must be convincing enough to turn fish from their intended route. Sometimes the broadside presentation is the only option available.

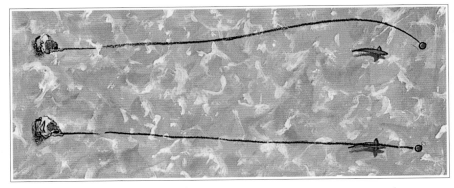

When bonefish are swimming away from your position, a curve cast is necessary. Be certain the fly line lands behind and to either side of the bonefish. If you "line" the fish with either fly line or leader, as illustrated at the bottom, a take is unlikely.

Going Away Presentation

When fish are moving away and a frontal presentation is not possible, presenting the fly without spooking them is difficult. The best chance is to throw a curve cast and show the fly slightly ahead and off to either side of the fish. Such a presentation is difficult but rewarding when it is successful. Present a fly that sinks quickly or makes a slight audible plop, which might temporarily turn bonefish in the direction of the fly out of curiosity. At other times, the noise may spook them. A slow-sinking fly is seldom adequate because, by the time it settles to the bottom, bonefish have passed.

Swim-Away Technique

This is similar to the rear presentation only more technical. It must be executed down wind, down tide, and down current or with the flow of surf surge. A "downstream" mend is built into the cast. Place the imitation in front of the fish. The water current and pull of the fly line will swim the imitation away from the fish and angler. An occasional twitch can be imparted. Once the belly begins to straighten out of the fly line, the fly begins to track back toward you. Usually, bonefish jump the fly immediately, and your only problem is hooking them.

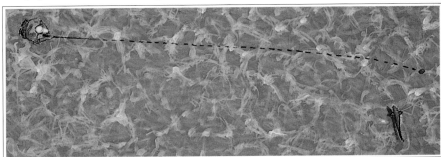

The overcast presentation is relatively easy. Place the fly ahead of and beyond the fish. Reposition the fly as necessary, keeping the fly line out of sight of bonefish.

Overcast Presentation

The overcast presentation is casting the fly in front of and beyond the projected path of bonefish. The fly can then be repositioned into the fish's path. This retrieve usually intersects bonefish at an angle between 45 and 90 degrees. This is an excellent technique for anglers who are less accurate in their casting. It is also useful when attempting to intersect bonefish that are annoyed and leaving the area but have not yet bolted or picked up speed. By overcasting their projected path, you can show the fly to several bonefish, and you might coax one into a brief stop for one last tidbit. The overcast technique is sometimes necessary when casting a heavy bulky fly in shallow water or when fish are feeding in deeper water. When time is limited, the presentation must be more accurate.

If possible, overcast the fly so fish must initially turn away from your position to inspect or take it. This lessens the chances of bonefish sighting you. This ploy is especially effective when fish surprise you in close, particularly next to the boat. Should you accidentally overcast fish (or cast short) when fishing over weeds, retrieve the fly as fast as you can without spooking fish to keep the fly from sinking into and snagging grass. A fly towing weed or snagged in grass usually gets the wrong kind of attention from bonefish.

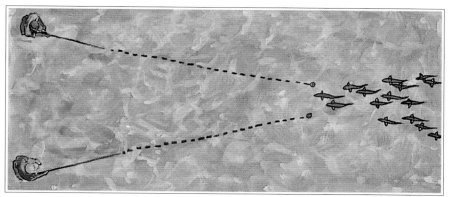

Anglers should position themselves to both sides of the school and cast slightly ahead and to each side of the lead fish.

Presentation Strategy for School Fish

Bonefish commonly associate in large groups, or schools, but singles, pairs, and small pods are also common. School fish are mostly uniform in size. Usually, the larger the school, the smaller the fish. Larger fish tend to be loners or to associate with their own kind. They swim and feed at a different pace and require slightly deeper water than the smaller fish. Larger fish often spread out in a frontal line. Smaller fish come together.

Why fish break up into small groups one day and school up

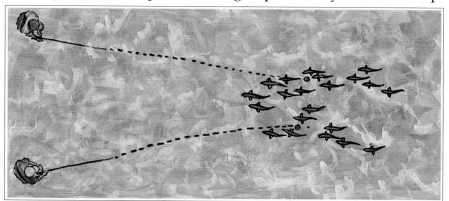

If the lead fish does not turn to either side to take the offering, the next fish in line often does. A long leader keeps the lead fish from swimming over the fly line and alerting the school before its followers have had a chance to grab it. Another ploy is to wait until half the school has passed over the fly or until several fish are within sight before moving it. The competitive factor comes into play. Sometimes the fly is picked up as it lies motionless on the bottom.

the next is not understood. Perhaps social reasons or weather conditions are a factor, or schooling may be a means of protection (safety in numbers). Whatever the reasons, bonefish group together more during low tide and when they enter and exit shallow areas. Schools usually number between 10 and 30 individuals, but schools may contain hundreds, even thousands, of bonefish. When frightened or pursued by predators, big schools whirl around, often creating considerable commotion.

School fish create internal competition. If bonefish are in an aggressive mood, this is an advantage to anglers. When your cast is

positioned so more than one fish sees it, the race is on. Another effective strategy is to place the fly ahead of a school and wait for several fish to swim near the fly before starting to retrieve it. Sometimes waiting for some of the school to pass over your fly before beginning the retrieve is effective. Sometimes a passerby may root out your stationary offering. I have seen a half-dozen or more fish fight over a fly. When one grabs it and takes off, others often follow. Often these "shadow" fish are interested in the fly, especially during the initial confusion. These shadow fish either still want the fly or are offering moral support.

Two of us were working the last flat of the day along the east coast of Andros Island. The sun was low, there was a patchy cloud cover, the tide was dead high, and there was a 10-mph wind. We should have been beachside sipping a cocktail and eating conch. We shuffled along halfheartedly, staring into the occasional light hole between waves when a tiny hole appeared in the cloud cover.

Suddenly there were bonefish scurrying right at our feet! We figured, "A few blind casts cannot hurt." Brian hooked a respectable bone. His fish zig-zagged within five feet of me, followed by a larger fish that was oblivious of me and intent on shadowing his companion. I flipped out my fly, made a pull, and felt the strong tug of a bonefish, but I missed it. Seconds later I had a second chance. Instantly, a fish was on. We had a double. The take was like that of a bank-feeding trout to a hopper. The fly had hardly landed when the fish had it.

When you hook a school fish, release tension on the hooked fish, allowing it to easily remain with its buddies. This gives your angling partner a shot at any groupies. During such competitive confusion and on other rare occasions, bonefish might grab your fly in mid-water or just subsurface. Always be ready.

Bonefish often swim in formation, scattered along a frontal line, traveling and pushing water in a V. The V wake is *behind* the bonefish. Cast ahead of the V. The point fish in a school are usually the most dominant and strongest fish; they are also the most picky. A small sparse fly often works best on these fish. Sometimes the largest fish travels in the center of the pack or school, as if surrounded by guards. A cast to the front or side of the school may break it up, possibly giving you a clear shot at the larger fish. Two anglers can sometimes work as a team. One angler draws small fish and the other angler concentrates on the larger fish. Sometimes you may be able to cast over small perimeter fish directly to the largest bonefish.

The feeding formation and travel speed of bonefish also influence the presentation. Their pace is usually between one and two miles per hour. They stop often to eat, change direction, and eat again. If possible, target a specific fish, but, if you miss, do not risk spooking others with another quick cast. Leave your fly in position and wait for another fish to discover it. If no other fish appears, wait until the intended target fish is far enough away before casting again.

All members of a school do not travel at the same speed. As the front of the school slows down, the rear ranks close up. When speed increases, the ranks space out. When your fly line is overrun,

Hard rock or dead coral flats at Bikini Atoll. When bonefish are hooked in this type of environment, keep the rod high!

let it lie. Many times the rear ranks seem to be green recruits on garbage detail; they are often easy to fool or desperate for leftovers. You might also find a break in the ranks that allows you to reposition the fly or make another cast.

When a school of bonefish is approaching two anglers, they should position themselves to either side of the school and cast slightly ahead and to the side of the lead fish. If the lead fish turns left or right, it may see one fly, as may some of the other followers. More importantly, if the lead fish does not take the fly, leave it in position and the fish immediately behind the lead fish might see it. If not, continue to twitch the fly slowly. These fish are aggressive and your chances of a hookup are great. Both anglers have an excellent chance of hookups with the inside and outside ranks or with those stragglers bringing up the rear.

When a school of bones is coming directly at you or if you are surprised by close-in fish, you should freeze, preferably in a sitting position with your rod low to the water away from the fish. Do not move until all the fish have passed. Sometimes they continue on, unaware that you are anything more than a misplaced mangrove. Bonefish that frequent the same area will not be fooled, even though they may not be overly alarmed. Such fish may move off a short distance and continue feeding.

When approaching bonefish sense or see you, especially in deeper water, but do not "spook," there may still be a chance for a hookup. If they skitter around you at 20 feet and slow down, make a cast. You have little to lose except your fly.

Anglers should note that there is a difference between traveling and feeding schools of bonefish. Traveling schools move faster in tight formation and are difficult to slow down and interest in a fly. A presentation sometimes only seems to irritate them. Consider leaving traveling schools alone. Hopefully, they settle down, break up, and begin feeding elsewhere on the flat. Do not herd or surround such bonefish.

Tight loops cast low to the water are usually best. Aim for an imaginary position two to three feet above the water's surface so the fly line and leader stretch out in the air, then fall two to three feet to the water rather than slapping down on the water. Randall Kaufmann near Deadman's Cay, Long Island in the Bahamas.

Presentation Strategies For Tailers

There are few sights in fly fishing as exciting as tailing bonefish, especially if the tails are tall. Once, in Biscayne Bay, Florida, we were tracking some on-again, off-again nervous water upwind in bright sun, but we could not see the fish. Suddenly, "boosh," a tall shimmering silver tail thrust up into glaring sunlight less than 20 feet away. Before we could position ourselves for a cast, the fish detected us and was gone. Our prize remains the memory of its unexpected brilliance and all that it symbolizes: mystery, and saltwater magic.

The best time to cast to mudding, rooting, or tailing bonefish is when they are tipped down or temporarily facing away to either side. A mud tailer likes to work against the tide because currents help clear the circle of mud and increase visibility. A mudding bonefish has impaired peripheral vision and is less likely to notice your cast. The hazy edge of this murky screen is where you want to place your fly. The bottom excavation activity of the fish helps mask any noise, shadow, or splash associated with the cast. The optimum angle of retrieve will be straight away from the front of the fish.

If your cast is on target and your retrieve is right, the bonefish might believe that your imitation is the intended prey. Your best chance for success is to cast to the nearest bonefish. Casting beyond one to reach another diminishes your chance of success. Tailers often drift and feed with the tide, which may be moving two or more miles per hour. When this is the case, anglers must move into position quickly.

A single tailer is likely to be more cautious than a school of tailers whose members, to some degree, are competitive with each other. When casting to a pod or to tailers strung out along a line, attempt to retrieve the fly in front of as many as possible. The retrieve should be very slow.

Cruising and Approaching Bonefish

Bonefish do not patrol a specific beat like trout, but individual bonefish often follow in the general path of other bonefish. This path may revolve around a specific water depth or a productive feed zone. It is most often a general course, but it can be a radical zigzag route. Pay attention to these paths and position yourself accordingly. If your casting is not perfect, cast your fly beyond and in front of bonefish and retrieve it across their path when they

It is best not to touch bonefish. If you must have a photo of a bonefish, this is the proper support position. Do not lift them high above the water.

Jon Covich

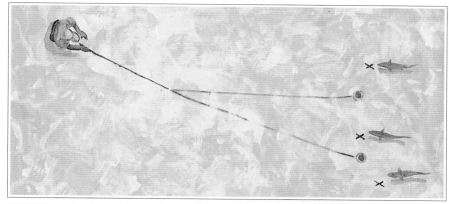

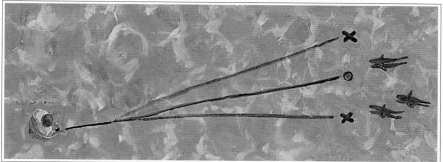

These illustrations depict two scenarios of presenting a fly to a trio of bonefish. Fly placement strategy depends on the positioning and number of bonefish. Unless you are targeting a specific fish, place the fly so that more than one bonefish sees it. This encourages the competitive instinct and speeds up response time. The more quickly bonefish respond, the better the chances of a hookup. If the cast can be positioned so that bonefish must turn away from your position to take the fly, so much the better.

approach. This eliminates casting errors that so often frighten bonefish. Be certain not to overcast fish that may not be visible in the foreground. Look carefully before you cast.

As you observe bonefish making their way across a flat, their direction may seem purposeful, almost as if they were following a map. When tracking records are analyzed, their ultimate destination is consistent, but their route is erratic. If different fly fishermen drove between Miami and Seattle and stopped at all their favorite fishing waters, their routes would be different, but the ultimate destination would be the same.

Big fish move more directly and slowly, and deceiving them is an art. Usually, it is best to wait for them to come to you. Don't move down the flat or cast long. If possible, wade on sand; it is quieter. Walking on coral alerts them every time. When big fish are in deeper water, they are usually more casual. If you make a bad cast, you may get a second chance.

If you notice bonefish are no longer approaching your position but are making a detour, perhaps they have found you out. A change in tide or wind may have alerted them, or one of their buddies that you released may have squealed. Position yourself at another point along their route. If you can conceal yourself in depressions or the mangroves, so much the better.

A fly line or boat can act as a barrier to fish's intended migration and feeding routes. A clear fly line can be an advantage in this situation. If you notice fish abruptly turn 90 degrees to the boat, they have sensed you. When you make a cast and fish change direction, it is obvious they have found you out. At other times bonefish only make subtle changes in direction or speed. Observe closely from the instant you make your cast and especially when they initially see the fly. Their body language reveals whether they sense your presence, how to best retrieve the fly, and what the chances are of a hookup.

Deep-Water Presentation

When bonefish are encountered in water four feet and more deep, an on-the-bottom presentation may be difficult. Your fly must reach the desired depth in a timely fashion and remain there during the retrieve. Larger, heavier flies may be needed.

Depending on water depth, a sinking line may be needed to best capitalize on deep-water situations. Anglers seeking large bonefish should scout water three to six feet deep. Larger bonefish often spend a great deal of time at such depths where they may feel more secure. Bonefish are more casual and are less likely to spook in deeper water. If you make a bad cast, it often is not a problem. When everything is right, they can be aggressive and relatively easy to fool.

Sometimes bonefish may be traveling at mid-level or even near the surface. When this is the case, cast ahead of them, allowing the fly to settle or swim to the bottom. Bonefish may drop down to attack it. Another ploy is to cast closer to the fish and swim the fly downward so the fly intersects the fish's path at or above their level. Bonefish have been known to attack crabs, shrimp, and other food at the surface. When you can entice bonefish to the surface, it is a never-to-be-forgotten thrill.

Another possibility is to present a fleeing baitfish imitation at the level they are traveling. Baitfish imitations are perhaps the most overlooked aspect of the bonefish game. Bonefish ingest smaller fish on a regular basis, and such imitations can provide exciting action.

Waist-deep water is considered deep on flats. At dropoffs, bonefish usually cruise a specific water depth, perhaps two to eight feet deep, which is sometimes referred to as the transition zone. Remain several yards back from deep water. Bonefish often swim the same direction. Walk toward the direction from which they are swimming. Because it takes longer for a fly to sink to a depth of four or eight feet, you must spot and lead bonefish accordingly. It might be advantageous to have your fly waiting on the bottom until a bonefish swims into view. One short pull should do it. Inside the lagoon at Christmas Island.

Casting Blind

I caught my first bonefish casting blind simply because I didn't know what to look for and because I got tired of looking and made a few casts. Since then, I have learned that casting blind is a useful technique. It is usually employed when visibility is poor. If you are walking a flat and a stiff wind or cloud cover makes spotting difficult, consider an occasional cast in the direction bonefish have been traveling. If weather is going to be a problem for most of the day, consider staking out a known migration route. Position yourself so fish are swimming toward or past your position and cast toward them. If you take this approach, fish do not intercept the fly line as often and have a better chance of seeing the fly.

My favorite ploy is to probe deeper water and drop-offs. This is the most likely place to encounter a cruiser (sometimes a big one!) that may not be overly concerned about you wading in shallow water. To lessen the chance of being detected, stand back from the edge. Select a fly that sinks deep and can be seen from a distance. If you hook a fish, stay put and make a few more casts; you might have stumbled onto a migration route.

Casting blind for bonefish is similar to fishing lakes or fishing for steelhead. The number one rule for finding fish is to cover the water. Don't stand in the same place and make the same cast until you hook a fish. You might be there forever. Keep moving and cast in a systematic manner. Use a fan pattern. Cast parallel along the drop-off in both directions. Pause and scan behind you, checking the shallow water.

Once, I was dropped off alone on a large flat and was to meet the boat on the other side in about two hours. The incoming tide also brought an incoming storm of gigantic proportions. I could see it coming, an awesome charcoal-colored fury of wind and water that was surely drowning everything in its path. A labyrinth of lightning illuminated the horizon. It was so frightening that I fully expected to see a funnel cloud and tidal wave! I would not have wanted to meet it on the open sea, and I did not wish to meet it on the flat either. I decided to stay put, wait it out, and fish blind in a cut where bonefish were swimming up onto the flat from deep water.

Octopus-like storm tentacles probed ahead of the storm center, whipping the water into a tempest and blowing my fly line straight up and holding it there. Incoming water from the tide and sky obliterated the last dry land, and, simultaneously, the storm was upon me. I was marooned, invisible, and insignificant, and I was overcome with loneliness. Was I ever glad to have a polypropylene shirt and rain jacket in my pack! Without it, I would have been in a world of hurt. Eventually, the wind calmed enough for casting, and the blind fishing was exceptional. After about an hour the storm blew out of sight, and I continued fishing toward the boat, a happy angler.

First-time visitors to the tropics often have a preconceived notion that the weather is always warm and pleasant. It usually is, but it can just as easily be *nasty.* During inclement weather, your first consideration is safety and comfort. Tropical flats anglers never know what the day will bring; *always* have warm clothing and rain gear at hand. Your next consideration is hooking bonefish.

This almost surreal image is created by light mirrored off the bottom and refracted from the undersurface of the surface tension. Underwater, molecules are attracted to each other in all directions. At the surface, water molecules are attracted on one side only—from below. This boundary of water and air acts like a thin, elastic membrane. Viewed from below this tension, or film, water appears slippery, smooth, silvery, and opaque. Colors and patterns are further distorted by movement of the surface film, either due to wind, wave, or tidal action. The angler's cap, head, and shoulder appear abstract above the water's surface. North Andros, Bahamas.

Chapter 14

The Retrieve

The day is sunny. You are relaxing in your lawn chair on the front porch after lunch when, suddenly, a 200-foot-long creature built like a vacuum cleaner bounds around the corner. To your disbelief and horror, it is sucking up your friends as they flee and pulverizing them in its jaws. What should you do? Run and hide? In panic, you dive into your house. . .but it is too late. The creature sees you, inserts its snout into your doorway, and sucks up everyone inside.

It's not a pretty picture, but you now have a faint idea of how flats animals respond when bonefish enter their neighborhood for a snack.

Animals that flee are almost always spotted and pounced on. Those that dive into their mud or sand shelters are treated like those fairy tale animals, the three little pigs. Those that rely on camouflage, keep their wits, and remain stationary might escape if bonefish do not detect their scent.

An understanding of bonefish feeding habits and the movements and response of prey helps you present your offering in a convincing manner. The retrieve should attract initial attention to your offering and excite bonefish to attack it. The retrieve often becomes a game of enticement, creating a great deal of anticipation for both bonefish and angler.

The basic retrieve used for bonefish is simply a pull, or strip, retrieve. It is easy to master. Hold the rod handle with one hand. Catch the fly line under the first or second finger of the rod hand, and press the line against the cork handle. With your other hand, grasp the fly line behind your rod hand with your thumb and first finger. Strip, or pull, fly line down and back while releasing tension on the fly line between your finger and the cork handle. Resume fly line tension against the cork when you are not stripping line.

Pay careful attention to the location of the fly line that has been stripped in. Make certain it is not tangled or trapped by your feet or objects in the boat; you must clear the line quickly when a fish is hooked. When two people are fishing from a boat, the angler who is not fishing should help keep the fly line free of obstructions. When you are stripping line, point the rod tip directly at the fly and keep the tip just under or at the water's surface. This ensures direct contact between the rod tip and the fly. The fly line should always be tight to the fly and under your complete control.

Eliminate as many variables as possible and make each strip count. Your best chance of success is during the first one or two strips. Each succeeding strip reduces your chances of a hookup. The further you strip a fly, the greater the chance it may snag the bottom, pick up a weed, or be detected as a fraud.

Various combinations of slow, fast, short, and long pulls interspersed with pauses can be employed. Remember, the retrieve is not always associated with movement. Sometimes a very slow-moving or even stationary offering is preferred. At other times a continuous series of short pulls ("ticks") keep fish interested and from getting a good visual fix on your imitation. The combinations are endless. The mood and response of bonefish dictate the most effective retrieve to use.

Adjust the speed of the retrieve so it is slightly faster than the speed of the bonefish. Deeper-swimming fish usually move faster and require a faster retrieve than those feeding in shallow water. Rooting or tailing bonefish are best enticed with a very slow retrieve, a twitch, or perhaps a short single pull and stop. Most anglers retrieve too fast and move the fly too often. If you are fishing from a boat, you might need to compensate for any boat movement toward the fly or fish, making quick, hard strips to barely move the fly. Water movement (tides) and wind also influence retrieve speed. When fishing cross tide, incorporate a variable speed, but not one so slow that a belly forms in your fly line or so fast that you pull the fly away from interested bonefish. If possible, position yourself to take advantage of water movement.

Always point the rod tip directly at the fly and keep it at or below the water's surface. This ensures direct contact between you and the fly.

When fishing with the current or wind, you need to retrieve faster to keep up with the natural drift. This is like controlling a fly on an upstream dry fly cast. The same holds true when fishing into incoming waves or swells. Incoming water pushes the fly, and you must compensate with a faster retrieve and, perhaps, a heavier fly. Sometimes tides move so fast that it appears you are fishing a river. Fast-moving water over a clear sand bottom is reminiscent of fishing transparent trout streams in New Zealand, and bonefish can be just as spooky as the trout.

A twitch is one to three inches. A short strip is three to eight inches; a medium strip is eight to 18 inches. A long pull is 18 to 30 inches. A slow strip takes about one second. A hard, or fast, pull is very quick. Under some situations a s-l-o-w hand-twist or twitch retrieve is in order. Remember, most bonefish prey moves slowly, even awkwardly, and retrieving too slowly is difficult—retrieving too quickly is easy to do.

Concentrate on the position of the fly in relation to the fish. Watching the movements of the fish helps you determine how to retrieve the fly.

Before you begin the retrieve, wait for the fly to settle to the bottom. You should usually select a fly that reaches the bottom on the count of three. If the sink rate is shorter, the fly is probably too heavy. If it takes longer, chances increase that fish may pass the fly before it reaches the bottom.

Ideally, the fly should lift up off the bottom on the strip and settle to the bottom on the stop. This is referred to as a "jig" or "hop" action. Flies with bead chain and metal eyes naturally lend themselves to this action, which simulates a fleeing crustacean. A shrimp swims in short, erratic spurts. Keep this in mind as you retrieve your fly. Better yet, get a face mask and snorkel and observe shrimp and crabs in their natural environment. The heavier the eyes, the faster you can retrieve without sacrificing this action. Flies without weighted eyes do not impart this action because they settle downward too slowly. They are reserved for very shallow water and must be fished slowly.

The retrieve is meant to attract attention and elicit a response. Usually, fish see the fly during the first strip and show interest. Fish usually take the fly when it is stopped between pulls. Do not pull the fly away. Allow the fish to tip down and grab it. Bonefish think this is a sure meal. If the first strip does not attract fish, twitch or strip the fly again and, perhaps, again. If a grab has not occurred after the first series of strips, usually three, your chances of a hookup decrease dramatically. I prefer to strip short once and stop, then two or three times and stop. After this, it often becomes a game of enticement and frustration. If a bonefish is close to the fly but does not see it, *twitch* the fly. A hard pull almost always spooks the fish.

Bonefish often play cat and mouse with your imitation. When this is the case, a series of short pulls and pauses often renews their interest and brings them in for a close-up view. Sometimes a two- to three-foot pull entices a grab as the fly settles. Bonefish rely partly on scent when feeding. Perhaps they are attempting to get a sniff of the unfamiliar offering. Do not allow the fly to sit too long, especially if it is not life-like or animated, because bonefish may detect it as a fraud and become suspicious or lose interest. When more than one fish is playing cat and mouse, the competition factor might elicit a grab.

You should not ordinarily put yourself in a position of speeding up the retrieve to hold their interest. Such strategy seldom results in a hookup. Instead, they follow right to the end of your rod tip and bolt, taking all their friends with them. If you do not feel fish are genuinely interested, it is better to stop the game early. Stop the retrieve or lift your fly carefully and gently out of the water, avoiding any liftoff noise or line spray.

Allow fish to move away, or cast to another fish that is farther away. If you lift a long length of line to make another cast, the liftoff noise and line splash may scare any nearby fish.

If bonefish appear genuinely interested, don't give up. Many times bonefish have seen you or the boat and are disturbed and plan to leave, but they may stop for one last morsel before departing. Slow down the retrieve to a series of slow, short pulls and stops in an attempt to finesse them to the fly. Many bonefish are hooked a rod's length away, even when you are in a boat. Remember that when fish are close in, you should kneel or crouch down.

The strip retrieve is simple. Catch the fly line against the cork handle and under your first or second finger Grasp the fly line with the thumb and first finger of your line hand.

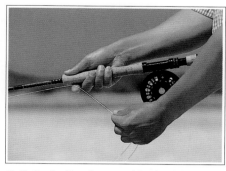

Pull the fly line down and back while releasing tension between your finger and the cork handle. The photo exaggerates releasing the tension. Assuming there is a tight connection between the rod tip and fly and there are no other variables, the fly moves as far and fast as you pull on the line.

Resume tension when you are not stripping

All bonefish destinations offer exciting opportunities to catch many species of fish. Each offers a unique experience and challenge. This school of mangrove snapper in the Bahamas may be more difficult to trick than this giant tarpon at Isla Holbox in the Yucatan. Both are fascinating quarries and tough adversaries. Don't miss the fun and excitement of other flats visitors.

Chapter 15

Fishing for Other Flats Visitors

Bonefish anglers are always on the lookout for movement and color variations, anything out of the ordinary. Not all irregularities, however, spell bonefish. Many other shallow-water fish inhabit the same environment, including barracuda, boxfish, milkfish, needlefish, sharks, and stingrays. Fish traveling erratically across flats or patrolling adjacent areas might be jacks (bar, crevalle, horse-eye, pompano), permit, snapper (cubera, Lane, mangrove, mutton, red, schoolmaster, yellowtail), snook, or trevally. These fish often attack bonefish flies and offer exciting angling. Larger specimens attack bonefish. An understanding of their individual habits and characteristics allows you to more easily and quickly identify them, ultimately resulting in more productive and exciting angling.

If any of these species are available, fish for them! They are great sport and many are easily hooked on small minnow or bonefish flies. Make a cast to any fishy places, including coral heads, channels, cuts, depressions, edges, mangrove holes, rip tide areas, slack water, deep water, eddies, rock outcroppings, wrecks, lobster condos. . .any structure or water character out of the ordinary. You may be pleasantly surprised!

Barracuda

Anglers often think they have spotted a grandaddy bonefish lazily swimming or resting motionless when, in fact, they have discovered a fair-sized barracuda. Barracuda, *Sphyraena barracuda*, are solitary creatures that often remain stationary, sometimes just

Barracuda are notorious for stealing bonefish from anglers and do not practice catch and release. Be especially careful when landing and releasing bonefish. You don't want barracuda eating your fish or your fingers. Either frighten them off or move to another area.

Let your guide release sharks and barracuda.

Barracuda are abundant at most bonefish locations. They are aggressive and jump wildly when hooked, providing anglers with excellent sport. Keep them in the water and handle them carefully. Use pliers to back out the hook and release them unharmed.

under the surface, waiting for an unsuspecting meal to come along. They often wait in deeper cuts or depressions or patrol channels. In contrast, bonefish are always on the move unless they are tailing or have momentarily stopped to pick up a snack. Closer inspection reveals radical physical differences. Barracuda are darker and more blue green in color. They have a broad black tail, two dorsal fins, a pointed nose, and a set of teeth any dentist would love to work on.

The presence of 'cuda can be a strong indication that bonefish are in the area. Barracuda are notorious for stealing bonefish from anglers, and they do not practice catch and release. Barracuda typically chomp a bonefish in half, leaving the head for the angler. _Do not allow barracuda to make a meal of your bonefish._ 'Cuda and sharks are like thugs and drug dealers—you don't want them in your neighborhood. Either frighten them off or move to another area. If a 'cuda does get on the trail of your bonefish, either break the fish off or release the reel drag. Be especially careful landing and releasing bonefish in the presence of barracuda. Barracuda move at hyperspeed, are very bold, and can literally steal bonefish from your hands! Just be careful they don't steal your fingers.

Brian O'Keefe, Mary Kaufmann, and I once came upon a huge school of "bibbling" bonefish in the Bahamas. This occurs in the Bahamas during late April and early May when smaller, two- to three-pound bonefish gather in schools of a thousand or more. They mingle tightly together and sometimes their heads, dorsal fins, and tails protrude from the water. Brian calls it "heading." This particular school was surrounded by several 20- to 35-pound barracuda, which are big enough to give you chills. Like sheep dogs, the 'cuda were herding their flock of bonefish.

Brian finally enticed a bonefish to eat his fly and a nearby barracuda went on the offense. Before I could shout a warning, the barracuda engaged its warp speed and instantly was between Brian's legs butchering his bonefish. The water erupted in turmoil and turned to blood. Mary screamed in terror and ran

for the boat. A petrified Brian practiced his walking on water technique. I was determining if Brian still had a leg or any fingers left! It didn't look pretty, but Brian was O.K. Shaken, Brian cranked in his line, retreated to the boat, and rigged up a wire leader. None of us was in any great hurry to wade back into the water. Brian soon had the 30-pound monster that had terrorized him. It leaped for the reef, but the bonefish in its belly slowed it down. It didn't make it.

Barracuda are abundant at most bonefish locations, especially in the Atlantic. Anglers seldom see them at Christmas Island, but there are some giants offshore. When no other species is willing to play "fish," you can always count on barracuda. They are aggressive and good jumpers. To hook them, all you need is a long fluorescent green, fluorescent orange, or pearlescent fly. Attach it to a wire leader and pull it quickly past their nose. You should soon be fast to a finned razor blade.

The aggravator technique also works well. Present your imitation six or seven feet in front of the fish and lift the line up as if to make a cast, zooming the fly past and away from the fish. Once or twice is usually enough. If the fish hasn't fled, it should jump the fly when you present and retrieve it.

Don't go flats fishing without a couple of wire leaders and barracuda flies! Don't forget the pliers—you do not want to release them with your hands! If you experience problems, cut the leader; the fish quickly work out a barbless fly.

You do not want barracuda eating you and you probably do not want to eat them. Not because they are not tasty, quite the contrary, but because barracuda are the number-one fish implicated with ciguatera. This is a nerve poison that begins with certain microorganisms associated with coral reefs. The microorganisms are ingested by small fish and passed up the food chain. Ciguatera kills 10 percent of its victims, but only a small fraction of the local predatory fish population carries the poison. It is indeed a remote possibility, and locals often eat barracuda without worry, especially those from deep water. Our guide once kept a 25-pound 'cuda. When I asked what he was going to do with it, he said "Eat it." I asked if he were concerned about the toxin. He replied that he would first feed it to his dog; then, if safe, the family would eat it! If not, they eat the dog! Symptoms include nausea, vomiting, cramps, and diarrhea followed by muscular pain and weakness.

Barracuda are solitary fish. They often lie motionless while waiting for prey to appear. Look for them patrolling channels and deeper cuts or waiting in depressions and around mangroves. Smaller ones patrol flats.

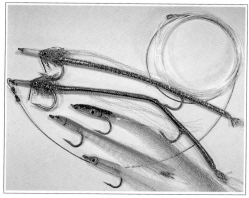

Randall Kaufmann

'Cuda flies must be tethered to wire. Anything long and green or silvery works. Retrieve fast!

Assorted snapper, jack, and barracuda flies.

Boxfish

Boxfish are a common sight on most bonefish flats. Belonging to the Ostraciontidae family, these odd fish are enclosed in a mostly solid bony box with holes for the eyes, mouth, fins, and vent. They are solitary fish that inhabit shallow water. Their fins and tails constantly flip and splash water in a rhythmic manner. They remain stationary until disturbed, then scoot off a short distance. Their underside is shaped like an oblong triangle. The females are dark blue with light spots. Males are much more brilliant. Their best defense against predators seems to be their ability to exude a toxin when they are frightened, which drives away predators. If not prepared properly, they can be poison to humans. Leave boxfish alone to pursue their peaceful lives.

Boxfish are a common sight on shallow flats and move with the tide. Their fins and tails constantly flip and splash water. These bizarre creatures should be left alone to pursue their solitary lives.

Jon Cavich

Jack crevalle appear similar to permit and are common throughout Atlantic and Caribbean waters. They readily jump streamer and popper flies and are strong contenders. Fish should never be brought into the boat. If you must have a photograph, hold them alongside the boat as shown here.

There are many species of jacks, and they come in all colors and sizes. They are all aggressive, swim quickly, and have an insatiable appetite. Sometimes they are compared to piranha. They provide anglers with great sport. Brian Jarvis, bar jack, Andros Island, Bahamas.

Jacks

Erratic and quickly traveling fish in Caribbean waters are most likely one of the many species of jacks, family Carangidae. This large family is represented in all subtropical and tropical waters. They are strong, fast swimmers and offer excellent sport to fly rodders. When encountered on flats, jacks have no qualms about jumping a bonefish fly on the run. Sometimes they attack a fly the instant it hits the water before bonefish or any other species have had a chance even to see it. Single fish and pairs are the most common, but small schools can also be encountered. Jacks often travel with permit and bonefish and trail stingrays. Pompano, *Trachiontus goodei*, are related to jacks but are less common. Anglers sometimes mistake them for permit. Pompano are quick, erratic swimmers and, unlike permit, leap from the water when hooked.

It is often difficult to determine specific species from a distance, but horse-eye and bar jack are common. Bar jacks, *Caranx ruber*, are also called skipjack (not to be confused with the skipjack tuna) and are plentiful throughout the Bahamas. They are blue gray above and silvery white below. Unlike most jacks, they occasionally jump when hooked. Look for schools in blue holes, in channels alongside flats, and in deeper flats. They are competitive and often rush nearly any fly in an effort to make the grab. Their motto seems to be, eat all you can, when you can.

Mary, Brian, and I were lounging on the porch of our waterfront bungalow in the Bahamas playing backgammon when we noticed a school of bar jacks swim into casting range in the channel out front. Yelling "jack attack," we grabbed our rods and tormented the little beasts until they wised up, at which time we returned to our backgammon game. Every few minutes another school would appear, someone would cry "jack attack," and the race to the water was on. This continued through the cocktail hour until dinner was served at sunset—an absolutely delightful afternoon—backgammon, jumping jacks, and rum with Coke. Life was good.

Atlantic horse-eye jacks, *Caranx latus*, are an Atlantic jack crevalle that is closely related to the horse-eye jack, *C. marginatus*, of the eastern Pacific. Another similar species, *C. sexfasciatus*, ranges the Indo-Pacific region from Hawaii to the east coast of Africa, and together they constitute a nearly circumtropical species complex.

Specimens have a large eye and are dark blue-gray above and silvery white or sometimes golden along the sides and below. A small black spot may be present on the upper edge of the operculum (the bony covering protecting the gills). The tail is yellow. Schools of horse-eyes have been observed to change their color from dark to light to blend with their surroundings.

Like bar jacks, look for them in deeper flats, channels adjacent to flats, and blue holes. Fly rodders usually encounter fish up to a pound or two, but they can exceed 10 pounds, and fish to 25 pounds have been reported. Horse-eye jacks are often misidentified as jack crevalle, *C. hippos*, or common jacks, which exceed 50 pounds. Horse-eye jacks have a lot of energy, and a half pounder will zoom frantically every which way before being subdued.

Permit

Guides don't usually get too excited, but, when a permit is within sight, you will know it. When you are in the Florida Keys, Yucatan, and Belize, the odds are strong that any unidentified visitor in medium-depth water is most likely permit (they are not found in Pacific bonefish waters). If you are close enough to see their big round eye, they have probably already spotted you. Key into their exit wake and put your scanner on infinity in an effort to spot the next one before it detects you.

Permit are the most prized and most difficult inshore saltwater fish to capture. The "phantoms of the flats," as they are called, are difficult to see and vanish easily. To be successful, permit anglers must condense all their knowledge and skill into one perfect package—tackle rigging, fly selection, hunting, stalking, casting, presentation, retrieving, hookup, battle, landing, and releasing.

The Atlantic permit, *Trachinotus falcatus*, family Carangidae, swims from the mid-Atlantic states south to Brazil. Permit are a silvery fish with dark, dusky, almost black fins and tail. They are usually bluish gray across the back, sometimes with a mottled patch along their side just behind their pectoral fin. A yellow patch is usually present before the anal fin. Permit are oblong in shape with a blunt face and large round eyes. They have a hard, rubbery mouth with a crusher inside that pulverizes crustaceans, their favorite food, especially crabs.

Native guides often refer to permit as palometa. Pompano, *Trachiontus goodei*, are sometimes confused with permit. Pompano can usually be identified from a distance by their quick, aggressive mannerism and their lighter-colored tail and fins. Pompano, unlike permit, jump when they are hooked.

Like bonefish, permit feed with their eyes, nose, and ears and are on ultrahigh alert. If the size of their eyes in comparison to those of bonefish is any indication of their visual prowess, permit have X-ray vision. Their senses of hearing and smell are equally good. Make the least noise or movement, and they do their vanishing act. Actually, when permit are tipped down feeding, it is believed their vision is limited to a small area, which might help explain why anglers think they have superman eyesight. Maybe they just do not always see the fly.

Unlike bonefish, permit are not smorgasbord feeders but rather connoisseurs of fine crab. Anglers often catch permit on live crabs, and permit seem to easily distinguish live crabs from imitations. Until 15 years ago, few permit had been fooled into taking a fly, and most were caught by accident by people fishing for tarpon and bonefish. Even today, relatively few anglers have hooked permit on a fly, and very few anglers have landed over a dozen.

Jack Samson, writing in his informative book, *Permit On A Fly*, states that Joe Brooks caught the first *recorded* permit on a fly in 1951. There are not many accounts of permit landed on a fly in the 1950s. George Hommell, of WorldWide Sportsmen fame, caught one. Florida Keys guide Bonnie Smith, fishing near Islamorada in the late 1950s, was the first woman to land a permit on a fly.

A few flats aficionados began specializing in permit during the 1960s and 1970s, including anglers Charles W. Walton, Bill Levy, and Del Brown, and guides Captain Nat Ragland, Captain Harry

When permit swim and "tail," or feed, in shallow water, their dark tail and sickle-shaped dorsal fin are easily recognized. Because of their shape, permit require deeper water than bonefish. Duncan Barnes casts to a single permit in Belize. Flats anglers may encounter them in good numbers in Florida, Mexico, and Belize, and sometimes in the Bahamas or Cuba.

This channel is a likely spot to find permit.

If any fish can steal the limelight from bonefish, it is permit. Their secretive and jittery nature, relatively small numbers, finicky appetite, and almost mystical physical prowess place them in a class all by themselves. Most anglers consider them the ultimate prize. When you spot, stalk, cast to, and spook them, you'll understand why.

Spear, and Captain Steve Huff, to name a few. Permit fishing didn't really generate much interest until the late 1980s when better crab flies and refined angling techniques became available. This expansion continues today as innovative anglers glean new insights into the world of permit and how and where to catch them.

To date, anglers have found the greatest concentration and the largest permit in the Florida Keys from the Content Keys west to the Marquesas. Ascension Bay in Mexico and "permit alley" south and west of Turneffe Island in Belize also have excellent populations of permit. Pockets of permit are also found in the Bahamas.

Permit are not a flats fish, preferring deeper water most of the time, but they often follow the tide to feed in shallow waters. Bonefish anglers can encounter permit anywhere, anytime throughout Atlantic waters. Their favorite haunts include coral and grass flats, coral reefs, and shallow bars. The windward side of reefs, bars, and islands is best, especially if there is a good tidal flow across such areas. They are also found over sand, along flats drop-offs, in channels, and in the transition zone between flats and deep water.

Tides are important factors when fishing for or planning a serious permit adventure. Full or new moon "spring" tides are usually best. During this time, more water is pushed onto flats, allowing deep-bodied permit access to areas that would otherwise be too shallow. Big bonefish and permit often prefer the same habitat and water depth. Water temperatures between 72 and 80 degrees Fahrenheit seem to be optimum for permit.

Spotting: If you can't spot permit, you can't catch them. There just aren't enough to cast blind to, and permit require an exact presentation. Bright sunny days are best, but cloud cover is welcome when permit are tailing. Wind is the permit angler's friend; a 10- to 15-mph breeze is ideal. Such conditions provide security for permit, and they relax and feed in a happy mode. Cloudy, ruffled, muffled conditions give the angler a slight edge and allow a margin for error.

Permit are most easily spotted when they are tailing in shallow water. Because of their deep bodies, they require relatively deeper water than bonefish. Depending on their size, look for them in water 18 inches and deeper. Water two to four feet deep is ideal. Look for their sickle-shaped black tail and smaller dorsal fin protruding from the water. Search subsurface for bluish and grayish colors, their black tail and fins, and their silvery sides. Scan for nervous water and surface wakes. Look for any out of the ordinary shadow or movement. Many spotting, stalking, and presentation techniques used for bonefish are valid for permit.

Like larger bonefish, larger permit are often solitary feeders, but schools of smaller fish may number a dozen or more. Smaller school fish tend to be more aggressive than singles and larger fish and are easier to spot.

Flies: Permit have been caught on nearly every bonefish and tarpon fly, but crab flies are the best choice. The best crab flies both look and act like real crabs. Knowing which crabs are indigenous to where you are fishing is of paramount importance. For example, in Florida, permit often eat one- to two-inch sand crabs. In the Bahamas, large blue crabs are often preferred. In Belize, fish feeding on reefs eat dime- to quarter-sized greenish- and brownish-gray crabs. The fly's impact, sink rate, and swimming characteristics are also important considerations. Most effective crab patterns available over the counter are useful to some degree everywhere, but crabs designed for specific locations are best. The crab flies pictured here are current favorites throughout the range of permit.

Presentation: Permit feed much more selectively and are more wary than the average bonefish. They are also fewer in number, and you don't get many shots, so make them all count. Execute a poor cast with an unrealistic fly or swim the fly in the wrong manner, and your quarry bolts for deep water. You can make a seemingly perfect cast with a perfect crab imitation and still find yourself staring at a foot-deep watery crater the fish left when it exploded from the area. Obviously, it didn't like something you did! Anglers accustomed to fishing for ultrapicky trout have not learned how to spell the word picky. It is spelled p-e-r-m-i-t! Permit are the most difficult saltwater fish to feed a fly to. They are

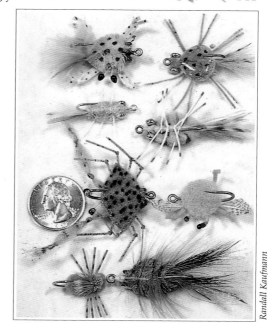

Crabs for permit are generally larger than those used for smaller bonefish. A general comparison is quarters for permit, dimes for bonefish.

Chernobyl

Captain Crabby

Rag Head

Epoxy

Turneffe Foam Crab

Randall Kaufmann

difficult to locate, even more difficult to hook and hold. They require skill and dedication.

You must consider many variables when you cast to permit. This is why a knowledgeable guide is indispensable. Pay attention to what your guide says and follow directions. Possible considerations or calculations include the weather, the speed and direction fish are traveling, the position and visibility of the angler and fish, and the casting ability of the angler. Other considerations include the fish's feeding pattern and rhythm, its food source and size, its degree of contentment, its reaction to the presentation, whether the fish saw the fly, the fly's size, and the tidal flow.

Once the fish spots the fly, read the permit's body language. This dictates what to do next. All these and many more factors must be deduced by angler and guide, which is why you want the best possible permit guide you can find.

Sometimes, however, permit fishing is straightforward, even easy. In a best-case scenario, you spot a happily feeding fish and present the crab imitation five or six feet ahead of travelers or as close as you can to tailers (drop the fly when they are tilted down). The permit sees the fly, and you let it drop or swim to the bottom. The permit rushes over and grabs the fly. You are off to the races.

If the fish does not see the offering, twitch it one to three inches sideways, just enough to attract attention to it, and then let it remain motionless. If the fish still does not see the fly, retrieve it slowly until the fish does see it, and then let it drop. Moving the fly often betrays it as a fraud, probably because the fly does not swim like a crab.

Another strategy is to cast several feet ahead and to one side of cruising fish. Move the fly forcefully to bring the legs to life, swim it sideways, and, once it is spotted, let it drop toward the bottom. The audible "plop" of the fly landing and the quick-escape-and-sink ploy often does the job.

Anglers should prepare themselves for the "permit rush." Upon sighting your offering, permit often rush the fly for a quick inspection. An instant decision is made to either eat or reject the offering. Their head is tipped on the fly and their tail is in the air. You await the grab. It often looks like the permit grabbed your fly, when in fact the fly was refused. This usually leaves anglers baffled. You must get used to permit rejection.

Sometimes, when it is mildly irritated or disturbed, a rooting permit will circle its feeding area much like a dog does when it is searching for a place to lie down. This is probably a survival mechanism or just a double check to make certain everything is O.K. When it is satisfied that all is well, the permit often returns to the exact place it was feeding. Have your fly waiting.

Imagine yourself a crab. A permit is looking for you, perhaps right at you! You are too scared to move or dig, hoping desperately that your camouflage does not fail. Just in case, you have extended your claws. Your eyes are the only things moving. At the first opportunity, you try a slow, tentative sideways escape, or you make a quick dash for your burrow. Uh oh! Wrong move.

When (if!) the permit tails on or picks up your fly, wait a second, and then make a slow motion strip-strike to determine if it has

Permit are where you find them. They often cruise into mangrove areas if there is a deep channel nearby. North Andros Island, Bahamas.

taken the fly. If it has, set up hard and get ready for a chase. Clear your line and get the fish on the reel as soon as possible.

Permit usually head for deeper water, sometimes at blistering speed. The first run is always the longest. Pay attention to your backing. If you are running low, make certain your guide knows to chase the fish. If there is any coral in the area, permit usually find it, sawing your leader or fly line. Once in deep water and after their initial burst of energy is spent, they dog it and pull broadside. Take advantage of angles, always pulling the fish sideways and keeping it off balance. Keep strong steady pressure on the fish, reeling in any line you can.

If you are lucky and skillful enough to land a permit, handle and release it carefully. Do not bring it, or any other fish, into the boat. Grasp it just in front of the tail fin, support it from underneath, face it into the tide or moving current, and move it back and forth until it is ready to swim away. Always smash the hook barb before fishing.

Tackle: Anglers geared with a 9-foot 8- or 9-weight rod can handle medium-sized permit. Anglers who specialize in large permit and cast heavy flies usually fish a 9- or 9½-foot 10-weight rod with an 11-weight line. This makes delivering a heavy fly in wind a little easier. Leaders should be stout enough to turn over heavy, bulky flies. Most anglers prefer a stiff butt section of hard nylon, graduating to a fluorocarbon front section and tippet. Leaders 10- to 14-feet long and tapered from .012 to .016 are about right. Bonefish-style reels are adequate. Expert permit fishermen like at least 250 yards of 30-pound backing.

Bonefishermen usually have (certainly should have) a spare rod. It should always be rigged with a crab fly and readily accessible when you are in permit country. If you are fishing on foot with a guide, have the guide carry the spare rod. If you are specifically chasing permit, rig the extra rod for permit. If you have a tangle, hang up on the bottom, or get a refusal, you have a second chance.

Improving Your Game: Bonefishermen should not dare to visit bonefish/permit country without some basic knowledge of permit—and the other species that inhabit these fascinating areas. _Permit are so electrifying and fun to fish that all flats anglers should make the most of their opportunities and be ready!_ All you need are a few flies!

This is a book about bonefish, not permit. There is a great deal

This is a likely place to find permit—flood tide on ocean flats with quick access to deep water. Their favorite haunts include coral, grass, and shallow bars. Because permit are often encountered in areas of extensive coral, especially in Belize, they are often difficult to land. Buck Buchenroth at Little Cayman Island.

more to the permit game than there is room for here. Anglers wishing to learn more about permit should read the literature cited in the bibliography. In addition, look for new publications and talk to anglers who are successful at hooking permit. Book a day or two with a good permit guide. They are available at all permit destinations, and they take permit fishing very seriously. Most important, just do it!

Caution: If you are one of those unfortunate rare anglers who carries the "PERMIT" gene marker, beware of permit fever. If you become infected, expect your life to change forever. Friends notice the progression of the disease long before you do. Infected anglers slip into a finned passion, one of crazed intensity. It might begin innocently enough with you staying up late camouflaging leaders so they look like turtle grass or notching the legs on your crab imitations. This quickly progresses to walking around the dinner table three or four times before you sit down. You become more selective about your food, eyeballing it closely, smelling it, and refusing to eat half of it. By the time your eyes begin to pop out and you start to blow bubbles, it is too late.

Permit have changed the lives of many anglers. Angling mania seems directly related to a species' size, rarity, and angling difficulty. Unlike trout fishing, which is available relatively close to most anglers, permit are found only in a few remote areas. They require travel; there are not very many of them; they are difficult to find and even more difficult to fool—all the ingredients of crazed passion. You can lose yourself, and any other excess baggage, in the pursuit of permit. It is the angler's never-never land.

South Pacific anglers may encounter the snubnosed dart, *Trachinotus blochii*, also known as buck-nosed trevally, swallowtail, and oyster-eater. They resemble permit and pompano very much. Their deep body is colored brilliant silver and washed in golden yellow with a touch of yellow orange on the belly. Except for their dusky golden dorsal, pectoral, anal, and caudal (tail) fins, they look amazingly like permit. They grow to 25 pounds.

Permit are found in relatively few places and in small numbers. They are difficult to find and even more difficult to fool—all the ingredients of crazed passion. You can lose yourself in pursuit of permit. It is the angler's never-never land. Greg Price plies a likely channel edge in Belize.

Milkfish

At a casual glance, milkfish, *Chanos chanos*, look similar to bonefish. More than one angler has had stalking and casting practice with them. A friend of mine related how he had spent the better part of an afternoon fishing an edge at the back of the lagoon at Christmas Island without hooking a bonefish. He said he made many perfect casts, tried every fly he had, and didn't even have a looker. Finally the guide came along and said, "No, milkfish. They won't take the fly." Milkfish are said to be plankton feeders, and a few have been caught with flies that look like algae. Pass on casting to milkfish unless you want to make a career out of trying to catch one. If, however, you can figure out a consistent method for hooking them, you might just forget bonefish—milkfish are formidable battlers.

Milkfish can be found throughout much of the Pacific. Milkfish and bonefish often swim together at Christmas Island, especially back in the lagoon, at the lagoon mouth, and along lagoon edge flats. At Christmas Island, they are farmed on a commercial basis and sometimes reach 15 pounds or more. A very large milkfish would be 35 to 40 pounds. Moana succinctly put the movement of bonefish and milkfish in perspective for me. He said, "You ask milkfish to go to the store for bread, and they stop at the gas station, the post office, and the tanning salon. Ask a bonefish to go to the store, and he goes directly there."

The lighter, silvery fish are bonefish; the darker fish are milkfish. Close inspection reveals that the bonefish are on the bottom and the milkfish are suspended above the bottom. Milkfish cast a larger and darker shadow and have an overall bluish color and darker greenish back. When milkfish swim toward you, they appear to have a third eye in the center of their head. This illusion is created by a dark spot between their eyes. When milkfish tail, only the top of their deeply cut, black-tipped tail protrudes from the water. Their tail is in constant motion, making a wide swing. In contrast, bonefish show their entire silvery tail, and it is stationary when they are feeding. Bonefish tails are not as radical or as deeply cut as those of milkfish.

To the uninitiated, milkfish look like bonefish, and you would not be the first angler to spend time casting to them. Not that they can't be caught, mind you, but you usually need to feed them an algae-type fly. Try an olive-colored worm pattern. If and when you hook them, be prepared for the run of your life because they are very strong and reach 15 pounds or more.

Milkfish are vegetarians, hence they are a relatively rare catch for fly anglers. However, they are exceptionally strong and offer excellent sport if you can catch them. Try a green lettuce or worm-style fly. John Hull hooked this milkfish at Christmas Island.

John Hull

A pair of stingrays cruise the mangroves at Grand Cayman Island. As they swim across the bottom, rays dislodge bonefish prey. Always cast behind stingrays in case a bonefish or other species are in tow munching goodies.

Stingrays are docile plankton-eating animals and mean no harm. Their barbed tail can be painful if it lashes you as they scoot away. Shuffle your feet when in stingray country, warning them of your presence so they can swim ahead, and you should never have a problem. This ray is settling in for a nap in the Queen's Garden, Cuba.

Rays

The undulating, rhythmic beat of the stingray's wings curling above the water is reminiscent of an underwater Drexasoras, a long-extinct relic of past millennia. On one occasion I was mesmerized as I watched a ray silently break the water's surface. Its dark wingtips looked like menacing shark fins. The creature looked huge, especially in such a thin environment. The ray continued its course toward me, and I wondered if a bonefish or two were tagging along. I cast to the near side and slightly behind the ray at the edge of its mud trail. Instantly, a bonefish exploded on the fly at the surface (a rare treat) and pulled free just as quickly. I frantically returned the fly to the same position, and, again, a bonefish pounded the fly and bolted away. This one was hooked securely, and I eventually released a strong four pounder.

While fishing near Islamorada, Florida, we encountered a big stingray. Our guide, standing on a poling platform, proclaimed, "Nothing there, nope!" I cast anyway, and a five-pound bar jack had the fly before it touched the water. My fishing companion, Jim Kenyon, said it would have hit a Griffith Gnat. Anglers should cast to all rays whether or not bonefish are visible.

Once, while fishing out of Deep Water Cay in the Bahamas with David Pinder, Jr., Mary, and I came upon two dogs paddling across a shallow flat. We couldn't believe how or why they were in the middle of bonefish country. David laughed and said, "Those crazy dogs; a shark will get them one day." They were two or three miles from the lodge via watery mangrove muck! As the dogs plowed and paddled through the shallows, they churned up the bottom and, sure enough, four bonefish were in tow!

Bonefish are opportunists. As rays (and dogs) swim across the bottom, they disturb it, creating long muds in soft areas and displacing coral and sand in others. What better way to obtain an easy meal than to let a stingray dig your lunch? More often than not, bonefish are found cruising behind rays, picking up prey dislodged by their progress across a flat.

Stingrays belong to the family Dasyatidae. They are docile, plankton-eating animals; they mean no one any harm when swimming across a flat. They are easy to spot. Look for their triangle-shaped wing tips breaking the surface or their dark bodies resting or moving along the bottom. When at rest, they bury themselves in the bottom strata. Wading anglers should be careful not to step on them as their barbed tail can be painful if it lashes you as they scuttle away. Shuffle your feet when in stingray country, warning them of your presence and allowing them to scoot ahead.

While poling for tarpon off Tarpon Cay in Belize, we came upon an eagle ray, *Obispo chucho*. Locals called it a leopard ray, and it is one of the most beautiful of the species. It allowed us close-up photos before settling down into the sandy bottom for a quiet nap.

Pacific manta rays, *Mobula diabolus*, are found in deeper water. They can measure 10 feet or more in width and usually swim close to the surface. They use water to support their wings much like birds use air. They flap their "wings" and glide gracefully through the water, gathering tiny fish and filtering suspended organisms with their large slot-like mouths. Mantas often "fly" up to visitors, enjoying their company. Remora fish often have a symbiotic relationship with mantas, eating scraps and removing parasites. Mary and I once rode a 10-foot manta ray while snorkeling in Tahiti. The sensation was thrilling and powerful, yet peaceful and calming. Atlantic manta rays, *Manta birostris,* reach up to 22 feet in width!

Flats and other shallow-water areas that have an abundance of fish life (needlefish, boxfish, rays, sharks, jacks, barracuda, and trevally) will probably also have bonefish. You might not locate or spot them as easily as these other species, but they are there, or soon will be.

Flats anglers who take time to snorkel can enjoy spectacular sights and learn much about the watery world of coral, rays, bonefish, and much more. Gorda Cay near Abaco in the Bahamas.

Sharks

Sharks are a common sight on most bonefish flats. Their wide bodies appear brown or black. Their steady, tail-swinging movement and ominous dorsal fins make sharks readily identifiable. Most sharks that swim on flats are 18 to 40 inches long, but six-foot and larger specimens may also be present, especially if deep water or a reef is nearby.

Black-tipped sharks, *Carcharhinus melanopterus,* are the most common species and are easily recognized by their tall dorsal and shorter secondary black-tipped fins. They are dusky golden yellow, usually two or three feet long, and can be a nuisance.

If you see two tall dorsal fins of about equal size, it is most likely a Lemon shark, *Negaprion brevirostris*, which is a dusky lemon-brown and usually three to six feet long. The lemon is very common on Caribbean bonefish flats and can provide excellent sport.

Bonnethead sharks, *Sphyrna tiburo,* have a wide, rounded head and a white edge on their fins. They are dark gray on top, light gray underneath. They average two to four feet in length and are not easily spooked by anglers or boats.

Bull sharks, *Carcharhinus leucas,* look like bullies with their rounded snout and body-builder appearance. They are gunmetal grayish blue-brown above and white underneath. They have small eyes and can be aggressive. Avoid messing with these brutes, which can exceed eight feet. They are considered dangerous.

Nurse sharks, *Ginglymostoma cirratum,* have a catfish-like face and tall, wide, sweeping tail. They are brownish and usually between three and five feet long.

Other species of sharks are also common at various locations.

Sharks are fascinating and mysterious creatures to observe. Look into a shark's eye and imagine yourself swimming through time. Sharks do not recognize humans as a food form. Attacks are usually by accident. The International Shark Attack File estimates that for every human killed by a shark, 10 million sharks are killed by humans. Populations of many species of shark are in trouble, being indiscriminately slaughtered for their skin, teeth, fins, and cartilage. Overfishing of species that sharks feed on is also causing a marked decline in their numbers. Sharks are an integral and vital link in the ecosystem. They deserve the same respect and protection accorded bonefish or any other flats species.

Sharks are seldom a problem in clear shallow water, but all sharks should be treated with respect and considered dangerous. In deeper water or in reef areas, it never hurts to be cautious. Pay attention. When large sharks are present or if smaller sharks seem overly aggressive, get out of the water. When water is cloudy, they might not be able to see you and could attack by accident. To avoid possible problems, step out of any mud cloud you may have created. Wiping bonefish slime on your pants can attract sharks. Jim Kenyon once had a shark nose his slimy calf. If sharks become too curious or aggressive, a quick kick in their direction or a wiggle of the rod tip in the water usually sends them scurrying away. If that does not work, a knock on the head with your rod butt should do it.

Brian O'Keefe, however, no longer antagonizes sharks with his

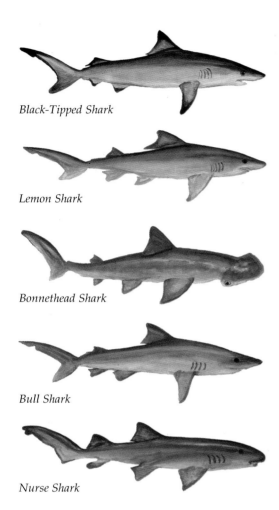

Black-Tipped Shark

Lemon Shark

Bonnethead Shark

Bull Shark

Nurse Shark

rod tip. A three-foot shark was casually swimming in front of him as we walked a flat off Deadman's Cay at Long Island in the Bahamas. He mischievously splashed the water with his rod tip. The shark whirled around and bit his rod tip off!

Another time I was trudging through a terrible flat of mucky moguls. I was tired and wanted to rest but was afraid to stop, fearing I might not be able to lift my feet out of the ooze. A murky cloud surrounded me and I knew this was a potentially dangerous situation. A small but aggressive black-tipped shark homed in on my trail, and it was all I could do to fend it off. I finally took my rod butt and knocked him between the eyes. Pay attention and stay out of the muck!

Flats that are heavily fished seem to have sharks that associate anglers with a meal of bonefish; sharks may shadow anglers, waiting for a hookup. This behavior should be discouraged. It is hard on the bonefish population and can be dangerous. I have had three-foot-long sharks swim between my legs in an attempt to grab my bonefish. Should you encounter such behavior, move to another location. Too many sharks and barracuda can keep bonefish from entering a flat or cause bonefish to leave or to be edgy.

When a shark or other predator is after your bonefish, you have two options: release the reel drag and hope the bonefish outruns the pursuer or point your rod at the bonefish and break the leader. Breaking the leader allows the bonefish the best chance of survival. Remember, bonefish are easy prey for predators immediately after a release; _landing bonefish in a timely manner is critical._ If you have a choice, release bonefish in shallow water instead of along a channel or deep cut where predators are likely to lurk. Sharks track bonefish after they are released and often run down tired fish. A surface commotion in the area where you have released a fish probably means there is a happy shark and one less bonefish. Make a game of seeing how quickly you can land and release bonefish.

Sharks, especially larger ones, are not easy to entice to a fly on the flats. Splashing water, vibrations, and other things attract sharks, but silence is required when pursuing the big players. Sharks have relatively poor eyesight, making the angle of presentation critical, especially in shallow water. For optimum results, cast to a shark as it is swimming toward you. Present the fly alongside the head and retrieve it in the same direction the shark is swimming, allowing the shark the longest possible view. Do not cast in front of the shark where it is difficult for it to see your offering. Sharks are attracted to poppers, but, because their mouths are positioned so far back under their bodies, they often have trouble getting a piece of poppers.

Small black-tipped sharks sometimes attack almost anything, including bonefish flies. Larger sharks require larger flies. Try 'cuda-style flies and 4/0 flies that imitate fish.

If you are not using a wire leader, you will not get your fly back. If you are using a wire leader, you may not _want_ to get your fly back. It is not advisable to bring sharks into the boat. Be extremely careful releasing sharks and release them unharmed. Use pliers to back out the barbless fly or cut the leader. A barbless fly may soon be ejected.

Every flats angler has a shark story. While they are indeed dangerous under certain circumstances, shallow-water flats anglers have little to fear. Treat them with respect and imagine how long they have prowled the oceans keeping other species strong. These gray reef sharks were photographed off the back of the boat at Bikini Atoll.

Sharks are an indicator of rich, healthy flats. They are present for the same reason bonefish are—to eat. They are not interested in eating you, but they eat bonefish if you let them. In the interest of protecting bonefish, either scare sharks away, wait until they leave, or move to another area. Seychelles.

Yellowtail snapper over turtle grass at Abaco, Bahamas. Most species of snapper, especially the smaller ones, are aggressive and provide anglers with plenty of action. However, they are smart and sometimes very difficult to fool, especially large ones and those that hang around bridges, docks, etc. Just try to hook one under a boat dock.

Productive snapper flies. Poppers, Clousers, and bonefish flies with rubber legs are good choices.

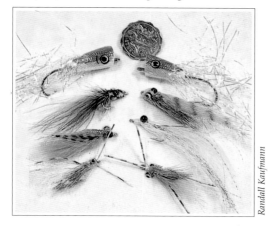

Randall Kaufmann

Snapper

Depending on the species, snapper can be found in all types of flats habitat. Large snapper, except mutton and sometimes cubera, are seldom spotted out in the open or on flats. They live adjacent to flats in cuts, in channels, and, especially, under mangrove roots. Locating most species of snapper is often more a recognition of suitable habitat than visually spotting them. The taller the mangroves and the deeper the "hole," the better the snapper fishing, especially for schoolmasters, red, and mangrove snapper. When the light is right, a school can often be seen along the edges of mangrove stands.

Red, mangrove, schoolmaster, Lane, and yellowtail snapper are plentiful in bonefish country. They eat and attack almost anything—bonefish flies, minnow imitations, and surface poppers. Most bonefish anglers encounter snapper up to two or three pounds—easily handled with a bonefish outfit. Make the cast!

Mutton snapper, *Lutjanus analis,* is highly prized both for its sporting nature and as fabulous table fare. If there is a mutton snapper around, your guide will definitely urge you to cast to it, hoping that you allow him to keep it. They are always disappointed when I free the beautiful muscular fish. Recognize them by the black spot located about midway along their lateral line. Their eyes are striking, colored red, yellow, and black. Their spiny dorsal fin extends from just behind their shoulder to their tail. The specimens I have caught in the Bahamas are bronze olive with orangish-red pectoral fins, tail, and underbelly. The anal fin and the rear edge of the dorsal fin are pointed rather than rounded like other snappers. They reach 20, even 30, pounds and are strong fighters. The Bahamas is one of the best places to fish for mutton snapper, but they are found throughout most of the Caribbean bonefish haunts.

They are suckers for poppers and Clouser-style flies and are sometimes hooked inadvertently by unsuspecting bonefish anglers. If muttons are present, *fish for them*!

Cubera, *Lutjanus cyanopterus*, is the giant of snappers, sometimes reaching 100 pounds. Body colors range from greenish to dusky gray, paler below, and may be tinted with red along the sides. Eyes are dark red. They do not have a dark spot on their bodies. They are often confused with the gray, or mangrove, snapper, which attains weights of only 10 pounds. Big poppers, minnow imitations, and wire leaders are the rules of the water for these body builders. Look and fish for cubera in deep channels from Belize to the Bahamas.

Lane snapper, *Lutjanus synagris*, is commonly found in shallow water and is sometimes hooked by bonefish anglers in Florida and the Caribbean. It rarely exceeds 12 inches, and its general coloration is rosy with longitudinal yellow stripes, paler below. Fins are tinged orange yellow, and the eye is red.

Mangrove snapper, *Lutjanus griseus*, is known as gray snapper. This is the most common species available to flats anglers. General coloration is gray above, paler below, with a tinge of red along its sides. There is no spot along its sides, and its eyes are red. Its pectoral fin is shorter than in other snappers. Look for them in deeper holes along mangrove groves, but don't expect them to be pushovers. Snapper in general are very cunning, and this species is no exception. I like to make a game out of fooling mangrove snapper. When a school is spotted at the edge of mangroves or back under the overhang, see how many you can fool. You might hook one on the first cast, but that might terminate the game. Sometimes, if you are stealthy and pull hooked fish away from others quickly, you might get another. I watched Brian O'Keefe pull five half-pounders

Cubera snapper are tough customers and highly prized by anglers. Turneffe Island, Belize.

Mutton snapper are beautiful, strong fish with an appetite for bonefish flies. Don't pass up a chance to make the cast. These mutton snapper, above and below, were photographed near Abaco in the Bahamas.

Schoolmaster snapper are common in shallow water in and around coral and structure. They are recognized by their small size, golden-yellow tail and fins, and the vertical bars across their backs.

Mangrove, or gray, snappers are the most common in bonefish country. They are grayish in color with a red eye, and their pectoral fin is shorter than on other snapper. Look for them in deeper holes along mangroves. There may be several, but don't expect to catch too many too often—they are suspicious and wary.

Cubera snapper are the biggest, baddest snapper in Caribbean bonefish country. Look for them in deep channels from Belize to the Bahamas.

from a choice snapper hole in the Bahamas. Mangrove snapper seldom reach 10 pounds; a two pounder is a great catch. What they lack in size, they make up for in numbers and intelligence.

Red snapper, *Lutjanus campechanus*, is the best-known snapper. Recognize it by its generally rose coloration, paler below. It has red fins, red eyes, and a black spot on smaller individuals. It has a long pectoral fin. Red snapper are considered a deep-water fish, but smaller specimens are available to flats anglers. Look for them around hard bottoms and structure, but don't expect to catch too many, as they are not easily duped.

Schoolmaster, *Lutjanus apodus*, are one of the smallest snappers with most individuals weighing less than one pound. A five pounder is a granddaddy that ate all its grandchildren. Recognize schoolmasters by their brassy-yellow coloring and vertical bars across the back. Fins are yellow. It is common in shallow-water flats, around coral, and near structure.

Yellowtail snapper, *Ocyurus chrysurus*, is easily recognized by a deep yellow stripe that runs from its snout to its tail, which is also deep yellow. All fins are yellow. They are mostly pale olive with yellow spots above and paler below with perhaps a tinge of violet. Most individuals weigh less than two pounds. Look for them in

channels, on flats adjacent to channels, and around structure and reefs. If you find one, there are usually several.

Various unidentified species of snapper abound in South Pacific and Indian Ocean waters. Some have been landed in the Marshalls, Solomons, Seychelles, Australia, and elsewhere, but many others have ripped off fly lines and at this time remain unseen and virtually unknown to fly rodders. Gear yourself accordingly! There is big sport awaiting adventurous anglers down under and beyond.

Snook

Common snook, _Centropomus undecimalis,_ are common in bonefish habitat from Florida south to Honduras, especially around mangroves and in brackish estuary waters. They are homebodies and hang around the same haunt. Anglers who find a choice "snook hole" never, ever talk about it. Like snapper, finding them is often a matter of understanding habitat or acquiring local knowledge.

They are easily recognizable by their prominent black lateral-line stripe, which runs from the top of the gill cover through the tail. Their snout is pike-like. Two dorsal fins are separated by a gap. Their back is often bronze, but it may be black, greenish, dark gray, or silvery depending on the season, habitat, etc. They reach weights of more than 50 pounds, but bonefish anglers encounter three- to 15-pound specimens. Snook are especially fond of mullet, but shrimp, crab, and baitfish imitations and poppers do the job. They are wary and sensitive to cold snaps. Snook are cousins to the Nile Perch, _Lates niloticus,_ in Africa and Barramundi, _Lates calcarifer,_ in Australia. South of the U.S. border snook are known as rabalo.

Look for snook almost anywhere in shallow Atlantic and Caribbean subtropic and tropical waters, including golf course ponds, canals, mangrove thickets, jungle rivers, and brackish estuaries. Large snook frequent Atlantic and Caribbean surf throughout Central and into South America. Mike Heusner, above, with a beautiful snook from the Belize River in Belize. A baby snook, below, jumps a popper on the last cast of the day in the Yucatan.

Tarpon, like this beautiful specimen, are relatively abundant in Cuba. Sharks often prey on exhausted tarpon. Anglers should use 12-weight rods, land tarpon as quickly as possible, and completely revive them before release. Tarpon are best photographed in the water.

Tarpon

Tarpon, *Megalops atlanticus,* are relatively plentiful, but they are seldom seen on skinny water bonefish flats. Anglers usually find tarpon in channels or adjacent to bonefish flats. Search the edges of mangroves, deep water, channels, cuts, bays, grass banks, and open water. They can also be located in lagoons, some rivers, and brackish sloughs.

Tarpon inhabit most waters in the Caribbean, Florida to Los Roques. In bonefish country, anglers will find the biggest and most tarpon in the Florida Keys. Belize and Yucatan can be good to excellent. The Bahamas offer limited tarpon action.

Look for laid up (resting) fish and migratory tarpon in water five to 15 feet deep. Sometimes they are suspended just below the surface or a few feet deep. Because of their size, tarpon are not difficult to see, especially if spotting conditions are good. Their dark backs are highly visible over light-colored bottoms, but they can be difficult to spot over grassy bottoms, especially if it is windy. Just look for fish up to five feet long!

Look for baby tarpon along mangroves, in mangrove channels, and in lagoons and canals. They are relatively plentiful throughout Florida, Belize, Yucatan, Cuba, and Little Cayman. Look for their dorsal fin and tail, which often cut the water's surface when they are milling about or in shallow water. Tarpon of any size offer spectacular aerial sport!

Eventually, all anglers infected with big-fish fever get hooked by *Megalops atlanticus.* You become obsessed with the air-shattering explosion of a prehistoric creature that is as large as you and is tethered to you by monofilament. Tarpon may make jumps 10 feet high and 20 feet distant each time they clear the water. Their gill plates rattle in the sky like a primeval exorcism. Their scales are the size of silver dollars and the color of mercury, and they scatter silver light like a holographic prism. You stand transfixed and bow to the mythological creature as it swims through the air and flies through the water.

Their power is awesome! It is the ultimate light-tackle "big pull," and it is all you can do to hold on. More than one angler has been yanked overboard or lost rod and reel to this Neptune of the sea. There are stories of 150-pound tarpon jumping over the boat or into the boat! What do you do when a giant tarpon jumps into your boat? Jump out!

Tarpon fishing is indeed heady stuff. These magical creatures are infectious, and they call you back again and again. Every time you hook a giant tarpon it is like the first time.

I know of one angler who became so possessed by tarpon that he moved across the country to the Florida Keys, sold his business, divorced his wife, and became a Keys guide, in that order. The Florida Keys are full of such anglers, and there is always room for one more. Do *you* dare hook the giant silver king?

History and Physical Characteristics: Megalops atlanticus is a member of the family Elopidae, a giant cousin of the bonefish and ladyfish. They are known by many names, including silver king, the king, bucket mouth, tarpoon, and iron man. Natives know it as Sabalo. Their history dates back to dinosaur times. Tarpon reach ages in excess of 55 years and are believed to be intelligent. They

Giant tarpon may make jumps 10 feet high and 20 feet distant each time they clear the water. Baby tarpon sommersault all over the place. Lance Kaufmann, Key West, Florida.

Capt. Tom Rowland

Tarpon flies are all similar in style. Both bright and subdued colors are popular. Most are 2½ to 4½ inches long.

Randall Kaufmann

look like giant herring. Their lower jaw points out and up, and their mouth opens up like a bucket. The inside of their mouth is hard and bony, and their teeth are small and fine like sandpaper. Their gill plates are sharp, and their body is covered with "armored" scales. They are greenish to bluish gray across the back and metallic silver along their sides and underside.

Larger fish are migratory. In Florida most migratory tarpon are caught from May through July. Tarpon feed on anything that fits down their throat, especially crabs and baitfish. In the Florida Keys, it is a common sight to see thousands of mullet panic into sky travel with tarpon in pursuit.

Donny Burks and Jeff Rose release a beautiful tarpon at Ascension Bay in Yucatan, Mexico.

Habitat: Tarpon are the most widely distributed inshore game-fish pursued by fly rodders, being found along the shores of three continents—North America, South America, and Africa. They inhabit warm tropical and subtropical waters—everything from clear saltwater flats to brackish lagoons to semi-freshwater ponds and canals. You are just as likely to find tarpon in a golf course pond or a downtown Miami canal as in the Everglades and the Venezuelan jungle.

Tarpon can tolerate rapid changes from salt to brackish water and tolerate water temperatures roughly between 65 and 100 degrees Fahrenheit, which enables them to survive in waters where many fish cannot. This is in part because of their ability to take air above the surface of the water. When tarpon "roll," they gulp air into their air bladder, which is saturated with tiny blood vessels much like our lungs. As a result, tarpon can live in almost stagnant water.

Giant Tarpon: Fish over 100 pounds and six feet in length are considered "giants." Until 1882, it was considered impossible to land giant tarpon with conventional gear. Sportsmen used harpoons to bring them to the boat. In 1882, Anthony W. Dimock, author of *The Book of the Tarpon*, landed one with rod and reel. His book was published in 1911 and republished in 1990. Julian Dimock took the spectacular photos. Modern anglers are amazed to realize such incredible fish could be landed and photographed by the methods of the day.

Today the classic deep clear-water sand flats and channels in the Florida Keys are where most aficionados of the sport prefer to hunt giant tarpon, but Homasassa on Florida's west coast is also legendary with fly fishermen. Fish over 125 pounds are common; some push the 200-pound mark. The jungle river mouths in Costa Rica, particularly outside the Rio Colorado bar, are also world famous and produce fish of 60 to 100 pounds. The Gabon coast in east-central Africa offers good numbers of tarpon over 200 pounds!

I well remember the first giant tarpon I hooked. I was fishing from a dugout canoe in a Costa Rican estuary when the six-foot giant saber-rattled out of the water 15 feet in front of me, leaping higher than my head. I was transfixed. I lowered my rod tip, and my mouth opened wide. The scene could have been a million years ago.

Fishing for giant tarpon is a game unto itself and requires specialized gear and technique. Anglers interested in pursuing giant tarpon should study the subject. Begin by viewing the excellent videos available. A guide who specializes in fly fishing for tarpon is invaluable. Florida guides have the best knowledge of giant tarpon—where and when to find them, and how to hook, land, and release them. They will put you on fast forward. Have a wild time!

Baby Tarpon: Baby tarpon offer fantastic sport for flats fly fishermen. Unlike giant tarpon, baby tarpon do not require specialized gear or angling techniques. They are found in good numbers in the Cayman Islands, Cuba, Belize, Florida, Yucatan, and Venezuela. Scattered populations are found at some Bahamas locations.

Tarpon up to about 40 pounds are considered "babies." Flats anglers generally encounter baby tarpon in the 10- to 30-pound range. They are aggressive. Attacks are spectacular; there is never a

Typical baby tarpon water near Cancun, Mexico. Angler is Steve Rewick.

The Sea Habit Bucktail is currently one of the most universal saltwater patterns, especially for jacks, tarpon, trevally, and bluewater species. The anchovy, flying fish, mackerel, and sardine patterns are popular. If you tie your own flies, vary the color and length to suit your needs.

Randall Kaufmann

Baby tarpon run up to about 40 pounds. They are common in the Caymans, Cuba, Belize, Florida, Yucatan, and Venezuela. Steve Rewick with a prime baby in the northern Yucatan.

dull baby tarpon take. When hooked, baby tarpon spend more time out of the water than in the water. Such fish put a healthy bend in an 8-weight rod and put the wood to you! Baby tarpon are resident fish so they are almost always available. Look for them in cuts, channels, lagoons, back bays, and rivers, and along and under mangrove canopies.

Fishing for baby tarpon is relatively straightforward and should be easy for flats anglers. After tarpon are sighted, cast as close as possible without alarming the fish. Point the rod tip directly toward the fish and strip the fly. They might attack instantly, or they might follow your offering back toward the boat. Be ready for an aggressive, explosive take. You'll see it all happen.

Tarpon have a hard, bony mouth. Sharpen your hooks and strip-strike them very hard, sometimes several times. The strip-strike is explained in the Hooking, Landing, and Releasing chapter. Be certain your line clears the rod guides without hanging up. Tarpon often take to the air immediately. When they jump, "bow," or lower your rod tip, thereby lessening the chance of breaking them off or breaking your rod! When they are not jumping or running, exert the maximum sideways "down-and-dirty" pressure. This is a short course on tarpon fishing. Like permit or bonefish, there are many subtleties to the sport, and a book could be written about them.

Tackle: Flats anglers fishing for baby tarpon can do so with bonefish and permit tackle. Eight-, 9-, and 10-weight rods are perfect. You need a few 30-pound leaders and an assortment of tarpon flies. I like size 1/0 flies, mostly in drab colors, but you should also carry a few bright patterns. Baby tarpon are also suckers for surface poppers. A floating bonefish fly line is O.K. for shallow water and surface-oriented fish, but you should also have a slow sinking or intermediate tarpon taper, especially in Belize.

In addition to baby tarpon, larger tarpon may also be available at most Caribbean locations. Belize offers perhaps the best clearwater, flats-style fishing outside Florida. Fish often run to 70 pounds, sometimes to 100 pounds. Yucatan tarpon reach 60 pounds, sometimes 100 pounds. Anglers fishing for these should have a 10 weight or heavier rod and size 3/0 flies. I like a 12-weight rod because it does everything a 10 weight does plus a great deal more!

Tarpon can be "laid up," cruising, or feeding anywhere in the water column. Your fly should intercept them at their angle of approach and at the depth they are traveling. A bonefish or tarpon taper sinking line allows you to present the fly at any depth up to about six feet. Once the fly has sunk to the desired depth and the retrieve is begun, the fly stays "in the zone." If you hope to maximize opportunity, gear up properly.

Landing and Releasing: Land tarpon *quickly and carefully*. They can be handled gently without fear of injury to you. Like bonefish and permit, in a weakened state tarpon are easy prey for sharks. Despite their size and strength, tarpon are fragile. Keep them in the water! Do not hold them in a vertical position. Don't let them bang on the side of the boat. Handle them carefully and do not hurt them. No one wants to see them dead. A good motto to fish by is *always do what is best for the fish.*

Randall Kaufmann

Trevally

Trevally, called "ulua" in Hawaii, is the Pacific counterpart to the Atlantic permit and jack crevalle. The difference between permit and trevally is that you can catch trevally more easily, lots of *big* ones! Pacific anglers who encounter fast-traveling fish on or adjacent to flats, along drop-offs, in channels, inside the surf, or along reefs are probably seeing trevally. They are numerous, aggressive, and addictive. They can be extremely bold even in shallow water. I have seen trevally of more than 50 pounds in water 18 inches deep eating bonefish. Over 33 species have been identified in the Pacific and Indian oceans. Common fly-caught species include the following:

Blue-fin trevally, *Caranx melampygus*, is common on flats and inshore areas throughout the Pacific and Indian oceans. It is a strikingly beautiful fish with its soft dorsal fin and tail often washed in electric blue, hence its name. Blue-fin can reach 30 inches in length and 20 pounds in weight.

Giant trevally, *Caranx ignobilis*, is the largest species in the Indo-Pacific region. Christmas Island fly anglers commonly hook fish in excess of 50 pounds, and gear fisherman throughout the Pacific have brought fish to the boat weighing over 100 pounds! Its identification lies upon locating the small oval-shaped patch of tiny scales on its breast in front of its ventral fins in the center of a larger scaleless area that is always present. Giants also lack an opercular black spot, and there is no black blotch at the base of the pectoral.

Great trevally, *Caranx sexfasciatus*, commonly called big-eye, is

Few angling thrills can compare to hooking and releasing a giant trevally, especially when they explode on a surface popper in shallow water. Randall Kaufmann tricked this 50 pounder at Christmas Island near Y site on Christmas day. Christmas Island guide Moana T. Kofe releases the beautiful fish. All trevally should be landed quickly, handled gently, and released in strong condition.

Anglers can fish trevally with 10-weight rods, but 12 weights are best. Wind, large bulky flies, and the chance that 40- or 50-pound fish may be hooked are reasons to use stout tackle. The author was using a 12 weight when he turned this trevally at over 200 yards inside the lagoon at Christmas Island.

Mary Kaufmann

Richard Humphrey

This giant trevally, landed and released by Richard Humphrey at Christmas Island, is bigger than the boat!

Jerry Swanson

Richard Humphrey has pursued trevally throughout South Pacific waters. He found this beautiful blue-fin at Bikini Atoll in the Marshall Islands.

Richard Humphrey

Golden trevally are relatively rare and a special prize. Richard Humphrey, Christmas Island.

widely distributed throughout the Pacific and readily available westward to Australia's Great Barrier Reef and Queensland. Juvenile fish are especially abundant over shallow reef flats. Look for large adults along drop-offs and at the edges of swift-running channels. Adult fish are colored silvery to silvery gray. The great trevally's breast is completely scaled, a feature that separates it from giant trevally. The gill cover shows a tiny black spot high on its rearward margin with a diffuse dark blotch below it. It reaches three feet in length.

Golden trevally, *Gnathanodon speciosus*, can reach lengths of four feet and weights of 85 pounds. They are usually found near reefs. Often called striped trevally at Christmas Island, young fish often glow yellow and have 10 or more black stripes across their flanks and back. Older fish lose their stripes over time. The golden trevally is the only trevally that does not have teeth.

Other possible trevally catches include:

Blue-spotted, *Caranx bucculentus,* also referred to as wide-mouth trevally. This is one of only a few trevally that is heavily spotted. Look for blue spots above the lateral line, which is heavily armored with sharp scutes. It reaches lengths of two feet.

White trevally, *Pseudocaranx dentex*, is also called silver trevally. It is easily recognizable by its conspicuous black blotch at the rear margin of its gill covers. Whites grow to 20 pounds and have been released at Bikini Atoll by Richard Humphrey. Black trevally has also been documented at Bikini.

You'll know trevally when you see them at Christmas Island, Bikini, Kanton, Seychelles, and elsewhere. *Be ready!* Many flats fishermen have turned into trevally fanatics after an encounter with these brutes. Richard Humphrey is one such angler. In conjunction with chasing bonefish around the world, Richard has become a trevally junkie. Besides having released several world records unrecorded (no reason to kill fish for your personal glory—who really cares how big your fish or ego is?), Richard has released over a dozen species.

Most Christmas Island anglers have their first encounter with trevally when one steals their bonefish. This is common. I once hooked a bonefish that couldn't get far enough away fast enough. It apparently ran into a hunting party of trevally and figured I was a lesser threat. It zoomed directly toward me with three muggers nipping at its tail. When the bonefish was nearly between my legs, the 35-pound marauders spotted me. For a split second I think they contemplated eating me! Trevally fresh from the open ocean show no fear and are known to eat small black-tipped sharks.

Trevally fishing at Christmas Island is a sport unto itself. These brutish bullies often travel in gangs. When 40-pound trevally are speeding across a shallow flat with their backs half out of the water, it is a sight not soon forgotten. Few spectacles in light-tackle fishing can compare. You move out of their way!

This account of his first big trevally by Steve DeMoulin is typical: "A huge mouth engulfed my popper. When the fish turned sideways, I thought I had made a mistake. The guide said 'run' and I was thinking, which way? Toward the fish or away from it?"

My brother, Lance, has visited Christmas Island many times and specializes in big trevally. During one visit he was hunting them along a drop-off on a two- to three-foot-deep flat when two huge trevally suddenly materialized out of the deep. The fish were only 40 feet away and traveling fast, but Lance got a good cast to them. Both fish turned on his fly, and his guide, Tyrone, shouted retrieve orders: "Strip! Faster! Faster!! Faster!!!" Finally, the largest trevally Tyrone had ever seen (pushing 100 pounds) grabbed the fly a rod's length away! Lance describes the ensuing hook up and warp-speed run as mind altering and worth the price of several Christmas Island trips. What happened? What do you think?!

Trevally are easy to entice to the fly. If you can get a cast to them and execute a proper retrieve, hang on! Small ones up to 20 pounds are relatively easy to land. Larger fish are very difficult to beach. If they don't clean you out, they break you off on coral. Being at the right place at the right time with a little luck always helps.

Moana, Mary, and I were fishing at the back of the Christmas Island lagoon on Christmas Day, casually hunting trevally in the cuts and along drop-offs. We had hooked some 20-pound fish and were relaxing on the beach when Moana spotted a huge single fish working our way along the beach.

I pitched an eight-inch popper 20 feet in front of it, gave a forceful four-foot pull, and the surface of the lagoon erupted like a volcano. Mary screamed from fright and excitement, and I had a 50-pound trevally heading to wherever big trevally go. All but 20 feet of my 300 yards of backing disappeared, and my 12-weight rod was pushed to its limit. There was no place for me to run, and everywhere for the trevally to run. I either had to turn the beast back toward me or lose my fly line. . .and the fish! Luck intervened. I was able to stand on a high bank and exert just enough pressure to turn the brute.

In about 15 minutes the beautiful creature was at our feet. Its electric-blue outline, golden-yellow highlights, neon-black markings, and silvery underside were stunning. It was one of those special fish of a lifetime. As its powerful slab-like body rested in my grasp, its beautiful yellow-black eye stared at me in confusion and fear. Mary and Moana helped me revive it until it was too strong to restrain. We smiled as it moved off in a deliberate and thankful manner. We were all very, very lucky. I'll tell you how to catch the king and queen of the flats if you promise to handle them gently and release them. . .*every one of them!*

Tackle: First, you need proper tackle or everything else is a moot point. Pack a 12-weight rod and a premium saltwater reel that holds 300 yards of backing. A 10 weight is fine for the smaller fish, but what are you fishing for? When the trevally of a lifetime swims into range, and it may at Christmas Island or other South Pacific locations, you'll need the 12 weight! A 12 weight also doubles as a blue water, tarpon, and king salmon rod. A few big streamers and poppers and some wire leaders round out your trevally gear. I like surface poppers because they are fun to fish and because their surface commotion attracts fish from a greater distance and heightens the level of excitement.

Second, hire a personal guide. Besides spotting far more fish than you possibly can, the guide can carry the trevally rod when

Richard Humphrey

Lance Kaufmann has visited Christmas Island many times and specializes in hooking giant trevally.

Dr. Jeff Sherman practices the ideal release with a blue-fin trevally at the Seychelles.

Assorted poppers are best for trevally. Wire leaders are usually recommended.

Blue-fin trevally exude neon-blue colors and seem to light up surrounding ocean waters like this beautiful one in the Seychelles.

you are bonefishing. When a trevally happens along, you are ready to fire off a cast. If you do not have the big rod and fly handy, forget it. The opportunity is lost.

Third, forget the bonefish. Fish for trevally! Prowl their haunts. They are often encountered cruising across flats and feeding on bonefish, but many more, and usually larger, fish are in the channels and cuts and along drop-offs and the reef.

Fourth, retrieve the fly in the same direction as the fish, making it seem to be fleeing straight-away in panic. Imagine a flying fish racing away from an invading trevally, and you'll get the picture. It is a physical impossibility to strip a fly too fast. If a trevally wants anything, it will have it. Pull your offering *fast!*

If you are a gear fisherman, casting pencil poppers off the reef in front of the hotel after a day's bonefishing is great sport. Usually, a fish or two is landed each night. Anglers need sturdy footgear, strong casting rods, 15-pound monofilament, and wire leaders. Cruising fish commonly crush six-inch plugs and *completely* mangle 3/0 treble hooks. Be prepared for some brutal action! Unfortunately, trevally are not as plentiful as they once were. Visiting Honolulu gear anglers and locals kill everything; it is not uncommon for locals to claim your catch and declare, "We eat." If you do not want to slaughter your beautiful trevally (and you promised me you wouldn't), say so and release it. It's your fish!

By the way, pencil poppers cost twice as much in Hawaii as they do on the American mainland, and double again in price at Christmas—when they are available. Anglers should bring all the gear they think they might need, plus more, just in case. Don't worry about spending a few extra dollars. Tackle money is insignificant compared to everything else you have invested in the trip. It is better to bring some gear home than not to have had enough. Any excess can be left with the guides.

Chapter 16

Hooking, Landing, and Releasing

Compared to other saltwater species, bonefish feed at a leisurely pace. This is because the creatures they prey upon are relatively slow, and bonefish feed in, on, or near the bottom by sight and smell. As a result, they do not attack a fly in the true sense of the word, and there is no arm-wrenching jolt. They take the fly softly, merely picking it up. If you do not tighten the line on the fish, it continues feeding. The instant the fish feels resistance, panic prevails. Its freedom has been curtailed, and it bolts for deep water as if its life depends on it—and it probably does. Bonefish know that any nearby predators sense their peril and that they are easy prey when restrained or crippled.

Bonefish kick into turbo quickly, and their exit from shallow water is one of the most exciting thrills in light-tackle fishing. It doesn't shake its head or jump, but as your line tears through the water, you can hardly believe the quickness and power of such a relatively small fish. The first run is the longest and most powerful. During this run the fish decides which direction to take and may make a course correction, usually toward deeper water. Whichever direction it takes, do not expect to slow it down on the first run—or perhaps the second, either! Don't expect the battle to be a delicate, easy-does-it affair. You need to fight brute strength with brute strength.

Toward the end of a successful day's fishing in the Bahamas, we came upon a school of bonefish on a flat that also contained several large sharks. Knowing that any fish I hooked would instantly become shark bait, I elected to break off the hook point.

The ready position. Line is stripped from reel and fly is in hand.

Roll line forward, back cast, single or double haul, and present fly.

Feed fly line through stripping fingers or finger loop.

Crouch position. Strip.

The ensuing session was hilariously entertaining and delightfully enlightening. When I stripped and stopped the fly, a fish would rush up, tip down, and grab it. Stripping again, I would pull the fly from its mouth. I could detect an expression of disbelief and resolve to recapture the escaped morsel. Sometimes a fish would run off a few feet with the fly and attempt to crush it, refusing to let go. Bonefish swim with their mouths closed, so it sometimes took a solid jerk to free the fly. Several times three or four bewildered fish would take turns grabbing the fly, jockeying for position. They appeared completely befuddled about why this food kept escaping their grasp. Eventually, the experiment was reduced to a game, and the bonefish seemed to be enjoying it as much as we were. They would come right up to the boat, unafraid.

The take was always easy and smooth, just a gentle pick up. When a fish had the fly, it casually looked for the next food object. When the fly was pulled from its mouth, there was no panic, just a resolve to eat it again. Such an interlude quickly teaches you what to look for and how to recognize a take. It is also guaranteed to put laughter into your world and give you another perspective on angler-fish interaction.

The Take: If you understand the feeding habits of bonefish and concentrate on watching the movements of interested fish, you know when it has the fly. They usually pick up the offering when it is still, but they may also take it when it is sinking or being retrieved. Bonefish do not reject a fly quickly, probably because they are accustomed to hard foods. When a bonefish rushes up behind a fly, or any suspected food, its tail works nervously as it moves into a taking position. When the fish stops moving, tips down toward the fly (its tail comes out of the water in shallows), and begins to right itself, it has picked up the fly. If you are not certain about the pick up, watch the leader for movement. When it moves, tighten up. Knowing when to tighten up on a bonefish is one of the major keys to success. Since bonefish and permit seldom charge a fly but, instead, suck or grub it off the bottom, detecting the pick up can be difficult. Anglers who know the location of their fly and concentrate on and understand bonefish body language hook many more fish. Watch the fish!

Strip-Strike: If you think a fish has your offering, *do not jerk the fly or raise the rod tip.* Point the rod tip directly at the fly and make a long, medium-speed pull—just enough to take the slack out of the line. If you tighten up and feel a fish, a quick, short pull on the fly line with your stripping hand will set the hook. This is called the strip-strike. If the fish does not take the fly, you have only moved the fly a foot or two, making it look as though the fly escaped. Nothing is lost. Continue the retrieve and give both the fish and yourself a second chance. If you cannot see the fly, keep retrieving until you have a hook up—you'll know when. Bonefish do not fool around and waste time. They get right to the business of running for their lives.

Clear the Line: When you have hooked a fish, your initial concern is to clear the fly line, to feed it safely through the guides, and to let the fish have its way. Point the rod tip at the fish; don't raise it. This lessens resistance during the first blitzing run. Watch your loose fly line, not the fish. Turn the reel handle away from the fly line and tuck the rod butt against your wrist, reducing the chance of line hang-ups. Use the thumb and index finger of your line hand to form a circle around any loose fly line and let it feed out, or shake and untangle the fly line as needed, allowing it to keep up with the bonefish.

The Fight: There is usually a short pause between the strike and the run as if the bonefish is unconcerned or momentarily confused. It is best not to apply excessive pressure during the first run. Once everything is going smoothly, raise the rod. Let the fish have its way, avoiding any sudden jolts or hang-ups. Keep the rod tip high and in a straight line with the fish, which applies the *minimum* amount of pressure. Attempt to avoid any obstructions such as coral and mangroves. If you are fishing near a drop-off and the fish heads in that direction, run to the edge. Bonefish do not dive but swim downward at an angle. Still, the fly line can be cut on the edge. If the situation warrants, get into the boat where you have a higher angle and can keep more line in the air and off the water. Stay as close to the bonefish as possible. This allows more control, and you can exert more pressure on the fish.

The instant the run slows, take command and apply maximum pressure, turning the fish's head to either side and pumping back on the rod and the fish. Do not arc the rod high or point it directly toward the fish when you are attempting to subdue it. Even though there is a bend in the rod, the fish is not having to exert much energy to hold or increase its position. Throw the fish off balance by applying low sideways and backward pressure with the rod. The rod should usually be parallel to the water. If the fish runs to the left, pull to the right. Constant reverse pressure is the key.

Always maintain pressure. At no time should there be slack line. Do not pump, or draw, the rod too far back. You pump the rod to turn the fish's head and keep it coming toward you. Pump too far, and you can't recover the line before the fish has turned away again. You should be reeling down on the fish, pumping back on the rod, frantically reeling as the fish swims toward you, or applying maximum pressure as it swims away.

When a bonefish is on the run, let it go. Attempting to subdue a bonefish on the move usually means you will be reaching for your fly box. If the run is explosive, point and thrust the rod toward the fish, which alleviates stress on the leader.

When fighting a fish that has gotten into the surf or any fast-moving tidal area, take advantage of the situation. When a roller is moving out, don't apply too much pressure. When a roller is coming in, exert more pressure, sometimes even surfing the fish into the shallows. Do not bring bonefish up on the beach. For the fish's safety, always keep it in the water.

Drag: Drag tension varies depending upon fish size and strength, tippet breaking strength, and your skills. I like a medium-strong drag setting that helps slow and shorten runs, ultimately allowing for a quicker, safer release. The drag should not be so tight that it breaks the leader when fish jerk against it. When you have a hookup, the first concern is to minimize the initial shock and get the reel turning without the line backlashing. If more drag is needed, the drag can be adjusted, or you can palm the reel spool. Remember, too, that drag increases as the amount of fly line on the reel spool decreases and as more fly line comes in contact with the

Bonefish pickup! Keep rod pointed at fish, come tight, strip-strike.

Lift rod. As fish bolts, begin to clear line.

Hold rod high to keep line drag to a minimum, clear all line, and let fish run.

Angler holds tired bonefish by tail and gently moves it back and forth while calming it by rubbing its head. If possible, keep fish in your shadow. If bonefish are not exhausted, simply run your fingers down the leader, back out the fly, and let the bonefish do the rest. No mess, no fuss, no danger—and more fishing time for you!

To quickly subdue fish in shallow water, always exert backward and sideways pressure. The orange line is correct angle; the dotted black line is incorrect.

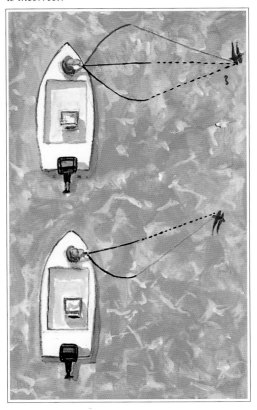

water. This is especially noticeable when fish make a right-angle turn after a long straight-away run. To prevent fly line from knotting up on the reel, always wind it onto the spool tightly. If the fish runs toward you, it may be necessary to strip in long lengths of line *quickly* to keep up with its movements. Wind loose line onto the reel as soon as possible. Again, always reel frantically and keep pressure on until you have the fish at your feet.

Landing, Releasing: It is important to land bonefish quickly and forcefully before they tire. A tired bonefish has a significantly reduced chance of survival. The longer you fight it, the greater the chance of losing it. *Land bonefish quickly.* Horse them in!

A 10-pound (1X-0X) leader is seldom too heavy for bonefish. With an 8-weight rod, a great deal of force can be exerted, *much more than most anglers realize.* Test a 10-pound leader by tying it to a stationary object and applying pressure with your rod. Try to break the leader, and you will understand how much force both rod and leader can sustain. *You should constantly be exerting the maximum force that the tippet and rod allow.*

When fish explode with a burst of energy, drop your rod tip to help reduce stress on the leader. It is estimated that a bonefish can run 25 miles per hour (36.7 feet per second) in short bursts. At 25 miles per hour, the handle on a spool three inches in diameter is turning at 46.7 revolutions per second! Your reel handle becomes a blur—unless your fingers get in the way. Be very careful: broken fingers and split nails are no fun.

Once a strong fish is close, get its head out of the water and glide it into your grasp. Many times, at this stage the fish is a leader's length away, and it is running around you in circles. It is amazing how difficult it can be to lift the head of a three-pound bonefish out of the water with an 8-weight rod when it is only 10 feet away! Keep the fish in front of you and pull in the opposite direction from the direction the fish wants to go. I prefer to keep the leader outside the rod guides. If your leader is inside the rod guides and the fish rushes off, immediately drop the tip and point and thrust it at the fish.

Once you are ready to land the fish, hold the fly line tightly between the rod and your index finger. Lift the fish's head out of the water, and, holding the rod high and behind you, bring the fish toward you. If you have reeled in too much line and leader, you cannot reach the fish. Usually, a 15-foot length of line-leader beyond the rod tip is required to bring fish to your feet.

When you have hooked a fish from a boat, try to keep the fish from swimming under the boat. Letting a fish go under the boat is an easy way to lose a fish and a rod tip. Bring the fish alongside the boat. Your guide will help release the fish if you like. If you are in a boat, you may have a net. If the mesh is not soft, it may be better not to use it. If you are landing and releasing the fish yourself, you may need both hands. Tuck the rod under your arm. *Slide your fingers down the leader, back out the barbless fly, and release the fish.* If you are having trouble and must touch the fish, wet your hands and turn the fish upside down. Fish seldom struggle in this position. *Do not squeeze the fish.* If you cannot back out the fly easily or if the fish swallowed the fly, use a forceps or smooth-nosed pliers to back it out. If you still cannot remove the fly, cut the leader. The fish will probably survive.

If you did everything right, the bonefish should not need reviving. If a fish needs to be revived, hold it by the tail and gently support it from underneath. Do not remove the fish from the water, puncture its gills, or squeeze it. When you handle bonefish or use a net, their protective slime coating comes off, which increases the chance of the fish's death. *Avoid handling them whenever possible.*

Photos: Anglers may want photos of some of their fish, but you do not need photos of *all* of them. When you desire a photo, set everything up in advance. A photo of you and your fish is best taken with the fish in the water. A fish-calming trick that guide Wellington Taylor showed Brian and me is to gently rub the top of a bonefish's head between its eyes while it is in the water. Fish do not swim away and they stay calm, allowing for close observation or photos in a nonstressful situation. Fish seem to relax and swim off in a calm manner. Again, keep fish in the water and handle them as little as possible. If you want an above-water shot, gently lift the fish *inches* above the water and take the picture quickly. *Under no circumstances should you bring bonefish into the boat.*

Bonefish are fragile. After you have caught a few, give yourself a handicap—consider casting only to larger fish or break off your hook point. Don't molest every fish you can. No one really cares how many fish you caught. After releasing a fish, check your leader for abrasion and the hook point for sharpness.

When landing and releasing bonefish, keep them in the water at all times. Calm bonefish by gently rubbing their head between their eyes. If landed quickly, bonefish do not need reviving. If they are tired, completely revive them before release. It is best not to handle bonefish as their body slime is easily rubbed off and handling increases the chance of injury.

Fish Size (pounds)	Hooking, Landing, and Releasing Time (minutes)
2	2
3	4
4	5
5	6
6	7
7	9
8	11
9	13
10	15

This chart is a general time line for landing bonefish. If you battle bonefish longer than these times, you need to increase the pressure. Expert fish landers release bonefish in half this time. Do bonefish a favor—get'em in and get'em off! Don't toy with them!

The perfect release. As you release bonefish, remain still until they swim away. Quick movement may frighten them unnecessarily. Note fish shadow. Jeff Rose, North Andros Island, Bahamas.

Chapter 17

Tackle and Gear

Vroom! You're hooked to a bonefish, the Ferrari of shallow-water fish. Zero to 20 in one second! The venerable "E" ride for anglers. Yes, bonefish demand tough tackle in good working order and specialized gear. Anglers must pay attention to detail.

Several species of fish are usually available in bonefish country; anglers wishing to fish for them should plan accordingly. Florida anglers and those bound for the Bahamas should consider jacks, snapper, barracuda, and, perhaps, permit and tarpon. Anglers with destinations in Mexico or Belize may fish for permit, tarpon, snapper, jacks, and other reef or bluewater species. Many attempt a grand slam—permit, tarpon, and bonefish all in the same day. Some add mutton snapper to the quest. Christmas Island visitors should angle for trevally. Visitors to Bikini should be geared for anything that swims in salt water—bar jacks to billfish.

Rods

I like 9- to 9½-foot rods. An 8 weight is the best all-around bonefish rod, but, because fish vary in size and the flies required to catch them vary in weight and because it is often windy, different weight rods may be required. Seven, 8, or 9 weights are good choices. I like 8 or 9 weights because they perform best in windy conditions, cast heavier flies better than lighter rods, and can handle an eight- to 10-pound bonefish. Florida anglers often use 10-weight rods to deliver heavy, bulky flies and subdue fish over 10 pounds. A 6 weight is O.K. for small one- to two-pound fish when

Tony Capone

Rod length is an important decision for traveling anglers. A nine-foot two-piece rod measures 56½ inches. A three-piece rod measures 38¾ inches. A four-piece, 30 inches; and a five-piece, 25 inches. A multi-piece carrying case is convenient.

A quick-change wire leader setup. In this case a wire leader barracuda rig was tied directly to the hook of a bonefish fly. Keep the line tight on barracuda so they can't reach the monofilament.

A popper or any other fly can easily and quickly be attached to a bonefish fly. Tension usually keeps the popper from slipping free.

This is my brother's saltwater reel bag. It includes 8-, 9-, 10-, and 12-weight lines on reels suited for everything from bonefish to tarpon. No one ever accused Lance of being unprepared or boring!

Tony Capone

conditions demand small flies and delicate presentation, but, with an 8 weight, fish have a much better survival rate because you spend less time landing and reviving them. Permit require a 9 or 10 weight. For average-sized or larger tarpon and trevally, you need a 10, 11, or 12 weight.

Bonefishing usually requires air travel. For convenience, I like five-piece travel rods that can easily be stashed in a suitcase or carried onto the aircraft. This greatly reduces the chance of theft, breakage, or a "no show" at baggage claim. You'll never notice the extra ferrules, but you will notice the rod's convenience and enjoy peace of mind. Three- and four-piece rods are also good.

If you ever arrive at your destination without rods, you may be shopping for a five-piece model. *Always carry a spare rod.* Considering fish, airplanes, boats, trucks, and guides, the chance of breakage is good. The chance of finding a replacement at most destinations is zero.

Seasoned anglers know that everything moves quickly in salt water and that opportunities appear and disappear just as quickly. Brian O'Keefe capitalizes upon all angling possibilities. If a jack, 'cuda, permit, tarpon, shark, yellowtail, or anything else swims within casting range, Brian is ready. He rigs up three rods, an 8, 9, and 10 or 12 weight. This covers most species. The 8 weight is rigged for bonefish; the 9 weight for permit or the second most available species. If it is snapper, Brian ties on a small streamer. He uses a popper or long thin braided-mylar tube fly in conjunction with a wire leader for barracuda. A 9 weight doubles as the perfect big bonefish rod and is a backup if you break the 8 weight. A 10 or 12 weight is the perfect third rod. Rig it for tarpon, trevally, yellowtail, or whatever else might be on the agenda. *Having two or three rods ready greatly increases your fishing enjoyment and ensures plenty of diverse and continuous action.* When a fish presents itself, you are prepared.

If you have only one rod, keep a popper or streamer fly rigged with a wire leader and a loop. In 30 seconds or less, you should be able to remove your bonefish fly, tie on the looped leader and make a cast. If you don't have a looped leader ready, simply hook your popper to the bonefish fly. These methods are not ideal but both are better than not making an effort.

Brian and I were lazing in the boat on a sunny afternoon as we passed over a deep channel while traveling to the next flat. Looking up the channel, Brian noticed a huge 'cuda lying at the drop-off. On a whim he quickly hooked a suitable 'cuda fly onto his bonefish fly and made the cast. After a wild battle, he landed a 25 pounder. If you think this is great sport, you are correct. That 'cuda somersaulted all over the channel and almost landed in our boat. That wouldn't have been such great sport. If you have ever seen 'cuda teeth up close, you know enough to let the guide handle them!

Reels

Comparing two look-alike reels, a guide asked if the materials were the same. When told they were, he had a puzzled look and asked why one was so much more expensive than the other. His clients remarked, affectionately, that he should not ask those questions. "Why would someone pay $100 extra to fish with you?" they asked. A smile of enlightenment crossed his face.

A good reel able to withstand the tortures of salt water and super strong fish is *mandatory*. Purchase the *best* quality reel you can afford. Stay clear of foolish economy. Salt water is murder on everything, especially reels. Freshwater reels cannot withstand the punishment of salt water and saltwater fish. A five-pound bonefish will outdistance *anything* you have caught in fresh water. Don't underestimate their strength. Bonefish can burn up a reel during one blitzing run. A reel must have a *strong smooth drag* and hold at least 125 yards of backing. Backing should be heavier than the leader tippet. I recommend 30-pound backing. Bonefish over eight or nine pounds may require 175 to 200 yards of backing.

A reel with a strong drag enables you to keep bonefish from running off the flat and helps you to land fish in a timely manner, allowing for more hookups and fewer lost bonefish. Don't embark on the trip of the year (or of a lifetime) without a reel that can go the distance. You won't find many for sale in Venezuela! Visit your local fly fishing specialty store or call a fly fishing mail-order house. Buy it right the first time, and you won't have to buy it again, and be frustrated in the interim.

A typical flats tackle arsenal—three rods are rigged and ready to fish for whatever comes within casting range. Footgear, head gear, and a hip pack containing a water bottle and assorted tackle are necessities.

Anti-reverse reels are designed so the reel spool turns but the crank handle does not. When fish pull hard enough against the drag, line feeds off the reel without the crank handle turning. This means that, when a fish is tearing line off at 30 feet per second, the handle is stationary. Otherwise, it may be turning 50 revolutions per second, which is fast enough to break your finger or split your fingernail if you get in the way. Anti-reverse reels also alleviate the problem of cranking on a fish at the wrong time and breaking your tippet. Many beginning anglers appreciate the no-brainer operation of anti-reverse reels.

With direct drive reels the handle crank turns when the spool turns. These are the choice of most anglers. They are lighter, more streamlined, retrieve line at a quicker pace, and are simpler mechanically. Anglers have more control over landing fish, and there is more of a hands-on feel. Just remember to stay clear of a wildly spinning crank handle. Your learning curve is quick; you only bang your knuckles once. After that you know better.

I like a reel with a large-diameter, or large arbor, spool because it retrieves line several times faster than conventional reels, especially when most of the backing has been peeled off. Other positives include a much lower startup inertia so the spool begins to turn quickly and easily (this is important to anglers using light tippets). When the fly line is spooled onto a larger diameter circle, it does not take a set as easily as when spooled onto a smaller diameter reel.

There is ongoing debate over which hand to use for reeling and casting. Do what feels natural. If you wish to reel and cast with the same hand, do it. If you can cast with one hand and reel with the other, you are in constant control of rod, reel, and line.

Backing

Backing is fine-diameter material tied to the back of your fly line and connected to the reel spool with an arbor knot. It functions when you make an extra-long cast (usually over 90 feet) and when fish take all the fly line from the reel. If you have 50 yards of backing behind a fly line and a fish runs that distance, guess what happens? If the weakest point between your fly and the end of the backing is the leader, the connection is broken there, and you lose the fly. If it is your knot at the reel or your backing, you lose a fly line and/or your backing.

Backing is available in different materials, diameters, colors, and breaking strengths. Like other components of a finely tuned outfit, every choice is a tradeoff. Braided Micron or Dacron is currently the material of choice. Pick any color, but I like something bright that I can see. A fly reel that holds 225 yards of 20-pound Micron or Dacron only holds 160 yards of 30-pound Micron or Dacron. I like 30 pound because it is more abrasion resistant and allows me to fish heavy tippets without the worry of the backing breaking before the leader. In addition, the larger diameter does not become compressed and dig into itself, especially when fish are on a tear and the drag is set tight.

Typical saltwater fly lines have a breaking strength of 30 to 40 pounds. If you have a 20-pound tippet and 20-pound backing, you risk having the backing break and losing the fly line.

Fly Lines

Fly lines differ for a reason: the variety of angling conditions. No single fly line performs best in water temperatures between 30 and 90 degrees Fahrenheit or in both calm and windy conditions. Saltwater fly lines are designed with a stiffer, braided monofilament core and heat-resistant coating. This provides the needed stiffness to deliver a bulky or heavy fly in temperatures up to 100 degrees Fahrenheit. Saltwater anglers often face windy conditions. A fly line with a shorter front taper helps turn a leader over in the wind. A medium-length belly helps make longer casts, and a longer rear taper helps facilitate smooth turnover of the line when false casting. As you can imagine, there is a big difference between a steelhead taper line (cold water and cooler air temperatures) and a bonefish taper line. A weight forward bonefish taper fly line is mandatory for flats anglers.

Micro balloons inside a floating fly line help float it. Because salt water is more buoyant than fresh water, fewer balloons are

Tropical saltwater fly lines are available in several colors. They are specially designed for warm water and weather. Most bonefishing is done with a floating line. Other species may require specialty lines. Always carry a spare.

needed for saltwater lines. This translates into a thinner diameter line that is easier to cast into wind. Saltwater fly lines are also stiffer so they cast better into wind.

If you intend to fish water over four feet deep or want better line control in windy weather, consider an intermediate or faster sinking line. Knowledgeable freshwater lake anglers realize that a fine-diameter slow-sinking or intermediate fly line drops below the water surface where wind cannot blow it about and create slack. You have a straight-line connection to the fly, which is necessary for control over the retrieve and over hookups. These lines also cast more easily in the wind, and line shadow is also reduced or eliminated.

Carry a spare line just in case a bonefish runs your line or backing over coral and cuts it. I have seen it happen, and the outer reef in Belize is no place to be without a fly line.

Clear fly lines are the least noticeable and can be a big advantage when fish are unusually wary, but they are recommended only for expert flats anglers. Their downside is that you cannot see them either.

Most anglers rely on the fly line to locate and track the fly. Being able to see the fly is paramount in knowing when to strike. When you can see the line in relation to the fish, you know when to, or when not to, strike or tighten the line. For this reason, use a color that you can see. Bonefish usually spook at the sight of any visible fly line. Besides clear, pale green, and tan are least noticeable. Present and pick up the fly correctly, and fish never see the line or any reflection from it, unless, of course, they overrun the line. If photos are a consideration, use a brighter fly line.

Heat is the number-one enemy of fly lines. Heat swells vinyl and squeezes chemicals to the surface. As vinyl cools, these chemicals cannot reposition themselves inside the fly line. A fly line lying in the back of your vehicle may be exposed to temperatures of 180 degrees Fahrenheit. A brief time at this temperature shortens the life of a fly line. Several hours at this temperature destroys a fly line. Extended exposure at temperatures over 130 degrees Fahrenheit is harmful.

Many chemicals damage fly lines. Insect repellents, sunscreens, and reel lubricants are the most common culprits. Some types of fly line lubricants have been shown to cause fly lines to crack.

For best performance, fly lines should be cleaned daily. Microorganisms and debris in water can cause a fly line to lose its surface slickness. Crusted salt is notorious for reducing casting performance. A liquid soap applied with a clean soft cloth and wiped off is effective if all the soap is removed. After contaminants are removed, use a nontoxic line lubricant. Using only a line lubricant does not solve the problem of dirt on the line.

Special Considerations: Today's high-tech angler has learned to take advantage of recent tackle innovations, especially in fly lines. Anglers match fly lines to prevailing conditions just as they match flies. For example, if you only fish out of a boat, you might opt for a clear sinking bonefish taper. The line is always on the boat deck, so you don't have to worry about it sinking when you are ready to cast. A sinking or intermediate line has a diameter two line sizes smaller than a floating line, allowing you to cast further into the wind. Remember that a clear fly line is invisible to both you and

Some anglers are gear freaks and want to be prepared for any and all contingencies.

R. Valentine Atkinson

Randall Kaufmann

the fish. Remember also that, if the fish doesn't take or changes direction, you must strip in more of a sinking fly line than you would a floating line before casting. It is easier to pick line *off* the water than it is to pick it *out* of the water. Advantages may offset disadvantages.

Suppose you are poling or wading along a deep-water cut 15 feet deep? If you are on foot, a sink tip is your first choice. If you are in a boat, choose a full-sinking line. Remember that salt water is more buoyant than fresh water, causing sinking lines to sink more slowly. Use a line with a faster sink rate than you would in fresh water.

What if you are tarpon fishing? What would be your first choice for a fly line? Think about the conditions: big, sometimes fast-moving fish, deeper water, and bulky flies. My first choice would be a 12-weight sinking tarpon taper; sinking because you are in a boat fishing deeper water. The thinner diameter line helps you cast farther. The tarpon taper has a short front taper for quick turnover. The short head and rear taper allow for quick casts with a minimum of false casting. The 12-weight rod is needed to handle the heavier tippet and fish. You are not casting all day or carrying your rod around. When opportunity appears, you want to be ready, no matter how big the fish!

Again, there is probably a very good reason why the angler in the other boat is hooking so many fish. The only way you can be that angler is to capitalize on all available resources, especially gear. The most effective anglers look and think before they fish.

Tackle Care

All your gear, especially rods, reels, and fly lines should be *washed in fresh water nightly*. Salt water corrodes everything and can cause the best of reels to freeze up, so lubricate them often. I protect my reels with a product called Boeshield. It displaces salt water, and the spray-on coating dries to a thin waxy finish. Coat the entire reel except the drag. It is also good for rod fittings, pliers—anything that corrodes. A salt coating on your line is very difficult to shoot through the rod guides. If a hose is not readily available, soak your gear overnight in a bucket of fresh water or in the flush tank of the toilet (if the water is fresh and clean). In addition, clean the line and apply lubricant at least once a day. This removes dirt and salt crust, and allows the fly line to shoot through the rod guides easily.

Leaders

An entire chapter could be written about leader selection and how to balance and taper leaders to a rod, fly line, and fly. Everyone has their own ideas. If you wish to construct your own, there are many materials and formulas to choose from. I keep it simple. I buy them pre-packaged and tie on a tippet. Short leaders with heavy butts turn over flies and allow you to land fish quickly.

I like to use the shortest and strongest leader that will do the job. A nine-foot leader is sometimes long enough, although I usually prefer a 12- to 14-foot leader. Windy conditions allow use of shorter leaders and tippets, which turn over more easily. Bonefish may or may not be leader shy. I once fished for three days with a four-foot 20-pound leader and caught as many bonefish as anyone. I have also seen bonefish bolt from a 12-foot 3X leader.

Saltwater anglers soon discover the value of good pliers and a good knife. Rinse all "hard" gear exposed to salt water and salt air in fresh water nightly. Keep flies dry. I like to take only what I need for the day just in case they go for a swim.

Jon Covich

Usually an 0X or 02X tippet is fine, but you should have some 1X and 2X for small flies, spooky fish, and flat water. The letter X denotes monofilament diameter. To determine the diameter subtract the X number from 11 and you have the diameter in thousandths of an inch. Eleven minus 1X equals 10, which is .010 of an inch. Eleven minus 4X equals 7 or .007. Casting dynamics and fish respond to diameter, not breaking strength. Remember, all 1X tippet does not have the same breaking strength. 1X of Brand A might test out at 10 pounds breaking strength. Brand B might test at 14 pounds. All things being equal, I would choose Brand B.

Bonefish leaders should have a butt diameter of at least .026 inch. This matches most bonefish fly line tip diameters and allows smoother casts. In contrast, rare conditions can be similar to freshwater spring creeks and might demand an 18-foot leader tapered to 3X with a size 10 fly. Fewer bonefish are landed with 3X tippet, but lost hookups are better than no hookups. Be prepared to adapt leaders to current angling conditions.

Be certain your leader is free of kinks and coils. A straight leader transfers energy smoothly during the cast, facilitating good fly turnover. It also aids in the retrieve, resulting in a direct connection between the rod tip and the fly. Straight leaders sink better than coiled ones. It is important to keep your leader straight. If it kinks, replace it. When you wind in your leader and fly, keep the leader outside the rod tip, otherwise it may take a set, or kink.

Tie on a fresh leader every day. I often tie a two- to three-foot fluorocarbon tippet section onto a nine- or 12-foot tapered leader. Clear leader material is usually best. Fluorocarbon is a tremendous advantage and is the favorite of many anglers. Fluorocarbon is nearly invisible underwater, has excellent wet knot strength, is abrasion resistant (especially useful around coral), and it sinks. It is unaffected by ultraviolet light and lasts almost forever. _Do not discard fluorocarbon in or near water._ It has a multidecade life expectancy and easily snares wildlife.

Many flats fish and species in areas adjacent to flats have teeth, and many are not leader shy. When fishing for toothy critters, it is necessary to rig a shock tippet. A shock tippet is simply a six- to 12-inch section of 30- to 80-pound monofilament or wire. Heavy monofilament tippets are not easily cut by most fish. The most voracious species with the sharpest teeth, such as wahoo and barracuda, demand wire. Because they are somewhat difficult to rig, many anglers opt for a prepackaged wire leader. That is what I do. Unless you love tying knots and are good at it, buy the wire and Bimini-style leaders. All you need to do is tie the leader to the fly line, perhaps tippet to the leader, and the fly.

Knots

If you can rig up for trout fishing, you can rig up for bonefishing. A few basic knots (nail, blood, and clinch) are all you need to know, but, like anything, there is always more to learn. Bonefish are unbelievably strong for their size; they really test your knots. Other species may require specialized knots.

Practice the following knots until you can do them upside-down and in the dark. If you don't possess dexterity, begin practicing using rope, gradually working down to regular-diameter monofilament.

The casting dynamics of the fly and the strength of fish determine leader choice. Anglers can choose from a complete selection of packaged leaders. All you do is tie the leader to the fly line and the fly to the leader. Pictured are Hightower poppers, excellent for trevally, dorado, jacks, etc.

The offshore popper (top) is rigged to a wire leader. The bottom popper is connected to heavy monofilament. Always straighten leaders before fishing. If leaders become kinked or frayed, replace them.

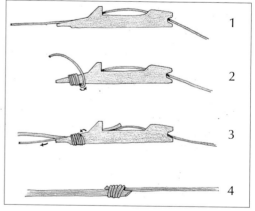

Nail Knot
1. Set leader in tool as shown.
2. Wrap leader backwards around tool five times.
3. Push the end forward under wraps. Insert fly line from front.
4. Pull wraps of leader off front of tool and cinch tightly around fly line. Completed Nail Knot. Be certain to trim ends as closely as possible.

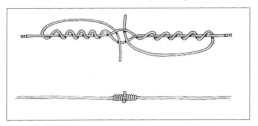

Blood Knot
Cross two like-diameter sections of monofilament. Twist each end around the other five times and insert the ends back through the middle loop in opposite directions. Wet knot before you pull it tight. Trim ends closely.
Finished Blood Knot.

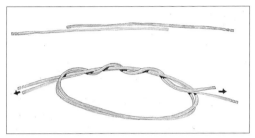

Double Surgeon's Knot
Place two leader lengths (about five or six inches) alongside each other. Make a two-inch loop and tie in three overhand knots. Pull the knot tight and trim.

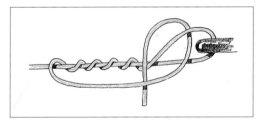

Improved Clinch Knot
Thread leader through hook eye and wrap end around leader five times. Thread end through loop in front of eye twice.

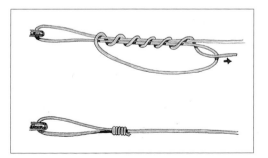

Duncan Loop
Thread leader through hook eye and bring end back parallel to leader. Form a loop by bringing the end back to hook eye and over doubled line. Make five turns around doubled line while passing through loop. Pull tag end until knot forms. Tighten the knot by pulling the tag end of the leader and the hook with pliers.

Anglers who are fishing bluewater or who plan to go after world records must learn the Bimini Twist and other knots. Those anglers should read *Practical Fishing Knots II* by Mark Sosin and Lefty Kreh, and *Bluewater Fly Fishing* by Trey Combs.

Nail Knot: This is the basic knot for attaching the leader to the fly line. With the Tie Fast Knot Tyer, it is a 15-second knot. Without the tool, it can take forever. Get the tool, and you will never again dread tying a nail knot.

A nail knot is rated at 95 percent breaking strength. It may not hold well on some saltwater fly lines with extra-tough cores. Laboratory testing has revealed that two nail knots tied back to back are 100 percent. To accomplish this with fly lines, strip the fly line down to the core. If you wish to smooth over the connection, coat it with Aquaseal thinned with Cotol. Do no not use Aquaseal with monocore lines.

The smoothest line-to-leader connection is a needle nail knot. Using a needle, the butt section is threaded through the center of the fly line end and popped out through the fly line about one-third of an inch up from the end. Use pliers to pull the needle and leader up through and out of the fly line. A nail knot is now tied. The monofilament butt section extends from the center of the fly line rather than running alongside the fly line. Shave the heavy monofilament butt section with a razor blade.

The easiest and most popular leader-to-line scenario is to secure an 18-inch section of .025 or .028 monofilament (known as a butt section) to the end of the fly line with a nail knot. Using a blood knot, attach the leader to the butt section. Subsequent leader changes are quick and easy—just blood knot the leader to the 18-inch butt section. Some anglers like a loop-to-loop system for changing leaders and fly lines. I prefer a smooth knot connection and like my fly lines on a spare spool. There are many sophisticated knot and rigging combinations, especially for big game anglers.

Blood, or Barrel, Knot: This is the preferred knot for connecting monofilament to monofilament. It is an often-used knot and you must be familiar with it. If you tie your own leaders, this knot connects all the sections together. When you tie a front section of leader (tippet) onto your existing leader, or tie a new leader to the butt section, this is the knot to use. I call it the "two hands and a mouth" knot because I use all of them to tie the blood knot. Two nail knots tied back to back are ideal for joining radically different diameters of monofilament. Next best is the surgeon's knot.

Double Surgeon's Knot: This is the quickest method of joining two sections of monofilament. It is especially handy when you must make do joining two radically different diameters of monofilament. The resulting knot is less smooth than a blood knot. It is about 95 percent, which means 95 percent of the strength rating of the monofilament.

Improved Clinch or Cinch Knot: This is the most popular knot for attaching the fly to the leader. It is simple, quick, and about 95 percent.

Duncan Loop (Uni-knot): This is a popular knot for attaching the fly, which swings freely on a loop but the loop tends to tighten on the eye of the hook under intense pressure.

Footgear

Footgear is critically important. No one shoe is perfect for everything. Wading shoes should be high enough to keep out sand, tough enough to protect your feet from sharp coral, sea urchins and other hazards, and rigid enough to provide support for your feet. I like a double-thick sole, some arch support, a high top, and speed laces. Neoprene socks should be worn with your shoes and neoprene booties. They provide comfort, dry quickly, and are easy to wash. Neoprene booties are good for boat decks, snorkeling, and wading on hazard free grass and sand flats but not for coral. Anglers fishing Belize, the Marshall Islands, and most reef waters need tough shoes for protection from coral.

Extremely sharp coral and sea urchin spines, which are very common on many flats, can puncture neoprene or almost anything else. Remove spines carefully and quickly, disinfect the wound, and apply antibiotic cream. If you cannot remove the spine or if it breaks off, see a doctor at once. These mishaps can ruin your trip by causing severe infection and illness. *Get proper footwear and watch where you walk.*

When wading, you stir up the bottom. This bottom sediment consists of mud, sand, and decomposed shells and coral, all of which cause discomfort inside your shoes. To avoid this, attach gravel guards over your pants and shoes. You'll wade in comfort all day. Rinse out your boots and socks each day after fishing so they are free of coral and sand in the morning. Always wear footgear. The sun can cook your feet in less than an hour, and you never know when no-see-ums may fly in for an uninvited meal. Cover your feet.

Flats anglers often do a lot of walking, sometimes over rough or decomposed coral. Good support and protection are important to both your safety and comfort. Sturdy, lightweight, and saltwater-resistant footgear is advisable. Is this blue crab protecting its territory, or is it attempting to steal this bonefish from the angler?

Appropriate clothing is as important as the right fly line. Clothing should be lightweight, comfortable, breathable, cool, and quick drying. It should also protect you from biting insects and ultraviolet rays. The author at North Andros Island in the Bahamas.

Tropical Clothing

The intense equatorial sun and humidity require clothing that is comfortable, quick drying, cool, breathable, and resistant to ultraviolet (UV) rays. UV is the part of the spectrum of invisible light between 200 and 400 nanometers (nm) wavelength. About five percent of the sun's energy reaches the earth as UV radiation. This is further broken down into UVA, UVB, and UVC rays. UVC rays are filtered by the ozone layer.

UVB rays cause the skin to burn visibly and can ultimately lead to skin cancer. These rays can also affect your eyes and cause snow blindness.

UVA rays tan the skin more slowly than UVB rays. They cause damage to elastic fibers and increase wrinkling of the skin and pigment damage, such as freckling. UVA rays are the most damaging to the eyes and can cause cataracts and retinal damage.

Proper clothing is as essential as polarized sunglasses and makes for a much more comfortable, enjoyable, and safe adventure.

Long pants and long-sleeved shirts are a must. Tuck long pants inside neoprene socks or gravel guards. This helps keep out sand

and coral, and reduces noise. If you are adjusting the hem of long pants, leave enough fabric to tuck them in. Shorts and short sleeves are also nice, especially around camp or when you want to enjoy a little sunshine. The best tropical clothing is made of Supplex Intera. Its tight weave filters out up to 95 percent of harmful UV light; it dries quickly; and it resists biting insects. It is so comfortable that I wear it around town, in the outdoors, and when fishing anywhere. By contrast, a cotton shirt allows about 50 percent UV ray penetration. When it is wet, an additional 10 to 20 percent passes through, and cotton doesn't dry quickly.

Other *essentials* include a rain jacket and a *warm* jacket or both light- and expedition-weight Capilene. Both layers are lifesavers when you are boating in rough water or during a torrential rainstorm. A wide- or long-billed hat that offers ear and neck protection and that has black under the visor is *absolutely a must*. A hat shades your eyes, helping you to see better. The dark under the visor helps keep light from reflecting into your eyes. Get a hat with a chin strap so you won't lose it. My favorite hat is the foreign legion type that has an oversize bill, breathable mesh and reflective foil top, black under the bill, and a removable Velcro-secured cape. It blunts the sun, breathes, cuts wind, and keeps pesky bugs off my neck. It is also nice in a rainstorm. I don't go anywhere without this hat.

Flats gloves are another favorite piece of equipment. These comfortable lightweight nylon/lycra fingerless gloves protect the backs of your hands and wrists from harmful UV rays and biting bugs. If you have ever seen the backs of hands that have been exposed to lots of sun, you know how important this is. *Do not venture onto saltwater flats without proper clothing.*

A typical selection of flats clothing. Pants, shirts, hat, gloves, booties, and a bag to carry it all.

Tony Capone

Sunglasses

Polarized sunglasses are the single greatest aid to spotting fish. All flats anglers *must* have them. Polarized glasses help cut through surface glare to reveal the bottom. Side shields also help reduce glare. Besides being a great spotting aid, good polarized glasses help protect your eyes from sun damage and errant flies. Ultraviolet radiation can be 180 times more intense on the beach or on the water than in areas with less reflection. Buy the best glasses you can afford. Flats glasses should block 99 to 100 percent of ultraviolet light to 400 nm. They should be distortion free, optically correct, have split-mirror lenses for intense light conditions, and be photochromatic, which means they lighten and darken according to available light. In addition, it is a good idea to have an antireflective coating on the inside of the lenses to reduce sun bouncing back onto your face and eyes.

Light-amber lenses are best for early mornings and late evenings because they offer the best contrast. Medium amber is best for bright cloudy conditions. Brown is best during ultrabright conditions, including midday sunshine, especially when you are fishing white flats. Frequent flats visitors and guides may carry two or three tints, knowing that, if they can't see fish, they can't catch them. An amber/brown is a good one-lens compromise. Like horse blinders, side shields help narrow your focus, reduce distracting side light, and protect your eyes from sunlight. By shading

Polarized glasses are the single greatest aid to spotting fish. They also protect your eyes from sun damage. Guess which photo is polarized!

Action Optics

Both direct and reflected light are intense on flats. Dress accordingly—protect your eyes, hands, and face. Jerry Swanson has a bit more face protection than most of us, seen here in the Seychelles.

your eyes, you keep your pupils open, which helps you see more. Remember, bonefishing is a visual game, and proper glasses are your best visual aid. You should have a protective band to keep your glasses in place.

The flats, like a glacier or extensive snow field in the summer, are no place to be without eye protection. Pack a clean towel or some tissue paper in a plastic bag to have handy to clean your glasses and camera lenses periodically throughout the day. Remember that plastic lenses can scratch easily in a salty environment, so use a liquid cleaner. Glass lenses are nearly scratch proof and are recommended. However, prescription glass lenses can be heavy and uncomfortable. Some of the best prescription glasses are available from your favorite fly fishing specialty store. Ask for a prescription sunglasses form and for frame and lens recommendations.

Forget clip-ons. You miss seeing too many fish and they do not provide the eye protection of good polarized glasses. One day of bonefishing should convince you.

Sunscreen

Today, the lifetime risk of developing melanoma is one in 75. Researchers have learned that UV light somehow eliminates T-cell activity, which means that it is not functioning when you need it most. Intense sunlight can also induce mutations in your DNA.

Physical reflectors such as zinc oxide and titanium oxide block UVA rays. A process that breaks these compounds down into micro pieces allows them to be used in clear sunscreens. Chemical barriers are also available. Currently, the best UVA-fighting active ingredient is Parsol 1789. For the best protection, make certain your selected product blocks the full spectrum of UV rays; is hypo-allergenic, dermatologist approved, nongreasy, waterproof, and PABA free; and contains no harsh chemicals.

Everybody has a brownish-black pigment in their skin called melanin that protects us from sun-related skin damage for a few minutes. Protection time varies roughly between 10 and 40 minutes. Light skin has less melanin than dark skin. Sunscreen is rated from SPF 4 to over 40. SPF means skin protection factor. An SPF 10 sunscreen protects you 10 times longer than the melanin in your skin; SPF 30 protects you 30 times longer. If you would burn in 10 minutes without sunscreen, SPF 30 would protect you for 300 minutes, or five hours. Many believe these ratings are optimistic. I apply SPF 30 or SPF 40 every hour, and I still get too much sun.

Do not be fooled into thinking that just because you have a great tan you can take the tropical sun all day or even for an hour. The darkest tan only offers an SPF of four—virtually no protection. Because ultraviolet rays are reflected off the water, these skin-burning and cancer-causing rays are 1½ times greater on the flats than on land. Intensity doubles from Canada to Florida and doubles again from Florida to the equator. Anglers taking photoactive medications (including tetracycline, antihistamines, Advil, ibuprofen, Motrin, Rogaine, birth control, hypertension drugs, and nonsteroidal anti-inflammatory drugs) need to be particularly careful. Check with your physician.

Apply sunscreen before you go out so it can penetrate your skin and provide the best protection. _Do not become a victim!_ Use _full strength_ sunscreen and _apply it liberally and frequently._ This is especially true for your nose, temples, and face; the backs of your hands and neck; and, if you are wading in shorts, behind your knees. Wading washes off sunscreen, even the waterproof type; you must keep applying it. Sunblock for your lips is also essential.

Don't forget to protect your feet when you are in the boat without shoes.

The backs of your hands take a beating from the sun, and no amount of sunscreen seems to alleviate the problem. Unless you want the backs of your hands to eventually look like chopped liver, wear a pair of fingerless flats gloves.

Some anglers think it is cool to come home with a deep dark tan. With today's knowledge about UV light, it is foolhardy. A little sunshine, especially behind a shield of SPF 30, will not kill you. If you want to expose yourself to sunshine, do so gradually and do it early or late in the day when the sun is low in the sky. To ease a painful sunburn, cover up and _stay out of the sun._ This means no fishing. Sitting outside in the shade still exposes you to ultraviolet light. Soothing lotions (100 percent aloe vera is very good) and sunburn medications help reduce pain. Drink plenty of water and take cool showers. Apply cool compresses but not ice, which can cause ice burn. For severe sunburn or when you experience nausea and vomiting, seek medical help. Pack twice as much sunscreen as you think you need.

If you run out of sunscreen, you might be able to learn something from sharks. Unlike other fish that sometimes die from long exposure in bright waters, sharks never seem to burn or get skin cancer. After sharks spent a month in shallow water, researchers noticed the sharks did indeed tan, which helps them survive in bright seas. Perhaps tanned skin is more than fashionable—it may be evolutionary.

Notebook and Pen

With each passing day, our memory fades and we are able to recall less from the past. What seemed forever etched forever on the emulsion of our mind two weeks ago soon dissolves and becomes distorted. Like looking at pictures, reading words from yesterday is perfect recall.

When I am fishing or adventuring, I always carry a pocket-sized notebook and pen in my shirt pocket. I carry it in a plastic resealable bag to keep it dry. Waterproof notebooks are also available. As interesting information, conversations, observations, or insights occur, I write them down. If I can't record them immediately, I do so at the first opportunity or in the evening. If I have

A pocket-sized notebook sealed in a plastic bag is perfect for recording observations and events.

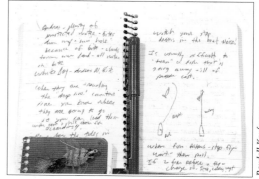

Randall Kaufmann

Topics to Include in Field Notes			
Date	Wind direction	Other destination ideas	Companions
Location	Wind velocity	Other names, special	Barometric pressure
Time of day	Sky conditions (clear, cloudy,	contacts (pilots, guides—	Moon phase
Presentation technique	cloud type, bright light, low-	addresses, phone, fax, e-mail)	Angling strategies
Tides (direction, highs, lows,	angled light, etc.)	Water conditions (clear,	Habitat type
water speed)	Travel time to fishing, etc.	cloudy, dirty)	Special gear, tackle
Water clarity	Water depth (rising, falling,	Fish species observed (where,	Spotting notes
Water temperature (rising,	steady)	when)	Flora, fauna
steady, falling, in relation	Fly patterns, size, colors,	Fish cast to, hooked, etc.	Unique observations
to depth)	new ideas	Prey species	Colors, sights, sounds
Fish size, condition	Historical interest	Reference material	Possible side trips
Map sketch of fishing area	General recap of events	How to phone the U.S.	Highlights of the day
Other activities	Photo notes	Local customs	Food
Funny dialog	Travel connections	Items to add/delete from list	Expenses

trouble remembering every detail, I ask the people I am with to help recall the information and to share their perspective. Any and everything I find interesting gets scribbled down. If something seems too personal to share, I really scribble.

When recording fishing data, I track all the usual stuff: weather, fly patterns, fish species, techniques, and so forth. Intermingled are field notes: flora, fauna, sights, sounds, and the inner workings of nature. The diary includes creative ideas—those fleeting thoughts of the moment that appear and disappear without a trace if not immediately recorded. I keep a combination field journal, fishing log, and diary. It has been said that you should write a diary as if no one will ever read it. Only then can your true and most secret thoughts be recorded.

This book is the result of years of field notes and would not be possible had I not taken the time to write it down. Everything from fishing techniques, strategies, observations, names, places, dates, times, weather, and historical facts is from my notes. Keeping a journal requires discipline, and it can be difficult to do on a consistent basis, but nothing else brings the past into the present or recalls fond memories and forgotten fishing information like your own written words. With each passing year, your journals become more precious. Besides learning to cast, my best advice is to keep a journal.

Consider incorporating items from the list above into your saltwater field notes. You won't be able to record everything on a consistent basis, but hit the highlights. I have a master check list, and every so often I fill in as much information as I can. A journal requires little time.

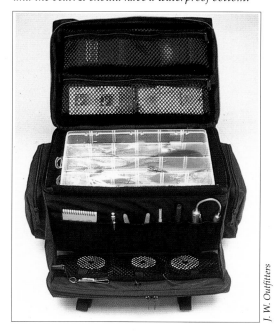

A combination travel and boat bag containing all essential gear is invaluable. Take it on the airplane and the boat. It should have a waterproof bottom.

J. W. Outfitters

Carry-on, Boat Bags, and Hip Packs

Traveling anglers should always carry their rods, reels, flies, camera, medicines, and other important gear onboard the aircraft. By doing this, you have the irreplaceable essentials regardless of where the airline sends your checked luggage. Some fine bags that take advantage of every square inch of space under an airline seat are available. If the bag doubles as a boat bag, so much the better. Once you are at your destination, your boat bag is your flats tackle bag, clothes carrier, and, most likely, your camera bag. Boat bags should have a waterproof bottom. This feature pays for itself many times over. Sooner or later your bag

Tony Capone

ends up in water, either in the bottom of the boat or in a rainstorm.

Anglers expecting to fish on foot should carry a few essentials in a hip pack. Hip packs allow easy access to any needed gear and are comfortable when you are walking and casting. Be certain it has one or two water bottles or one that accommodates a water bottle. Water is the most important reason to have a hip pack! You cannot drink too much water in the tropics. Stay hydrated. Soda or beer does not keep you hydrated. Hip packs can be positioned off to either side or in front or behind you. Chest packs are also useful if they have a water bottle. Backpacks are not advisable because of difficult access. If you have attempted to locate a small piece of gear in the bottom of a backpack while you are knee deep in water with no place to set down the backpack, you know what I mean. Consider packing an empty lightweight duffle to bring back things you did not take on the trip or to pack wet items in.

As you can see, there is more to a successful bonefishing trip than casually stuffing some gear into a suitcase. Being properly prepared and packing for a saltwater adventure is an important ingredient for success. It is a huge advantage to have an expert walk you through the process of selecting gear or to do it for you.

Getting Outfitted

Bonefish anglers require specific tackle and fishing information. This may be because they are new to the sport or they are frequenting unfamiliar areas or fishing for multiple species. Desired information may include details about fishing locations, times, technique, tides, flies, knots, leaders, fly lines, footgear, and rods, or simply, "There is a four-foot tide; be careful where you

A hip pack carries your on-the-water stash of tackle and miscellaneous gear. Being prepared is an important ingredient for success.

Richard Humphrey

Items to Include in a Hip Pack	
Water	Nippers
Pliers	Flies
Leaders	Tippet material
Sunscreen (face, lip)	Knife
Thermometer	Snack
Camera, film	Flashlight
Toilet paper	Notebook, pen
Nail knot tier	Hook hone

wade." Knowledgeable anglers can expound for hours about the nuances of Christmas Island or the Bahamas; the Bahamas is a big place. Conditions and angling techniques may vary from location to location. The same is true of Christmas Island.

Like professional sports players on the road, anglers away from their home waters are at a disadvantage. A tiny edge can make a huge difference in your fun level. "Coaches" or tackle consultants can make all the difference. They outfit and prepare you to make the perfect cast. They also prepare you mentally. It is important that your expectations match reality. This avoids disappointment and ensures that you are properly equipped. Every tackle consultant prepares clients differently. Your degree of preparedness is directly related to your consultant's knowledge and their ability to transfer that knowledge to you. Experience makes a difference.

It takes years to become an expert on fishing for various species, understanding food sources, and using appropriate angling techniques. There are no shortcuts to the knowledge gained from fiddling with every reel and casting and field testing rods. It takes years to learn the intricacies of fly lines, leaders, knots, flies, fly tying, entomology, etc. Throw in guiding, teaching experience, and relating to anglers on an individual basis, along with a working knowledge of destination travel, and the expert becomes a consultant.

Many fly fishing specialty stores have one or more knowledgeable consultants on staff. If you cannot locate a local expert consultant, get on the phone. Some of the best in the business are at mailorder houses. The best are usually low key about their expertise. Ask how much experience they have and whether they are familiar with where and when you intend to fish. You'll soon know if they are good at what they do. No one has personally visited every location, but they should be educated about it. Most rely on their extensive network of traveling anglers, guides, and lodges to obtain timely information.

Spend as much time as possible with a consultant/outfitter or trip leader and have a prepared list of questions. Clients can often set up an appointment for one-on-one coaching after hours so you have uninterrupted time. Many trip leaders offer special small client group seminars or clinics that cover everything from fishing basics, to knots, to lines, to hook sharpening, to specialty casts and anything else you need to know. They have as much fun as their clients. It is very satisfying to put anglers on the fast track and have them report that the info was right on target and that it helped them have a more enjoyable time.

Like golf clubs, there is more than one 8 weight fly rod, and all are different. A rod for one person might not fit another's casting style or preference. If you already have some rods that you like, you might purchase something similar. If you are a surf, steelhead, or salmon fisherman, you probably have a strong double haul and can cast into wind. You probably like faster rods. If you cannot double haul, a slower rod may be best for you. Outfitters can cast with or talk to clients for a few minutes, assess their general casting skill, and recommend a good rod. Everyone has a few pet rods that everyone usually likes, and outfitters usually don't hesitate to recommend those to almost everyone.

How do you know if your consultant is recommending the best rod? An angler called a supply house and asked what rod was best for his intended fishing. "Ours is," was the reply. When asked what rod was second best, the answer was, "Brand A." The angler then called another supply house and asked what rod was best. "Ours is," was the reply again. What is second best? "Brand A." There are only so many premium rod manufacturers, and the same two or three names always surface. The moral is, don't blow your money on inadequate, unproven, or unnecessary equipment.

Consultants pride themselves on giving their customers the edge. They accomplish this by "custom outfitting" clients and going the extra mile. They never sell anything that is not needed, but they make certain their clients have what they need. This logic is simple. If you arrive at Christmas Island without a hip pack with a water bottle and some sparsely dressed flies, you soon realize that you do not have what you need to fish effectively. Consultants build their credibility and earn your repeat business by doing their job better than anyone else. That means setting you up with the trick gear.

Once you have your gear, learn how to use it! Know how the drag on your reel functions, practice tying knots, and sharpen your hooks. If you tie flies, get busy! Collecting, organizing, and packing your gear is all part of the fun. Packing your gear so that it is always handy is an art. Before a bonefishing trip, lay everything out and check it off a master packing list. Saltwater and salt air corrodes everything, so place nearly all your gear in resealable plastic bags. This helps protect it and helps you organize it. Label everything as to where it goes once you're at your destination (boat bag, hip pack, room, etc.) Within 10 minutes of arrival, you should be ready to fish.

It takes just as much gear for a week as it does for a year. Collecting, organizing, and packing it is all part of the fun. Checking in at Christmas Island.

Your carry-on bag should contain everything you cannot replace at your destination (reels, lines, flies, personal medicines, travel documents, sunglasses, etc.), and you should always carry it on the airplane along with at least two five-piece rods. These are short enough to travel under the seat of a helicopter. Without rods you are not going to do much fishing. You only have to let your irreplaceable stuff out of your control once to learn a hard lesson! Pack all nonessential items in a duffel bag or suitcase and check it.

When I am bonefishing, I have two tackle bags—a boat tackle

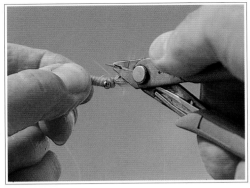

Smashing barbs not only makes releasing fish a snap—it also makes it much easier to remove the hook from your skin or clothing if your cast goes astray. Use a smooth-nosed pliers.

bag and a hip pack. I wear the hip pack when I am wading. It contains everything I need. My boat bag contains a duplicate of everything in my hip pack plus extra clothing, rain gear, spare reels, spare lines, flies, tackle, and specialty stuff. Get into the habit of always putting everything in the same place. By doing so you always know where everything is. When you need wire-cutting pliers or a popper fly, you need it now. Remember saltwater opportunities appear and disappear quickly—be ready!

Finally, maintain a good attitude. Don't beat yourself up because travel connections did not come off as planned, or you didn't get the guide you wanted, or you blew the last five bonefish. Relax. Make the cast that you can make without concern for others' expectations. The most successful fisherman is seldom the one who catches the most and biggest fish, but the one who has best attitude and the most fun!

Gear Checklist

Airline ticket
Alarm clock
Backgammon, etc.
Backing
Bandannas
Binoculars (for birding)
Boeshield
Books
Camera accessories—carry case, lenses, tripod, batteries, lens cleaner
Camera and film in double plastic bags (lead shield bag for airport X-ray)
Camp shoes; flip flops, sandles
Carry bag, waterproof
Cooler—doubles as waterproof boat box for camera, clothes, lunch. Secure lid with strap or tape.
Dictionary, English-Spanish
Ear plugs (for noisy airplanes)
Emergency telephone numbers
First Aid (include antiseptic, cortisone, and antibiotic cream, antihistamine, antibiotics, Imodium or Lomotil, tweezers, sunburn lotion, After Bite, Micropore paper for covering line burns on fingers. Consider motion-sickness medicine if you plan to fish offshore). Check with your doctor for a complete Third-World medicine kit.

Flashlight, high quality lightweight; extra batteries
Flats clothing (long pants, short pants, shirts)
Flats gloves
Flats hat (foreign legion style), cap
Flies
Fly tying materials and equipment
Hip pack
Hook hone
Insect repellent
Jacket, fleece
Knife
Leaders
Line cleaner
Lines (spares)
Maps
Medicines (carry on plane and pack 50 percent more than you need)
Miscellaneous clothing (polyester, lightweight and expedition-weight top and socks, dress clothes if needed)
Money (lots of ones, fives, tens, and twenties for tips, etc.)
Nail knot tool
Neoprene booties
Neoprene socks (2 pair)
Nippers
Notebook and pen in plastic bag
Passport, visa (keep copy separate)
Pad, inflatable

Personal effects, toiletries
Pillow
Plastic bags to pack wet articles
Plastic spoon, fork
Playing cards
Pliers—stainless steel for barb crimping, wire cutting
Pocket knife
Polarized sunglasses; strap, lens cleaner
Rain jacket with hood
Rain pants (for wet boat trips and torrential downpours—optional)
Reel lubricant and repair tools
Reels
Resealable plastic bags for food, flies
Rods
Snacks
Snorkel, face mask, fins, booties
Sunscreen (for general use and lips)
Swimsuit
Tape, repair type
Thermometer
Tippet, fluorocarbon (04x, 02x, 01x, 0x, 1x)
Toilet paper in plastic bag
Vouchers
Wading shoes
Water bottle (full)
Water filter (optional)
Wire leaders (crimp sleeves, wire)

Chapter 18

Guides

Our guide, David Pinder, Jr., poled the boat quietly along the mangrove border of a deserted cay. I sat on the bow of the boat to relax and scan the shoreline for any hint of feeding fish. Tall, spindly Australian pines bent with the stiff wind, and small creeks and mangrove hideaways penetrated the shoreline every so often. An occasional narrow sandy beach broke the monotony of the green shoreline. The low tide, coupled with windy and cloudy conditions, made for a slow morning. During such days you want to make every fish count.

A half-hour passed without any action, and I used the time to discuss bonefishing with David. I asked him what his biggest problem is in getting his clients into fish. "Casting. If they can cast 30 feet quickly and accurately, I get them fish. If not, very difficult." His second biggest problem is getting clients to follow casting and retrieving instructions. A good guide could talk a blind angler into fish. I decided to fish the next fish blind.

A few minutes later David's tone and body posture changed to that of a hunter concentrating on prey. Crouching low and speaking softly, he said, "Bonefish! Single, in close, moving right. Cast short, 20 feet, 2 o'clock. Let it drop! Moving right; cast again, 10 feet right, 3 o'clock. Let it drop. Good! Let it sink. Wait! Strip short, strip short. Stop! Stop! He turned. Strip short again. Wait. He's looking at it. Short pull. He's there; long pull; he got it. Oh!! Let it rest. Wait. Strip short. . .again. . .again. There he is; he's got it now!" I never looked for or saw the fish. I relied completely on David's commands to cast, retrieve the fly, and hook the fish, a beautiful

Australian pines frame the author at Gorda Cay near South Abaco in the Bahamas. The combination of grass, sand, and mangrove flats offers near-perfect habitat for bonefish.

bonefish that would otherwise have escaped my notice. A good guide, it seems, can almost talk a bonefish into grabbing your fly. They can certainly talk an angler to the fish, but they cannot make the cast.

Unless you live in bonefish country and have your own boat or have road access to bonefish habitat, you need a guide. Having boat transportation and knowledge of where and when bonefish are feeding are worth the guide fee. After all, did you come to see and hook bonefish or to spend your time looking for them?

Most bonefish anglers travel to a destination resort where everything is included: food, lodging, boat, and guide. There are very few locations where bonefish are available to anglers without a boat. You do not need to interview or hire a local guide. The lodge has already engaged the winners, and everything from lunch to gas has been planned. This is one of the great advantages of a lodge trip. Guesswork has been eliminated. Your fun time is maximized, and your stress is reduced, which is partly why you came in the first place.

If you are doing your own a la carte package, you must be able to function on _mañana_ time and arrange everything—food, lodging, transportation, boat, and guide. The exception is Florida, where guides are excellent and easy to contact. Most can arrange accommodations.

To avoid unpleasant surprises, do your homework. Determine in advance what level of guiding is available. If guides are not accomplished or do not speak English, plan accordingly. Seek a guide who has experience guiding fly fishermen. Expert anglers can work with a guide who has limited experience with fly anglers, but beginners cannot. If your guide claims to understand fly fishing for bonefish, he should be able to discuss bonefish prey, fly selection, and so on.

Your best source of information about guides and lodging may be recommendations from friends, locals, etc. Here are a few questions to keep in mind:

What is the type, age, and condition of the boat and motor? These factors determine function, comfort, speed, and safety. Are seats comfortable? Is there storage? Room for an ice chest? Seat cushions?

Does the boat have a poling platform? Is the pole wood or fiberglass? This determines the style and effectiveness of fishing.

Is there extra gas to travel to the most distant location? In most areas gasoline is expensive, and guides may try to conserve fuel. Make it clear that you want to go where fishing is best. If fuel costs extra, offer to pay for it.

What safety equipment is included (radio, life preservers)?

What is and is not included in the stated cost?

Is the guide experienced with fly fishermen?

Does the guide fly fish or tie flies? (Ask about favorite patterns, what gear they own, etc.)

Is language a problem?

Is lunch provided? What does lunch include? Water? Drinks?

Does the guide understand that you want to release the fish you catch?

What are the departure and return times?

How far and how long do you travel to reach fishing areas?

When and where is the best tide? The ability of a guide to find fish at various stages of the tide is priceless. This may entail an earlier or later start so you are fishing during the best tidal flow.

Is the guide in good physical condition? Make it plain that you expect them to arrive on time without a hangover. Conversely, so should you. If you arrive late, you lose fishing time and frustrate your guide.

What level of casting skill is required? What type of fishing conditions can you expect?

Fishing from a specially designed flats boat is a big advantage for both angler and guide. A few obvious advantages visible here include the comfortable seats, poling platform, push pole, and smooth fishing deck, to say nothing of boat speed!

If you are fishing from a boat and you must have a photo, this is how to do it. Grand Bahama Island, Bahamas.

Richard Humphrey

This inquiry list may seem excessive, but, if you are on your own and want to cover your bases, this is the only way to do it. The more questions you ask about what you can expect of the guide and the fishing, the better. Both you and your prospective guide can decide whether or not you are right for each other.

As you make your inquiry, assess the guide's attitude, honesty, and level of enthusiasm. If you do not "click" over the phone or have a positive initial impression, you might try another guide. On your first meeting, many guides outside the U.S. are shy and low key. You might be a bit dubious about them or their gear, but give them a chance. If the gear is good, the guide is usually good. If the gear is poor, the guide is not necessarily so. Most open up on the water, love to chase tall tails, and are very good.

You expect your guide to be up front with you, and you should be candid with the guide. If you are a beginner or have any physical limitations, say so. Be honest about your casting expertise. Tell your guide if you are left or right handed. This can make a difference where he fishes you in relation to shorelines and wind. Arrive organized and rigged, ready to fish. Guides appreciate you washing your feet each time you have been out of the boat.

In undeveloped areas or where there are few guides or where a lodge operation might tie up all the good guides and boats, it may be difficult to hire an independent. Often you must settle for a boat handler and second-rate boat, not to mention less-than-

Everything is working in this photo. Coki, the guide, is pointing to and explaining the location of bonefish, while directing the retrieve. Jon Covich concentrates on finessing the bonefish. His rod tip is in the water, and his strip is accurate, which almost guarantees a hookup. If not, the skiff can quickly, safely, and comfortably take him to the next spot.

ideal accommodations. If there is a good lodge available, take advantage of it. You almost always get more bang for your buck. There are no destination lodges in Florida, and anglers must make their own a la carte arrangements. First-time anglers sometimes book more than one guide during a multiday trip in an effort to experience variety.

At established lodges there are always one, two, or perhaps three "best" guides. Sometimes camps rotate guides. If it is possible to reserve a specific guide, do it. If you wait until the last minute to book your trip, do not expect the best guide or the best room. A regular in-the-know customer or booking agent has already gotten them. My advice? Book early with a good agent.

Professional guides understand both bonefish and angler. They attempt to match the skill level of the angler with the difficulty factor of angling conditions. As an example, beginning anglers are best suited to light-colored flats, plenty of fish (usually smaller), and casting with the wind. Expert water may include a mottled bottom or fewer, but larger, fish in deeper water requiring casts angled into the wind.

You can tell the ability of guides by where and how they fish you. If they put competent anglers into mudding fish rather than on singles or small pods of cruising and tailing fish, they have much to learn. If they are slow, quiet, and cautious, it is a good

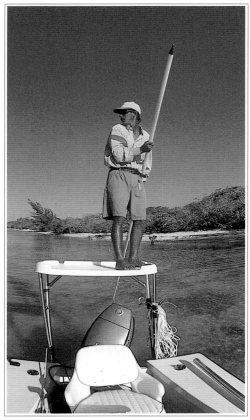

A three-foot-high poling platform makes an incredible difference in spotting fish. Lest you think it is easy to pole a boat all day, just try to stand on the platform. It gives you a new appreciation for what a guide does. It is very hard work.

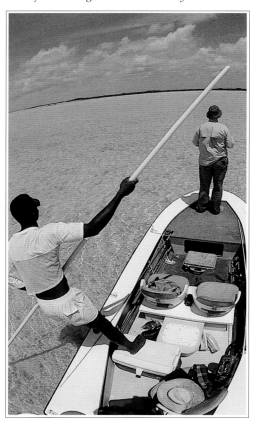

sign. Having a selection of flies and tying their own is another good sign. Expect the most from Florida guides, the least from undeveloped locations. There are some outstanding Bahamian guides. The best usually have their own Florida-style boat, tie their own flies, fish on their day off, and can cast better than you. Andros Island probably has the largest concentration of the most astute guides in the Bahamas. Some, such as the Smith family, Charlie and his sons Andy and Prescott, take bonefishing very seriously. There are also excellent guides at other islands. Some may not have the best gear, but they know where the fish are and how to catch them!

Most bonefish guides (especially outside the U.S.) live a simple, relaxed life. They are happy when you hook bonefish but do not get unhappy when you do not. Your trip is much more enjoyable if you have the same attitude. Your guide might tell you, "There will be another bone, mon. Don't worry; plenty of fish. You see." Relax; you are on island time.

Most guides love what they do and have been doing it for years. It is hard work. If you don't believe it, just try lifting their water-soaked wooden push pole. Veteran guides have collected a great deal of fishing information. I always look forward to sharing their ideas and knowledge. Don't be afraid to ask questions.

I often ask if there is anything I should do differently or pay particular attention to. This gives them an opportunity to make suggestions and relate observations without causing offense or making them feel inhibited. It also sends a message that you want to learn and are open to advice. You may be surprised what you learn or need to learn. If you ask, expect the truth.

Many guides speak English, but you may not easily understand their dialect or accent. Your time is too short and the guide's information too valuable to allow any words to slip by without you understanding them. When you are in doubt or have trouble deciphering his speech, tell the guide you want to know and understand everything they say and that you don't understand their accent. Ask them to slow down.

As you begin your first day of guided fishing, limber up the rod so the guide can assess your skill level. If you can cast with either hand, let them know. Determine how long a 30-foot cast is so you know how far to cast when they say, "Bonefish, 35 feet, 3 o'clock." The bow of the boat is always 12 o'clock. When you are on foot, the direction you are facing is 12 o'clock. If you have trouble locating fish, use your rod as a pointer. Some guides use their push poles as pointers. Do not point your rod tip at close-in fish because such movement can spook them.

Every angler desires something different from a day of guided fishing. You might prefer a particular type of flat, plenty of small fish, stalking individual fish on foot, a more relaxed schedule with a break on the beach for lunch, or perhaps some snorkeling. If you are interested in other species, speak up. Tell your guide in advance what you hope to experience. This gives them time to plan a schedule or make any special arrangements for gear, gas, or food. If you are working out of an established camp, they set the schedule, usually an eight- to nine-hour fishing day. Sometimes the camp might be flexible, depending on their arrangements or safety factors.

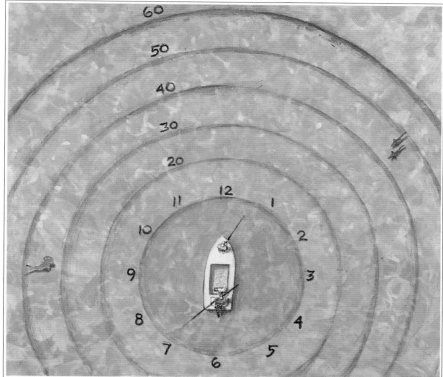

The bow of the boat is always 12 o'clock. When you are on foot, the direction you are facing is 12 o' clock. In this illustration, the guide would alert you to incoming bonefish at 2 o'clock, 40 feet. This is an easy presentation, especially for left-handed casters. Right-handed casters must be careful not to hook the guide.

A guide's duty is to show you fish; to be helpful, courteous, encouraging, and entertaining; and to get you back safely. Guides cannot control the weather, cast for you, or make fish grab your fly. A good guide puts you in the best place at the best time. They understand tides, winds, and bonefish. They become your eyes and talk you through the cast, retrieve, hookup, and release, commanding you as the drama unfolds. They probably know more about bonefishing than you do, and you can learn a great deal. A good guide is a people person and thoroughly in tune with the surroundings. They are happy, good natured, and talkative—always providing information about bonefish plus the local flora, fauna, and history.

Your guide is there to make your day more productive and enjoyable. Help them do that. Be kind, courteous, and gracious. *Pay attention.* Show your appreciation when they do well. If a good relationship develops between angler and guide, both of you will look forward to the next day on the water. If a problem arises with a guide, whether it is in relation to fishing, boat handling, or safety, do not hesitate to speak up. Remember, you are paying the bill.

Guides in developing countries may not always exercise the best judgment. There may be times when you need to voice a strong opinion or even take control of a dangerous or potentially dangerous situation. Do not be bashful if you feel threatened.

Once, while fishing at Placencia, Belize, two of our party were late in arriving back at camp. When they finally arrived near dark, I could tell by their tired and long faces that everything was not right. Their guide had happened on a partially sunk boat on a reef. Thinking he could salvage and claim it as his own, he asked, or shanghaied, his clients to help right the boat so he could tow it home. The guide ran the boat onto the reef drop-

Staking out for lunch near Turneffe Island in Belize. Pictured is the best boat equipment, which can mean the difference between a good day and an exceptionally good day. It can mean the difference between an unsafe or safe day of travel to and from the fishing. If you have a choice, go with the best gear.

Jon Covich

Be careful entering and exiting a boat with rods. This is when damage is most likely to occur. Pictured is the best method for keeping your rods safe.

When you are fishing on foot, your guide may stay at your side and spot fish and advise you on the cast, hookup, and help with the release. This angler is "clearing the line" on the first run. Keep the rod high and feed the loose line through the guides.

Angler and guide share a happy moment—the quick release. Abaco, Bahamas.

off, and the three began bailing the wrecked boat. Glancing back at their own boat, they noticed it was about to sink! The guide had been running without the boat plug in place and, in his haste, had forgotten to put it back in before leaving the boat. Working together, the three of them kept the motor from going under.

Hours later and near exhaustion, they barely salvaged their own boat but not before the clients lost all their camera gear and broke two rods. The potential for a dangerous night afoot on an offshore reef with an incoming tide was obvious.

It is entirely possible that your guide may turn out to be less than satisfactory, especially on a do-it-yourself trip. I once hired a guide for an 8 a.m. departure, and at 9 he still hadn't arrived. A local passerby drove to his house and rousted him out. His unkempt appearance and rum breath were disturbing, and not exactly what I had in mind. It was a fishless morning. The guide didn't want to be there, and I did not want to be there with him. Cut your losses and try again.

Not every trip or every day is going to turn out like the videos and magazine articles you see and read. Weather and fish do not always cooperate. Travel connections do not always come off as planned. Guides may not show up. Be realistic and do not expect every day to make the record book. In a week's fishing, if you have three excellent days of weather and fishing, two fair-to-good days, and two poor-to-fair days, you have beaten the averages. The same can be said of trips: some are picture perfect, and some are stormy.

Regardless, remember that you are on vacation to have fun. Complaining and blaming others for events beyond their control only makes matters worse for everyone. In addition, aggressive, competitive, and boisterous behavior is sure to alienate your hosts and fellow anglers. Leave the attitude at home and truly *relax.*

Pay your money, take your chances, and enjoy the day no matter the weather or fishing. In my book, any time spent on the water with friends and good company is a joy. There is always knowledge to find and beauty to be seen, and there is always tomorrow. Smile! Enjoy yourself! You are only here for a short time.

Tipping

Tipping is not required, but any amount offered is appreciated. Your tip usually comes back in extra service, extra time spent on the water, or special effort above and beyond a normal guide day. As a general rule, 10 to 20 percent is the standard tip. You may want to tip more if you are in a generous mood or had an exceptional time, or if the guide worked overtime or went the extra mile.

If you are rotating guides, tip after each day's fishing. If you are fishing with the same guide for more than a day, you can tip each day or on the last day. You may get more mileage out of a daily tip. Tackle and other commodities are sometimes useful, but nothing beats the U.S. dollar anywhere in the fishing world.

Chapter 19

Adventuring

L ike skiers searching for perfect untracked powder, climbers seeking unclimbed summits, and surfers chasing the endless wave, bonefish adventurers seek undiscovered flats, reefs, and lagoons that hold the mother lode. Most of the easy-to-reach bonefish locations have been explored, mapped, and exploited. Few anglers go to the effort required to reach those that remain unexplored. Most wait until others do the groundwork and report on how to do it. Once the adventurers and pioneers move on, the masses move in.

Adventuring on your own for bonefish can be a wonderful experience. Wonderfully good or wonderfully bad, depending on your outlook—and your luck. Bonefish adventures often begin the same way. You are told, in strictest confidence, about a faraway tropical paradise where man has seldom trod and bonefish are large and gullible. As with stock market tips, you absorb the information greedily and make every conceivable excuse to check out your treasure map.

Following are two very different bonefish adventure stories. How lucky do you feel?

Over the Edge

The adventure began as Brian O'Keefe and I boarded the interisland flight, which, in retrospect, set the tone for the week. To protect the innocent (us), our destination must remain secret. The aircraft was crowded, stuffy, and loud. Earplugs barely made the 1½-hour flight bearable. The in-flight snack packs contained Minute Maid

orange juice (expired four months earlier), a Cadbury bar that had crumbled into sugar, stale Planters' peanuts, and a Rich's honey-flavored bun. I inspected the Rich's bun for an expiration date and found none. The bun consisted of 39 unrecognizable ingredients. It didn't need an expiration date. This palm-sized biscuit was built to last longer than its plastic wrapper. Why would anyone make something like this, let alone eat it? I pulled out an Oregon apple I had smuggled into the country.

We had arranged to stay with a local family that would meet us at the airport. When we arrived, it became obvious that every other passenger had arranged the same ride. We shared pickup truck space with eight others, plus baggage, two oversized tires, and a leaky barrel of gasoline. Progress was slow as the overloaded truck negotiated continuous potholes. We figured the road had been used for bombing practice during the last drug war. As we bounced along, it looked like almost everyone had left this desolate rocky rubble of an island. Clusters of homes were abandoned everywhere, their shells standing eerily empty.

We arrived at our upstairs apartment in an oasis of concrete blocks, stucco, crabgrass, and a shade tree. The family was very hospitable and made us feel welcome. We unpacked, readied our gear, and located our guide at the bar down the road. He said it was too late to fish that day. We bought a round of drinks for the bar, bought lunch for our guide, and prevailed on him to fish after lunch. He was slow and unorganized; by the time he got his boat in the water, it was 3 p.m.

We soon realized that we had a boatman who halfheartedly aspired to become a guide. We decided to have Charles babysit the boat while we wandered on foot toward the back of the lagoon in

Twilight, the time of magic, is upon me. Colors pale, and my world becomes a silhouette of land, water, and sky. Bonefish tails continue to break the water's slick surface. Time for one more cast! Darkness comes quickly in bonefish country, ushering in balmy air of romantic topical nights. The first stars glitter, and tails become difficult to detect. There's one! Last cast. Hurry!

A shockingly powerful bonefish explodes upon my fly, shattering the peaceful evening air. The bonefish wants my fly more than I do and leaves my adrenaline dangling like my leader.

When you camp in the land of bonefish, nature serves up the best of the tropics—nonstop, 24 hours a day. By day, I wander through colorful waters, observe nature, and hunt tall tails. After dark, star clusters and constellations stir the imagination. On a clear dark night thousands of stars are visible. Tonight I count roughly three to four thousand, then stare into the campfire. Tomorrow I will count bonefish tails. It's the life. North Andros Island, Bahamas.

search of bonefish. Much to our disappointment, our boatman soon motored into the lagoon. Bonefish in panic mode zoomed in every direction. Chalking the first day's angling up to experience, we opted to head back. The motor wouldn't start. We poled, drifted, and pushed toward town until the motor sputtered to life. After we got back to the dock, the 15-mile drive home along the cratered road took an hour.

We made arrangements to get a 7 a.m. start but realized we needed food. The only store was at the airport, back down the same shelled road we had travelled earlier. Our host offered to drive us (for $50 U.S.) and get the owner to open up. The store was a combination hardware store, feedlot, emporium, and soft drink distributor under a tin roof atop a concrete slab. We gathered enough junk food to open our own minimart. A plastic bag of homemade yellowed ice cost us $8 U.S. Brian paid with two new-issue U.S. $100 bills. The clerk laughed and asked what kind of funny money we had. Realizing this was the real thing, he meticulously inspected it by sight, smell, feel, and taste. We accepted his funny money in change without fanfare.

Back home we had dinner from a can, readied our gear, and reset our mental attitude for a new day. A hot shower would have been a good end to the day, but both the toilet and shower worked with a bucket of rusty water stored on the porch, so I passed.

Last fish of the day.

Exhausted, I lay down on the bed and found plastic sheets, which are noisy, slippery, and clammy. It was stuffy so I opened a window to an unmoving air mass. Mosquitoes poured through tiny holes in the screen and soon I felt their bloodthirsty attack. I turned on the flashlight and noticed an oversized cockroach on the wall. I knew they would be all over our food, so I put everything in the

Lost! How do we get out of this maze of creeks, channels, and mangroves? Never mind, I see bonefish!

Conch trees! This is indeed a strange place.

Finally, bailing became a futile exercise and we had to abandon ship.

refrigerator. I closed the window and turned on a portable fan. In a few minutes I discovered the generator was right outside my window.

I changed rooms, closed the door, and put on socks and long pants, figuring extra warmth was preferable to bug bites and full plastic sheets. I set up a pop-up mosquito net, slipped my upper torso inside, and hoped for sleep. It was midnight. I ignored the whine of the fan, but I couldn't ignore the whine of the mosquitoes. The little buggers were difficult to see and even more difficult to kill, and there were plenty to replace those on the front line. The room temperature was in the 80s, and my body temperature was rising with each mosquito bite. I tried counting bonefish and pretending I was in a five-star resort and that I was merely hallucinating in a steam bath. Nothing worked. I felt like I had a hangover.

At 2:30 a.m., the rooster began its predawn solo. By 3 a.m., I was almost out of control. I tried to shower the bird with a bucket of water. He was wise to this ploy. He moved a few paces and crowed a satisfying laugh. In my stupor I accidentally smashed a cockroach with my hand, and, before I realized it, a swarm of fresh mosquitoes entered my room.

I heard Brian stumble into the restroom, curse the bugs, and spray Black Flag. (There were over 100 bodies in the tub the next morning.) He had a floor-to-ceiling bug net that allowed him relative comfort. I asked if he wished to sell or trade his netting. That was good for a laugh. If you don't have the right gear, you can pay a high price.

At 4 a.m., I hadn't slept. It was just as well because the dogs began barking at the rooster. Soon several goats struck up an ongoing conversation. I was living a McRandall's farm nightmare. By 5 a.m. the sky lightened, and somehow I snuck in 30 minutes of fitful sleep before the kids began their hour-long screaming match with the pigs, goats, dogs, rooster, and each other. They played an interesting game of bumper bicycle and crash-your-wagon-into-the-wall. The generator was, by now, running full time, its annoying staccato pounding driving me to the edge. No, I was over the edge and trying desperately to get back to the edge. I stumbled into the kitchen, battled ants, flies, spiders, and cockroaches; washed out a cereal bowl (I boiled the water); and had breakfast outside. The morning air had a calming effect and promised peace.

We hustled our gear to the road and were ready at the appointed time. True to *mañana* time, our guide was an hour late. I was in no condition to ask why. We endured the hour-long ride to the dock and finally boarded the boat. We motored off to quiet flats that promised tall tails.

Fishing with an inexperienced guide is almost as bad as not fishing. Our guide had no idea where the bonefish were and whether the tide was up or down. We took control of our destiny and began trudging across a huge flat. We found some fish but nothing worth the effort. Our guide dozed, ate lunch, and didn't think to come across the flat to pick us up. We gave him explicit directions at the next drop-off point. We fished hard until a heavy rainstorm drenched our bodies and spirit. We had had enough. Back at the dock we invited everyone to the bar for rum and Cokes. We played the juke box and pool, and visited with the locals.

We hitched a ride to a local restaurant-poolroom-domino bar

for dinner. The snapper and rice dinner was excellent, but the place was a bit rowdy; several out-of-control drunks attempted to befriend us. The TV volume was on maximum, but there was no picture, only static—not our idea of entertainment. Domino players increased the volume to 90 decibels. We walked home and mentally prepared ourselves for night battle. The animal farm performed on time.

Our host had arranged for a new guide to pick us up across the highway the next morning. At the beach we waded 100 yards out into the water where his boat was anchored. It looked like the toy boats I used to play with in the bathtub, only mine didn't leak. Our guide pulled the starter rope once, twice, three times. It started on the ninth pull. "Anything under 10 is good," Brian said.

Just offshore the water was pale green and very clear. Suddenly we were in the middle of a 30-foot by 40-foot inky blue hole. "Plenty blue holes," said Victor, pointing east. Tropical water always mesmerizes me, and this day was no exception. Pearlescent white foam striped the sea like lanes in a swimming pool. Colors constantly changed as I watched the bottom detail of sand, coral, and seagrass glide beneath our boat. Gradually, all detail disappeared, and only the smooth color of water remained.

We headed downtide and downwind, moving at eight to 10 miles per hour. I asked Victor how long he had been guiding bonefisherman. "First time!" he exclaimed. "Used to lobster, but too hard and too old; hope to bonefish now." Brian rolled his eyes, and I laughed to myself.

After a very long time in the cramped boat, we finally stopped. Fishing was fast for three-pound school rats. I took photos while Brian released several of the silvery battlers. Wanting a shot at larger fish, we motored on, stopped, looked, walked, and, unimpressed, decided to bag it. Besides, we knew it would be a long slow ride back.

The motor labored into the wind and tide. I triangulated on the shoreline, and 30 minutes later we were still in the same place. Our craft had been worn by unknown years of salty service. It had been riveted, nailed, fiberglassed, bolted, stapled, wired, and duct-taped together. If there had been a fourth person in the boat, we would have sunk. Several inches, and pounds, of water slowed our progress. I had been bailing for an hour. My body was suffering from lack of sleep, and my arms were suffering from bailing fatigue.

We joked about what we would do to the friend who had given us this treasure map. We discussed how to pass time until the plane would come in two days and about what we would do if the plane didn't come in two days. I kept bailing, laughing, shivering, worrying, and watching the distant shoreline. I looked to the west and watched as the sun sizzled below the horizon, throwing magenta and fire-orange banners into the pale blue sky. It was another calendar sunset, and we were happy to be alive.

On the beach, Victor asked us what time for the next day. I asked him how much for today. He said, "Whatever's fair, mon." I gave him $125 U.S., thinking this was very generous. He politely asked, "Can you make it a bit more, please, sir?" I made it $150, and said we would contact him if we wanted to fish tomorrow. It

Randall Kaufmann

Just another average bonefish? There is no such thing. They are all special!

Like a mirror, bonefish light up their surroundings.

Heading home. I think I see the dock.

was our fault for not following the guide-interrogation rules from the start. We knew better, but Victor had been recommended by our hosts. We decided to cut our losses, relax, read, write, and play backgammon until the plane arrived.

We discussed the plight of the locals. We were the first visitors this hamlet of 200 had seen in months. Some expressed gratitude that we had come. Most houses had a TV antenna, boomboxes, Reggae music tapes, and Nike shoes and shirts. They watched satellite basketball but didn't play. They sat in their doorways, but would not pick up the trash that littered their yards. There was no motivation. They just sat on the dock watching the tide roll in. We showed them what we did and explained that we hoped to send more anglers, but we realized this would not be a viable destination.

In the end, we figured we donated to charity, left a positive impression, and came away appreciating America all the more. Every American should see the Third World. It would make us a better country and improve our own lot. The total tab for four days on the island, including 2½ days fishing, but not including airfare, came to $1,600. We didn't do the trip to save money; there wasn't a local lodge or established guide service. This was the only way to explore new territory. Sometimes this costs a little extra.

I had survived the sleeping conditions. Whether it was the food, the water, or the force of the moon, I had some powerful dreams. Visions and insights allowed me to better understand human nature, Mother Nature (especially cockroaches), my world, and the world of bonefish. This was one of my better learning experiences. Brian took our adventure in stride. He learned a little about pigs, goats, chickens, kids, mosquitoes, cockroaches, dominos, drug runners, treasure maps, and backgammon. He ate the Rich's bun and drank the most rum.

Fishing is a means by which we learn about ourselves, about others, and about the world around us. If hooking fish were the only reward, it would be a dull pursuit indeed.

Correct way to hold and photograph bonefish above the water.

Floatplane and Kayak to Bonefish Paradise

Brian and I flew to Nassau, Bahamas, with another bonefish treasure map. The exact location must remain secret to protect the large, gullible bonefish.

At Nassau a band played Calypso tunes and put us in a tropical mood while we waited our turn at customs. Once the agent learned of our purpose (bonefishing) and destination, he was friendly and talkative. We proceeded outside, procured a taxi, and loaded our gear. The trunk wouldn't close, but the driver said he would drive slowly. It felt good to be moving on land toward our destination, which was a nearby floatplane dock.

Bahamians are always friendly, inquisitive, and talkative. Our taxi driver was no exception and told us of his recent marital fortunes. He said, "The wife, she always say she leaving. One night I come home, she packed up all her clothes, mon. She left! I go to sleep. I not even look for her. A week later I get a summons for legal separation. She say she leave. I say okay, do you need a taxi? She say she look for greener grass. I say don't let it get brown. If it gets brown, don't come back here!"

Ellen was our floatplane pilot. She was casual, dressed in shorts, well tanned, and pretty. She was serious about flying and proud of her new airplane. Ellen said the life expectancy of a floatplane in the Bahamas' salty environment is only three or four years, reason enough not to own one.

When we showed her our gear, she was not amused and said there was only room for necessities. We sorted through our gear twice, and I concluded that I was indeed down to necessities: food, water, first aid kit, tackle, photo gear, tent, sleeping bag, pad, and pillow—all important stuff one cannot go camping without. Brian didn't bring a sleeping bag, pad, or pillow but had a two-person inflatable kayak. He knows his priorities; I know mine.

Brian and I dragged our 120 pounds of bulky gear onto the narrow dock, and Ellen did the loading. Being the lightest, I was doomed to be cramped into the odd space she left open in the back seat. I took a last deep breath before being shrinkwrapped into a hunchback position with my nose pressed against the window. I

Miles of deserted mangroves, flats, channels, cuts, and open ocean—perfect for bonefish, and us! At low tide it is easy to spot flats and possible bonefish avenues. We select a centrally located campsite and minutes later are setting up camp.

First cast at the edge of the flat nets Brian this chunky bonefish. We chose well.

Randall Kaufmann

Our camp is quiet and remote, just the way we like it. The driftwood furniture is home-made.

A room with a view. Sunrise and bonefish tails nearly at our feet.

Curved-tail lizards made friends with us. They peeked into our tent and followed us around camp. We had to be careful not to step on them. They love doctor flies.

At sunrise the light is too low to see the bottom so you fish the edge of the tide for early arriving tailers.

looked at the floats and noticed water washing over the top. Ellen, sensing my concern, said, "As long as they float, we are O.K." I knew this would be a long takeoff, if indeed there would be a take-off! We taxied to the very end of the lagoon and slowly, laboriously, and noisily plowed forward through the water. The nose rose slightly, and the floats struggled to break free of the water. We cleared the shoreline trees with room to spare.

From the air, the ocean was a deep cobalt blue, and whitecaps were scattered across its surface. As we approached our destination, the ocean shallowed and lightened. Every imaginable pigment of blue, green, and tan swirled together, creating visuals that are unrivaled outside the world of bonefish. Outlandishly beautiful flats and campsites were everywhere. Ellen circled a prospective site and, having deemed it safe to land and take off, descended onto a turquoise tongue that extended into deep-blue ocean water. The landing was flawless. After securing the plane in the breeze, we quickly carried our gear to shore. After the plane was unloaded, Ellen pointed it into the wind and soon disappeared into a sky as blue as the water. Brian and I looked at each other, grinned, laughed, and said, "How lucky can we be? Yes! This is for us!"

We set up camp, and Brian readied the kayak while I explored the beach. Our narrow strip of camp sand was five feet from the water and provided an exciting view of the channel and distant cays. We watched the sun set, enjoying its fading light while we could. Darkness slowly spread across the sky and clouds encircled the pale horizon. A quarter moon backlighted big puffy clouds, diffusing them like cotton candy. Stars appeared like city lights at dusk, and soon the Milky Way glittered like the Las Vegas strip. At our feet stretched the ocean—deep, dark, and mysterious. Space stretched overhead—deep, dark, and mysterious beyond imagination.

A jet passed overhead, heading to Florida or perhaps New York. The sights and sounds of the mechanized world are more and more difficult to avoid. Airplane and boat traffic, beach litter, lights, and pollution are everywhere.

I wrote by flashlight, kept my food cool with ice, slept in a Gore-Tex tent, and had reached this near-idyllic spot by float plane. I am mechanized, but I would gladly do without many conveniences if I could do the picking and choosing. I fell asleep wondering what I would choose.

A strong wind charged off the ocean, causing the channel in front of us to roar like a Class III rapid. The rising tide lapped against the rocky shore with small waves. The two sounds, ocean and river, were confusing. Sounds are magnified in darkness and can take on a sinister tone. Twice in the night I was awakened by scary water sounds. Would my tent be inundated? I imagined Brian's camera case and our film, passports, and stash of $100 bills rocking out with the kayak as it was set adrift on the wild ocean waters. Twice I shone the light about and, while the water had risen, all was safe.

I thought about other times when night and dreams have worked their dark, confusing ways on me. Once on the Deschutes River in Oregon I pitched my tent about 20 feet from the railroad

track. Sometime during the night the train came rumbling down the track shaking the ground and screaming its terrible whistle. I half awoke in a confused state of panic. I still remember exiting the tent, screaming, "Run for your life, the train is coming!"

Another time, on Alaska's Goodnews River, I thought I was dreaming that there was water in my tent and sleeping bag. I had a rude awakening when I realized it was no dream! The tide had backed up the river, and I was soaking wet at 5 a.m. So, as you can imagine, I am cautious about water noise in the night.

The night was cool, and it took Brian a while to warm up in the morning and coax his stiff body into motion. He had on all the clothes he had brought and was not a comfortable camper. I almost felt guilty for having sprawled in my down bag and snuggled with a full-sized pillow.

The morning sun and wind were behind us and parallel to the shore we intended to fish. What luck! We had a quick breakfast of cereal and juice and paddled the kayak across a 30-foot-wide and 15-foot deep side channel to a beautiful flat of sand, grass, and semisoft muck with a mangrove fringe. Bonefish tails appeared within minutes. My third cast brought a good fish to the fly. Brian photographed it, traded the camera for a fly rod, made two casts, and had two beautiful bonefish. Working the drop-off, he spotted another and was three for three. I made another cast and hooked another average-sized bonefish for this flat—five to six pounds. We concentrated on photos the rest of the morning and greatly enjoyed the low-angled light and our good fortune to have landed in bonefish paradise. Brian named the flat Morning Glory.

Floatplanes are great transportation. There just aren't many available in bonefish country.

An explosive take from a huge bonefish. The biggest bonefish sometimes slip into the shallows at nightfall. We could hear them well after dark.

We returned to camp for lunch and beached the kayak. Brian soon noticed it was adrift 50 feet across the channel. Stripping down, he swam the channel and rushed after it. The 15-knot wind caught the boat sideways and the race was on. Like a spectator at the racetrack, I placed my bet and watched the action unfold. For most of the race, the kayak was ahead by a length. As the water grew deeper and the sand softer, Brian slowed and the kayak gained distance. Brian tried to swim, but could not keep up. His energy was almost expended as the kayak drifted dangerously close to the ocean channel. If it had reached deep water, my dream of the previous night would have been realized as our camera, film, passports, and wallet full of $100 bills were on board!

After 100 yards, the race was too close to call. My horse was tiring, and the kayak showed no fatigue as it glided effortlessly with the wind. Suddenly, the kayak seemed to stall within inches of Brian's grasp. In a last-ditch effort, Brian made a lunge for it. He had it! My horse won! Brian rolled onto the top of the kayak and didn't move. The soft muck bottom, 18- to 24-inch-deep water, wind, and tide had taken its toll. That lunge had been his last burst of energy.

After regrouping, we headed across the ocean channel to a huge series of flats. Each flat was separated from the others by a narrow channel too deep to wade. Without the kayak we would not have been able to fish any decent water from our campsite. We encountered bonefish on every flat when the tide was rising. Tim Borski's Super Swimming Shrimp was the hot pattern. I noted that

After nearly losing the kayak, the author isn't taking any chances!

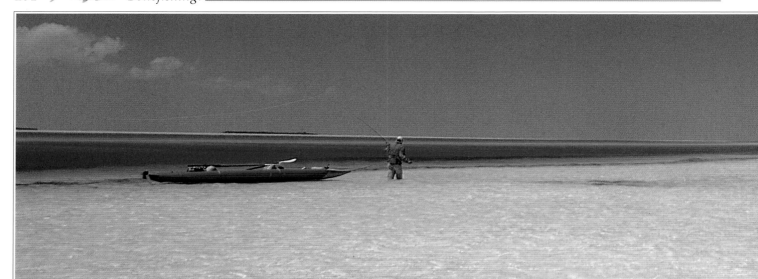

its colors perfectly matched those of the flats, which were a combination of tan sand, tan mud, and olive grass.

At one point, I heard a huge commotion in the water behind me. A big predator had something. The dark shape was patrolling the drop-off 100 yards behind me. I looked briefly, dismissed it as possibly a shark, and turned away. I looked again. This time I saw a 50- to 60-pound permit! Quickly switching to a crab fly as I hurried into casting position, I watched, disappointed, as the permit sank from sight, its dark shape changing to blurry emerald green as it became one with the channel. I was 10 seconds too late. Remember, think and act quickly, everything around you does.

Fishing slowed on the low tide, and we headed back to camp. Stepping ashore, we were instantly attacked by doctor flies, a type of horsefly. They attached themselves to any bare skin and proceeded to chew off a chunk of flesh. They were so intent on their diabolical duty that they paid no attention to their enemy, which was us. They were easily swatted, and one could quickly pile up 100 bodies. I put on long pants, gloves, and a hat. Brian sprayed himself with Cutter's and continued swatting. Finally, he put on navy blue pants, but the flies continued to land on him. They seemed to avoid my light-blue and white clothes.

Curved-tail lizards made friends with us in camp, and we were careful not to step on them. They were inquisitive, peeking into my tent, perching atop our gear, and generally entertaining us with their antics. When doctor flies were around, the lizards followed us everywhere and ate the flies at our feet as fast as we swatted them down. Charles Darwin would have appreciated their quick adaptation and our symbiotic relationship!

The afternoon of the last day we packed up and waited for

Ellen. Brian sarcastically wondered why we were packing out the trash. We had never seen so much broken glass on a beach. Some was half buried, some wedged in rock—it was everywhere. Plastic was present in all shapes and sizes, too, everything from six-pack holders to boat hulls. Other debris included tin foil, cans, polyethylene foam, balloons, ribbon, plates—anything you might find on a boat. Nearby was a wooden pallet with two pair of baby shoes balanced on it. The beach was like a municipal dump—you could find anything. Local inhabitants, visiting yachts, and cruise ships caused this mess. Everyone, it seems, throws everything into the sea.

Brian and I contemplated the industry that bonefishing has created, mostly in the past 10 years. We would not have been on the island if it were not for bonefish. Of all the fish in the sea, bonefish do it all the best for fly fishermen.

We heard our plane before we saw it. The pilot was Ellen's husband, and he landed directly. He was dressed in shorts and sandals, and doctor flies begin chewing his flesh immediately. He held the airplane with one hand, slapped at the flies with the other, and shouted for us to hurry and load the airplane. He did a wild dance and almost went berserk. Once we were airborne, I spied a stowaway—a doctor fly. We were flying at 2,000 feet and 125 mph when it was sucked out the air vent. I wonder if it was dazed, or stunned, or if its wings were ripped off. How far can they fly and swim?

Total cost for three days, from Nassau, was $1,000. You would need camping gear and a kayak (with a tie-down rope), and you must be able to protect yourself from man-eating flies. We did the trip to experience remote fishing and camping, to get some unusual photos, and to view the galaxy. We can't wait to do it again.

Indigo skies, emerald water, pearly sand flats covered with bonefish as far as the eye can see, and no one within miles. Can bonefishing get much better? I don't think so.

Randall Kaufmann carefully lifts a hefty Bahamas bonefish for a quick photo.

Chapter 20

Bahamas

There are two Bahamas. One is where the tourists go—Nassau, Paradise Island, and Freeport—which are extensions of Miami. The other is the outer islands, the *real* Bahamas. This is a country apart from the tourists that offers many wonderful and enchanting places to chase bonefish. Each area has a unique charm and a different style of fishing.

A few areas are conducive to do-it-yourself trips. Most are not, and a complete package from a reliable agent is advised. If you do not book and reconfirm all your air, ground, car, hotel, and guide reservations in advance, you must be flexible, patient, and resourceful. Generally, it is best to book at an established camp where everything is included. Then it is the camp's responsibility to have a boat, lunch, ice, drinks, and the guide waiting on the dock each morning or the taxi waiting to take you to the airport. Remember, the Bahamas are on *mañana* time and do not function around the hands of the clock or even the turning of the tide.

If you plan to rent a car at any of the out islands, don't expect a national company to have the car washed, gassed, and ready to go. The last time I rented a car, it turned out to be an old rusted station wagon with bald tires, worn-out shocks, and no gas. We nick-named it the "roachmobile" after we discovered a family of cockroaches dining on our munchies. We handled the entire rental over the phone; when asked if there were a rental agreement, the owner said, "No worries, mon, you can't go far. Everybody knows everybody's business. Call me when you leave." And so it is in the real Bahamas: friendly, trusting, honest people who have so far

Bonefish have an undiscerning appetite and feed on almost anything they can get into their mouths. Bahamas bonefish are no exception. They enjoy almost every known food source in a wide range of habitat. This sand and grass habitat attracts various other species, too! Be prepared.

Imagine walking barefoot in the sand while chasing bonefish on Abaco Island in the Bahamas. How lucky can you be?

managed to escape the drudgery and excess encumbrances that plague much of the world. Hopefully, you'll appreciate bonefishing and the easy-does-it pace in the Bahamas.

History

Arawak Indians, called Lucayans, met Christopher Columbus when he landed in the Bahamas on October 12, 1492, somewhere in the vicinity of San Salvador Island, the exact location being a point of contention. Columbus was searching for China and the Indies. The Lucayans are believed to have emigrated to the Bahamas around the 8th century A.D. The Spanish explorer Ponce de Leon visited the Bahamas in his futile search for the fountain of youth. His historian described the water as *bajamar* (pronounced *bahamar),* Spanish for shallow water, hence the name Bahamas.

The Spanish subsequently enslaved most of the inhabitants to work the mines in other areas of New Spain. In 1629 England claimed the islands and settled on Eleuthera (from the Greek word for freedom). The crops of the day (cotton, sugar cane, and tobacco) were raised, but corruption soon allowed pirates and their nasty business to flourish. In 1717 Captain Woodes Rogers became the first royal governor of the Bahamas; he cleaned up the lawlessness. Except for a few minor interruptions, such as the capture of Nassau by the U.S. Navy in 1776 and a brief surrender to Spain in 1782, the Bahamas government has been an orderly affair ever since. In 1783 the Spanish signed the Peace of Versailles, ceding the Bahamas to Britain and ending nearly 300 years of disputed ownership.

Following the American Revolution, thousands of Loyalists emigrated to the Bahamas. Many brought their slaves with them. The United Kingdom Emancipation Act of 1834 brought an end to slavery, but it was some time before real equality was achieved. During the Civil War, Nassau became a base for the Confederacy, and trade thrived until the South lost the war. This defeat ended the blockade-running and plunged Nassau into an economic depression. Blockade-running and smuggling once again became good business for the Bahamas during the U.S. Prohibition years. Rumrunners prospered until Prohibition came to an end, once again plunging the Bahamas into an economic depression.

During World War II the Bahamas became a strategic location

for the U.S. military. Today, a Navy installation and missile-tracking stations are located there.

The same secluded islands that sheltered pirates, blockade-runners, and rumrunners sheltered modern-day drug runners. The U.S. Coast Guard, with the aid of the Bahamian government and the latest electronic surveillance equipment, has, for the most part, ended the Bahamas drug trade. Anglers often notice overflights by the Coast Guard. "Fat Albert" blimps, which used to be tethered on long cables, were filled with surveillance equipment and said to be capable of telling what fly pattern you tied onto your leader from miles away.

Since 1973 the Bahamas have been a sovereign state but remain a member of the Commonwealth of Nations with the British monarch as head of state. The Bahamas have a two-house parliament, a ministerial cabinet headed by a prime minister, and an independent judiciary.

Today, no descendants of the Arawak Indians survive. Current residents can trace their ancestry to early English settlers, pirates, U.S. emigrants, and the days of slavery.

The population of the Bahamas is over 200,000. Bahamians are gentle, fun-loving, happy people. Leave Nassau and you leave one Bahamas behind and enter another country where peace and order are the rule. Regardless, when traveling anywhere, stay alert and keep your valuables safe and out of sight. If you have it, don't flaunt it. Every society has its criminals.

Tourism accounts for 70 percent of the country's income. Other income comes from lobstering, farming, and a banking structure that attracts out-of-the-country investors. Plant, bird, and fish life is abundant and attracts many tourists. There are no snakes. Flats

Brian and Randall tussle with a double hookup at Long Island. Many anglers believe, incorrectly, that flats in the Bahamas are soft and not wadeable. There are firm flats at every destination. Anglers wishing to wade can do so.

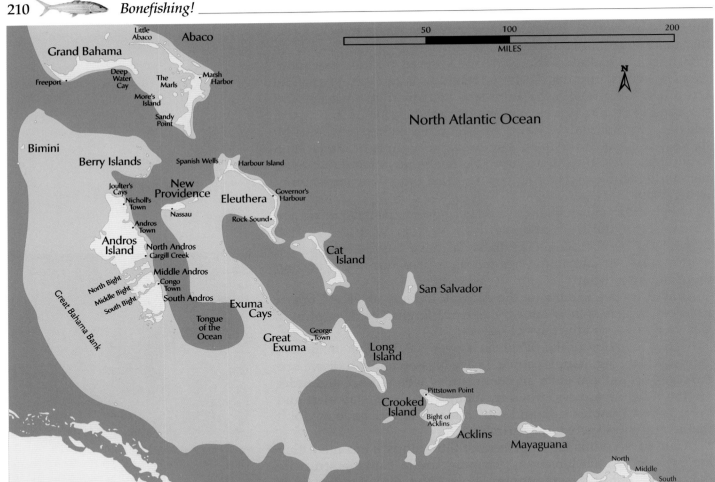

50   100   200
MILES

Little Abaco   Abaco

Grand Bahama

Freeport •   Deep Water Cay   The Marls   • Marsh Harbor

More's Island

Sandy Point

North Atlantic Ocean

Bimini

Berry Islands   Spanish Wells   Harbour Island

Joulter's Cays   **New Providence**   Governor's Harbour

Nicholl's Town   **Eleuthera**

Nassau   Andros Town   Rock Sound •

Andros Island   North Andros
• Cargill Creek   **Cat Island**

North Bight   Middle Andros   • Congo Town   **San Salvador**

Middle Bight   South Andros

South Bight   South Andros

Great Bahama Bank   Tongue of the Ocean   **Exuma Cays**

Great Exuma   George Town

Long Island

Pittstown Point

Crooked Island   Bight of Acklins

Acklins   **Mayaguana**

North   Middle   South

West Caicos   **Caicos**   **Turks**

CUBA

Great Inagua

The Bahamas are only 75 miles from Florida and offer anglers from the states easy access to some of the best bonefishing to be found. Guides and accommodations are plentiful, and air service is easily arranged. Yacht anglers can explore seldom-visited waters on a continual basis.

anglers will see various species of herons and egrets, plus spoonbills and frigate birds. Mosquitoes and no-see-ums are sometimes a problem, especially when the wind goes to bed, so pack repellent.

Geography

This stunning archipelago lies scattered over 500 miles of shallow emerald seas. The northern end of the chain begins about 75 miles west of Palm Beach, Florida, at Grand Bahama Island and continues for about 500 miles in a southeasterly direction to Great Inagua Island about 75 miles from Cuba. Geographically, the Turks and Caicos Islands are part of the Bahamas, but they are under different political jurisdiction. There are said to be over 700 islands and 2,400 cays, most of which are tiny and uninhabited except by the high tide, mangroves, and hermit crabs. A casual glance at a map reveals about 18 major islands. Total land area is estimated at 5,000 square miles, but 70,000 square miles of shoal water provide the most extensive bonefish flats in the world.

Cat Island holds the elevation record of 208 feet, but most islands and cays are less than 10 feet above sea level. In sharp contrast, the narrow Tongue of the Ocean between Andros and the Exumas is 5,000 feet deep. Many of the most extensive flats occur in bights or adjacent to shallow channels that weave through small clusters of islands or separate larger land masses. Other shallow areas are predominantly located on the southwest sides of the islands, with deeper water along the northeast shores.

Travel

You need a passport to enter the Bahamas. The legal tender is the Bahamian dollar, which is on par with the U.S. dollar. Both are accepted. Resorts usually accept cash or traveler's checks. Many do not handle credit cards or personal checks. In the British tradition, some restaurants and resorts request that you dress for dinner (sport coats for men). If you did not pack one, the restaurant or resort can sometimes supply one. Check before you make reservations.

Many visitors find the interisland airline, Bahamas Air, to be woefully unreliable. Book well in advance, confirm your reservations, and arrive early. It is common for flights to depart early or not at all. If the worst happens, use a private charter. Many resorts have private air strips, and a private charter offers quick, relatively inexpensive, and hassle-free travel from the mainland or between islands.

Food

The Bahamians have borrowed culinary delights from most of the world, and you may need to extend your belt during your stay. When it is in season (August to April), the lobster is wonderful, but grouper, snapper, dorado, ahi (yellowfin), and marlin vie for your dining attention. Tropical fruits are plentiful, and the rum drinks can seriously impede your fishing skills. All resorts have potable drinking water, and I have never had any problem except for a bad bout with food poisoning from the Nassau airport. Use common sense when outside resorts, but, for the most part, the food and drink are safe.

Bahamian cuisine ranges all over the spectrum—everything from lobster bisque and crêpe suzette to meatloaf-like bonefish balls. Conch (pronounced *konk)* is the white meat from those beautiful deep-pink snail shells that are commonly seen in photographs, sold in curio stores, neatly aligned along walkways, and piled high in every village. This "snail of the sea" is served as a snack, hors d'oeuvres, salad, soup, chowder, sandwich, steak, fries (fritters), and, probably, an aphrodisiac. It reminds me of abalone, and the salad or seviche are especially tasty. If you don't like it, you may go hungry on more than one occasion during your Bahamian visit because, in one form or another, it is served with almost every meal.

Paul Bruun is based in Jackson Hole, Wyoming, where he writes for the award-winning newspaper, *The Jackson Hole News.* A renowned storyteller and connoisseur of fine cuisine (especially hot sauces and wines), Paul never travels too far from good food and has never gone hungry in the Bahamas or anywhere else! In the following short story, Paul searches for tasty foods and his fly line.

Hey, wait a minute. We've got plenty! One more and we might not get back!

Conch and Kalik—standard evening fare in the Bahamas.

Angler Brian Jarvis with a typical Bahama bonefish at Andros Island.

Whew—who cares if we don't see any fish? Let's feel the sand beneath our feet and gaze at the colors. Maybe we can go for a swim and drift with the tide. Let's go!

The Flavor of Bonefishing
By Paul Bruun

Bonefishing has assumed more complexity than in the 1950s when I was a youngster growing up in South Florida. A 30 h.p. Johnson, six-gallon Cruise-A-Day gas tank, and a 15½-foot fiberglass skiff regularly bounced my buddies and me down to "the flats" and back home with fumes to spare. Today, sleeker, quicker skiffs can reproduce the same experience in more comfort and in a fraction of the time. Struggling with Miami's constant automobile and boat traffic still tarnishes my personal excitement.

Every year bonefishing becomes more of a traveling game. The Florida Keys, Bahamas, Caribbean, and newly discovered Pacific atolls beckon. I still sometimes wonder why I go to all that trouble when my old haunts around Soldier's Key, Sands Cut, the Featherbeds, and Elliott Key in lower Biscayne Bay still offer opportunities for double-digit silver speedsters.

The adventure of bonefishing improves when spiced by the flavor of a foreign country. Perhaps it's the martini-clear water with satisfying wading opportunities over endless white sand flats. You're free of jet skis and commercial jets throbbing overhead. Perhaps it's the unlimited casting targets provided by great schools of prowling fish. Perhaps I simply enjoy amusing the natives by dressing in outrageously colored flats-wear ensembles I'd never dream of wearing around home.

Foreign guides usually introduce a certain appeal. They can be primitive yet sophisticated. Many can see better without Polaroids than I ever believed possible. Their excitement is contagious, especially when excitable situations cause their instructions to become totally incomprehensible. They can become discouraged just as quickly when casts are bungled or fish refuse to strike. Their antique brand of personality differs from the polished and professional competence delivered by shallow-water Florida guides. By turning the clock back to a kinder, gentler time, a foreign trip simplifies what we've somehow escalated into *the business* of bonefishing.

I realize now that on my last several foreign bonefishing outings I sought a different satisfaction than just nabbing fish. For instance, immediately after escaping customs, I pitched into a detailed analysis of chilled local beverages until I found *the* perfect beer. This was as mandatory as rearranging my tackle bags. With the cold drink job semicomplete, my next task was finding a market to examine local hot sauces, limes, peppers, and fruits. I have a limited understanding of geography, but analysis thus far indicates that bonefish are frequently found in areas where rum is popular. So investigating the trip-enhancing potential of fermented sugar cane products is as imperative as checking the tides.

Many veteran bonefish camp guests eagerly seek their guides even before locating their rooms and measuring the height of the rod-tip-crunching ceiling fans. I'll delay such important details in order to pay a cordial visit to the lodge kitchen and a chat with the staff. Once I memorize the nightly entree schedule, I'll know which evenings demand to an early arrival for the joys of grouper, pork, and lobster.

It doesn't take an epicure to recognize that most tropical lunches surpass my normal U.S. fare of bread separated by Louis Rich reduced-fat turkey pastrami, mushy Seven-Eleven sandwiches, or Tom's peanut butter crackers. In the Caribbean, a little kitchen searching usually uncovers an addicting treasure. This camp staple is a mouth-warming mixture assembled from chopped cabbage, *habañero* peppers, cloves, and vinegar. This spicy concoction miraculously zips up everything from cold fish and raw conch to even the dullest sandwich. Gentle coaxing often wrangles a personalized jar of the mixture plus leftover dinner meats for supremely civilized skiff consumption.

When the old Belize City public market was open, I eagerly grabbed a few handfuls of fresh *habañeros*, papayas, mammy fruit, and limes to stuff in my tackle bag. I'd snoop around the back where turtles were sometimes butchered and marvel at how the hearts keep pumping long after being separated from the remaining body. I never missed a chance to stock up on spices, jars of original Melinda's Hot Sauce, and extra liters of inexpensive Durley's and Caribbean rums to haul home. Return airport trips often are so hurried that last minute shopping is lost in the rush.

In addition to fine eating, my foreign bonefishing trips seem to revolve around unplanned adventures. Combinations of broken outboards and tackle add memories that I can later turn into delightful articles and columns.

Once, a malfunctioning outboard lower unit totally disappeared. Taku, our thoughtful guide, rigged a giant Hefty trash bag between a crossed mast of my fishing rods. Rather than drifting, we actually sailed for help.

When my overstuffed suitcase aboard a runaway baggage cart

A bonefish reflects silver in the late evening sun. Dusk can be a wonderful time to be on the water.

Don't forget to put your face under the water! There is more to bonefishing than catching bonefish.

Raz Reid gets spooled in the Berry Islands. Don't make the mistake of believing that your single action reel is good enough for bonefish. Eight-weight, even 9-weight, rods are mandatory in the Bahamas because you never know when a double-digit fish may clean you out. Just ask Raz.

Time out! Brew pub, Bahamas style.

Rum and hot sauce—the breakfast of bonefishermen.

vaulted off a dock runway, it took three of us to haul its bloated contents out of the water. Back in Miami, a friend's house was brilliantly decorated with drying flies, clothing, and tackle for days afterward. The plunge silenced my travel alarm, quieted a portable radio, and swamped numerous fresh spices.

The most exciting foreign bonefishing trip I *never* made was my carefully planned Christmas Island trip with a group of long-time Jackson Hole angling pals. My outing came to a breathless halt in Hawaii even before it started when I was felled by pneumonia.

Chasing bonefish anywhere is a game of numerous rewards. Locating the fish, making a good cast, and savoring the sound of a whirring drag as line disappears from the reel are only the beginning. One day I dumbly watched as a brand-new fly line disappeared behind a hooked fish. At first I thought my carefully crafted line-to-backing knot had failed. While reeling in, I noticed several feet of running fly line were still attached to my backing. The fly line itself had broken.

'Don't worry, Mister Paul," my guide, Roy, comforted. "We catch up with that line." And we did because, without any rod pressure, the fish stopped. As Roy poled up to the line I grabbed it, only to have it break again as the fish raced off on another run.

"We get him," I was assured. However, after 15 or 20 more minutes of poling an expansive bay and adjacent flats, I accepted defeat. Then I saw the line limply floating in the distance. As we got closer, I used the topwater plug on my casting rod to snag the line. After breaking off more of the weakened running line, I whipped a nail knot to the backing and finally landed the determined adversary.

"Mr. Paul, you done fought that same bonefish three times!" Roy puffed.

"You're absolutely right. Now, you need a break. Let's eat!"

"You right about that," he grinned.

I'd slipped a batch of cold lobster tails and *habañero* magic into our cooler that morning along with the sandwiches. I like to add a little more to bonefishing than you read about in the magazines.

Paul Bruun
Jackson, Wyoming
December 1997

Hundreds of square miles of deserted flats await anglers in the Bahamas. It is rare to encounter another angler. These anglers work a combination coral, grass, and sand flat in Abaco.

Weather

During the northern winter, every angler dreams about escaping the cold, dreary days that drag the human psyche into the doldrums of hibernation. The southern attractions are obvious: the allure of warm sunshine, clear waters teeming with bonefish, cocktails by the sea, and breezy star-filled nights. Who wouldn't exchange the snow shovel for the fly rod? If you live and work in any northern city, an escape to the Bahamas is like an other world experience. Leave your topcoat, cell phone, mace, and aggressive manner behind. Bring your sunscreen, appetite, fly rod, and a smile. No grouches are allowed.

Located roughly between 22 and 27 degrees north latitude, the Bahamas are semitropical. There is some mean temperature variation between the northern and southern islands, but, overall, the climate is mild. Temperatures seldom drop below 60 degrees Fahrenheit or rise above 90 degrees. A look at the official government average temperature and rainfall chart, for Nassau, on the following page shows you what to expect.

Weather is a major determining factor when planning a bonefishing trip to the Bahamas. I have enjoyed very good fishing every month during the winter, but I have also encountered rainstorms, cool water temperatures, and wind. Water temperatures can momentarily fall below the acceptable range for bonefish when a cold front drops down from the north. This is possible anytime from December through mid-March. January and February can be very good if a cold front has not driven fish into deeper water. Even so, anglers can sometimes head farther south and find plenty of fish in the shallows. Conversely, during the summer head a bit north to escape a little of the heat.

Water temperatures can temporarily rise above acceptable limits from mid-June through September. Anglers fishing during these times should expect the possibility of fewer fish and may need to modify their fishing times to take advantage of cooler tidal periods. The most consistent fishing months are late October through mid-December and mid-March through mid-June.

Hurricanes are infrequent in the Bahamas, but the official season is June through November. Satellite forecasters generally give adequate warnings, and every television set in the country is

January weather at Fernandez Bay Village, Cat Island.

A combination of mangrove, grass and marl is a good bet for big bones.

Important thoughts of a bone fisherman. "Looks like a good flat; let's check it out! Jeez, this beer sure hits the spot. Conch fritters for dinner! I might never go home."

perpetually tuned to the many Miami stations. You can obtain current weather conditions by calling the National Weather Service, which is listed in the phone directory under the U.S. Department of Commerce, or check their web site.

The Bahamas are perfectly situated to receive the effect of the Gulf Stream, which is one of the most powerful of all the ocean currents. At its peak off the coast of Florida, the stream runs about six miles per hour and is about 3,000 feet deep. It carries warm, nutrient-rich equatorial waters past the Bahamas and eventually becomes the warm benefactor for Europe. Prevailing trade winds, like the Gulf Stream, come from the southeast. Local winds are generated by cooler air over the ocean colliding with warmer air rising over land masses, which creates gusty winds 10 to 20 miles per hour, sometimes reaching 30 miles per hour. During the warmest summer days (July through September), winds sometimes cease, and the humidity becomes almost unbearable.

Average Temperature (°F) and Rainfall (Inches)—Nassau				
Month	Average Low	Average High	Average Temperature	Average Rainfall In Inches	Days Without Rain
January	65	77	70	1.9	25
February	64	77	70	1.6	23
March	66	79	72	1.4	26
April	69	81	75	1.9	24
May	71	84	77	4.8	22
June	71	87	80	9.2	18
July	75	88	81	6.1	17
August	76	89	82	6.3	17
September	75	88	81	7.5	15
October	73	85	78	8.3	18
November	70	81	74	2.3	21
December	67	79	71	1.5	25

Fishing

The Bahamas have a well-deserved reputation for being one of the premier angling destinations in the world. Few places can match Bahamian angling for the variety of gamefish available on a year-around basis or for accommodations for visiting anglers. Bluewater species include white and blue marlin, sailfish, yellowfin tuna, king and cero mackerel, wahoo, dorado (mahi-mahi), oceanic bonito, grouper, snapper, and many more. Some permit and tarpon are available and jacks, snapper, and 'cuda are plentiful.

The Bahamas are a bonefishing mecca. Nowhere else in the world are there so many accessible flats with such great numbers of bonefish. The Bahamas are also *the* place to catch large bonefish. Most saltwater anglers sum up their first trip to the Bahamas by saying, "I thought I had fished bonefish before, but I hadn't!" It could only be better if the Bahamas were located astride the equator. For anglers who have access to a yacht and a flats boat, the Bahamas are paradise. There is no other place in the world where you can fish a different unfished location day after day. Sailors anchor at the edge of flats and scout with skiffs. It's the life.

Many anglers believe, incorrectly, that Bahamian flats are soft and must be fished from a boat. While there are many soft flats, there are an equal number of firm, wade-able areas. Anglers who desire to wade fish can find ample areas, but fishing from a boat is usually more productive because you have better visibility and mobility. The drawback, of course, is that only one angler can fish at a time. I often prefer to spot and watch because I learn more that way.

John Randolph is the editor of *Fly Fisherman* magazine. His travels have taken him to distant lands for many species of fish. Bonefish are still his favorite, and he is just doing his job when he travels to bonefish country. Following are some remembrances of fishing the Bahamas that convey the ambiance of stalking the "silver sides."

On the Flats
By John Randolph

When I was a boy—in the '50s—my father wrote the "Wood, Field and Stream" outdoor column for *The New York Times*. His work took him to Andros Island in the Bahamas on assignment to cover the bonefishing at a place called the Lighthouse Club, a new watering spot for jet set sportsmen. At Andros I first tasted bonefishing on a fly with world famous angler Lee Wulff. That's a little like taking batting practice with Babe Ruth, thrilling but intimidating.

Forty-five years later, I can still recall the cooing of wild pigeons from the pines bordering flats that shimmered in Bahamian azure. My hands still tremble with the anticipation of fins flashing, backlit by the sun, where tailers nose their way happily up a bank like children frolicking across a pasture. My eyes ache pleasantly with the strain of searching for telltale signs—a ripple here, a distant splash heard faintly there, a shadow on white sand, or gray slivers in a ghostly geometric pattern moving my way. I know the lonely longings of the flats fisherman, for on Andros I was introduced to them when the whole world was young and new and I had set out to discover it with a fishing rod.

Bonefishing remains an adventure of discovery for me to this day. It has changed, too. Today, it's enough to be there where the fish are. I am more the voyeur than I was then, when I was a pure hunter. Now the flats dramas are as much my meat as the fish.

At Sandy Point on Great Abaco, a morning ocean breeze riffles the palm fronds as you stand on a waterfront porch and look out past the wet street leading to the dock and the bay beyond. Once on the flats, you can be off on your own, stalking schools of bones here and there until your calves and thighs burn with fatigue, and

When presenting flies on flats with a mixture of grass and sand, it is often best to place the fly over sand where it has less chance of snagging and a better chance of being seen.

Larger bonefish in the Bahamas are often found in deep water and in soft mucky habitat. When such is the case, flies should sink quickly, and they can seldom be too big. "Big flies, big fish" is a useful axiom. Don't forget to include a few snapper, jack, barracuda, and permit flies.

Sharks are fascinating to observe and always stir your imagination. Lemon sharks (or any other species this size) are best avoided and observed from the boat. Don't allow sharks to make a meal of a hooked bonefish. If sharks are present, either frighten them off or fish some other place. If they do pursue your hooked fish, break it off as soon as possible.

you long for a Kalik beer that has raised beads of sweat on the glass.

Standing on a long flat with a guide one day, I spotted something that didn't fit the flats karma. "What's that up there, Richard? Is that a school of bonefish?"

"I don't know, mon. If it be bonefish, they be beeg bonefish."

"Let's have a look."

We eased forward some 200 yards up the sandy bottom and into a shallow lagoon. Ripples marked a spot where a school of fish circled first this way and then that way like a mob of sheep being herded by a border collie.

"Look at those two lemon sharks, Richard! They're herding those bonefish as though they were captives. Why don't those fish just swim away?"

Richard wasn't saying much. He was watching intently, taking a short step now and then toward the melee of bonefish and sharks.

They swam as though in a slow-motion *tableau vivant* of predator and prey, each mesmerized by the close presence of the other. It was a slow predator/prey cheek-to-cheek dance there in front of us. We wondered how would it end.

The minuet continued, with the large lemon first attempting a rush and a bite and then the small one lunging heavily and unsuccessfully at this bonefish and that. The bones swam languidly, circling around the sharks this way and then that way at what seemed perilously close range, two feet from the teeth that had for eons chomped their kin and kind.

Sharks are inherently cowards. As I approached, the big lemon shot off and up the flat, followed by his partner in crime. The bonefish school moved away, gathering speed and confidence as it went. We stood there watching. Then, from somewhere on the side, a large barracuda knifed in a flank attack on the school. Fish fled this upside-down and sideways in panic, and one shot into the air. The flat turned red and brown with blood and mud.

In an instant it was all over. The school of bones sped up the flat, and I could see their bow wave until they slowed and settled into the normal rythm of the flats as the tide slowly reclaimed the shallows where they would feed.

This is what is important to me now. I am aware of the sharks that prowl the flats on the hunt for bonefish for their next meal. I am more concerned about the welfare of the bones I stalk than I am about catching them. I am worried that I will hook that double-digit bone of a lifetime and, while the fish is tethered by my line, a blacktip or lemon will hear the thumping or the thrum of the struggling fish and race in and chomp before I can pull back and break off.

It happened innocently enough. I had been stalking the sweetest school of big, black-backed bones I'd ever seen near Gorda Cay in the Bahamas. They wouldn't let me get within casting range. Like a pack of coy cheerleaders, they kept edging away just out of casting range. They'd angle this way and I'd lose them in the late afternoon glare. Then I'd spot them again farther up the flat. I'd stalk and then rest and look, shading my eyes from the glare that made my skin burn. My back ached with the fatigue of bending to look, my knees slightly bent in anticipation of the moving school and the need to make a fast shot ahead of them. Why wouldn't they settle down and feed?

Almost as an aside, an afterthought, I caught a movement

Bonefish this size can run for a mile if you hook them on foot.

A great day for spotting tails, V wakes, and nervous water. Abacos, Bahamas.

Bonefish inhabit a transparent world of liquid colors that capture the imagination of everyone who visits. Note the dark stripes across the back. Besides taking on the color of their surroundings, bonefish exhibit stripes when they are tired or stressed.

ahead and to my left. A five-foot black-tip eased my way, moving in that languid shark motion that makes them look indolent, even stupid. He kept coming.

I looked for the school of double-digit bonefish. There. They had moved up the flat and were slowly turning, moving closer, returning obliquely along the mangrove edge. I glanced sideways at the shark.

He stopped at about 50 feet and then came on deliberately as though curious about the sound of my wading. I did not move. I fixed him then with an intent, frozen glare. He lumbered slowly toward me.

At 12 feet I began to whomp the water with my rod. It had always worked in the past. This time it didn't. He halted momentarily, but, without evident concern, then came on, still slowly. . .deliberately.

I beat the water more emphatically. No dice. After a pause, he advanced, cautiously, suspiciously. I poked the rod under water and hit him with the tip. He stopped and seemed to consider his situation for the first time, as if to say, "What is this thing that does not flee but pokes me in the nose? Is this something to eat or not?"

He tried an advance again, and I poked him hard in the face. I was willing to sacrifice a $500 rod to save myself. I thought about my next move if the rod trick failed. If he attacked, I could jump over his back, an old Keys guide trick.

The black-tip tried to approach once more. This time, at about three feet, I hit him with the butt of the rod. He halted and then began slowly to move away, stopping to look back and then moving off again. I watched him a long time. I gave no thought to the school of big bones. I returned to Richard at the boat. Shaken.

"What he do out dare, mon?"

It was a while before I answered.

So it goes on the flats. I am a voyeur and somewhat of an adventurer. I am less an adventurer now. More of a voyeur. Come to me, you big bones!

John Randolph
Editor/Publisher
Fly Fisherman *Magazine*
Harrisburg, Pennsylvania
May 16, 1997

Abacos

Located about 175 miles east of Miami and 75 miles north of Nassau, the Abacos lure divers, sailors, and anglers searching for a lifestyle that has disappeared from most of the world. Little and Great Abaco islands form a crescent around Great Bahama Island, and the northern tip of Little Abaco is known as the tip of the Bahamas. The two islands are narrow and about 130 miles long with a scattering of cays located both on the inside and outside of the land mass. The outside cays face the deep water—Africa is the next land east. The inside cays lie in the Little Bahama Bank and offer some of the best shallow-water bonefish habitat.

The area from Cooper's Town to Sandy Point includes about 100 square miles of bonefish flats that are punctuated with hundreds of tiny islets. Treasure Cay is located near the midpoint. South of Bluff Point is an intriguing 300-square-mile area of remote mangrove islands known as The Marls. This secluded area offers thousands of aggressive bonefish that weigh between two and three pounds, some to seven or eight pounds.

From Cooper's Town west are many hard, wadeable flats, some with dense beds of turtle grass and bonefish that average three to five pounds. The top of the land mass drops south and breaks up into many small cays (including Cave, Cross, Daniel's, and Smith) with extensive flats offering some bonefish over 10 pounds. Some of these flats are wadeable, but many are not.

Many of the Bahamians who live here are descendants from Loyalists and pirates who once headquartered in the Abacos. An estimated 500 Spanish galleons sank in this region, and locals tell stories of occasionally finding gold doubloons (coins of Spain and Spanish America, circa 1600-1625) on the beach. Today, these

Bonefish flats tend to calm the spirit and soothe the soul.

Grand Bahama, left, and Abaco, right. The western end of Grand Bahama Island is located a scant 60 miles due east of West Palm Beach, Florida. Direct charter and scheduled flights offer easy access to this fabulous bonefish country. The Marls can be seen at the extreme right center off the western coast of Abaco. On the east coast are Marsh Harbor and Cherokee Sound. Sandy Point is the left point at the southern end of Abaco. Follow the shallow water to More's Island, halfway between Abaco and Grand Bahama. Continue to a group of islands divided by channels at the eastern end of Grand Bahama. This is the location of Deep Water Cay. Continue to the bulge of land to locate Freeport.

NASA

Miles of wadeable flats await anglers at Andros Island. This habitat could produce bones, permit, and jacks.

Zillions of bones scatter at our feet. North Bight, Andros Island.

islands mine their own treasure from underwater enthusiasts as the Abacos are the second-most-visited islands in the Bahamas, behind only New Providence (Nassau-Paradise Island). Accommodations are excellent, and some good guides are available.

Sandy Point on the south end of the island group offers some excellent angling along the southwest point on nearby wadable flats that have plenty of bones in the three- to five-pound range, some larger. Offshore at More's Island there are some very fine flats and bonefish, but ocean conditions have to be right. Closer in is Gorda Cay, a beautiful piece of tropical paradise with a small mangrove lagoon on the north end, a miniature bay fronting deep water on the west, and a small sand beach with coconut trees and a sloping shoreline on the east. It is a perfect castaway island. That is precisely why Disney bought the island and turned it into its Caribbean cruise ship resort called Castaway Island. Big permit and bonefish frequent the area, and some very fine mutton snapper action is available during their spring mating. This area of Abaco is for serious bone fisherman and is probably the best place to land a Bahamas grand slam—a permit, bone, and mutton snapper in the same day. Late April through mid June is the best time for a shot at all three species.

Andros Island

Andros Island is located 170 miles southeast of Miami and 30 miles west of Nassau. The largest of the Bahamas Islands, it is 100 miles long by 40 miles wide. Its mostly flat 2,300-square-mile surface is inhabited by about 5,000 people who live along the east coast for the most part. Andros is actually divided into three main land masses: North, Middle, and South Andros. At the end of the road on North Andros, arrangements can be made with local boatmen to take you south to Mangrove Cay (Middle Bight). Free government ferries transport you between Mangrove Cay and South Andros.

North Andros is easy to reach with daily 15-minute flights from Nassau to both Andros Town and San Andros (Nicoll's Town). There are also some flights to Congo Town on South Andros, and there is a small airstrip at Mangrove Cay. Flights can be erratic. Also, be certain you know where you are going and have all necessary connections nailed down, or you could find yourself temporarily stuck where you do not want to be. Rental cars are scarce; getting off the airplane and driving to an intended destination is not always possible. Accommodations and guides range from fair to excellent.

Andros Island has more wilderness flats and big bonefish than anywhere else in the Bahamas. The North Bight (a bight is a bay-like channel in the Bahamas) forms one edge of an immense interior archipelago whose erratic edge cuts through the entire width of Andros Island. It eventually merges with the Middle Bight to the south and forms hundreds of beautiful flats that nearly defy description. Nowhere have I seen a more captivating collection of cream-colored flats superimposed with every color in the tropical rainbow. Every flat and smoothly contoured island edge bombards the senses with so much visual pleasure that you forget the bonefish and want to stop and absorb the beauty.

North of Fresh Creek to Nicholl's Town is a wide variety of inside and outside flats, creeks, and mangrove lagoons that produce some excellent action for the few anglers who visit. Off the north coast from Lowe Sound to Rum Cay are 20 miles of clean white sand flats known as the Joulters' Cays.

The interior of Andros is one of the largest unexplored tracts of land in North America. It is riddled with fresh water, brackish water, saltwater ponds, and channels. Access is limited, but some interesting fishing is possible for those willing to go the extra mile.

Accommodations on Andros are good to excellent. Bonefishing is steeped in history here and almost everyone from taxi drivers to school children take fly fishing very seriously. Some of the best bonefish operations and guides in the Bahamas are found on Andros. All other considerations aside, Bahamas anglers searching for a shot at big fish while fishing with great guides in a diverse landscape can't do much better than Andros Island.

I once asked Sydney, a veteran guide at the famous Andros Island Bonefish Club, how many flats there are in this area. He replied, "Everywhere you go there are flats. Yes, everywhere. I ain't seen them all yet. Bonefish come from all directions." The variety of flats is limitless, and many are beautiful pure-white sand. Big Wood Cay alone offers miles of sand, and big bones cruise toward the shallow shoreline in pairs and small pods. Other flats offer mud and grass bottoms, and escape from the wind is nearly always possible. The South Bight is not as extensive but it, too, offers plenty of fishing to keep a smile on your face.

It takes an hour to boat from the east end of Andros to the west end through the Middle Bight. Once on the western shoreline, you face the Great Bahama Bank and the Gulf Stream. The ocean tapers into a narrow band of shallow water fairly quickly, which gives way to mucky mangroves, lakes, and swampy areas that are like a mini-Everglades. To the north and south are over 50 miles of some of the greatest bonefish waters. Numerous small creeks and "holes" sometimes hide tarpon and many other feisty species too numerous to mention. Because of its secluded nature, resort operators usually fish at least two boats in case of engine trouble. This is as close to wilderness bonefishing as you can get without having your own yacht and flats boat.

Every angler who has fished the Middle Bight or the west coast of Andros has a fish tale. Anglers tell of getting 15-pound, even 20-pound bonefish to eat their fly and setting up hard on them four or five times before the fish just spit out the hook. They talk about losing fly line and 250 yards of backing on the first run. They don't call this country the land of giants for nothing!

We recently motored into the Bang Bang Club to talk to legendary guide Charlie Smith, who was working on reopening the once-famous club. Charlie told us about the colliding currents that bring super bonefish into the area and gave me a couple of his original Charlie patterns. We were hoping to continue on to the west coast, but weather conditions were not right. Because of prevailing winds, the west coast is generally best February through August; the east coast October through January.

The east shoreline of Andros Island is paralleled by the second-longest *underwater* barrier reef in the world. The reef

This spectacular view of Andros Island clearly demonstrates why it is one of the premier bonefishing destinations. The north, middle, and south bights divide the island, creating an incredible amount of interior flats. The west coast is unpopulated and remote. This shoreline graduates from mangrove marsh to the fertile Great Bahama Bank. Much of this shoreline is a perfect example of beach flats. There is no reef, surf is relatively light, and the water gradually deepens. The Joulter's Cays are visible in the northeast corner. The dark blue water along the east coast is the Tongue of the Ocean, whose currents continually rejuvenate and refresh. This entire picture spells bonefish.

NASA

Bonefish live in water that is often as clear as the air. Note the physical characteristics—scale pattern, color, shape, flattened head, eye placement, and its shadow. Beautiful creatures, bonefish.

The Berrys are little more than sand dunes poking above the surface of the ocean. Some of the most extensive sand flats in the Bahamas are found here.

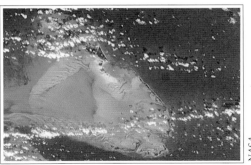

drops vertically over a mile into the Tongue of the Ocean, which is 140 miles long. It is the playground of innumerable sea creatures and a favorite haunt of American submarines. The east shoreline offers some very fine flats, including those of Fresh Creek. Many of these flats are within sight of Autec Navy Base. Some are wadeable; others are not. There are two blue holes (deep oceanic wells) in Fresh Creek that might offer a shot at tarpon, but, in general, the Bahamas do not have consistent tarpon fishing. However, many of the back country interior waters offer fantastic baby tarpon action plus many other species that have never tasted steel.

Berry Islands

Beginning 35 miles northwest of Nassau and 150 miles east of Miami, this 30-island chain extends in a western and then northern arc for about 25 miles. The Berry Islands are at the east end of the Great Bahama Bank and at the top of the Tongue of the Ocean. These islands are removed from the normal tourist route, and many are private.

Great Harbour Cay is the largest in the chain. Its 3,800 rolling acres of rock and scrub have been the haunt of the rich and famous.

There is a golf course, a marina, a great beach, and waterfront accommodations. About 500 people live on the island, which is about eight miles long and 1½ miles wide. There isn't much of a town—a small grocery, condos, and a couple of restaurants. Hooking an occasional bonefish from the beach is possible, and huge, beautiful flats are located just to the south. Some large bonefish can be hooked in this area.

Chub Cay is the only Berry Islands spot with civilization as we know it. It is located at the southern end of the Berries. Bluewater fishing in this area is world famous, and Chub Cay has been an exclusive retreat of the jet set big game angling crowd.

There are some decent bonefish haunts. As with elsewhere in the Bahamas, be certain you have reservations before you embark. Accommodations and transportation are not always available, and the local bonefish guide may be off diving for lobster or conch.

Angler wades Infinity Flats, also known as Lonesome Flats, in the Berrys.

Bahamas Special—a favorite with big bonefish hunters.

Water fills the mangroves on a high tide, then rushes out on the ebb. Bonefish ride the wave both directions. Be patient and wait. This is the perfect place at the perfect time.

Bimini

Located 50 miles off the Florida coast, Bimini is at the point where the Gulf Stream meets the Bahama Banks. It is the self-proclaimed big game fishing capital of the world, a past rum-running capital, and the place where the legendary fountain of youth supposedly flowed. Ernest Hemingway came here to fish and write *Islands in the Stream* and much of *To Have and Have Not*. This 7½-mile-long hook-shaped island covers only nine square miles, but there are numerous accommodations, restaurants, and happy-hour establishments that cater to the drinking and carousing fishing crowd. Some very good guides are also here.

There is not a great deal of bonefish water available, but some very large fish have been landed over the years, including both the 12-pound and the four-pound line-class world records, both 15 pounders. Local guides like to tell stories of seeing 20-pound fish. March and April seem to be the best months to hook the big boys. Some fishable flats are adjacent to the island, but the classic fishing takes place on the Big Flat, which extends from the hook point of North Bimini to the shore of South Bimini. Most of the fish are two-pound schoolies, but big fish are a possibility. Be advised that these fish have doctorates in bonefish flies and have probably seen more of them than you have.

Cat Island

Cat Island is located midway down the Bahamas archipelago, about halfway between Eleuthera and Crooked islands and 130 miles southeast of Nassau. It is about 50 miles long and averages about two miles wide. The highest point in the Bahamas, Mt. Alvernia, towers 208 feet above the Atlantic surf. Father Jerome, one of the century's great ecclesiastical architects, came here to live out his final years and built a small hermitage on this peak.

Many claim Cat Island offers the best beaches. It certainly has some of the most secluded and deserted stretches of inviting sand. Tall cliffs provide a spectacular scene along the east coast that is second to none in the Bahamas.

Cat Island is off the tourist circuit, and its 2,000 inhabitants depend on fishing and farming. Electricity only arrived in the early 1990s. (Crooked and Acklins still do not have electricity but should shortly.) Another Cat Island distinction is that it has the only clothes optional resort in the Bahamas.

To land fish in the shortest possible time, keep the rod low to the water and off to either side. This fish is being pulled off balance sideways. As the fish reaches the 12 o'clock position in front of the angler, switch the rod angle from right to left, again pulling backwards and sideways on the fish. About the only time the rod should be high overhead is when the fish is moving quickly away and you are not in control.

It is said that the most gifted obeah witches live here. Obeah is the English-speaking Caribbean's answer to voodoo, which is popular in nearby Jamaica and Haiti. Instead of a doll, its prop is a bottle, sometimes empty, often filled with secret liquids and flowers. Visitors see bottles hanging in agricultural areas. These are a warning not to eat the fruit or pick the flowers lest you suffer horribly or even die, especially if the potion is potent.

Ask your guide to share some of the folklore about bonefish. Some stories are funny, others are serious. I heard a story that bonefish like the rain because they like to sip freshwater off the surface of saltwater.

Cat is one of the best outer islands for families. Resorts, such as Fernandez Bay, offer everything—fine dining, canoeing, beach combing, tours of blue holes and bat caves, and snorkeling. You'll see trigger, box, and trumpet fish, beautiful sea fans, sponges, flamingo-teeth shells, spider crabs, and grouper. Blue holes are steeped in legend and folklore. Islanders tell stories of encounters with mystical sea creatures. Guess what you'll see in the bat caves? Swimmers and divers should exercise caution in unfamiliar blue holes. Currents can be treacherous, and it is possible to become disoriented when soft sediment is churned up.

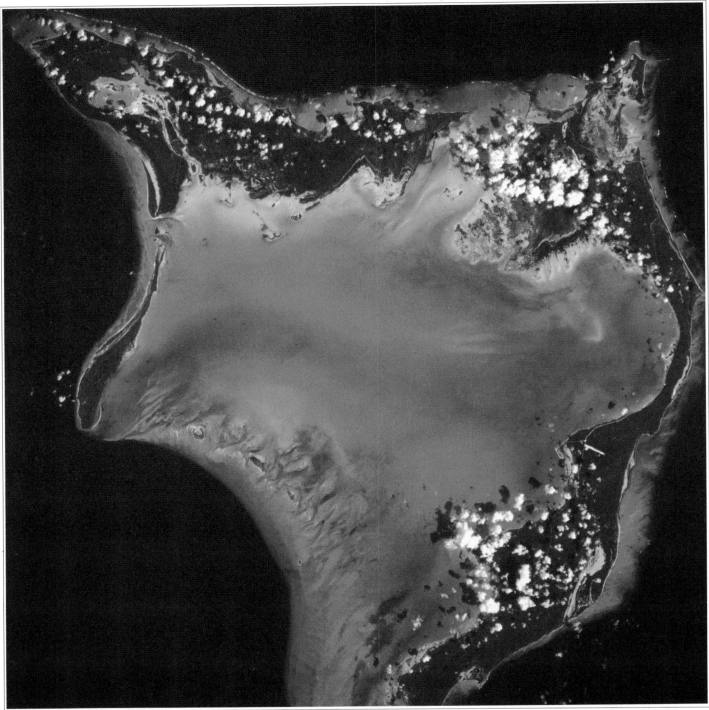

NASA

Crooked Island is at the upper left, with Pittstown Point at the extreme upper left. Fortune Island is immediately south of Crooked Island. Acklins Island extends along the right side of the photo. Salina Point is just out of the picture at lower right. The Bight of Acklins shelters flamingos, permit, jacks, 'cuda, and, yes, bonefish!

Crooked and Acklins Islands

Columbus came this way 500 years ago and landed at what is now Pittstown Point. He became friends with the Taino Indians and set up a temporary base camp. Columbus called it Fragrant Island because of the aroma of its many herbs, including cascarilla bark (used in a local liquor and exported). Rumors of big bones in the Bight of Acklins had finally pulled us to this quiet island 225 miles southeast of Nassau, and we, too, landed at Pittstown Point.

Today, Crooked Island is still remote and quiet enough that the local taxi doesn't bother to meet arriving flights. We had to bum a 20-mile ride in the back of a pickup with a local to reach our

hotel—and we weren't certain if the hotel was open or if any rooms were available.

There are actually three islands—Crooked, Acklins (limited services and accommodations), and Fortune. Together they form 2½ sides of a square. The inside of the bight offers miles of near-virgin flats where we saw more bonefish in two days than in the previous two weeks. Unfortunately, the bones were schooled up and did not provide the fishing we had hoped to find. Big fish were absent, but we were assured by our guide, Robbie, that they exist and usually provide exciting action as singles and doubles crisscross the beautiful sand and mud flats, most of which are wadeable. Subsequent visitors have confirmed this. The disadvantage is that the best flats are 45 to 70 minutes away from accommodations. Guides, transportation, and accommodations are limited.

The Bight of Acklins, as the bay is called, is extensive and very beautiful and a few anglers are making the trip to this relatively remote and unexplored area. It supports good populations of both sea and bird life. Flamingos are often seen. Bonefish (sometimes huge schools of them) of two to 10 pounds swim over clear sandy flats. A shot at an occasional permit is a possibility. The outside reef is inviting for anglers; everything from bonefish to jacks is probable. Jacks are eating machines. If you get a cast to one, it is almost a certain hookup. Reef fishing often requires relatively low surf and tidal conditions. Sand flies and mosquitoes can be an occasional annoyance.

Flats anglers usually have miles of water to themselves. It is an event to see another boat. In the Bight of Acklins.

Eleuthera—Spanish Wells and Harbour Island

One of the most popular islands with tourists, 100-mile-long Eleuthera is 50 miles east of Nassau and has gorgeous quiet beaches and wonderful resorts but only limited bonefishing areas. The east coast is mostly rocky and deep. Even the sheltered inside west coast is too deep to wade, being mostly over 10 feet deep. There is some fishing near Governor's Harbour, but the best flats are reached from St. George's Cay and Harbour Island off the northern tip.

Spanish Wells is located on St. George's Cay a half-mile off the northwest corner of Eleuthera. It is 1½ miles long and a half-mile wide. This was the last stop for Spanish galleons heading home, and crews dug a two-foot well in the sand here, hence the name "Spanish Wells." Ponce de Leon noted his layover day here before returning from his fruitless search for the Fountain of Youth. He at least found water so he could survive to continue to search for the magic fountain.

Fewer than 30 years after the founding of Plymouth, Massachusetts, a group of Puritans fled England and eventually

Jeff Rose and an average-sized Bahamas bonefish.

Hibiscus, bougainvillea, and oleander are common throughout the Bahamas.

Dunmore Town is friendly and one of the prettiest in the Bahamas. Its colorful, well-kept saltbox houses sport white picket fences and beautiful flowers.

Randall Kaufmann, Bonefish Joe Cleare, and Brian O'Keefe at Dunmore Town, circa 1990.

Bahamian 10-cent pieces feature bonefish.

settled on St. George's Cay. The American War of Independence set the stage for the next wave of immigrants (1776-83). Many of these new arrivals wanted to establish a plantation economy, complete with slaves. The religious belief of the established residents would not tolerate this, and, eventually, it became a slave-free colony that was blacklisted and shunned by other islands.

Most of the economy is tied to the lobster trade. One would think that a lobster dinner would be reasonably priced here, but it is not. In general, the food is not what you would hope to find in the Bahamas. The village is neatly manicured and many of the brightly-colored houses (some of which date back 200 years) have beautiful flower gardens. You can walk anywhere, and no one locks up their houses, cars, or valuables.

The fishing? It can be good on the flat off the north beach in front of the hotel for two- to four-pound bonefish if the tide is right. Toward the eastern end of the island, channels apparently allow easy access to bonefish. You'll find both tailing bones and heavy local boat traffic, which does not put down the fish. A lagoon on the north side of Russell Island also offers plenty of fish, but flats are limited in the area. Try the Ragged and Lobster cays and Curry Sound about five miles down the Eleuthera mainland.

Harbour Island lies two miles off the north end of Eleuthera. It is one of the oldest settlements in the Bahamas and was settled before America became a nation. It is perched on the side of a steep hill overlooking the sound. Harbour Island is best known for its broad pink-sand beach that runs the entire length of its three-mile-long eastern shore. The beach is protected from ocean breakers by an outlying coral reef, which makes it one of the safest swimming beaches in the Bahamas. The island is only a half-mile wide.

Harbour Island is a popular destination for couples and families. It provides excellent accommodations, swimming, diving, snorkeling, beach combing, plain relaxing, dining, and fishing. Dunmore Town is friendly and one of the prettiest in the Bahamas. The tropically painted and neatly kept saltbox houses sport white picket fences and beautiful flowers, including bougainvillea, oleander, and hibiscus.

The fishing area is not extensive but runs from Nurse Creek flat to the Dixie Cays, where large (but not stupid) tailing bonefish can be found. Most flats consist of turtle grass and are wadeable. They are close enough to allow you to return to Dunmore Town for lunch if you like. Harbour Island has been a popular bonefishing destination for decades. There are some excellent guides, many of whom have been trained by the legendary Bonefish Joe (Joe Cleare), including his son, Stanley. Bonefish Joe is continually optimistic and cheerful; a day with him is worth the trip. A nonstop talker, Joe entertains you from sunup to sundown and eats lunch with the push pole in his hand.

Stanley M. Babson, who wrote *Bonefishing*, published in 1965, fished with Joe. The Babson home in Dunmore Town is still in the family. The flight from Nassau to North Eleuthera takes about 30 minutes. Then it is a mile ride in a taxi to the ferry dock and a two-mile ferry ride to Dunmore Town.

Exumas

The Exuma chain of islands begins 35 miles south of Nassau and extends southeast for 100 miles. This chain of 350 cays is mostly uninhabited and unspoiled. When viewed from the air, the brilliantly clear water sparkles with dazzling aquamarine colors that turn transparent opal as they wash onto some of the most beautiful beaches in the Bahamas. Nowhere else in the Bahamas are the views so magnetic. Sailors, pilots, and anglers in the know feel the Exumas have it all, except easy access.

As you fly over this enchanting display of land and sea, you can't help but notice the transition zone between the two. This is the area bonefishermen (and beach fanatics) can't take their eyes away from, and it is indeed special. Sand beaches melt into shallow sand flats, which dissolve into multicolored channels and cuts, which ultimately turn into the deepest ocean blue. Shallow waters of the Great Bahama Bank contrast brilliantly with the 5,000-foot-deep cobalt waters of Exuma Sound to the east.

Most anglers visit George Town, which is near the southern terminus of the Exumas. The Tropic of Cancer passes through George Town, as do thousands of tourists. There are great beaches, excellent accommodations, food stores, an international airport, and a protected harbor. It is a mecca for sailing, water sports, and bonefish enthusiasts. There are extensive flats, creeks, channels, and cays made up of grass, sand, mud, and a combination of the three. Bonefish run to five pounds or so and see plenty of anglers. There are numerous guides in George Town.

The Exumas are a 100-mile-long strand of gem-like islands that are far removed from the urban world. Nearly all offer untrodden beaches and unfished flats. This is the haunt of secluded estates, private aircraft, luxury yachts, and foolish bonefish.

Excellent accommodations and numerous guides are available at George Town.

Turtles are relatively scarce on Bahamas flats. Turtle tracks (below) are a rare find. Turtles ascend sand beaches, dig a hole, and deposit their eggs. When the young hatch, they descend the beach and swim into the water.

Notice how the bonefish blends with the habitat. The author at Grand Bahama Island.

The Caribbean Marine Research Center has a station on Lee Stocking Island. There is also a mysterious cave to explore.

The best way to enjoy the Exumas is to get far from the crowds and boat to some of those intoxicating spots that are so easily viewed from the airplane. By the way, there are 11 airstrips in the Exumas, of which all but two are private. Visitors are not welcome at these private strips.

The area north of George Town has been designated the Exuma National Land and Sea Park, which offers fabulous sightseeing, but no fishing is allowed. Snorkeling doesn't get much better. Limited private accommodations can sometimes be arranged near this area, but you are pretty much on your own for guides. My brother, Lance, and others have stayed at a private island compound near Staniel Cay and had a fabulous time. The Thunderball Grotto, where the James Bond film *Thunderball* and the film *Splash* were filmed, is worth a look. The Grotto is located on a rocky islet facing the Staniel Cay Yacht Club.

Grand Bahama

Grand Bahama offers luxury hotels, casinos, an international bazaar, and almost any activity. It is the haunt of some of the world's most famous people, many of whom have homes in exclusive developments. The Freeport International Airport is one of the largest privately owned airports in the world and has good facilities and connections to the U.S.

Freeport/Lucaya is an excellent place for a getaway with a non-fishing partner. Shopping, numerous activities, supurb accommodations, and fine cuisine are all within close proximity. Resorts have excellent boats and guides.

Fishing in the Freeport area is on the flats at Dover Sound and Water Cay. There are about 100 square miles of mostly unexplored, wadeable flats with plenty of nice bonefish. On the opposite end of the island is McLean's Town. Most fishing is in the area of Deep Water Cay.

Deep Water Cay is a private one-square-mile island off the east end of Grand Bahama. The resort caters to bonefishermen. It is situated among a complex and extensive aggregate of remote cays and channels that stretches for 30 miles from Jacob's Cay north to the topmost islands of Abaco. These flats are world famous and offer the visiting angler 100 square miles of seclusion. Many famous saltwater angling writers have headquartered here and fished with the legendary Pinder family, including A. J. McClane.

The creeks are composed mostly of soft sand bottoms, patches of turtle grass, and clusters of mangroves. This luxuriant environment is ideal habitat for shrimp and crabs, two favorite bonefish foods. Many flats are adjacent to creeks and mangrove cays while others are isolated. Bonefish are usually scattered, but anglers sometimes find themselves in the enviable position of not being able to decide which tail to cast to. Because of the intricate arrangement of creeks and channels, tidal flows are complex. It is possible to fish a particular stage of tide at various locations during a two- or three-hour period.

Bonefish average three to four pounds, but many fish over eight pounds are routinely taken. There are also some very large

permit, averaging 35 pounds, but they have lockjaw. Deep Water Cay had a standing offer of a free trip to anyone who caught one on a fly. However, if you didn't, you paid double! To my knowledge, no one ever took up the offer.

Great Inagua

Great Inagua is the least visited and the southern-most island in the Bahamas archipelago. Matthew Town is the main settlement, and Morton Salt is the primary industry. There are miles and miles of desolate inland salt flats. Few fishermen visit this dry crusty landscape, and there is little organized bonefishing. Bonefish are, however, present, along with good numbers of baby tarpon and some snook.

Remember that the largest fish are usually found in or adjacent to deeper water like the angler fishes here. Landing, top, and release, bottom.

Approaching Long Island from the north looking toward Cape Santa Maria and Stella Maris.

Bahamian churches are almost always colorful and surrounded by flowers. Some of the most interesting are on Long Island, like these near Deadman's Cay. An especially unique church is located at Clarence Town. Climb the turret for a great view.

Long Island

Located 160 miles southeast of Nassau, Long Island is 65 miles long and averages one to two miles wide. The east coast faces the open ocean and is a series of lovers' coves sprinkled with beautiful and remote beaches that are separated by high (178 feet) headlands and cliffs. The west coast is more erratic, sheltered, and shallow and is characterized by bays, sounds, and points. Flats are mud and white sand, usually fringed with mangrove. Quaint native settlements dot the coastline.

Columbus discovered Long Island in 1492, and a monument at Cape Santa Maria commemorates his visit. The view from this promontory overlooking the vast waters of the Atlantic and the beautiful pink-sand flat is worth the effort, especially at sunset.

Both Cape Santa Maria and Stella Maris resorts offer beautiful beaches, excellent accommodations, guides, and good fishing for tailers along mangroves and over beautiful white sand. Glinton Sound, Hog Island, and the area north to the Cape are all good.

This is one of the better destinations in the Bahamas for non-angling partners. Many things, including diving, tennis, beach exploring, and relaxing beside the pool are at your discretion.

Clarence Town is the most picturesque town on the island and is noted for its two Moorish-style churches built by Father Jerome. Climb the steeples of the west hillside church for great views. To the south, Hard Bargain is well named. It is the location of the saltworks and provides a look at how salt is obtained. Go elsewhere for fishing.

Deadman's Cay is the largest town. Locals are friendly; they farm, fish, and race sailboats. The Knowles family provided us with wonderful hospitality during our early trips. They are serious sailors who build their own boats and compete in races throughout the Bahamas. They have been consistent winners in the annual Long Island Sailing Regatta that is held in late May.

Area sightseers can view the remains of early Arawak Indian life or visit the luminous limestone caves. Bring a flashlight.

New Found Harbor at Deadman's Cay offers the most extensive bonefish water on Long Island. The areas around White Sound

	J	F	M	A	M	J	J	A	S	O	N	D
Bonefish	F-E	F-E	G-E	E	E	E	G-E	F-E	F-E	G-E	F-E	F-E
Permit	P-F	F	F-G	F-G	F-G	F-G	F-G	P-G	P-F	P-F	P-F	P-F
Tarpon	P-F	P-F	F	F	F	F	F	F	P-F	P-F	P-F	P-F
Barracuda	G-E	G-E	G-E	G-E	G-E	G-E	G-E	G-E	G-E	G-E	G-E	G-E
Snapper	F-G	F-G	F-E	G-E	G-E	G-E	G-E	F-E	F-E	F-G	F-G	F-G
Jacks	G-E	G-E	G-E	G	G	F-G	F-G	F-G	G	G-E	G-E	G-E
Shark	F-G	F-G	F-G	F-G	F-G	F-G	F-G	F-G	F-G	F-G	F-G	F-G
Wind	M-H	M-H	M	M-L	L	L	L	L-M	M	M-H	M-H	M-H

P=Poor F=Fair G=Good E=Excellent
L=Light M=Moderate H=Heavy

Angling conditions and locations vary greatly in the Bahamas. These are *average* conditions that anglers *might* encounter. It is quite possible permit fishing may be excellent at one location in March and poor at another location. Tarpon are available at limited locations. Remember—fishing is not productive during major storms, especially hurricanes!

On the beach flats at Long Island.

Casting poppers into shoreline structure can produce any number of surprises, including snapper and jacks. Long Island.

Cay, Conch Cay, and Upper and Lower Channel cays are all good. Scheduled air service and private charters reach Long Island. Accommodations and guides are best reserved in advance.

Turks and Caicos

Located at the southern end of the Bahamas, the Turks and Caicos are politically separate but geographically like the Bahamas. There are many beautiful and extensive flats on the lee side of these off-the-beaten-track islands. A few flats are hard sand and marl and are wadeable; others are too soft to wade. Some flats are easily accessed from shore.

Rumors of deserted sand flats teeming with bonefish have circulated around the Caribbean for years. If you had been here at the time of Columbus, there were probably bonefish aplenty and plenty of big ones. If you visit today, there are few bonefish close to resort areas because locals keep them under control with nets. If you are in the Turks for diving or other activities, it is worth taking a rod, but it is not worth a special trip unless you have a yacht and can fish the far-off unexplored flats.

Bob Guard, dressed for rain showers and rough running in the boat, gently lifts a beautiful bonefish at Grand Bahama Island.

Chapter 21

Belize

Belize fronts the Caribbean Sea along the eastern coastline of Central America immediately south of Mexico's Yucatan Peninsula and east of Guatemala. The mainland is about 180 miles long and 70 miles wide. Many recognize it as British Honduras, its name until September 1981 when it gained independence from Great Britain.

The history of Belize dates from ice age man but is more commonly understood in terms of the Mayan people, slavery, and pirates. Today Belize is a peaceful sovereign democracy that is patterned after Britain and the United States. English is the primary language. Its income comes mainly from agriculture, small manufactured goods, and tourism. Fifteen years ago Belize was mostly unknown to tourists, but that has changed. Fishermen, divers, photographers, birders, boaters, and retirees have all found Belize.

Belize City is the entry point to Belize and gives visitors a close-up view of the Third World, complete with open sewers. It is easy to get into trouble there, especially after dark. The only reason to go is to deepen your appreciation of America and to make connections to the outlying resorts, which are a world apart.

Geography

The northern half of Belize is flat and mostly covered with mangrove swamp, but the land rises in the south and west in the Maya Mountains to over 3,000 feet. Numerous jungle rivers drain the lush tropical rain forest, creating ideal habitat for an incredible variety of wildlife. The mainland coast is mostly swampy and inaccessible and has few beaches.

The most striking physical characteristic of Belize is the Belize Reef. This barrier reef extends 180 miles from the tip of Mexico's Isla Mujeres to Sopidilla Cay in the Bay of Honduras. In northern Belize at Ambergris Cay, Cay Caulker, and Cay Chapel, the reef is less than half a mile from shore, but elsewhere it is 10 to 25 miles offshore. The three atolls—Turneffe Island, Lighthouse Reef, and Glover's Reef—are outside the Belize Reef. Between the mainland and the outer reef there are over 200 recognized cays. This offshore habitat is a mosaic of hundreds of reefs and flats that resemble a jigsaw puzzle scattered about the table. Bonefish habitat is some of the most diverse and includes coral, sand, mud, and grass flats edged with mangroves, plus countless reefs that break the incoming surf.

Weather

The climate in Belize is mostly subtropical with temperatures averaging 79 degrees Fahrenheit. Flats anglers usually experience temperatures between 70 and 85 degrees. Occasional "northers" from North America cross the Gulf of Mexico bringing rain, cool temperatures, and strong winds from mid-December through mid-March. Strong winds are common January through March but can occur at any time.

The dry season is November to May, but rain falls whenever it likes. Don't forget to pack rain gear and carry it in the boat. When it rains, it really rains! Rain gear is also useful when traveling in the boat, especially in choppy water. Midsummer is referred to as the "mauger" season—when the air and sea are calm. At this time, the weather can be uncomfortable, but tarpon fishing can be extraordi-

Belize offers some of the most diverse habitat, including coral, sand, mud, grass, and mangrove flats. Reef flats add another dimension. In this scene in Turneffe Island country, the angler makes a less than ideal cast across the wind and current to four o'clock. A right-handed angler must be careful not to hook the guide.

nary. Summer and fall are hurricane season, although Belize has only experienced a few in the past half century.

The weather and fishing can be wonderful anytime. The best weather is usually November through May. Like most fishing trips, you pay your money and you take your chances. If you don't hit it right one trip, you may get lucky the next trip. Fortunately, during most visits a few days are perfect, some are O.K., and others may be snorkle days.

Fishing

Belize has been a popular destination for a small group of bonefish anglers since the 1950s, but it has only come to the attention of most anglers since 1980. The late Vic Barothy started a modern fishing camp on the Belize River after he was forced to flee his resort on Cuba's Isla de Pines in the early 1960s. Outdoor writers like Joe Brooks and A. J. McClane soon followed and reported on the wonderful fishing opportunities. Today, resorts are scattered offshore on private islands including Ambergris Cay, Turneffe Island, South Water Cay, Glover's Reef, and Lighthouse Reef. Other diving and fishing resorts are located on the mainland or along rivers.

Belize offers flats anglers a potpourri of angling possibilities perhaps unmatched elsewhere in the Western Hemisphere. Knowledgeable anglers consider Belize one of the best locations to accomplish a grand slam: landing a bonefish, permit, and tarpon all in the same day. Some anglers have even added a fourth fish, the mutton snapper, considered a formidable opponent and sometimes difficult to take with a fly. This is referred to as a royal flush. Barracuda, snapper, and jacks are also available to flats anglers. For

bonefish and permit, many of the same flies and terminal tackle are adequate. Tarpon anglers need more powerful gear.

Many rivers flow into the ocean and offer excellent fishing. The Belize River runs right through Belize City and offers excellent sport upstream. The most unusual rivers are in the south. Some become a broad apron of murky water long before reaching the coastline, spreading out into mangrove and low jungle. Others, like the Monkey River, flow strong almost to the sea. Tarpon are usually the main attraction and can be found in the slower holes and along and under dense vegetation. Tarpon and baitfish gather there to eat and be eaten because there is shelter. Other river species include snook, bay snook, assorted snappers, and other exotics. If you have the gear and courage, try for crocodile!

Bonefish: Most fly fishermen initially come to Belize for bonefish or permit. Anglers visiting Belize should understand that, while some excellent bonefishing is available, it is not available everywhere nor is Belize considered the best place to fish just for bonefish. Belize is, however, one of the best destinations to experience the big three: permit, tarpon, and bones. Some areas offer fishing for school or mudding fish that average one to three pounds. Bonefish four to five pounds are common, and big bones are available. The best bonefishing is found at selected locations along the reef and at some selected cays in the northern half of the country. Turneffe Island is a favorite destination. I believe the best bonefishing is along the outer reefs and the transition flats just inside the reefs. This exciting, powerful habitat offers the best tailers and a chance of double-digit fish.

Fly selection and presentation are the keys to fooling these persnickety feeders. Craig Mathews, who operates Blue Ribbon Flies in West Yellowstone, Montana, is one of only a handful of anglers who consistently dupes these clever bonefish. Craig says that big Belizean bonefish often search out small sea urchins and mollusks as they patrol the shallows of the flats and reefs. He calls these shallow-water-patrolling bones "reef rangers." When you watch these large fish working the shallows, you can see how slowly they root around, turning and tumbling everything on the bottom as they feed. These large bones seldom chase minnows or fleeing shrimp—the coral provides too many escape routes for quickly darting shrimp and minnows. Instead, the bones leisurely root along in the coral, mud, and turtle grass feeding on their favorite creatures—the slow-moving crabs, urchins, and mollusks.

If the angler attempts to strip a weighted size 4 or 6 bonefish fly by these reef rangers on the shallow flats or in the reef areas, the fly will often hang up on coral or turtle grass. This causes the fish to move away or to spook to the next flat. Urchins and mollusks, and to a lesser degree crabs, move very slowly or not at all and are not imitated well with heavily weighted or traditional bonefish patterns.

Craig and local guide Winston "Pops" Cabral discovered that small lightly weighted flies often work best when fishing for bones in six to 18 inches of water on the reef or on the extremely shallow flats. By properly incorporating the right deer hair into the fly, you can create a pattern that becomes weed and coral proof and that lands softly. This is often important because, again, when a fly hangs up on coral or weeds, the big fish spook.

A full box of Belize bonefish flies. You may not use them all, but they are ready for duty when you do need them.

Randall Kaufmann

Popular Belize flies include small and light tan and olive patterns that represent crabs and urchins.

Randall Kaufmann

Craig Mathews' Bonefish Bitters patterns. These are some of the most effective for the shallow water reef rangers. When tied properly, Bitters land lightly and sink slowly.

Randall Kaufmann

Fly color can make a difference depending on light condition, bottom makeup and color, water depth, tide stage, and the time of day. The proper fly color can even vary from one flat to another. Craig believes colors such as olive, tan, and amber work best in the mornings, during bright sunny conditions in heavy coral bottom areas on the reef, or in extremely shallow water when the fish are often half out of the water while rooting and feeding. In Belize the fish tend to work the reefs during low tides or at the beginning and ending of tides; you will want to fish subtle colors at these times. Bright green, white, and orange work best in late afternoons, on cloudy days, and during strong tides associated with the full moon and high pressure systems; also in deeper water with a mud or soft bottom.

Two important shallow-water bonefish patterns have come out of Craig's and Pop's fondness for fishing the shallow-water reef rangers. The Pop's Bonefish Bitters imitates small sea urchins, crabs, and mollusks. The Turneffe Crab imitates the tiny crabs so important to bonefish in Belize. These crabs are tan, white, olive, and green. Other effective patterns include Winston's Urchins and the Hermit Crab Bitters.

Tied with little or no weight, a tiny clump of deer hair, and mini rubber legs, these flies land lightly and sink slowly. The hook rides up, and they can be cast close to and retrieved away from the wisest bonefish without causing suspicion. The retrieve is slow. Leaders must be fluorocarbon, 14 to 16 feet long, and tapered to 01X or 04X (10 to 18 pounds). The coral eats up anything else. Seven- and eight-weight rods are usually best.

Standard bonefish flies including Charlies, Gotchas, Clousers, Baited Breath, Turd, Mini Shrimp, Puff, Flats Master, Christmas Island Specials, and crabs work when you are fishing for bones over sand and marl, but they don't work on the reef rangers.

Permit: Bonefish anglers armed with 8-, 9-, or 10-weight rods and crab flies are ready to cast to permit. That is what you will most likely be doing—casting. Nevertheless, stalking and casting to permit is so thrilling that you shouldn't mind seldom hooking any! The swirling water twister they leave behind after a hookup or after being spooked is action enough. If you are lucky and skilled enough to hook one, be prepared for one of the most electrifying fish battles of your life.

Permit anglers should consider fishing during a spring tide, which allows permit enough water depth to feed on most flats. Permit have excellent eyesight, hearing, and sense of smell and are far more spooky and selective than bonefish ever dreamed of being. Crab imitations are the most effective flies. The more realistic they are, the better because permit usually inspect them with microscopic vision. They should sink fairly fast, like a real diving crab.

The most widely accepted method of hooking permit (besides chumming or attaching a live crab to your fly) is to present a diving crab imitation. If permit see the fly, do not retrieve it. Crabs remain motionless when under scrutiny and rely on camouflage for survival. They might look up from the bottom with their claws outstretched, but, for the most part, they remain stationary. This is how permit are used to seeing them. Twitch the fly only if the permit turns away. Incorporate the knowledge you have about bonefish,

Turneffe Island offers some of the greatest variety of bonefish habitat to be found. Sand, grass, muck, marl, hard coral, soft coral, reef, mangrove, skinny water, deep water, fast tidal flows, surf. . .it is all there, sometimes all mixed up into one package. Some bonefishing is ridiculously easy; some is as tough as it gets. You can fish the smoke and hook small bonefish every cast or stalk double-digit bonefish that seem uncatchable. That's why they're big!

Look at the expression on this handsome bonefish. It probably made the first wrong call of its life, thinking that shrimp was real! While it looks a bit confused, it also looks relieved at its imminent release.

Aside from the clear sand flats and deeper channels north from Belize City and at Ambergris, Turneffe, and selected cays, most tarpon fishing in Belize takes place in bays, backwaters, lagoons, river mouths, and channels. The water is usually muddy, and you either hope tarpon are there below the surface or you see them rolling or swimming at the surface. A sinking tarpon fly line is often needed.

and you have an excellent chance of hooking a permit. . .but don't get greedy and expect too many! Some anglers consider Permit Alley, the area between Tobacco Cay and Gladden Cays, to have the best permit fishing anywhere.

Tarpon: From a distance the quarter-mile-long, crescent-shaped south shore of Tarpon Cay was quiet and calm in the early morning light. As we motored closer, the sights and sounds of the pelican rookery that occupies the mangrove-lined shore came into focus. Numerous birds were fishing in the shallow water, their clumsy dives amazingly effective at capturing baitfish. Dense schools of baitfish were clearly visible over the shallow white sand bottom, as were several tarpon. These long dark shapes patrol the flanks of baitfish schools whose silvery sides reflect terror and panic when tarpon rush into their midst. At Tarpon Cay, everything is visual. You spot the fish, make the cast, begin the retrieve, and anticipate the heart-stopping attack.

Poling along the lagoon in 10 feet of water, we spotted five tarpon of 40 to 80 pounds lolling just under the surface enjoying the early morning sunshine. I tossed the silver-blue baitfish imitation ahead of the fish and let it sink. A long strip attracted the attention of the lead fish, and it swam closer to investigate. After two more enticing strips, I saw the fly disappear into the huge bucket-shaped mouth. My mouth was also shaped like a bucket as I struck the fish repeatedly and watched the line pull tight, angle upward toward the surface, and quickly slice into the air. The fish shook its head, rattled its gills, and climbed still higher. I lowered the rod and pointed it directly toward the fish in an effort to lessen the shock to my leader. The tarpon's powerful surge forced me to tighten my grip on the rod, and I tucked it against my body for better control.

The tarpon continued to somersault away, pulling line from the reel at an awesome pace. My rod seemed stressed beyond recovery. Each jump was five feet high and 10 feet long. Everyone in the boat

Fan coral is beautifully fragile. Forget about landing any fish here! Permit Alley, Belize. Tarpon, bonefish, and permit can be found in this habitat of coral, grass, and sand.

was on their feet screaming meaningless instructions. I heard only blurred excitement, intent only on hanging onto the 70-pound monster that was trying to take me overboard. I never had a chance to recover any line. The tarpon continued to move into deeper water, and soon the line went slack. In slow motion, everyone became quiet and sat down, still pointing at where the giant was last seen leaping for its freedom. I was shaking from excitement and physical abuse as I reeled in the limp line and passed the rod to the next angler whose turn at *Megalops atlanticus* had arrived.

A 70-pound tarpon is not big in the world of tarpon, but it is big enough to require a 10-, 11-, or 12-weight rod and a reel capable of withstanding severe punishment and holding plenty of backing. Besides the rod and reel, you need a few tarpon leaders, some shock tippet, saltwater pliers, a hook file, a dozen flies, and, perhaps, a fly stretcher. The stretcher holds your flies pre-attached to stretched leaders ready to fish.

Visitors to Belize should consider taking advantage of the tarpon possibilities and gear up accordingly. It is a thrill you will never forget. Who knows, you might jump a tarpon twice the size of your biggest dog and stronger than a gorilla! Belize offers three sizes of tarpon. Baby tarpon weigh under 40 pounds and are usually found along mangroves, in small lagoons, and at the mouths of creeks. Medium-sized tarpon weigh 40 to 70 pounds and require heavier gear. They are found in cuts, larger lagoons, and channels. The *grande* tarpon are over 70 pounds and provide a tremendous challenge.

Other Activities

Belize is not just a fishing destination. It is one of the most popular diving spots in the world. Its bird life is also world famous, and bird watchers rack up dozens of species each day. If this isn't enough, there are Mayan ruins. Belize was once the center of the ancient Mayan culture, and many ruins are open to the public.

Tropical sunsets always stop traffic, which is only foot and boat in Belize. A toast to your good fortune to enjoy such splendor is in order.

The underwater world is fascinating. Hours can be whiled away snorkeling with friendly schools of fish.

American flamingo, Phoenicopterus ruber, *has a uniquely shaped bill that is bent sharply downward, which sets it apart from any other bird. You will recognize flamingos by their characteristic pink color. They inhabit tropical flats, lagoons, and shallow waters throughout the Caribbean and elsewhere. I have seen flocks at Ascension Bay, in Belize, and in the Bahamas, and they always are an exciting find.*

Diving: Most fishing resorts are also in the diving business. The Belize Reef is world famous. Besides the reefs and steep walls, the adventurous tourist can explore secret caves and previously undiscovered shipwrecks from the pirate era.

Diving lessons and gear are readily available and world-class snorkeling is almost always at your doorstep. Bring your own mask if you like, but you can usually find fins and a mask.

Ruins: The Mayan civilization is considered one of the greatest of all time. The Mayans developed a written language, charted the universe, farmed, and created dynamic architecture. Ruins dot the lowland forests. Most are in a continuing state of decline and are besieged by tomb robbers. Altun Ha is 28 miles north of Belize City and covers about 25 square miles. Xunantunich (meaning stone lady or maiden of the rock) is the home of El Castillo, one of the tallest structures in Belize. It is a favorite destination southwest of Belize City, as is Caracol, perhaps the largest Mayan site in the country, and Tikal, which flourished over 1,500 years ago.

Archaeologists estimate that a million Maya once lived in the area that is now Belize. New Mayan sites are being discovered each year and date back hundreds—or thousands—of years. Be advised, though, that most are located inland in the rain forest and require at least a two-hour drive from Belize City. There are no services at the ruins, and many require you to walk. Dress accordingly—insects thrive in the jungle.

Birding: If you are a serious bird watcher, you already know about Belize. From the reefs, marsh-rimmed shores, fruit groves, and vegetable fields to the highest jungle-covered mountains, exotic birds are the norm, not the exception. There are more birds to watch in Belize than at almost any other location in Central America. One of the most spectacular is the toucan, which is the national bird of Belize. The jabiru stork, with a wingspan of nine to 12 feet, is the largest flying bird in the Americas; while they are very rare elsewhere, Belize has a healthy population.

One afternoon while motoring the Monkey River, which flows through true jungle in southern Belize, we identified over 40 species of birds. Other animals were also visible, including iguanas and howler monkeys. In the oceanside channels we observed a pair of shy manatee. You may also see jaguars, pumas, ocelots, tapirs, deer, peccaries, and numerous snakes, including coral, moccasin, tropical rattler, and fer-de-lance. Care should be taken when exploring the Belizean jungle. It is best to have a guide.

Speaking of guides and snakes, Ralph and Lisa Cutter visited Belize in search of adventure and their first bonefish. They operate a guide service and the California School of Fly Fishing in Nevada City, California. Ralph is a free-lance writer and author of *Sierra Trout Guide.* Both are accustomed to the unusual and routinely seek out the untamed, so it was only natural for them to be in a rough Belizian bar when they hired Otto to take them bonefishing. Following is their story.

Of Boas and Bonefish
by Ralph Cutter

Otto was not the talkative sort. He stowed the fly rods amid a tangle of rusting trolling gear and wedged the tackle bag between

an ice chest and a greasy box of outboard motor parts. With a grunt, he motioned for Lisa and me to sit on the ice chest. He walked the skiff to deeper water and jumped in. We roared off toward a pastel horizon peppered with palm-studded islands.

The night before in a seedy Belizian bar, we had been introduced to Otto and were assured he was not only versed in the ways of bonefish but skilled in the art of the fly. His green eyes, black skin, and wavy hair spoke of ancestors from several continents. I don't think Otto uttered a word; he let those around him do the talking. Through the rum- and smoke-filled evening, we heard him variously described as pirate, gun runner, drug smuggler, and fishing guide. We couldn't have been happier.

We've always considered fishing a good excuse to go somewhere. Catching our first bones was a good excuse to travel to the southern border of Belize. Turneffe and San Pedro Islands were the obvious bonefish destinations, but we wanted more than that. We wanted jaguars and snakes and jungles and ruins. We wanted adventure.

We couldn't find anyone who had fished southern Belize, but everyone agreed it should be perfect for bones. Two months later we were in Otto's excuse for a boat.

About 40 minutes from shore, Otto cut the motor and let his skiff glide to a stop over the silky clear water. A dozen feet below, brightly colored fish darted amid the carpet of dense turtle grass. Otto never uttered a word; he simply dove over the side and swam to the sea floor trailing a silver stream of bubbles from his nose. With powerful frog kicks he maneuvered over the bottom and collected what appeared to be several large stones.

He surfaced at the boat's edge and lobbed the conch over the gunwale and then pulled his glistening black self in after them. A few pulls on the rope and we were once again roaring out across the Caribbean Sea.

Another 20 minutes passed before Otto slowed the boat and eased it into a bay formed by two overgrown cays. He cut the motor, and we slid to a halt some 50 feet from shore. Frigates danced like medieval kites overhead while spoonbills and ibis cavorted in the mangroves. Some 20 feet beneath us the crystalline sea was smoky with churned mud. Faint flashes similar to those made by nymphing trout winked from the murk. Otto pointed to the semaphores and grunted, "Bones."

While Lisa and I watched for fish, a wicked looking knife

Iguanas are friendly and delight visitors with their climbing and free-fall antics.

Ralph Cutter enjoys a lunch of cerveza and bonefish sashimi, prepared by his guide, Otto.

Otto, Ralph, and Mr. Boa.

Lisa Cutter

No worries, mon; life is casual in Belize.

Future bonefish guides.

appeared in Otto's hands. He deftly carved small cubes from the living conch. Without a word he picked up Lisa's rod and pulled the Crazy Charlie from its keeper. He speared a chunk of conch on the fly and then started peeling off the feathers.

"Scares the fish," he muttered. Without any preamble he tossed the baited hook overboard and pulled line from the reel. He handed the rod to Lisa and wiped his knife off on a dirty rag. Within seconds a slender gray form materialized from the boat's shadow and arrowed toward the bait. The rod bucked lightly. and the barracuda sliced the line razor clean.

Sensing that Otto's fly fishing skills weren't quite as keen as advertised, we decided to change gears and use his local knowledge to best advantage. I explained to Otto we weren't really into fishing this morning and that we'd rather catch boa constrictors.

He looked at us sideways and asked, "You want to catch snakes?" "Yeah," I explained. "I'd like to catch a boa and these islands look like perfect habitat."

Otto clearly warmed to the suggestion. He grinned, and, with perfect white teeth gleaming in the tropical sun, he pointed to the horizon and said, "I know a place with many boas." The grin never faded as he steered us toward a distant cay.

At the cay Otto announced that we needed food before looking for snakes. What Otto lacked as a fly fisherman or conversationalist, he made up for as a cook. He made us a lunch of barracuda seviche, cold lobster salad, and sweet rolls topped with warm mangoes picked about 30 feet up the beach. After lunch, Otto rolled himself a fat joint while Lisa and I sipped icy Belikan beers and wandered up the narrow beach looking for boas in the dense tangle of mangroves. We expected to find boas; we found bonefish.

Lisa saw them first, a pair of glassine fins twisting and dipping amid the mangrove roots. Without a word, we looked at each other, grinned, and raced for our rods. Otto was sound asleep in the shade so we just guessed at the choice of flies. Lisa quickly tied on a small white Charlie. We had seen numerous small shrimp that looked more like a Hare's Ear than any bonefish pattern in the box so, in my blissful ignorance, I tied on a Hare's Ear and matched the hatch.

Our only knowledge of bonefish came from devouring books on the subject. The authors could agree on only two things: bones were incredibly difficult to see, and they were terrified of their own shadows. Our bone couldn't have been easier to see if he wore ribbons in his hair, but he was sure to be spooky in such skinny water.

On hands and knees we approached the tailing fish. Lisa finally made a 40-foot sidearm cast that landed on the fish's head. I cringed and waited for the explosion of silt that would mark the terrified departure. In less than a second the water detonated, and the fish raced towards the deep with Lisa's fly in its mouth.

The little Hardy shrieked as the bone streaked away. Lisa was ecstatic: "It's not big enough to pull out *that* much line *that* fast!"

During its second run, I noticed a shadow patrolling the shoreline. With an abbreviated cast, I dropped the Hare's Ear in ankle-deep water and waited for the fish. Half a minute later the bone was within a couple feet of the fly. I gave it a slight twitch. The shadow bolted to the nymph and inhaled it like a thousand trout had done before.

Our first bones and a double at that! We spent the rest of the day wandering our private island and jumping singles, doubles, and small schools of bonefish. They weren't too hard to see, nor did they seem particularly concerned about our fly selection. All we needed to do was make common-sense presentations and not make ourselves too obvious.

The fish were small, maybe three pounds at the biggest, but they were our first bones. We were hooked—hooked on the stalk, hooked on the grab, and hooked on the unbelievable runs. Most of all, we were hooked on the world of bonefish. We didn't find our first boa for another three days, but that's a different story.

Since that experience a lifetime ago, we've journeyed from North America to the South China Sea and to all points in between in search of bones. Every trip, every fish, and every cast has reinforced our belief: fishing is still the best excuse to go somewhere. Hunting for snakes is a close second.

Ralph Cutter
Truckee, California
February 1998

Ambergris Cay

This is the largest cay along the Belizean coast and is the most popular. The thin sliver of land extends south from Mexico and is near the northern terminus of the Belize Reef, which is located a quarter mile offshore. To the west are shallow flats and mangrove swamps all the way to the featureless and mostly deserted Mosquito Coast. In between are 200 square miles of clear water dotted with cays, mud and sand flats, bars, and mangrove islets, all uninhabited. This is the best tarpon country in Belize and the only classic tarpon flats area outside of southern Florida. South of Ambergris Cay are miles of shallow mangrove islets divided by deeper channels that offer one to three pound bonefish. Many flats are soft. Permit are occasionally seen.

San Pedro is the hub of Ambergris and is the most popular resort in Belize. Small airplanes constantly shuttle passengers back and forth to Belize City, 15 minutes away. The runway is on the edge of town; if you had to, you could walk, although plenty of taxis are available. San Pedro is a laid-back worry-free community with brightly colored cinder block and wood buildings and sand streets. Hotels and restaurants dot the waterfront, which has numerous piers with dive boats tethered to them.

San Pedro is still an old-style Belizean fishing village with upscale resorts. Accommodations are adequate but not glitzy. Fishing guides, tour operators, and dive opportunities are numerous. Day trips to Caye Caulker and Hol Chan Marine Reserve for snorkeling are a nonfishing possibility, as are diving and trips to jungle river ruins or to the Mayan pyramids of Lamanai. Visitors who have time should visit the unique Tackle Box Bar. Friendly people stop in at this waterhole to watch the sharks, bonefish, and sea turtles in the tank, mingle with who's who in San Pedro, and drink a Belikan beer or sip a tropical rum drink.

Belize is a birder's paradise. Casual observers see dozens of species, especially close to and on the mainland.

Time to slow down and savor today and dream of tomorrow.

Accommodations in the Caribbean are usually beachside.

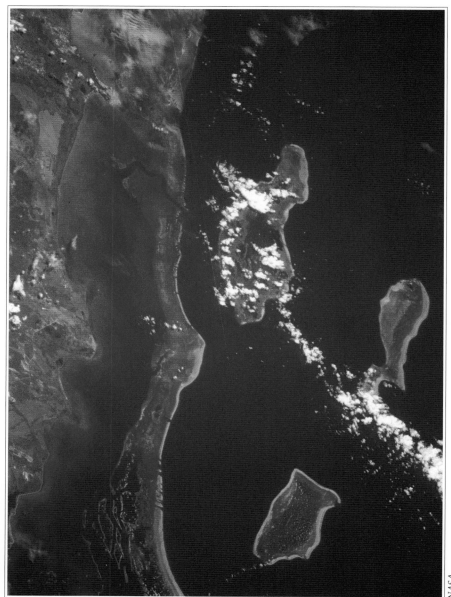

NASA

Turneffe Island (center with cloud cover), Lighthouse Reef (far right center), and Glover's Reef (bottom lower right) are all beautiful locations removed from the mainland and located outside the barrier reef. Access and accommodations are limited. Fishing and diving are excellent.

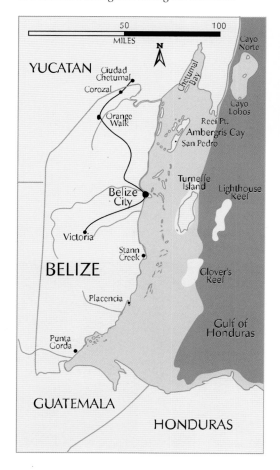

Glover's Reef

A tropical fairyland of reefs, coral, and sand, Glover's Reef may be the area least visited by fishermen. It encircles an 80-square-mile lagoon of stunning beauty. Located 75 miles southeast of Belize City, this is a diver's paradise. It does not have a program for bonefish anglers, but small bonefish are plentiful. They average between one and four pounds, but bigger ones frequent reef areas. Some permit are also available, as is offshore fishing when the ocean is not too rough.

Lighthouse Reef

Lighthouse Reef is primarily a dive destination. It is made up of a series of secluded cays 50 miles offshore from Belize City. The inside waters of this emerald-colored atoll are 30 miles long by eight miles wide and are the location of the famous Blue Hole, which was popularized by Jacques Cousteau. Flats fishing is limited, but some wadeable flats are located at Northern and Sand Bore cays and selected other areas. In front of the only resort is a

sand flat and around the corner are grass flats edged with mangroves. There are also some submerged coral heads that offer a variety of species. Some of the larger bonefish and tarpon are found in water three to 10 feet deep. Fishing is from a boat with sinking fly lines. Reef and bluewater fishing are available.

Access to Lighthouse Reef Resort on Northern Cay is either by boat or by small plane from Belize City. Accommodations are very nice; the setting is dreamily romantic.

A good day to run to distant flats.

Placencia

Located about 125 miles south of Belize City, Placencia is the southern-most destination of most fly fishermen. It is located at the end of an 11-mile-long peninsula that offers some of the best beaches on the mainland. The village itself is small and has a two-foot-wide sidewalk down the middle. Life is laid back to say the least. There are ample accommodations and a few guides. This area is best known for its permit fishing, especially along the outer cays, which are 10 to 20 miles distant. If the water is rough, and it often is, this is a torturous trip. Tarpon fishing is hot and cold, but a day at Tarpon Cay or the murky Monkey River is worth the long boat ride even if you don't catch any fish. There are better places to fish for bonefish. Snorkeling, diving, and reef fishing are excellent, but, again, it can be a *long, rough ride.*

Flats in Belize offer every type of habitat.

South Water Cay

Located at the edge of the barrier reef, South Water Cay is surrounded by white sand, coconut palms, blue water, and perhaps the best permit flats in Belize. The permit flats are a short, easy run with no rough water to cross, making this the best cay, logistically, from which to fish permit. There is limited bonefish and tarpon fishing.

Turneffe Island

Located 25 miles offshore from Belize City on the reef, Turneffe Island is a collection of 125 cays and offers the best and most consistent bonefishing in Belize. While there are some inside flats that provide good fishing, the best action is found along the outside reef and on the beautiful flats found just inside the reef. The largest bonefish are found here, and competent anglers have a chance at double-digit fish, although they are rare. Schoolies are plentiful inside the reef; most range from one to four pounds.

Tarpon fishing at Turneffe can be good; the best time is from April through June. Permit are also available. Snorkeling, diving, beach combing, and secluded bathing is at your doorstep. Surf crashes against the reef, and stars light the night sky. Access is by boat from Belize City. Trip time is about 90 minutes.

It is the dream of many anglers to live, work, play, and fish in a tropical paradise. What could be better than running one of the best fly fishing lodges in the tropics? All of one's passions compressed into one reality. A dream come true! Doug and Nancy Jorgensen had dropped out of the corporate scene to ski, fish, and backpack the West and were enjoying a carefree lifestyle until Craig Hayes, one of the owners of Turneffe Flats

A beefy Turneffe Island bonefish ready for release.

The reef environment attracts visitors from afar and is a beautiful place to chase permit, bonefish, and tarpon.

Lodge in Belize, gave them just such an opportunity. Following is Doug's insightful summary of some highlights of life in the tropics.

Don't Stop the Carnival
by Doug Jorgensen

Spring came. Skiing ended. The guiding business at Taos was enough to make a living, and we had been infected with New Mexico fever. Life was good. Then Craig Hayes called: "Please call me. I have a small fishing lodge in Belize, Central America, our present managers are leaving, and I would like to talk to you."

Several conversations later, we were on a plane to see the lodge and talk with Craig.

After an hour-long boat ride from Belize City, we rounded a mangrove point and gazed upon a stretch of white-sand beach dotted with coconut palms. A beautiful piece of the earth, Turneffe Flats.

Destination	Bonefish	Permit	Tarpon	Snapper	'Cuda	Snook
Ambergris Cay	F-G	F	G-E	G	G-E	F
Glover's Reef	F-G	F	P-F	G	G-E	P
Lighthouse Reef	F-G	F	P-F	G	G-E	P
Placencia	F	G	F-G	G	G	F
South Water Cay	F	G-E	P-F	G	G-E	P
Turneffe Island	F-E	F-G	F-G	G	G-E	P
Belize River	F-E	F-G	G-E	G-E	G-E	G

P=Poor　F=Fair　G=Good　E=Excellent

The week went by quickly. We caught a few bonefish and decided we would move to Belize in six short weeks. The "I'm sure, but I'm not sure" feeling gnawed at our subconscious and was our only topic of discussion during the next weeks.

We returned to Belize to what the locals call a norther—strong enough to delay the boat departure by a few hours. With seas of 10 feet or more, we crawled toward the islands of Turneffe. Waves broke over the bow of the boat. "This 30-foot boat isn't all that big after all," we thought. Was this an omen? We had arrived with a three-year contract!

Being a mountain boy, I had always dreamed of the tropics. I had visited and wanted to stay but had always been drawn back to the north. I had dreamed of lounging on the beach after a great day chasing saltwater creatures that take flies, with the sun setting, a tropical drink sweating cool droplets in my hand, and the smell of lobster dinner in the air. At no time did this dream reveal corroding brass and steel, salt-rotted lumber holding up porches, alkaline-damaged electrical wires buried unnoticed underground, outboard engines failing at the most inopportune times, shortages of fresh water, dead generators, or a hundred other now very real problems. I did read the required manual for managers in the Caribbean, _Don't Stop the Carnival_, and thought, "This can't be what it is really like."

Somehow I had imagined that this would be the best opportunity I could have to learn a lot about saltwater fly fishing. Of course, I expected this to be an immediate fulfillment. Not in my wildest nightmare did I think that a year would disappear without my fishing or tying a fly. As the year flew by, I listened with jealous ears to the nightly stories—guests being spooled by runaway bonefish and losing entire fly lines to wild tarpon. There were excited stories about golden bonefish, first permit on a fly, and grand slams.

Our learning curve that first year was steep. We learned about electrical wiring and saltwater knots, about emergency plumbing, and about casting 12-weight rods. We learned about finding parts and getting work permits in a Central American country. We learned that Creole is a foreign language and that it's possible to understand all the words and still not comprehend the meaning. We learned about Murphy's Law. I learned humility.

My ocean piloting began with a crash course in learning to run a 31-foot ocean-going twin-engine power boat. After several dual trips across the seas in all kinds of weather, I was turned loose for solo trips (with much trepidation on the staff's part). Things went along without incident for many months, building my overconfidence.

One supply day nearly a year later, the weather was terrible. Rain was coming in heavy squalls, and above-average seas were the order of the day. After I finished a hectic day in town

Time to head home and relax on the beach, enjoy a lobster dinner, and perhaps tie some permit or tarpon flies for tomorrow.

Turneffe Flats Lodge is located at the northern end of Turneffe Island on an ocean flat just a short cast from the reef. You can swim, snorkle, watch the sun set, or exercise bonefish after dinner—or is it the other way around?

and loading the boat with a week's supply of beer, soda, groceries, paint, fuel, and lumber, the weather got worse. Should we leave or should we stay? I was, after all, an accomplished pilot. We left.

It should be mentioned that the trip to the island involves crossing two reefs, one that guards the coast and one that guards Turneffe Atoll. We made slow forward progress and approached the first reef crossing. Suddenly it was there, directly in front of us. A sickening crunch told us how close we were. We had struck the reef. The engines shut down. Would I lose the boat, not to mention all the cargo?

Quickly, I stripped and dove under the boat. The boat was intact but solidly aground. The unnerving crunching continued as the surging water threatened to chew a hole in the bottom. One engine started. We tried to summon help with the radio. For a half hour we were in and out of the water, checking the hull and watching the rising tide. With the help of the tide and our remaining engine, we finally pulled free, drifting into deeper water. A final check of the bottom showed some deep scratches but no holes. We made our way back to Belize City. They say if you drive a boat in the waters near Belize that sooner or later you will find a rock that has your name on it. The bent outboard drive shaft hangs on my wall as a constant reminder of the humbling lesson I learned that day.

The second year I chased and caught bonefish. My emphasis shifted from large schools to larger singles and pairs cruising the skinny water next to the sharp coral reef. Many were hooked, but few were landed.

When I think of selective bonefish, I remember a particular afternoon. A good friend and I had been walking the flats for several hours and had cast to numerous schools of bones without hooking any. We switched to doubles and larger singles in the surf line. We took turns approaching and presenting our flies, still without reward. Frustration crept in, and we began trying extreme methods. We tried 20-foot 6X leaders with size 14 flies. We might as well have tossed our flies into the sea—the five- to eight-pound bonefish made short work of our delicate leaders. We went back to stronger leaders and larger flies. Soon my friend was landing a nice bone. I looked through my fly box and soon had a couple of noticeable refusals. My partner was fighting another bone. I couldn't stand it. I started moving toward him. As I approached, he glanced at me with a silly grin.

"What're you using?" I asked.

"Turneffe Crabs," he replied.

"I tried those without any luck. What size?"

"Oh, they vary," he said, reaching for the box in his pocket. I saw a half-dozen small green crabs crawling around in the box. "I wasn't having any luck with my flies. You had told me to be innovative. What could be more innovative than stripping most of the dressing from a size six Charlie and putting on a live crab?" he asked. "I pinched the barb down."

I could do nothing but chuckle. We decided that it was close to beer-thirty and started the walk back to the boat, talking about whether these fish would take a Pheasant Tail or, perhaps, a Mister Twister on the back of a size 6 Bitters. How about a rubber crawfish?

"Glass" minnows are a favorite food of bonefish, jacks, snapper, and tarpon.

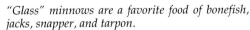

Tarpon armor! Their mouth is mostly bone, and their scales are like thin metal discs. They seem to be survivors from when dragons ruled the skies. Sharpen your hooks!

Belize has hundreds of remote cays. If you are camping, it is best to stay on those without too much vegetation—unless you don't mind biting bugs.

We clinked Belikans to newly found ideas. Much has been discussed and written about where fly fishing begins and ends. We pushed the envelope. Will a spring creek trout taking size 24 tricos take a red Woolly Bugger? Will a selective Turneffe Flats bonefish take a Pheasant Tail?

During that second year we also hunted, hooked, and jumped tarpon. Strip-strike, don't lift the rod, don't jumble the line on the deck, clear carefully. Our style of tarpon fishing can be trying. We locate the tarpon by watching for them breaking the surface (rolling) and then cast to them. Sometimes they are moving back and forth, covering as much as a quarter of a mile.

I was taking a short reprieve from the lodge and enjoying an early July with bluebird skies and light winds. I staked my skiff in a small creek flowing through the mangroves where a few tarpon were rolling. I stood on the deck and cast for 30 minutes, a tiring affair. I took a short break before getting up on deck again for another 30 minutes of casting. Fishing is supposed to be fun. After two hours my shoulders were aching, so I decided to sit and watch. What I failed to notice is that I had not brought all of the line in and the current was carrying the fly out. Yes, you're right in your thinking: the rod tightened, the reel sang, and both disappeared over the side with the first jump of an 80-pound tarpon. A $1,000 outfit was water skiing toward oblivion. I started the outboard to chase the rod and reel.

The tarpon took me to the reef before slowing enough to allow me to throw the anchor and exit the boat to chase the rod on foot. I finally snagged the rod. Much to my amazement, the fish was still solidly attached. Sometimes tarpon are easy to hook!

It is an inevitable conclusion that, if you spend enough time saltwater fly fishing, you will eventually pursue permit. I knew that I should be able to catch one. I spent time with all the Turneffe Flats guides chasing these critters. My ears still ring with, "Permit no eat flying crabs, mon;" "Too close, too close;" "No line the fish;" "Too much fly time in the air;" "Don't strip; strip; slow; slower!" and "Permit 11 o'clock; cast now."

I had spent several years in halfhearted pursuit of permit. One particular day I was walking my favorite permit flat. I had seen a few fish and even gotten a cast to a nontaker. My experience at this point told me permit were never takers.

Another hour or so with no sightings convinced me to turn back toward the boat. I had covered half the distance when I spotted four permit headed straight toward me. Happy fish, moving, tailing, mudding, moving again, and straight toward me. My hopes began to rise—150 yards, 100 yards, and still happily closing. I readied for the cast, 70 yards, 40 yards, still feeding and happy. I tried to still my shaking. At 25 yards, I started the cast. I wanted to aim eight feet in front of the lead fish. It was time. The cast landed where I intended it to land. The fish did not spook. I was shaking.

As the fly sank, the lead fish saw my fly and rushed toward it. The other three joined the rush, and all tailed down. There was no slack in the line. Then, the take! I used a solid strip set. I had him! The permit was on the reel, running, deep into my backing. Finally he slowed, and I began to bring him in, keeping the pressure on. A second run, again into the backing but not so far this time. I

"Permit! Twelve o'clock, edge of grass, moving left, 40 feet. Cast! Cast!"

The perfect end to a perfect day.

brought him back toward me. The others were now gone. After another short run, he was ready to be landed. The fly line was in the tip top. My first permit was nearly in my hand!

As he got close, I looked at him closely. Funny thing—from 20 feet I could tell that I had hooked and landed a 28-inch nine-pound bonefish that was traveling with the permit. I've caught a lot of bonefish and a few pretty large ones, but I've never been so unhappy to catch such a beautiful bone. My first permit continued to elude me.

Before we could take a deep breath, the busy season was in full swing. I had gone zero for dozens of permit. There's not much time to fish when the lodge is full, with all six boats in constant use. The intensity of running a camp that in truth is a small city takes precedence. Once in a while, we needed an extra guide.

I have guided trout anglers for years. What could be so hard about guiding on salt water? My first outings were wading the bonefish flats. "See the fish near that small mangrove, moving left to right? Cast! Short. Cast 10 feet more. Strip, stop, slow strip. He's on it; he's got it; strip-strike. . .good fish!" You take the anglers out and they catch some bones and learn something about saltwater fishing. How hard is that?

One day one of the regular guides was sick and could not go out. I decided to take the guests. They wanted tarpon and permit. I knew the places. A 20-minute skiff ride brought us to a great flat with deep

Caribbean accommodations are usually beachside under coconut palms and a thatched roof.

water next to it. It was ideal for permit. The tide was right. I pulled onto the flat and set up to pole it. Let it be known that, at this point, I had poled a flats skiff some but only when alone and when I could pick the places and never while looking for fish.

I was on the platform with a fisherman on the deck. I just needed to keep the boat straight and look down the bar for approaching fish and adjust the boat for the wind so casting is easier (and so I would not get hooked). I thought, pushed left, turned right, then pushed left and turned left. I tried to keep the boat straight. The current was pushing me out. I pushed left, looking for a fish I thought I'd seen, then pushed back toward the bar, but we were now in water so deep the pole would not reach. I had to start the engine to get back. The noise would spook any fish. I set up again, concentrating on keeping the boat straight. A guest asked, "Is that a permit?"

"Yes," I replied, "It's a fish coming this way." By now I was drifting back into the deep water. I could no longer see the fish. I had to start the engine again. It's not a compliment to your guiding ability when your client suggests moving to an easier spot.

What flies worked? Again, the information filtered in. Pop's Bitters is a good choice. Small (6, 8, and 10) and light (no eyes). Charlies and shrimp patterns were consistent. Out came the fly tying vise. After nearly two years of nonuse, even in an enclosed plastic bag, the harsh elements had somehow turned it into a rusted piece of iron. Much scraping and polishing later, I began to turn out tempting bonefish morsels. Surely I could devise a fly that would work without fail! Hours of tying and experimenting led me to a conclusion: when they eat, they eat; when they don't eat, they don't eat.

The next problem was leaders. My trout mind told me that if

Bonefish and crab mounds on an inside flat at Turneffe Island.

Flats in Belize offer a little bit of everything: sand, grass, mud, coral, and mangrove.

they refuse your offering, try lighter leaders. Well, they do work. However, I quickly learned about sharp coral. Going to six- or eight-pound soft-mono tippets produced takes, but it was equivalent to opening my fly box upside down over the water. I went the other way. Hard mono was much thicker, but it gave much better results. My hooking percentage remained the same, going up very gradually with experience, but my landing percentage increased dramatically. I discovered that attaching the flies to the heavier mono with loop knots (Homer Rhodes, perfection, or Duncan) gives the fly more free movement and seems to attract fish. The percentage edged up.

I finally decided that a size 8 Pop's Bitters or shrimp pattern and an 11- to 14-foot leader, heavy-butted and stiff, with a 10- to 13-pound hard Mason tippet was the combination that allowed good turnover in the ever-present 15-knot wind. It allowed a decent presentation. I found bonefish to be a neurotic lot—at times they refused everything, including bait! At other times I'm sure they would take a cigarette butt on a 2/0 hook. A guest, after becoming satisfied following earlier frustration, said, "I came here thinking that these are just dumb ocean fish. If I'd drop my fly somewhere near, they would rush over and fight to eat it." The years have taught us that bonefish are no different from trout. They are selective, frightened by noise and abnormal movement, and prone to eat something seen as natural in size, color, and movement.

I have gone back and reread *Don't Stop the Carnival.* I now know that running a resort in the Caribbean is everything that Mr. Wouk described, times 10. The stories of three permit in one day; of being flashed by local conch fishermen; of fishing off the dock, reaching for what was thought to be a barracuda and discovering at the last second that it was a crocodile; of falling asleep with a drifting tarpon fly and having your rod and reel disappear to a leaping 80-pound silver king; of broken generators; of running out of fresh water; of transport boats with no engines; of broken 12 weights; of nighttime crocodile hunts; of dock fires; of beach parties and crab races; of tears, frowns, laughs, and smiles that make us realize that this carnival is nonstop.

Doug Jorgensen
Turneffe Flats, Belize
March 1998

The following is a peek into a solo adventure in Belize by Brian O'Keefe. He left Belize River Lodge near Belize City in an inflatable Zodiac to explore, camp, and fish on the outer barrier reef while heading south to Placencia. Brian was on assignment to take photographs and write an article for *Field & Stream* magazine and to do a video for TNN.

This 100-mile-long wilderness offers countless coconut palm-fringed cays, bonefish flats, tarpon lagoons, and some of the best permit waters known. In addition, there are conflicting ocean currents, heavy winds, submerged boat-busting reefs, ferocious biting insects, drug runners, and pirates. In this no man's land, you are on your own and you best be able to take care of yourself. Readers should keep in mind that adventuring for bonefish is often a question of surviving while getting from one place to another. Adventuring is, after all, to engage in daring undertakings. If you deem yourself an adventurer, the sirens of Permit Alley are calling! What the heck, you only live once. If you believe you live twice, you've nothing to lose. Go for it!

Pirates, Permit, and Manatee
by Brian O'Keefe

After more than a dozen trips to Belize fishing most areas with guides, I began to wonder about bringing my own boat to this beautiful country and doing some off-the-wall adventuring on my own. After all, I did own a 13-foot Zodiac.

The 35-horse outboard started on the third pull and, after a "thank you and good-bye" to the fine people of Belize River Lodge, I motored down the Belize River to begin a fantastic 15-day solo adventure with charts and a basic game plan. It did not take long to appreciate the qualities of the solo experience. Every bend in a river and each new flat provided an opportunity to see wildlife, catch fish, or snorkel very remote parts of the barrier reef. I will describe some of the most memorable and challenging situations.

A few days out, I made camp on a small island surrounded by tarpon haunts and permit flats. Fishing was good. I lost a 50-pound tarpon on the third jump, which was just fine as landing big fish alone can be a problem. I had also released two bonefish and found a bunch of snapper for dinner right in front of camp.

An idyllic setting for camping, snorkeling, fishing, and relaxing— until the pirates showed up!

Slasher Cay—paradise by day, the isle of terror by night. It's the life of Brian O'Keefe.

Just before dark, a rogue-looking fishing boat sailed into view and anchored nearby. Two small dugouts headed my way with one person in each. Across the water I heard Spanish, which meant they were not Belizian, probably Hondurans fishing illegally. I knew that some Honduran gill netters were bad news and were responsible for taking more than bonefish. If things got ugly, I did not have much room to maneuver on my half-acre island. The unwelcome ruffians came ashore and launched into rapid-fire Spanish. With hand gestures and limited Spanish, I came to the conclusion that they wanted pot. I said, "No ganja," and they understood. I started working on a project that was a disguise for finding my coconut knife, a 14-inch Crocodile Dundee clone.

The Hondurans went over to my boat and were very impressed with my motor and snorkel gear. Then they went to the other end of the island to work out their plan. I would not be the first nomad to become bonefish chum or shark bait. I was pretty sure they were going to kill me and take my boat. I turned on a light, sat on a log, and worked on a coconut with my big knife. When they returned, I took a couple slightly theatrical chops with the knife. The scruffy amigos stared at the shiny weapon in silence, then got into their dugouts and paddled back to where they came from. I guess they had seen the movie! On the chart, this place is called "Slasher's Cay." What a basis for nightmares!

Several nights later, I anchored the Zodiac on a nice flat on an incoming tide. The ocean side was all sea fans, staghorn coral, and other leader-snapping structure. The inside was sand and turtle

Pirates of the Caribbean transformed into chickens of the sea by Brian O'Keefe.

Because of their body shape, permit require deeper water than bonefish. They also require more patience and specialized techniques. Their personalities and finicky nature makes them a fascinating quarry, and anglers are usually content (for a little while) just to make the cast.

Coming into South Water Cay. It's not a good idea to fly your flag in this no man's land. Besides, it is best to save it in case you lose your shorts!

Resupplies in this country mean beer, soda pop, and water, if you can find it.

grass. Permit can be on the soft stuff, but nine times out of 10 they are in the rough coral that has sunk ships for centuries. Today was my lucky day. Three permit were feeding on grass patches in 18 inches of water. I cast a Merkin 10 feet in front of the trio, one of 12 pounds and two at about 18, and let the fly settle on the sand. When they were four feet away, I gave the fly a slow pull to create a small sand trail. A fish moved to the fly, tailed, and I came tight. It was a perfect scenario, and it ripped me big time, but it never went to the coral. I managed a quick photo on automatic timer and released the fish. That day I cast at seven more permit. No hookups, but I did find some tarpon ripping through a school of baitfish and managed to hook, fight, land, and release a 30-pounder.

The next day I headed north along the barrier reef. The wind was picking up, so I decided not to cross over to Turneffe Island but to stay on the leeward side of the larger islands. It was a day to explore. I saw a permit tail here and there, but I had to find a good camp in case the weather got worse. I preferred small islands with more sand than vegetation because the bugs were thick on the lush islands. At 3 p.m. I pitched my tent on a little island 100 yards long and 30 feet wide. There was great snorkeling. After a lap around camp, I dried off and rigged up a 9 weight for snapper. I planned a fish dinner.

A short ride in the Zodiac found me at an island where, by luck, I found a break in the mangroves that opened up into a huge lagoon. Deep water and tall mangroves equal big snapper. I tied a foam popper onto 30-pound shock leader. Almost every cast was crashed by a shark, 'cuda, or snapper. It was heaven. I was out of the wind and having nonstop action on surface poppers, but my dinner plans were looking bleak. Every shark and 'cuda broke off, and the snapper were too big to keep out of the mangroves where they rubbed me off.

I poled a long distance up the lagoon and fished some potholes

far from any mangrove roots. My popper was instantly sucked up. After a long tug of war, I had an eight-pound cubera snapper flopping on the floor of the Zodiac. Back at camp, I built a fire out of dried coconut husks and wrapped the snapper, with butter and coconut milk, in foil. Twenty minutes later I ate sweet cubera snapper for dinner, had a Snickers for dessert, and tallied up the $30 worth of poppers lost in dark water to mean fish.

The trip south toward Placencia passed too quickly. The fishing was good at the many river mouths for snook, snapper, 'cuda, and jacks. I planned to fish the Placencia area for about five days.

On the last morning I was 15 miles east of town skimming across glassy crystal-clear 82-degree water when a large coral patch came into view. I slowed down uptide of the reef and got out my mask, snorkel, and fins. This looked like a perfect place for a morning dive! My only concern was that I would be in wet shorts for a couple of hours after the swim, so I took them off and dove in. I held the bow line and drifted with the tide over a beautiful forest of elkhorn coral and the aquarium-colored fish that called it home.

Suddenly, out of the corner of my eye, I saw a large gray shape swimming straight at me. I wheeled around and got into an aquatic kung fu position ready to fend off a shark attack. The 500-pound shape was not a shark; it was not even a fish. It was a manatee. She swam to within five feet and circled me three times trying to decide what to do with me. After a few minutes, she turned for deep water.

I climbed into the Zodiac. My Nikonos underwater camera was on the floor. Missing were my Patagonia shorts. The inside of a

It is easy to imagine being startled by a creature this size! Manatee are gentle, plant-eating aquatic mammals that live in shallow waters. They are sometimes called sea cow and can grow to about 13 feet in length. Like most saltwater creatures, their worst enemies are sharks and man. Because they live in shallow water, boat props are a continual danger to them.

Zodiac is not very roomy—there were not many places for shorts to hide. Blown overboard. I still had lots of gas, plenty of sunscreen, and all day to fish. That evening, on the way back to town, I decided to run the boat full speed up to the beach and then dash 50 yards to my room. That plan worked fairly well. No more than a dozen people were yelling at me, pointing, and laughing. At the door to my room, I realized the key had been in the shorts, so I sprinted to the nearest clothesline and borrowed a towel.

At home I wondered: After countless trips to the Bahamas, I've always wanted to camp and fish northern Andros. I've got the charts, and I do own an inflatable sea kayak. . .

Brian O'Keefe
Bend, Oregon
March 1998

	J	**F**	**M**	**A**	**M**	**J**	**J**	**A**	**S**	**O**	**N**	**D**
Bonefish	F-G	F-G	F-E	G-E	G-E	G-E	F-E	F-G	F-G	F-E	F-E	F-G
Permit	P-G	P-G	F-E	G-E	G-E	G-E	G-E	F-G	F-G	F-E	P-E	P-G
Tarpon	F	F	P-F	F-G	G-E	E	E	E	G-E	G	F	F
Snook	F	F	F	F-G	F-G	F	F	F	F	F	F	F
Barracuda	F-G	F-G	G	G-E	G-E	G-E	G-E	G	G	G	F-G	F-G
Snapper	F-G	F-G	F-G	G-E	G-E	G-E	G-E	G	G	G	F-G	F-G
Jacks	F-G	F-G	F-G	G	G	G	G	G	G	G	F-G	F-G
Shark	G	G	G	G	G	G	G	G	G	G	G	G
Wind	L-M	H	H	M-H	M	M	L	L	L-M	M	M	M

P=Poor F=Fair G=Good E=Excellent
L=Light M=Medium H=Heavy

Most Belize flats are wadeable and consist of coral, sand, and grass. The author casts to tailers at Turneffe Island.

Chapter 22

Bikini

Bikini Atoll is one of the most remote and beautiful ocean locations in the world. Located 800 miles north of the equator and 2,300 miles west and a little south of Honolulu, Hawaii, Bikini is "out there." When you are at Bikini, the rest of the world is only a rumor. Unlike Christmas Island, Bikini is well vegetated. This blending of reef, sand, coral, vegetation, and water creates an astonishingly beautiful realization of the proverbial south sea paradise.

During World War II, the Marshall Islands and Micronesia were the scene of many fierce battles. Ironically, the end of World War II signaled the beginning of suffering for the people of Bikini. During the 1940s, the U.S. government moved all native islanders off Bikini and began nuclear testing. The largest atom bomb in history was exploded there in 1954. In essence, the U.S. government selected one of the most strikingly beautiful places on earth and subjected it to the most horrible of calamities. Visitors see bunkers and the mile-wide crater created by the 1954 blast. Nature has healed many of the scars, but others are still slowly recuperating. Visitors also see untouched ocean beaches and flats that offer some of the greatest unexplored fly fishing opportunities.

Bikini has been in a time capsule for 50 years and off limits to everyone, except U.S. Department of Energy scientists who have closely monitored radioactivity. The International Atomic Energy Commission says it is safe to walk on all the islands, and, although the residual radioactivity is still higher than on other islands in the Marshall chain, it is not hazardous to health at the levels measured.

Bikini is roughly an equal distance from Hawaii, Australia, Philippines, and Japan. It is 2,300 miles from Honolulu, which is the closest city. If there weren't a landing strip, you wouldn't think of making the journey. There is; you did! Your thoughts, however, focus on the spectacular ocean flats that separate the tiny coral islands and lagoon from the surging ocean. Visions of fishing for virgin fish in iridescent waters and in total isolation are about to become reality.

Steve Danchok with an exotic long-tom. You never know what might jump your fly next. This fish fought like a tarpon, jumping continuously.

Steve DeMoulin

The air and salt water are safe, but cesium is still in the ground. Any food that is grown becomes poisoned, hence, the native people cannot yet return. No one lives on Bikini permanently. The absence of human habitation has created a de facto saltwater wilderness.

The Bikini government is allowing a limited number of visitors, most of whom are divers and fishermen. Brian O'Keefe was the first American fly fisherman to visit there. Jerry Swanson, who manages Kaufmann's Fly Fishing Expeditions, Inc., led the first organized group of anglers to Bikini and later that year organized a second group of anglers. The photos and fishing discussion in this chapter have been drawn from the experiences of Brian, Jerry, and other group anglers.

All consider Bikini one of the most exciting places for anglers who are self-sufficient and adventurous. Anglers find every imaginable species from puffer to billfish, many that have never been seen by fly fisherman. Divers rate Bikini one of the top five "must see" places. The transparent waters, steep walls, and lagoon with its many sunken ships are a diver's paradise.

Habitat

Bikini is a unique "flats" location, offering much more than the usual bonefish destination. While there are beautiful sand flats, some with scattered coral and vegetation, most angling takes place in "harder" habitat. Many areas of coral are hard and relatively smooth. This is usually dead coral. Live coral areas are rougher. Substantial footgear is a must.

Some coral areas are extremely rough and present a challenge to anglers. When fish swim through coral landscapes in panic mode, flies, leaders, fly lines, and backing are easily destroyed. If you lose a fly line and have a spare, you are fishing within minutes. No big deal, unless you don't have a spare line! Keep your rod high and exert maximum pressure to subdue fish quickly. When fish swim into a coral hole, the game is lost unless you can reach the hole and clear the line. Bikini anglers must use stout rods and leaders and have plenty of flies!

Because you are often wading deep, it is advisable to have a waterproof camera or a shoulder bag that is waterproof. Boat rides can be rough and wet. Protect your rods and carry rain gear.

The extensive lagoon is about 13 by 23 miles and up to 180 feet deep. Between the 20-odd islands that have vegetation and encircle the lagoon are channels that lead directly to deep ocean. Coral heads dot the lagoon, and it is great sport to motor up to one, toss a streamer over it and watch what comes out to play. Once a fish is hooked, it becomes an immediate tug of war of keeping the fish from returning to the sanctuary of the coral. You can lose a lot of flies playing this game. Numerous species patrol the currents that race in and out of the lagoon. Some of the most exciting possibilities happen in these channels, along the reef, at drop-offs, and in blue water.

On the ocean side of the islands lie expansive flats, sometimes backdropped by huge silvery waves that literally explode over the reef. Some ocean flats are sand, rock, and relatively smooth, dead coral, but some are rough, uneven coral. The better locations can be as tough and wild as it gets for anglers. Anything can happen, and any type of fish can swim within range. Be ready!

Whether fishing the channels, lagoon, reef, or blue ocean waters, anglers might cast to trevally, shark, dogtooth tuna, or snapper, all on consecutive casts. Jerry Swanson, casting behind a ray, once hooked three different species on three casts! Like a conveyor belt in a sushi bar, every species imaginable is on parade, either eating or

Accommodations are surfside where the tide and blue Pacific sweep your thoughts to distant places and times. As you relax after a memorable day of exploring, your rods are at ready just in case!

Jerry Swanson

Jerry displays a colorful grouper. They come in all colors and sizes, some larger than you.

The close proximity of lagoon and ocean creates diverse habitat and fishing situations.

Blue-fin trevally over coral on an outside ocean flat.

A quick do-it-yourself, do-not-touch-the-fish photo of a blue-fin trevally.

being eaten. That is part of the fascination at Bikini—you never know when or where your next target will appear or what it might be. Because of this quick-paced and varied fishing, anglers must have the proper tackle and know how to use it.

Fish Species

Bikini is unique among bonefish destinations because it offers the widest variety of species. It is possible to release 20 or more, some of which you may not be able to identify. Some of the most common fish anglers are likely to encounter include, trevally, grouper, sweetlips, emperor, snapper, goatfish, coronation trout, squirrel fish, coral trout, jobfish, bass, swallowtail dart, tuna, dorado, wahoo, marlin, and many species of shark.

Trevally is the most available species at Bikini, and it is the perfect fly rod fish. Besides being beautifully colored, trevally are aggressive, quick, and powerful, and they get big. They literally explode on surface poppers. This audible and visible explosion is one of the most exciting experiences an angler can have in shallow saltwater. Imagine skating a seven-inch dry fly for trout! The experience is not soon forgotten. What more do you want?

Anglers should note that when the wind is disrupting the water surface, trevally may be difficult to interest in a surface popper. If the choppy surface makes it difficult for fish to detect the popper, use a larger popper and pull it *fast!*

Many record-size trevally swim in and out of the lagoon waters and prowl the reefs at Bikini, including blue-fin, *Caranx melampygus*; great (big-eye), *C. sexfasciatus*; giant, *C. ignobilis*; golden, *Gnathanodon speciosus*; black; yellow spotted; and others not yet identified.

Richard Humphrey accompanied Jerry on the first organized trip to Bikini, and he landed record-size blue-fin. Richard also hooked a 60-pound giant trevally 10 feet off the beach! Brian

O'Keefe talks of hooking 20 to 30 pounders on poppers until he got bored or until he didn't want to stress his arm and rod any longer. Bill Leahy, a Colorado angler who was a member of Steve's group, was trolling back to camp one evening when his plug disappeared into a huge watery vortex. It looked like an underwater twister exploded at the surface but turned out to be a trevally of incredible proportions, perhaps 150 pounds! Bill's fishing partners couldn't lift it into the boat even if they wanted to, which they didn't. It was released back into the lagoon.

One fisherman once watched doubles and triples come out of the deep like fighter jets. They would strafe the flat, and smaller fish would scatter in every direction for safety, sometimes using the angler as cover. Trevally would whirl about him, completely unafraid, eating everything possible. Watching the frenzied action was better than fishing.

Another time, walking the beach between sand bars when the tide was running just fast enough to obscure the bottom, an angler flipped his Sea Habit Bucktail 20 feet, and five famished trevally materialized. The angler felt like he was energized into another world. The feisty five raced for his fly, and his line shot through the rod guides. He could see the fly in the corner of a trevally's mouth with the others in eager pursuit. It looked like a street fight was about to erupt—four fish attempting to steal the fly from the mouth of the one that had it. He watched water erupt and didn't know whether to reel or give slack line so the trevally could get away. Suddenly the fly came flying through the air back toward the fisherman. As it hit the water, another fish grabbed it, this time deeper in its mouth and out of sight. Later he released a beautiful long-nosed sweetlips, *Lethrinus miniatus*, that had beat out the blue-fin gang of five. These wild looking sweetlips are commonly called emperors.

There are many varieties of sweetlips, and they are widely distributed throughout the Pacific and Indian oceans. The long-nosed sweetlips is recognized by its long pointed head and especially large tail—a measure of its speed and power. Its body and fins are silvery pearlescent with tints of pale green, even electric blue. When captured, they develop dark blotches and cross bars, possibly as a warning to other fish or because they are frightened and stressed. Keep them in the water, where they are much happier, more electric, and more photogenic. This is true of all fish.

Bonefish run three to eight pounds with bigger fish patrolling reef areas.

Richard Humphrey and a long-nosed sweetlips. These are strong, aggressive fish, and they vary in color.

Richard Humphrey

Bikini bonefish seem to be unusually broad and well muscled. This ocean fish was caught on the reef.

Richard Humphrey

An average bonefish hooked off the beach by Rod Bourke. Bikini bonefish are tough customers and are often sighted in strong tidal flows. You don't catch a lot of them but when you do. . .

Coronation trout are beautifully colored and are strong battlers. Jerry Swanson hooked this one from shore. Fish are not selective at Bikini so it is seldom necessary to change flies for the various species. Just tie a big one that sinks onto a stout leader and go for it!

Jerry Swanson

They are exceptionally robust and strong. This might be explained, in part, by their habitat, which is harsh and always in flux. Brian O'Keefe described his first encounter with Bikini bonefish this way: "Bonefish were holding like trout in a quick-paced tidal current. They rested from the current behind structure—rocks, coral, shells. I had never before seen stationary bonefish. I positioned myself up current and drifted and swung the fly in front of them. When hooked, they took full advantage of the current and were very difficult to land. They were big and incredibly strong!"

Other anglers have encountered bonefish over sand bottoms, inside the reef on ocean flats, and feeding along the margin of the lagoon. All have commented on their strength. Bonefish are not present in big numbers at Bikini. Anglers target them as they would any of the many other species. When you find them, make the cast!

Walking the beach into the tide is a good method of intercepting fish. Jerry Swanson was working his way toward a coral point against the tide when he spotted what looked like a big rosy jobfish, *Pristipomoides filamentosus*, or king snapper, holding in the current. King snapper grow to over three feet and are ferocious battlers. In a playful mood, Jerry tossed an epoxy bonefish fly across the tidal current, which caused the fly to swing and skate over the fish. Mr. Snapper chased it downstream. Fish on! It peeled fly line and backing across the flat and stopped in a coral hole. Jerry wanted a photo of this fish so he waded out across the tide to the obstruction. Chest deep in current and barely keeping his feet under himself, he probed the coral hole and came up empty handed. His narrow focus now turned to getting back without some larger creature thinking, "Look what's coming for dinner!"

Jerry tells of a green jobfish, _Aprion virescens_, also referred to as king snapper, that swam into a blue hole after crossing a flat from the ocean. Blue holes on the flat are like watering holes in the desert. They are rich in food and attract many species, all of them there to eat others. At Bikini these aquariums can produce a different fish every cast. Jerry was false casting to another fish when the jobfish came into range. He changed casting direction and presented the fly. The jobfish whirled 90 degrees to take it. Realizing its mistake, it returned to the ocean and left Jerry without a leader and fly. He was lucky to keep his fly line!

Goatfish, _Parupeneus rubescens_, and others are another interesting species in that they have two long white fleshy whiskers growing from their lower jaw, which they use to locate food. They seldom exceed three pounds but are an interesting catch. In some parts of the Pacific, goatfish are known as dreamfish because they can cause fish poisoning characterized by vivid dreams. Eating one of these could turn your adventure into a dream trip.

Coronation trout, _Variola louti_, is one of the most colorful fish commonly caught with a fly. It is brilliantly colored in hues of magenta, tangerine, and lemon with crimson and purple spots. Its tail forms a perfect semicircle that is edged with canary yellow. You can't mistake these; they are too beautiful to remove from the water.

Coral trout, _Plectropomus maculatus_, are considered royalty. They can reach several pounds, but a five- or six-pound fish is a prize catch. They have various color phases, but coral with purple spots seems to be the most common. Others look like a brown trout, and still others may be almost black. Bikini anglers find these

Richard Humphrey

Coral trout have various color phases, and this one looks like a brown trout. Note how the coloration of this fish matches the surrounding coral. Angler is Matt Hollis.

All aboard! The "hammerhead" was the early mode of transportation. It plows through the roughest seas and looks like it survived the 1950s. Note: Some of the photos of fish in this chapter were taken inside the "hammerhead." Because of its high sides, it was the only way to photograph them.

Steve DeMoulin

Rod Bourke displaying a bass. Note the big streamer in its mouth and the rough and tumble landscape it calls home.

Richard Humphrey

Swallowtail darts are one of the most beautiful, exciting, and plentiful fish at Bikini. They are found in the same habitat as bonefish.

Jerry Swanson

Bikini atoll viewed from inside the lagoon. The larger islands are vegetated but have sandy beaches.

in heavy coral, and they are always difficult to land. The trick is to get their head up and keep it up.

Red Bass, *Lutjanus bohar*, are present to over 20 pounds, but a five pounder can attack your fly so savagely that it is difficult to keep them from running for the coral—and freedom. They are darker on their upper sides and back, shading pink to red underneath. Usually, the larger the fish, the darker its colors. Red bass have been implicated in tropical fish poisoning, or ciguatera, and should never be eaten. Symptoms may appear within two to 24 hours and can be complicated by alcohol. Muscle weakness; nausea; vomiting; tingling of the lips, fingertips, toes; numbness; temperature sensation; and even respiratory paralysis are all possible. Because it is impossible to tell how severe the poisoning may be, it is advised you get to a hospital at once. Better yet, don't eat fish that you can't identify or that are known to carry the toxin!

One of the most exciting and beautiful fish at Bikini is the swallowtail dart, *Trachinotus velox*, also known as southern swallowtail or southern dart. They are perfectly suited to bonefish tackle and smash poppers, streamers, and Clousers. Swallowtails have a deep, slender body, a swallow-like tail, and sickle-like anal and second dorsal fins. They are smooth, clean fish with a toothless mouth and average five pounds. Expect them in shallow-water sand flats, along beaches and drop-offs, and in cuts. The snub-nosed dart, *Trachinotus blochi*, is closely related to permit and is found at Bikini.

Fishing offshore in deeper blue water is an unknown quantity in virgin sport fishing grounds. Brian O'Keefe was one of the first American fly fishermen to test the waters. He rigged up a seven-inch popper on a 12 weight and within 15 minutes a billfish of unknown variety swooped in for the grab, and that was it. Brian re-rigged and hooked another tackle buster 30 minutes later.

Jerry Swanson was trying his luck at trolling outside the lagoon

and was rigged with a billfish popper, 8/0 hooks, 20-pound class tippet and three feet of 80-pound wire. The rig was not in the water 30 seconds when a mystery fish bit through the 80-pound wire. Jerry didn't feel so bad after the sailboat captain lost a fish that broke him off on 300-pound test while he was hand lining! The line was about the diameter of parachute cord.

One angler relates a story of trolling big flies offshore for dorado, *Coryphaena hippurus*, commonly called mahi-mahi. "I watched as the bulls jumped from wave top to wave top smashing bait. Watching these colorful speedsters leapfrog each other to be first on the scene was a never-to-be-forgotten sight. When one was hooked, the school would stay together and surround the boat. Others were soon hooked, and many times five anglers would all be fast to dorado streaking in every direction. It was difficult to determine which fish was yours."

Dogtooth tuna, *Gymnosarda unicolor*, are not considered a tuna or a bonito as previously classified but, rather, the lone species in its own genus. Dogtooth tuna get their name because they bark when chasing prey and howl when hooked, especially when the moon is full. If you believe that, you should believe everything in this book! Actually, they have large dog-like conical teeth and are scaleless except for over the corset, a region near the pectoral fin, and along the lateral line. They are indigo blue across their backs, shading to pale blue and silvery along their sides, with dull yellow fins and big eyes. They commonly grow to over 150 pounds but don't expect to land any that size. Cast your fly to 20 or 30 pounders. These are tough customers on a 12-weight rod and will

As you wade flats, you are both in the water and in the sky. Both seem to extend to infinity, and you can't help but notice your insignificance. Note the mixture of sand and coral and the waves on the distant reef.

Richard Humphrey

Richard Humphrey and a red bass.

This mahi-mahi was landed and released a short distance offshore.

Jerry Swanson

Bikini is extremely rich in bird and fish life. Birds and predator fish know where to find food. Locate the birds and you are in for some wild ocean action.

Richard Humphrey

Coconut crabs are the largest living terrestrial invertebrates and grow to two feet in width. Their claws can break a man's leg.

South Pacific flies.

clean you out. They can be found in the faster, deeper channels, off shore, and sometimes at lagoon entrances.

Skipjack tuna, *Katsuwonus pelamis*, is a coveted migratory fish that is fished commercially throughout the Pacific and ends up in cans marked light-meat tuna in spring water! Skipjack often swim with yellowfin and are common to 30 pounds. They are guaranteed to put the hurt on your gear. Skipjack are easily identified by the four or more dark stripes on their belly that run from their pectoral fin to their tail, and because there are no markings or pattern across their blue-black back.

Yellowfin tuna, *Thunnus albacares*, is one of the most sought after and respected of saltwater game fish. I have seen tuna fight anglers to exhaustion, and that is no lie! Sometimes yellowfin run fast at the surface, ultimately running the angler out of line. At other times they sound deep and are impossible to move. When big fish go deep, back off the boat so you can exert rod pressure at an angle. Otherwise, you can't move them.

If you find the birds, you often find yellowfin and everything else. Smaller tuna usually chase baitfish at the surface. If you find them, hope that the tuna are not too big. Look for yellowfin in the deeper, faster channels and offshore.

Wahoo, *Acanthocybium solandri*, are found beyond the reef. They are one of the greatest game fish. Wahoo look like a cross between a barracuda and a mackerel. They have razor-sharp teeth, can leap like flying fish, and have the strength of billfish. Wahoo are one of the fastest fish, attaining speeds of 50 miles per hour. They'll do zero to 60 in a second! They are common up to 40 pounds or so but can tip the scales at 150 pounds. Very few fly anglers have landed wahoo. You'll know when you hook one! Anglers interested in offshore fishing should read *Bluewater Fly Fishing* by Trey Combs.

At Bikini it is possible to walk to the edge of hard rock (dead coral) flats at low tide and, using a shooting head fly line, reach deep water and pelagic fish. Casting to mahi-mahi, yellowfin, skip jack, dogs, and monster trevally from shore is rarely possible. Don't miss the opportunity.

Tides

Tidal fluctuations vary between one foot during neap tides to five feet during spring tides. Like anyplace, Bikini fishes differently according to the tides. During higher tides, currents channeled past sand bars and islands speed up and run from the ocean into the lagoon. During the highest tides, fish cruise at the edge of the main current within an easy cast from shore. In many places, this creates river-like conditions complete with seams, riffs, and eddies—plus dangerous undertows! All this makes for some very dynamic and thrilling fishing. Be careful when fishing near deep moving water. Brian's hat blew off at such a place, and it was on its way to New Guinea.

Always be careful when releasing strange fish. It is possible that they may have unusually sharp or poisonous spines, razor-sharp fins and gill covers, or teeth that can cause you harm. Ask the locals how to handle them. When in doubt, don't touch them. It is best to keep fish in the water, run your hand down the leader to the fly, and back it out with pliers.

At Bikini both the fishing and the sense of creation overwhelm you. You could hook a fish that is the size of a half-sheet of plywood, is colored like a prism, or swims faster than almost any land animal runs. If you have "been there and done that" and are looking for a challenge, Bikini is the place.

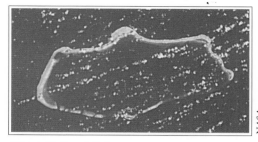

Bikini Atoll and its lagoon.

Hundreds of species inhabit Bikini, and they come in all colors and sizes.

Man overboard!

The fluidity of color and form in the underwater world of bonefish are astonishingly beautiful. Bikini Atoll.

Chapter 23

Bonaire

One of the most frequently asked questions by bonefish anglers is, "Where can I take a nonfishing friend?" That answer depends on what activities are desired and whether the emphasis is on fishing or other activities. Some compromises must be made!

If swimming, birding, relaxing with a good book, and hanging out on the flats are fun without too much emphasis on accommodations and dining, then many locations are excellent. If land and water sports, restaurants, and a little shopping are necessary, a few locations would work. If a selection of five-star restaurants, spotless accommodations, and Fifth Avenue shopping are on the agenda, nonfishermen should consider spending the week in Miami, Nassau, or Honolulu while the angler fishes his fly off at Christmas Island or at the out islands in the Bahamas. Many anglers go to Christmas Island and spend the week before or the week after in Hawaii with the family. Everyone has a great time! Or, on the radical side, the nonadventurer can spend the week in London or Paris and the angler can sail the Seychelles!

Some destinations offer excellent accommodations, a selection of fine restaurants, and some shopping. Others offer none of the above, and many fall in between the two extremes. Many nonfishing friends have a wonderful time at bonefish destinations. It can be the perfect tropical getaway to sunshine and sand, especially if a casual and relaxed lifestyle is desired. Lounge on the beach, swim, snorkel, dive, bike, beachcomb, sail, windsurf, read, shell, bird watch, exercise, or simply vegetate. All destinations are not created

Jon Covich

A typical Bonaire bonefish. Notice the scales and intricate color scheme and how perfectly they blend with surrounding colors.

equal. What works for one couple may not work for another. Don't get lured into the wrong place.

Jon Covich is a fishing manufacturers' representative and free-lance photographer living in Seattle, Washington. Jon used to travel to distant lands with one thought in mind—fly fishing from dawn

Rainbows bring good luck. Look for the school of giant bonefish that always swims under the arch.

to dark, maybe beyond. Nothing else mattered. . .until he met Fran Doniego. Now the word "vacation" has taken on new meaning and there are other considerations. I am certain many anglers can relate to this dilemma! Following is Jon's story.

"Whatever You Want, Honey"
By Jon Covich

November through March can be frustrating months for North American anglers. I am no exception. My busy season as a fly tackle sales representative is over by November when nothing is more important than escaping to a tropical environment and wading bonefish flats. I usually rationalize this extravagance by telling myself that part of my job is to become a well-traveled expert angler. Besides, it's theraputic and a good investment in my mental health.

This rationalization worked perfectly until I met the girl of my dreams. As most nonbachelors realize, love often alters the angling scene. Fran likes to fly fish but questions why every vacation must be centered around it.

Looking for a compromise, I queried friends who had visited Bonaire on a scuba-diving expedition, which is located 100 miles northwest of Caracas, Venezuela. They raved about the fantastic underwater sites, the island's unique scenery, its funky resorts, and its bonefish. Bonefish was the magic word. We decided to try it. We arrived shortly before the peak dive season and rented a rusty micro van—perfect transportation for Bonaire's rough roads and for stowing wet dive gear and flats boots with guiltless abandon.

Jon Covich

Bonefish are best photographed in the water.

Jon Covich

Jon decided to visit Bonaire which is located about 100 miles northwest of Caracas, Venezuela.

Jon Covich

Jon Covich

Bonefish are available close in and right along side the road. Guides can take you to remote areas.

Coral gardens are prolific and many are almost on the beach. Pack a picnic, fly rod, camera, and swim gear and enjoy the tropical ambiance.

Jon Covich

We checked out all the resorts and small inns, looking for just the perfect accommodation. We like the adventure of not booking lodgings in advance, but this is not advisable. Nonetheless, we lucked into a beautiful poolside room complete with a kitchenette and a view of the ocean.

Kralendijk is the largest town, and it offers civilized life. We found a number of classic ocean-front bars and excellent restaurants. There are also plenty of tourist shops and a well-stocked market. Bonaire has a European flavor, Dutch currency, Dutch beer, and casual dress on the beach. It didn't take long to get into the groove of island life.

I lobbied for starting each day with an early trip to the bonefish flats at the south end of the island. I claimed tidal timing and that the midday heat might be too grueling in this salty mangrove country. "I'm just concerned that you have a good time dear, so let's fish early and spend the rest of the day doing what you want." I thought I had fooled her at the time, but I've come to realize that she recognizes fish lust.

Driving south on the island's coast road, we discovered water on both sides of us. To the right was the ocean and to the left interior flats, some of which are used for salt production. Part of this area is a flamingo sanctuary. When we ran out of no-trespassing signs, we began looking for bonefish habitat. At several places the road passed over cuts that led to and from the ocean. We followed

these cuts inland to where they fanned out into about four square miles of wadeable flats, much as we imagined the bonefish did.

We soon spotted several bonefish tails glimmering in the calm water. We caught fish each day, sometimes a few, sometimes several. Bonaire is often windy but it was unbelievably calm during our visit, which made the bonefish skittish. We were successful only after long stalks and landing small flies delicately in their path. Guides are available and probably would have increased our catch, but we were on our own adventure. Each fish was very rewarding. Productive patterns included the Gotcha, Turd, Baited Breath, and pearl or tan Charlies. Bonefish ranged between two and four pounds.

At Lac Bay on the island's southeast corner there is a beautiful flat that opens up to the ocean where small sets of waves break. Locals told of catching tarpon out of boats at the bay's entrance when the tide was changing. I gave it a try wading but only enticed a few small barracuda. Locals said that a day of guided boat angling in the backcountry mangrove area at the interior of Lac Bay should reveal snook, baby tarpon, and rooting bonefish.

Bonaire makes it easy for divers and snorkelers to explore the underwater coral and fish life, which is fabulous. Although organized dive trips are offered through all the resorts, it is easy to do much on your own. We found dive sites with the aid of a courtesy dive map. Yellow-painted numbered rocks that correspond to those on the map are found along the road. The water surrounding Bonaire is shockingly clear, partly because sediment is not stirred by dramatic tide fluctuations. Every dive was unique and remarkable. At one site we swam through an incredible coral forest, at

Jon Covich

Water surrounding Bonaire is shockingly clear. Roadside dive and snorkel sites are easy to access and provide wonderful sport. Beaches are often deserted—do what you like best.

Jon Covich

Jon and Fran with scrappy bones. Fish this size rip more line than trout several times this size!

another we were shadowed by a huge barracuda, and at yet another we saw several turtles.

One of the first things that struck us about Bonaire was how unpopulated and arid the island is. Many first-time visitors visualize Caribbean islands as lush and tropical, when in fact many are not. The landscape at Bonaire is barren, broken only by mangroves and cactus. If you rent a four-wheel drive, Slagbaai National Park at the north end of the island is worth the trip. A bumpy dirt road leads through endless cactus forests where you can view iguanas and wild goats in great numbers. We were always pleased when the view revealed the deep blue waters of the Caribbean or the inland lake that was crowded with flamingos. The park also has numerous secluded bays that are ideal for diving, snorkeling, and doing other fun things. Travel through this area is slow, however, so plan on spending the better part of a day here.

Bonaire is a bonefish destination that can satisify couples seeking a diverse vacation. It is part of the Dutch-speaking Lesser Antilles and unlike nearby Aruba and Curacao, Bonaire does not cater to cruise boats, and is relatively unknown.

Bonaire has much to offer. We went there to have a vacation that was more than just fly fishing. We got just that. On our last morning on the flats, however, only hours before our plane was to leave, Fran spotted, cast to, and hooked her first bonefish without any assistance. It made a burning run through water only inches deep, took a right turn around a mangrove, and broke her off. She reeled in, and we left. During the trip home, she talked of little else besides that fish and how we need to take more trips to bonefish destinations. Whatever you want, Honey!

Jon Covich
Bend, Oregon
February 1999

Fishing? Right now? Maybe later. The beach looks pretty inviting. This tranquil scene is in the Cook Islands.

Chapter 24

Cayman Islands

Located about 500 miles south of Miami, the Cayman Islands are best known for world-class diving, international banking, and stable winter weather. Daytime temperatures run between 70 and 80 degrees from November through April. January through early April is the driest season, although heavy tropical rain can occur anytime.

There are three islands: Grand Cayman, Cayman Brac, and Little Cayman. Grand Cayman is the center of the tourist activity and is home to 28,000 of the country's 30,000 inhabitants. Most visitors stay here at upscale beachside resorts that offer all the amenities. The famous seven-mile beach is one of the most beautiful in all the Caribbean. Families find plenty to do, and anglers can fish the many flats for bonefish or take a short 75-mile flight to Little Cayman for a day of expertly guided permit and tarpon fishing. At Grand Cayman, productive bonefish flats can be waded from shore at many points, including South Sound, Prospect Point, Frank Sound, and the northwest corner of North Sound. Tarpon are also found in nearly every pond and ditch on Grand Cayman and sometimes can be hooked off the beach. Fish run one to 10 pounds; some off the beach may reach 40 or 50 pounds!

Cayman Brac caters mostly to divers, but there is some bonefishing along the southwest end of the island. Walk the beach and spot cruisers and tails in shallow water.

Little Cayman has 100 inhabitants and countless species of wildlife, especially fish. Relaxed resorts offer all the amenities and specialize in fishing and diving. Water clarity is fantastic. At least a

There are plenty of places to cast a fly at Little Cayman. Tarpon Lake is on the right. Notice the huge muds at the center.

thousand species of plants and animals are found on the reefs and reef walls offshore, including 60 species of coral and 30 species of sponges. The red-footed booby colony is one of the largest in the Western Hemisphere. Several species of parrots are found on the island.

Bonefish and permit are plentiful on surrounding flats, and good numbers of aggressive baby tarpon inhabit shallow Tarpon Lake. Fishing is excellent, either on your own while walking the beach or boating with a guide. Excellent guide service can be arranged on an hourly or half-day basis. Schedules are flexible, allowing you to return for a beachside lunch or to fish only during peak time. Or, take the day off and snorkel, dive, or relax. This is the perfect place for couples whose favorite pastimes may include diversions other than fishing. You won't be bored!

Buck Buchenroth and his wife, Jules, operate a guide business in Daniel, Wyoming, and guide at the Southern Cross Club at Little Cayman during the winter. Buck has fished on the U.S. World Fly Fishing Team and is an angler extraordinaire. In the following piece, Buck shares many valuable insights about the angling opportunities this unique island offers.

Fly Fishing Little Cayman Island
by Buck Buchenroth
Note: If you were casting a full sinking fly line with a sink rate of one foot per second, it would take about seven hours of descending through noth-

ingness before your #2/0 deep water Clouser snagged the seabed at the bottom of the Cayman Trench 25,000 feet below.

An isolated seascraper towering up through the Caribbean abyss, Little Cayman Island rises from the depths in a sharp vertical spike. Only 10 miles long and one mile wide, the landmass is oriented with the narrow ends pointing easterly and westerly with long northern and southern coastlines. The 10 square mile top of the seamount reaches a mere forty feet above sea level at the summit of Sparrowhawk Hill.

Surrounding terrestrial Little Cayman, sea life flourishes. Fly fishermen find the tiny isle an astonishing microcosm swarming with an abundance of diverse sport fishes. Unlike many fishing destinations where anglers may walk or be poled for miles looking for the same fish species, conditions and species change rapidly as you move along the shores of Little Cayman.

Bonefish, tarpon, and permit are the three species most sought by the fly anglers who visit the isle. Due to the unique layout of Little Cayman, opportunities to fish to all of the "big three" present themselves every day. Indeed, the island is a location where a fly-caught grand slam is relatively common.

Donna Stewart with a decent bonefish from the flats inside the reef.

The large variety of species swimming the flats of Little Cayman interested in flies provides ample opportunity for anglers to add the word "super" in front of their well-earned permit, bonefish, and tarpon grand slam. This is accomplished by also landing a mutton snapper, ocean triggerfish, or perhaps a 25-pound horse-eye jack. All of these and many more strong-swimming fly rod species are common, but not overly numerous, on the flats of Little Cayman.

Be warned! Anglers who want to catch large numbers of any specific species—bonefish, for example—risk disappointment. Little Cayman is simply too small an environment to provide anglers with big numbers. Little Cayman is not *world class* for catching any one fish. What Little Cayman offers fly fishermen is diversity. The close proximity of the shoreline to deep water creates a situation where fishermen commonly see, fish to, and catch species rarely accessible elsewhere. As a friend of mine put it, "There is a lot more action for bonefishermen on Little Cayman than just bonefish."

I learned this lesson well the first time I fished Little Cayman in 1986. I was staying at what was then and still is the only fly fishing destination lodge in the Cayman Islands, the Southern Cross Club. A lifelong friend of mine, who coincidentally guided for the club at the time, had lured me down. My friend had talked about bones and the isle's famous landlocked Tarpon Lake, but it was his whisperings of permit that resulted in the purchase of those plane tickets. "Permit up to 35 pounds swim the flats of Little Cayman year round, but, come spring, when the water over the grass flats really begins to warm up, they are as thick as sand. While fishing at high tide, you won't be working singles, but rather pods of fish averaging 11 to 18 pounds. "

The following spring a local fisherman spotted me wading the turtle grass flat in front of the Southern Cross Club. It was the morning after I had arrived; the tide was up. Intrigued by my fly-rodding antics, the Caymanian watched me closely. He observed

Sunsets can be spent fishing, swimming, cocktailing, or dining. All are within a few paces of your accommodations.

my very first cast and thus witnessed the very first time I spooked a pod of permit.

With a "swoosh," their sickle tails swirled a cataclysm of seawater. Then, knees trembling, I stood pondering on the now empty plains of Permit Central.

I snapped back from my reverie, hearing the native bystander kibitz, "Ah, you crazy mon; dem bonyfishes won't eat no feaders."

After being humbled by that group of spikers (permit), I would have viewed even friendly salutations as fighting words. With that comment, in that situation, I thought, "Hell, at least I know the difference between bonefish and permit. "

Giggling and brimming with good-natured camaraderie, the big fella continued, "Did ja gib it up? Der right der; show us how you cotch dem bonyfishes wit dat fly rod."

"Idiot," I thought. "He's an idiot. Spooked; they are spooked. You can't catch a permit that is spooked." Ready to tell the fellow a bit about the sport of fly fishing I looked up. "Hey!" I exclaimed. Then, before I could continue, my polarized vision spied a movement that made my knees start trembling again. Swallowing my rebuke, I inquired hoarsely, "What's making that huge line of nervous water?"

"I done told ya, mon," he said smirking and shaking his head. "You see what I say now? Dem bonyfish been feeding along all quiet like, but now, I'd say about 60 of dem buggers is about ta run ya down."

"Idiot," I thought. "I'm an idiot. "

After quickly stripping a sufficient length of fly line from the reel, I checked the fly. I was fishing a size 6 brown snapping shrimp. I had been assured, and later came to prove for myself, that stealthy slender patterns that ride hook up, like the snapping

Buck Buchenroth and Donna Stewart score a double hookup. They both could have bonefish or "isbutain'ts."

shrimp, murder anything feeding over the grass. Attempting to ignore my skeptical audience, I made a cast, "Wait for it; not yet; let the lead fish pass the tippet." As I talked myself through the moment, it occurred to me, what if bonefish here really "don't eat feeders?"

"And den it happened, right der in front of dat big fella. I hitched my line and den hauled up a big fly-rod-cotched bony-fish." Or, so I thought.

I was so proud. After getting the leader touch, which is enough for me to count coup, scoring another one to the life's list, I planned to lift briefly the battled bedraggled bone from the water. Showing off for the amused Caymanian seemed a grand plan until I reached for the fish and realized that it wasn't a bone. I had caught my first Little Cayman "isbutain't."

The dreaded "isbutain't."

"Isbutain't?" For the uninitiated it's a silly but appropriate phrase applied when you know it "is" one kind of fish "but" it "ain't." On your hook is some other species altogether. One of the quirks about fishing such a diverse ecosystem as Little Cayman is that you don't always catch the fish you have seen. The overlapping of many flats species feeding side by side provides many unseen opportunistic fish the chance to strike your fly before your intended quarry can. In this case, the fish turned out to be a five-pound yellowjack. Shaking the weariness from the wrist of my rod hand, I realized that some species of "isbutain'ts" ain't so shabby.

This experience further taught me that, while all flats fishing requires the awareness of a heron, wade fishermen on Little Cayman must pay attention to all water depths because permit, bonefish, and others are frequently feeding simultaneously on the same flat. Darting out from a pod of permit or school of bones, the unavoidable fly nabbers will foil 30 percent of your best-placed casts.

Members of the jack and snapper families are the most common culprits. Both groups of these aggressive fish are avariciously attracted to yellow. This color attraction, practically an addiction, is so strong that anglers seeking these species need only to strip anything yellow, and they will soon have one.

This is an excellent training method. I frequently teach beginners the fundamentals of stripping, striking, landing, and releasing fish by having them fish a size 4 yellow epoxy fly. I'd think nothing of a student landing six or more species in a lesson while he or she casts the durable epoxy fly over any of the isle's coral flats. The compulsion to strike yellow makes it a color to be avoided in patterns aimed at more classical targets like bonefish lips. Burnt orange and dirty pink are the safe pigments of choice for flies that require color.

Flies that have been proven effective on other fishing grounds are found equally appetizing by these fish, and all of the traditional patterns work fine. Due to the shallow nature and bottom texture of many flats, it is helpful to augment most patterns with a monofilament weedguard. Smaller hook sizes are preferred. If you would normally go with a size 4, tie on a size 6. In many situations a size 8 or 10 will outperform a larger fly. Light olive, tan, and root beer are favored colors because they match most bottom hues.

Cayman sunrises and sunsets are always worth the effort to see. Sometimes tailers are easiest to spot at this time if the tide is right.

Life is laid back in the Caymans. Even the fish seem to be relaxed as they feed on urchin, which are certainly on slow mode. Fish a little, eat a little, perhaps dive or snorkel, play tennis, soak up the sunshine, or nap. Many species of fish keep anglers interested. Grand Cayman Island.

Regardless of color, big bright eyes peer out from the body of all of my ties. Serious attention needs to be given to the sink rate; bead chain eyes are sufficient for deeper water or days with more wave surge, painted-on or mono eyes for the skinnier water conditions. Metal eyes are typically unnecessary except for fishing muds.

I realize that some folks may not be this critical, but, when it comes time to select a fly for any species on Little Cayman, my rule is, if I had only one cast at a world-record fish in this situation, would I cast the fly in my hand? If the answer is no, put it back in the box. Little Cayman isn't going to show you enough targets to justify a fly selection refusal.

One food item common to Little Cayman that is frequently overlooked by fly fishermen is urchins. Because of the diversity of species that frequent the flats of Little Cayman and love to munch urchin, it is a "must" fly. Patterns should be tied to imitate either the reef urchin or, even better, the rock-boring urchin. Tied on a size 2 black or red-stained hook, the overall body diameter should be no greater than 1/ inches.

The most difficult aspect of fishing an urchin fly is knowing when and how to strike. Getting the fish to eat an urchin is easy. Throw the fly in the water—not so close that it causes a spook, just so the fish sees it—then let it settle to the bottom. Now, wait for the tough part—when to strike.

Although different for each specie, I break the correct timing and hooking method for an urchin fly strike into two categories: fish with rubbery lips and fish with teeth.

Fish with rubbery lips—permit, bone, and Nassau grouper—tend to tail down hard, smashing the exposed urchin against the sea floor. For rubbery lips, strip strike just after the fish tips down. The strike begins with a slow draw strip, not enough to move the fly, just to take the slack out of the line. When the line comes tight—and if the quarry is tailing—strip strike. Make a short hard strip strike, then hold the line tight and *do not* raise the rod tip.

Of course, you have to be ready to guide the slack line cleanly onto the reel. You'll need to get that rod tip up extra high so the line doesn't rub into a coral as the fish races about. That all has to wait. Fish that eat urchins expect to be pricked and don't take off

after being hooked the way previous experience using other fly patterns suggests they should.

After strip striking an urchin pattern, it is not uncommon for the fish to stay right where it is. While it continues to smash the prickers attempting to nibble on the protected tidbit, you go crazy. It's unnerving. You stuck him 15 seconds ago, the line is light, and you can feel the vibration of his head movements shivering up the fly line. Don't worry; he will take off once he figures you out.

Fish with teeth, whether they are super hard-lipped like certain parrotfish species or semirubber-lipped like most members of the trigger family, seem to prefer picking the urchin up and then turning it over before biting the tender and less protected underbelly. More often than not they are carrying the fly as their heads come up. On these species, make the strike just as they lift their head up after tailing down. This is not a strip strike but rather an aggressive back-cast strike. If you miss the fish, ripping the fly away seems to create confusion as the fish looks for the missing morsel. Typically, when you present the urchin a second time, the fish will nail it. If you strip and miss the hookup, the fish tend to sniff suspiciously at the suspended pattern as it settles back to the bottom. This is time to change patterns or find a new fish. That one's done with urchin.

I cannot tell you the number of times I've caught fish or the number of different species I have caught while fishing the urchin fly. I've been amazed by the times when these fish have urchin spines still stuck in their lips from a previous meal. Each time I laugh, recalling my Labrador sheepishly returning home after playing with a porcupine—for the second time.

The long north and south coastlines of Little Cayman are composed of an array of differing fishing flats. The isle's beachfront and flats vary radically along the 20 miles of fishable coastline. The bottom diversity of the beachfront shallows and the corresponding smorgasbord of tasty critters most sought by sport fishers are two of the key ingredients that create the excellence of angling found on Little Cayman.

Approximately two-thirds of Little Cayman's fly fishing flats lie in bays protected behind an exposed barrier reef. The remaining

Grass, sand, and coral flats attract bonefish, permit, jacks, and snapper.

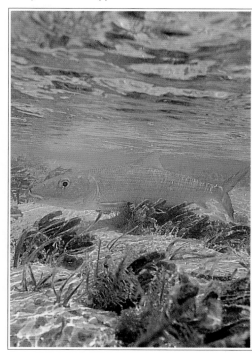

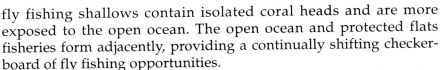

fly fishing shallows contain isolated coral heads and are more exposed to the open ocean. The open ocean and protected flats fisheries form adjacently, providing a continually shifting checkerboard of fly fishing opportunities.

Little Cayman Highway No. 1 circumnavigates the entire island. The alternating dirt and pavement road has an "island time" speed limit of 25 mph. In many areas the road is located near the water's edge and provides excellent road fishing opportunities. In areas where anglers cannot clearly see the flats, side roads have been blazed through the jungle, providing easy access to all of the flats. An interesting note for walking fishermen is that, although more than one-half of Little Cayman's flats are contained within the Cayman Islands Marine Park zones, fishing from shore is not restricted. All beaches below the high tide line are considered "Queen's Land" and are open to everyone.

The orientation of the isle, as it stretches from east to west, offers many advantages from prevailing summer southerly and winter northerly trade winds. The land mass often favors fly fishermen by placing one long coastline or the other in a fishable lee. Fly casters on Little Cayman curse the "downeaster." The island's alignment is additionally favorable because of the wind's effect on tidal flow. Little Cayman's high-to-low tidal fluctuation is less than 20 inches. Consequently, the prevailing wind, through its force and direction, always influences, and at times radically distorts, predictable tidal movement. This occurs as the wind literally pushes water up onto windward flats while pushing it off leeward ones. This is not an unusual event worldwide, but on this small island knowing the tide level is of paramount importance when determining where to fish. Fortunately, the Isle's two dominant flats configurations fish best on opposing tides.

Scrappy jacks often appear from nowhere and beat bonefish and permit to your fly. Donna Stewart releases a green jack at Little Cayman.

The grass or sand flats that form inside protected bays are quite shallow. These flats sport more feeding fish when the water is from mid- to full tide. Breaking off the high, as the water begins to fall, is premier time to catch fish feeding on grass or sand flats.

During low water in the tide cycle, coral flats are where the action is. Because of the depth, flats denizens are more accessible to anglers at low water. For a couple of hours before low tide and as the water begins to build up again, fish feed aggressively over the coral flats. At dead high tide and slack low tide, the fish are sluggish and can be off the bite.

Due to the frequency and direction

of heavy winter storms, the northwest corner and east end tip of Little Cayman are hammered. Lapping at the shore of these buffeted ends, the water is deep and offers fly fishermen little. The land confronting these seasonal furies has been denuded of vegetation, and the remaining coral coast is so heavily eroded that locals refer to it as "iron shore." These poor fly fishing zones are proportionally small, leaving the rest of the island a bountiful resource for flats anglers.

The largest areas for fly fishing are the flats that form behind continuous protective barrier reefs. These connected barrier reef formations create numerous bays. These range in size from small bights 300 yards long by 50 yards wide to many relatively large bays. For example, Mary's Bay on the north coast, east end, is four miles long by a quarter of a mile wide. Charles Bay, which lies on the south coast, east end, is three miles long by a third of a mile wide. Located on the south coast, west end, South Hole Sound is the largest bay. South Hole Sound is a classic "blue lagoon." In addition to being home to myriad of fish, it is where the Southern Cross Club is located. Three hundred yards southeast of the club, an 11-acre key called Owen Island lies sheltered in the calm waters of the sound. Although fishable all the way around, the west side of Owen Island is an outstanding grass and sand flat always inhabited by bonefish.

Regardless of its size, the basic physical nature of every protected bay on Little Cayman is remarkably similar. Long, pure, white sand beaches dominate bay shorelines. Locations more directly in the path of prevailing storms find the sand beaches strung with head-sized coral cobble, driftwood, and the ever-present plastic litter. In leeward areas, red mangroves, with their root systems home to all levels of the aquatic food chain, grow out into each bay.

There are several naturally occurring "cuts" in the barrier reefs that enclose the bays of Little Cayman. These channels provide fantastic after-dark fishing for many species. The most common catches include horse-eye jacks running from five to 30 pounds and tarpon from 40 to a 100 pounds. Both species take 2/0 to 4/0 white or yellow streamer flies stripped though the continually flowing current rushing out of the bays.

Because these flats are enclosed and are not blown out by wave action and current, bay bottoms are sand with occasional coral heads. A healthy and diverse mixture of seagrasses, in particular turtle grass, manatee grass, and midrib seagrass, grows throughout these shallows. The average depth is three to four feet and is never greater than eight feet.

As is common throughout the world, when the wind is up or the weather is stormy, the bonefish of Little Cayman will leave the shallow flats. They head for the deeper water of the bays, school up, and begin mudding. In South Hole Sound it is usual to observe two to eight muds every day, depending on wind direction and intensity.

One facet of fishing a small ecosystem is that you must have an alternate plan to be successful in all weather conditions. The guides on Little Cayman developed a chumming method in the early 1980s that provides bonefishing action regardless of conditions. Chumming isn't actually necessary for catching mudding bones;

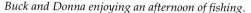
Flowering Bougainvillea brighten any landscape.

Buck and Donna enjoying an afternoon of fishing.

fan casting and short strip retrieving a weighty fly is simple and works well. The chumming method utilized on Little Cayman creates the added feature of giving anglers a target to shoot for when casting and frequently brings the fish out so they can be visually targeted.

The method consists of repeatedly throwing small groups of fine fry minnows from the deck of a skiff into the stirred-up waters of a bonefish mud. The fry are thrown so they land in exactly the same location with each toss. The fisherman "matches the hatch" by tying a size 6 unweighted minnow pattern to a 2X tippet. After each cluster of four or five minnows lands in the water, anglers cover the zone with their fry fly.

Although unorthodox, chumming can create bonefishing action during inclement conditions and can also attract fish into the casting reach of neophyte fly fishermen. Because of the consistency of the target area, chumming also creates an opportunity for two rods to be up on the deck, both looking for a fish at the same time. With two people fishing simultaneously, double hookups are an additional plus. In the bays of Little Cayman, bonefish schools are full family groups; fish range in size from young banana bones to 12 pounders. It is entirely possible to land a 26 incher or a nine incher followed by a 16 incher.

One third of the flats fisheries form behind independent coral head formations from 50 to 200 feet in length. These formations create excellent surf break while still allowing good movement of water and migration of fish along the shoreline. Behind these sectional barrier reefs, the bottom is a mixture of coral cobble with sand or gently sloping hard-pan coral. The combination of water circulation and uniquely changing bottom topography creates habitat for a plethora of fish food.

Crustaceans, crustaceans, crustaceans. . . from shrimp to crabs, fly boxes prepared for coral flats must contain a large variety of crustaceans.

There have been many excellent crab patterns developed in recent years. For Little Cayman choose stealthy patterns that ride hook up and are weed guarded. Various colors are effective, with plain tan topping the list. Shallow flats and calm conditions require crabs as small as size 8. Be prepared with a size 1 to 2/0 tan crab haywired to a shock tippet for predators. Crab patterns are my favorite flies for the lemon, reef, black-tipped, and nurse sharks that roam the island.

Pale olive and ivory with red bands are my favorite shrimp body colors. Translucent tan or gray-bodied shrimp patterns are equally important. Regardless of the coloration, bodies should give the appearance of being segmented. As always, eyes are important and should be placed at the bend of the hook with two long antennae extending out from beneath them.

There are two excellent ways to fish a shrimp pattern effectively: as an attractor pattern or as a well-camouflaged critter attempting to hide. Attractor patterns use odd coloration and odd behavior to entice the strike. After making the cast, move the fly with short darting strips. Repetitive short strips create a succulent shrimp scuttle. Roving fish are used to seeing shrimp attempting to flee. Keep the tiny twitch retrieve going. You may end up with leader in

Sunsets like these stop all activity at Little Cayman.

the line guides. It's not over. Strip the shrimp until you get the strike or the player spooks.

Camouflaged shrimp patterns need to fulfill two goals. First, the body color of the fly tied to the tippet should blend with the bottom. Both the brightness and color of the bottom should be duplicated as closely as possible. Second, the fly must be tied with a weed or snag guard. When fishing a camo shrimp, I use a hip-hop retrieve. This is done by beginning the strip slowly. After retrieving a foot of line slowly, I finish each strip with an ultra quick four-inch pull. Completing each strip, I let the fly settle back toward the bottom. Just as I believe it may have contacted the sea floor, I begin drawing it up again with the slow strip.

Fly fishermen fishing bones over the coral flats will find large singles, five to nine pounds. Pods are common. Pods are typically four fish ranging from three to five pounds. Smaller schoolie bones run in tight packs with never more than 30 fish. Permit feed over the coral flats and are seen daily. By Little Cayman standards the permit that feed here are the big boys. Fish of 16 to 28 pounds are common, with the largest being 35. Although a 20 pounder isn't large by world standards, these permit tail aggressively in three feet of water.

Seeing big permit in shallow water is hard on the heart, but other species besides permit produce an adrenaline rush. Look left, at nine o'clock. Yes, he's four feet long, probably over 50 pounds. No, not a barracuda. Although big barracuda are present in plague proportions, that bright emerald-green body with orange bead and tail is a super male rainbow parrotfish.

Rainbow parrots, which often feed in pairs, are unusually sensitive to motion, vibration, and sound. Other sport species, especially bonefish, permit, and mutton snapper, are aware of how skittish the big parrots are and use them as a safety barometer. It is very common to see permit feeding closely behind an active pair of parrots. In addition to rainbow parrotfish, spotted eagle rays and southern stingrays are frequently companioned by species sought by fly anglers. This is a promising situation because the sport fish aren't simply relying on the host for protection—they are feeding aggressively in the wakes of their lumbering companions. While all flats fishing requires stealth, when fishing around hosts, anglers must emulate a blue heron. Angling mistakes will make hosts bolt for deep water more readily than any other fish on the flats of Little Cayman.

Spook one, and you've spooked them all. Serious consideration must be given to the fishing approach. I prefer coming at them from out in the ocean. After wading out, I position myself so host and quarry are swimming toward me, not straight at me but with 20 to 40 degrees of side angle. The setup should be situated so they are swimming forward toward an easy cast on my downwind side. In this situation, select a fly that doesn't require a strip retrieve to be enticing. Size 4 or 2 urchin or crab patterns, designed with the hook riding up with a snag guard, are well proven.

One of the treasures of this mecca of fly fishing is Little Cayman's landlocked Tarpon lake. With an aura reminiscent of All Hallows Eve and Jurassic Park, swimming within the waters of this lake are fish that simply aren't normal. Tarpon Lake is a gigantic

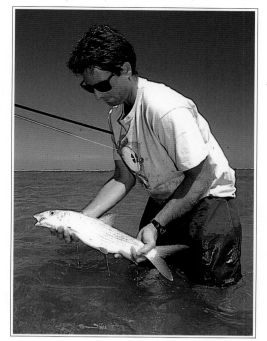

There is plenty of water inside the reef where all species can be spotted.

Dolphins and turtles frolic along the edge of the Cayman Trench and often entertain and accompany divers and anglers.

fish bowl where fly rodders can fish to tarpon at any time. Having been refreshed by Hurricane Gilbert in 1988, this rich and healthy lake is home to only two kinds of fish—the prey and the predator.

The prey are gambusia minnows. The gambusia are a continually rejuvenating food source with a biomass containing millions and millions of individuals. They are so densely packed, it often appears as if the lake's surface is being rained upon because the fry create a perpetual dimpling of the water.

The predator, tarpon, range in size from 12 to 40 pounds. These bucketmouths are so well fed they are awesome to behold. Not large by ocean tarpon standards, the landlocked fish are nonetheless healthy to the extreme. When you do battle with these fish, come prepared with a strong 9-weight rod or better, a 10 weight. Any rod lighter is like bringing a knife to a gunfight. These fish can beat you!

The lake is essentially a mangrove swamp that can only be fished from a shallow-draft rowboat. As the boat is rowed around the edge of the lake, two fishermen can simultaneously cast for the tarpon. The question of leader construction is a difficult one. Wild leaping and running tarpon can quickly tangle monofilament in the mangrove limbs. The entire leader, not just the shock tippet, needs to be built from an abrasion-resistant material. Knots in the leader tend to hang up as the fish bulldog their way through the maze of their escape route. The simplest solution is to forget the science of shock tippet leader building. Instead, Albright knot one end of a nine-foot length of 30-pound hard Mason to the front taper of your floating fly line, tie a fly on the other end and start casting. Many traditional tarpon flies, sizes 2 through 2/0, have produced strikes from these fish. Deer hair and foam surface poppers can induce strikes when the fish are quiet and the wind slack. Rattle bodies with big painted-on eyes and colorful collars and wings are favorites. In general, chartreuse, hot pink, and orange are the colors of choice.

Although tarpon can be seen popping and rolling all over the

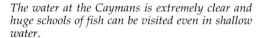

The water at the Caymans is extremely clear and huge schools of fish can be visited even in shallow water.

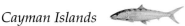

lake, the feeding fish are working the mangrove edges. Here they can easily crowd the minnows into a ball in preparation for a kill. While they can be observed feeding and are catchable at any time of day, dusk and the crack of dawn are the two best fishing times. Dawn fishing can be incredibly exciting because that is the time when many tarpon will gang up in a frenzy on the fry. During frenzies, the fish can create up to two inches of foam on the surface of the water. They are so intent on feeding that anglers are not just wishing they were jumping tarpon, they are doing it.

As a saltwater guide, when I first meet a new fishing client, I always inquire what method (meaning fly or spin) they like to fish with and what kinds of fish they would like to pursue. A season or so ago, I asked my standard question to a fisherman who had brought his school-age son to Little Cayman on a three-day fishing package. He replied, "With fly gear, I'm better than my son, but considering he can throw a clean loop 50 feet into the wind, he's no slacker. With monofilament, let me just say that every bass in Louisiana without a hearing aid has heard this boy's name. As for the kind of fish we want to catch, that's simple—if it swims, it is in peril."

If it swims, it's in peril? His response put me off a little. The guides and management at the Southern Cross Club are especially vocal about sport fishing ethics. We practice catch and release, fish barbless, and, in general, promote the successful return of sport fishes to their saltwater homes.

Thankfully, I came to learn that few anglers are as conscientious about correctly fighting and releasing fish unharmed as those two were. They were excellent fishermen, but this was their first flats trip. For them, "if it swims, it's in peril," simply meant that once they had experienced one fish, they wanted to learn about and have fun catching something else. They were right up Little Cayman's alley.

During their three days of fishing, we kept a list of all the different species they landed. Sadly, four nice bonefish were unintentionally killed while on the line. These deaths convinced us that intentionally killing two other fish might be justified. You be the judge:

The bones died after being brutally mauled by the same five-foot barracuda. He would not settle his appetite by dining on one fish but satisfied himself by taking only a belly bite from each. He would then leave the substantial bonefish remains to be gobbled by smaller "reefies." Following the boat as I poled along, he struck each fish we hooked up. After four, we decided to try to turn the tables. The father, casting a size 6 olive shrimp pattern, caught a bar jack when it flashed in to investigate the blood plume created by the barra's last conquest. I quickly live-rigged the jack on a size 1/0 treble hook haywired with size 7 single-strand wire. The big barracuda had been consistent in his belly biting, so I buried two of the hook barbs in the jack's stomach, clipped the wire to a swivel on a 15-pound spinning rig, and made a cast. He jumped three times and fought well, as barracuda do in shallow water. It was good to see him jump with the live-rigged bar jack still twitching between his half-inch-long teeth.

Caymanians say, "Wee's sendin' him ta Jesus, mon," when they

When fishing isn't on the agenda, just relax on the beach, snorkel, or go for a swim.

Nonfishermen can relax poolside and let the tropical ambiance overtake them.

Poolside dining at the Southern Cross Club.

Just off shore the ocean depth is measured in thousands of feet. Choose your dive or simply snorkel along the shoreline.

Maybe I'll fish today, maybe I won't.

mercifully dispatch a fish by whacking it between the eyes. Any angler who's been in a similar situation can understand why I said this to that bonefish-eatin' barracuda.

Besides the bone, barracuda, and bar jack, the father and son team landed 22 other species during their three days of fishing. Some species on the list were the son's first permit and the first tarpon for both. Along with the permit and bar jack, other members of the jack family included yellow jack, horse-eye jack, palometa, and blue runner. A 52-inch hound fish was measured and released. Hound fish, which are incredible tail-walking aerial fighters, grow up to five feet and have a serious set of teeth. Speaking of teeth, the father and son also caught three species of shark, the largest being a nine-foot female lemon. No great quantity of any of the 25 species was caught. They only landed seven bonefish (that didn't get eaten) between the two of them. A percentage—like that bone-eatin' barracuda—were taken on spinning tackle, but most were taken on fly gear. Either way, when they departed, they had 25 stories to express why fishing with the philosophy, "if it swims, it's in peril," leads to such serious fun.

Extending beyond the zone of fishing flats and barrier reefs, the aquatic top of the seascraper encompasses land in a narrow ring. As the coral pan of the reef top slowly descends outward from land, it reflects light in a dazzling blue halo. Then in water as shallow (and excellent for scuba divers) as 18 feet or as deep as 180 feet, the mountaintop ecosystem that is Little Cayman suddenly ends.

Old Caymanians call it "De breakoff." Modern scuba divers refer to it as "the wall." Once beyond the top ledge of the seamount, land falls away so vertically it is as if you have stepped off the edge of a mile-high skyscraper. For the myriad reef and shallow-water fish that reside near Little Cayman, the edge of the dropoff is the end of the known world.

For fly fishermen, it means they are all right there. Practically every shallow-water sport species found in the Caribbean, right there. It is no wonder Little Cayman's fishermen have all adopted the motto, "If it swims, it's in peril."

Buck Buchenroth
Little Cayman
March 10, 1998

	J	F	M	A	M	J	J	A	S	O	N	D
Bonefish	F-E	F-E	G-E	G-E	G-E	G-E	G	G	G	G-E	F-E	F-E
Permit	F-G	F-G	G	G-E	G-E	G-E	G	G	G	G	F-E	F-G
Tarpon	G	G	G	G-E	G-E	G-E	G	G	G	G	F-E	F-E
Barracuda	F-G	F-G	G	G-E	G-E	G-E	G	G	G	G	G	G
Snapper	F-G	F-G	G	G-E	G-E	G-E	G	G	G	G	G	G
Jacks	F-G	F-G	G	G-E	G-E	G-E	G	G	G	G	G	G
Shark	F-G	F-G	G	G	G	G	G	G	G	G	G	G
Wind	L-H	L-M	L-M	L-M	L	L	L	L	L-M	L-M	L-H	L-H

P=Poor   F=Fair   G=Good   E=Excellent
L=Light   M=Moderate   H=Heavy

Christmas Island

Dolphins, thousands of them, were swimming across the surface of the lagoon. Their sleek bodies reflected the pink afterglow of the intense tropical sunrise. A dozen or more swam playfully three feet off the bow of our boat; everyone reached out to touch them. Dolphin spray coated our faces. I felt they had a message for us.

Billowy low clouds seemed to rise up and separate from the lagoon, allowing sunbeams to scatter across the water's surface. The low-angled light skimmed across the wave tops and colored our faces with a warm glow. The turquoise of the lagoon was reflected on the underside of the low clouds. Everyone was at the front of the boat playing, laughing, and talking to the dolphins, which seemed to fly through both the water and the air.

In the near distance the low light and moist air combined to form a perfect double rainbow. It glowed neon in the concentrated light and appeared to be three-dimensional. Everybody reached out, but no one could touch it. The rainbow followed us for a while then faded into the misty sky.

As we left the dolphins behind, a school of flying fish suddenly began fleeing away from the bow wake. Flying fish feed on plankton so they are always found near the water's surface. Their pectoral fins are long and can be extended at right angles to their body like wings. Their ventral fins are also elongated and their tail can be broadened into a great paddle. When disturbed, they leap from the water and commence a side-to-side sculling motion with their tail that creates an intense audible vibration. They extend their

Mary spotted this tiny puffer, or toadfish, family Tetraodontidae, *scurrying about in two inches of water. When we gently picked it up, it puffed itself up many times its deflated size. Its inflated body was soft like a soufflé fresh from the ocean. Puffers have a lethal history dating back to biblical times. Captain Cook almost died in New Caledonia after tasting a puffer. The alkaloid poison tetraodotoxin (TTX) produced by these fish has no known antidote. It is one of the most potent nonprotein poisons (neurotoxins) known. In the Caribbean, a TTX compound derived from puffer fish is known as Zombie Dust.*

The lagoon at Christmas Island is vast and no one has fished all the flats or even counted them! Many are tiny, others extend for miles. In addition, there are over 100 miles of reef flats!

"wings" and glide through the air. The distance covered depends on the wind and swell direction, but distances up to 150 feet are often achieved. As they flew away from our bow wake, their effortless glide left us entranced. It looks so easy, why can't I do that?

All too soon we eased up onto a pristine flat of white sand surrounded by coral heads and deep aqua water. The colors were so intense and surreal I was on freeze frame. My eyes quit moving until I spotted three beautiful bonefish working the edge. I looked at my friends, inhaled the perfect air, and realized what the dolphin were celebrating and trying to tell us. *This is as good as it gets!* Captain Cook never had it any better.

History

The Samoans first visited Christmas Island around 1400. Captain James Cook officially discovered the island on Christmas Eve of 1777. On Christmas Day, Captain Cook sent his navigator, Bligh (who would later become Captain Bligh of *The Bounty*) to explore. He declared it uninhabited because of the absence of fresh water but was fascinated by the abundance of bird life and the turtles—which, over the next 150 years, were slaughtered for meat by passing sailors. The British annexed Christmas Island in 1888.

During World War II, Christmas Island was a strategic staging area for thousands of Allied forces. I met one such soldier who was bonefishing at Christmas Island, and he told stories of troops blasting the reef with explosives to catch fish. Fortunately, they did not know about the bonefish in the lagoon.

The United States and Britain tested nuclear weapons in the atmosphere off the southeast end of the island and at the Malden

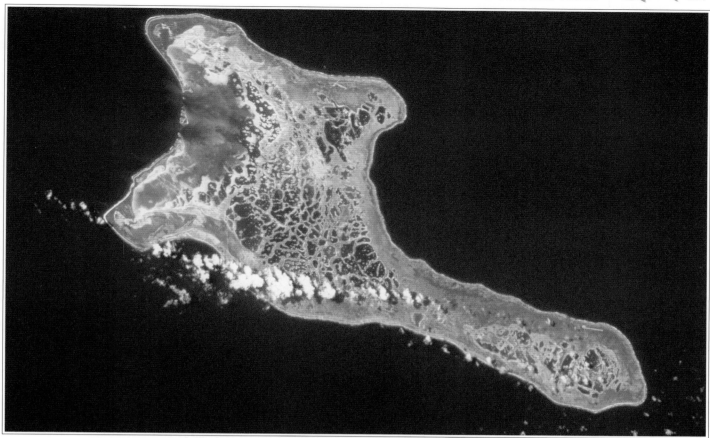

Islands from 1956 to 1962. The British tests blinded millions of sea birds and exposed thousands of servicemen to radiation-related diseases. In 1962, Britain loaned Christmas Island to the Americans to use for a crash program of 40 nuclear tests before the Partial Test Ban Treaty with the Soviets came into effect in 1963. One U.S. missile launched from a Polaris submarine off California exploded a half-megaton bomb near the island. Afterward, coral disintegrated when touched. The rest of the bombs were exploded 18,000 feet in the air over the ocean. No measurable radioactivity remains, only a lot of junk and shadowy reminders of a reckless era of unaccountable and shameful government and military officials.

Today, Christmas Island comes under the socialistic jurisdiction of The Republic of Kiribati, pronounced kerr-a-boss, which gained independence from Britain in 1979. The locals know Christmas Island as Kiritimati, the Kiribati spelling for Christmas. Kiribati is the official language of the island. The capital of the country is the island of Tarawa, located 1,500 miles to the west. The republic's territory extends roughly 3,000 miles east to west and 500 miles north to south, an area over 1½ million square miles that crosses the international date line and straddles the equator. Kiribati includes 33 low-lying islands of which 25 are inhabited. It includes the Gilbert, Phoenix, and Line islands (Christmas, Washington, and Fanning islands). Total land mass is less than half the size of Long Island, New York, and Kiribati has the largest sea-to-land ratio of any political unit on earth.

The 8,000 inhabitants are mostly indentured

Christmas Island looking toward the northeast. The lagoon entrance is visible at the center left of the island. This photo shows the lagoon at low tide. Note the many exposed flats. High tide floods all flats. Most of the outer reef is also bonefish country.

The village of London is on the lagoon-ocean point to the north. The village of Poland is at the southwestern point. The Captain Cook Hotel is about midway along the top half of the island.

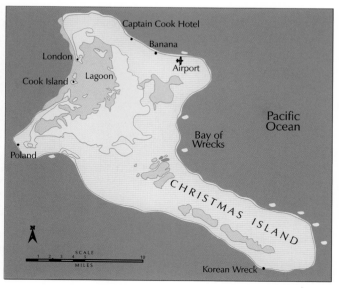

Randall Kaufmann

Sooty terns, Sterna fuscata, *are one of the most abundant nesting birds in tropical oceans. They gather at Christmas Island in December and January by the millions to mate and raise their young. Recognize them by their pointed black bill, black legs and feet, deeply-forked tail, and 34-inch wing span. They are colored snooty black above and white below with a white forehead.*

They can be seen soaring high above Christmas Island for extended periods, and it has been suggested that they sleep on the wing. It is believed that snooty terns cannot stay in the water long because their plumage becomes waterlogged. When feeding, they hover gracefully over water and pick up small fishes in their bill. At Christmas Island, snooty terns gather over schools of tuna to feed on fish that are chased to the surface. Fisherman rely on them as tuna spotters. Mary makes friends with a nesting colony.

After fishing everyone gathers on the beach for cocktails, sushi, sunset, and tall tales. The crashing waves, birds, and trevally fisherman provide additional entertainment. Dinner is served after dark.

Gilbertese (known as I-Kiribati) laborers employed on the government copra (coconut) plantation. They live in three villages: London, Poland, and Banana. Locals also fish, dive for lobster, and engage in their favorite pastime, socializing. They do not have to work all day to survive, and their requirements are minimal. Christmas Islanders are friendly, fun loving, easy going, inquisitive, hospitable, and sometimes bold. Visitors can easily mingle with the people.

Geography

Christmas Island, located about 1,200 miles south of Honolulu, Hawaii, has a land mass of about 140 square miles and is the largest atoll in the world. Typically, an atoll encircles a lagoon and is itself surrounded by a coral reef that has been formed by countless corals over the millennia.

Christmas Island used to be a volcano. From the air imaginative visitors can perceive the horseshoe-shaped lagoon as the caldera. Today, after 500 million years of erosion, sediment collection, and coral growth against a rising sea, the inside of the volcano has been transformed into a gentle, mostly level, coral and sand flat. The lagoon is protected from excessive wind and waves. It is one of the most productive bonefish habitats known.

Because of prevailing winds and ocean waves, the northwest coast is slightly higher than the rest of the island, but nowhere does the land mass reach more than a few yards above high tide. In fact, the highest natural point on Christmas Island is about 60 feet, and that is the top of a coconut palm. Arriving passengers can easily see the copra plantations from the air. Because of their unmanicured nature, they almost appear to be natural groves. The swaying green fronds break up the dry starkness of the white-to-tannish land. Nowhere is the solid land mass more than two miles wide, but it is about 30 miles long. The outside shoreline of about 100 miles is deserted beach piled high with shells and broken branches of blanched coral. There are many small saltwater lakes and brackish ponds in the deserted interior.

Christmas Island is not Bora Bora. Don't expect South Pacific scenes of lush tropical vegetation, wide crescent beaches, towering pinnacles, and topless beauties. Christmas Island is none of these. You encounter litter, rusted junk piles, slimy brown ponds, and an oily harbor at London. You will also experience some of the most beautiful bonefish flats imaginable, tame birds, flying fish, dolphins, tropical water the color of your dreams, and open spaces that remain mostly untouched by civilization.

The Captain Cook Hotel is located along a deserted stretch of beach far from the noise and clutter of the village. Nights are quiet and peaceful, and no lights pollute the night sky. If you are lucky, huge breakers will be crashing on the reef.

Accommodations

The best accommodations are at the government-run Captain Cook Hotel, which consists of a bar, dining room, 26 single-story 1950s motel-style cinder-block rooms (most with air conditioning), and six thatched-roof duplex bungalows. The bungalows are comfortable. Each motel and bungalow room has a small refrigerator, two single beds, a fan, a private bath, and a desk suitable for fly tying. The bungalows are close to the beach, and, at night, the thundering surf is your constant companion. After a day's fishing, I like to sit on the beach with a tropical punch, watch the crashing waves and trevally fishermen, listen to the cries of terns, and write in my journal until darkness and hunger drive me to the dining room.

The evening seafood fare is very good and includes trevally, yellowfin, wahoo, and other local fish. Breakfast and lunch are seldom anything to get excited about. Fresh milk is sometimes available. I usually bring my own fruit, cereal, milk, and other goodies, but most visitors eat what is served. Meats and vegetables are flown in from Hawaii, and stomach problems seldom arise. Groups are treated to an outdoor luau featuring fresh roasted lobster or, perhaps, a pig, along with traditional native dancing and singing. Drinking and cooking water is collected from rain. Sink and shower water is from a well and should not be consumed.

The Frigate Bar keeps a good selection of beverages on hand but does not have everyone's favorite libation. I suggest you bring

Native singing and dancing at the Captain Cook luau is a highlight for all visitors.

Blue-footed booby, Sula nebouxii. *Young are hatched on the ground.*

Red-footed booby, Sula sula, *above and below.*

Boobies are streamlined birds generally white with distinguishing colors that delineate their genus. They have straight bills, long pointed tails and wings, strong legs, and fully webbed feet. Their apparent lack of fear of man makes them easy to catch and apparently earned them their name. They have survived by nesting in remote places. They are fond of flying fish and often follow boats, knowing that boats disturb flying fish.

Urchin shells and trevally poppers. Notice the small to large round knobs, or bosses, which are the base attachment for the spines, and the small holes, or pores, from which the tube feet are extended. If one of these shells is broken open, the basket-like Aristotle's lantern may be seen.

your own. During one visit we ran out of Myers Rum on the third day (patio and tying guests consumed most of it), and we were forced to visit the local store. Walking up to the open-front establishment, it became obvious that cleaning agents, rice, flour, sugar, and cases of beer and soda made up the bulk of the available goods. With the help of an interpreter, we finally obtained the one and only bottle of liquor on the shelf, which happened to be a bottle of Jamaican rum, but only at a great price.

Phones and faxes have arrived at Christmas Island. There is a small medical facility in London. Because airplane service is only available once a week, anglers should plan ahead. A valid passport and visa are required to enter Christmas Island. If you require a visa to enter the United States, be sure you have a multiple-entry U.S. visa. There are no snakes on the island, and visitors are seldom bothered by biting bugs or mosquitoes. Dress is informal; tipping is appreciated. Camping is not permitted at Christmas Island.

Activities

While there are some wonderful outdoor diversions for nonanglers, it is not the place for everyone. Some anglers leave nonfishing partners in Hawaii for the week or meet them in Hawaii after fishing at Christmas Island.

Snorkeling and diving are excellent. The lee shore between North West Point and Paris is the safest area. At least once during the week, I like to snorkel and swim over the coral heads in the lagoon while the boatman stands watch. I also like to snorkel the flats and observe the tidal flux and the many foods that bonefish eat. I have never seen a large shark, but there are some dangerous ones around. Lobster divers report numerous harrowing encounters.

Much of Christmas Island is a bird sanctuary, and it is estimated that up to 18 million birds are scattered about the remote parts of the island. Large colonies of sea birds nest on Cook Island and Motu Tabu inside the lagoon; about 18 species of rare migratory birds are found at Christmas Island, and all are very tame. Millions of sooty terns nest in June and December. Other tame ground nesters include noddies, fairy terns, boobies, tropic birds, frigates, shearwaters, and petrels. Visitors can walk right up to nests, which are on the ground or in low vegetation. Boobies and frigate birds

often visit solitary anglers and hang motionless within arm's reach, probably wondering about the intent of this huge flightless creature. Birds have various breeding seasons, but March to July and October to December are peak nesting times.

When fishing in the lagoon, you should always troll between the flats. Watch your popper closely—don't let the birds pick it up. It is not fun to unhook a screeching, clawing, pecking, panicked frigate bird!

Visitors who are, however, appreciative of wild saltwater environments and wildlife find plenty to enjoy and marvel at during their stay. Beachcombing is a favorite pastime. Wonderful shells are everywhere, and glass floats are a possible find. Deserted stretches of shoreline invite the sun bather and naturalist. Nonanglers often enjoy just tagging along as there are always exciting sights, sounds, and places to explore, both on land and underwater.

The protective reef that encircles Christmas Island causes huge waves to form, creating both a visual and audible spectacle for visitors. The winter season offers the roughest surf, although it is flat some days. Perhaps the most adventurous visitors are surfers who arrive to ride the big waves into the narrow lagoon entrance, which provides a long, safe ride past the otherwise unsurfable reef. It's perfect surf for those looking for that endless wave on the ragged edge of the sport.

Combine world-class surfing and bonefishing, and you have the ideal playground for Yvon Chouinard, who has checked out all the best places. Yvon Chouinard is a world-famous innovator, adventurer, and author. His company, Patagonia, is the world leader in outdoor apparel and corporate tithing, the donating of money to nonprofit organizations fighting to protect the environment. In the following vignette Yvon discusses the zen of passionate sports and life in London Village.

Measuring Time
by Yvon Chouinard

When a man reaches a certain age, he begins to measure his wealth not in terms of how much he has accumulated but in how much time he has—or has left. Often, panic sets in. Forget about the *process* or Zen of activities like fly fishing or mountain climbing; the process takes too much time. He doesn't want to learn how to climb well; he wants to bag summits. He doesn't want to *merely* fish; he wants to *catch* fish.

Mountain guides, bonefish guides, hunting guides, river guides—all these exist to help the client hit the bull's eye without having to spend a lifetime learning a chosen craft.

My father was a tough French Canadian from Quebec. Papa completed only three years of schooling before he had to begin working on the family farm at the age of nine. In his lifetime he learned to become a journeyman plasterer, carpenter, electrician, and plumber. In Lisbon, Maine, where I was born, he repaired all of the machinery in the Worumbo Woolen Mill. One of the profound memories of my early childhood was seeing him sitting in the kitchen next to the wood-burning stove, drinking a bottle of whiskey, and proceeding to pull out his teeth, both good ones and bad, with his electrician's pliers. He needed dentures but felt the

A nice bonefish from the back of the lagoon caught blind casting from a point in off-color water.

This bonefish beached itself in its haste and confusion. I backed out the hook and the next wave carried it outward.

Big surf and spindrift near London.

Yvon Chouinard catches a good one in one of the reef passes.

local dentist was asking too much money to do a job he could just as easily do himself.

Because I inherited some of those genes, I have a preference for learning and doing things on my own and a visceral dislike of authority—like the old-school Florida bonefish guide who barks orders like a Marine drill sergeant: "I said one o'clock, not 11! Strip! Strip! Not too fast! Strip again!"

The classic example of excessive guiding can be seen on Oregon's Rogue River. The guide asks you to let 60 feet of line out from the stern of the dory and tells you to hold the rod with both hands. "Keep the tip up, and don't move it," he orders. He then ferry glides your fly right into the mouth of the fish. There is no doubt that the guide is doing the fishing and, with luck, the client may be doing the catching. What should be a deeply personal and fun experience can turn into "surviving a blizzard of micro management," as Tom McGuane described an encounter with a particularly zealous guide in South America.

I prefer to walk and wade my home river, the Snake in Wyoming, but I may go through the whole summer never seeing another angler on his own—just one drift boat after another with the "sport" throwing Pepperoni Yuk Bugs at the bank. One shot at each fish, and the floating shooting gallery drifts by. Anyone with that view of the sport can't possibly have an experience like the time I worked on a big feeding cutthroat for over an hour. I finally put it all together with a combination 7X tippet, a difficult reach cast to the precise location, and a stripped down size 20 PMD dry that I converted into a "physically challenged" emerger. The final solution was to put spittle on the tail end so it floated at just the right angle in the surface film.

My most memorable fishing experiences have not been the days when most of the fish were spotted for me by my guide but, rather, those singular experiences when I worked out a tough problem on my own. Don't get me wrong, I fish with guides. I've fished with great guides. The best have seen their role as teachers, not manservants.

These are just a few flashes of pleasant experiences and fond memories. They are enhanced by a sense of satisfaction and confidence gained in each case by exercising a degree of self-reliance.

The best bonefish guide I've ever fished with is Moana from Christmas Island. One time I did "Moana's Walk" with him. It's a six-mile all-day affair. You can only do this walk during the right tide cycle when the water isn't too deep to cross the cuts and when you can hit the different flats when there are fish on them. Moana only has one eye, but there is no way you can spot a fish before he does. You have to listen as he says quietly, "Over there, 30 feet." He won't tell you how to fish or rush over to take the hook out of your fish—unless that's what you want. If you ask, he will teach you the identity of every bird in the air or tell you the life history of the *Edward Scissorhands* manta shrimp and how his grandfather taught him how to catch them. He will show you what bonefish eat at Christmas Island and explain why the biggest ones come on the flats during the August full moon. We caught a lot of fish on "Moana's Walk," but that's not what I remember. I remember watching a master fisherman work those flats perfectly, so in tune with the environment and so adept at his craft that he has no need

It looks like we are having mantis shrimp for dinner.

Dig in!

Richard Humphrey

Bernie Baker

to actually catch a fish. I'll probably never do that walk with Moana again, but I've got two halfway decent eyes and two strong legs. There's nothing to keep me from trying to become as good a bonefisherman as Moana.

On my last few trips to Christmas Island, I've taken along my surfboard and fly rod and stayed in a shack in London Village—near the dock. My daily routine consists of getting up early, grabbing my surfboard, and walking barefoot along the coconut-palm-lined path to the surf break at the lagoon entrance. I often hear someone singing in the distance or see a young girl brushing her sister's long black hair. They smile when I walk past and, since they don't see many surfers here, a few kids and dogs follow me out to the point to watch. There's a lot of fish action at the lagoon entrance. Once, a friend had a giant black trevally busting at his surfboard leash as he rode down a 12-foot wave at 25 miles per hour.

The inhabitants of Christmas Island, the Kiribati, are not necessarily seafaring people. Most of them are uprooted farmers from Tarawa who were dumped on this barren atoll. I witnessed a near disaster during the occurrence of the largest surf of the year with the waves closing out the mouth of the lagoon. An unseaworthy old barge laden with 80 souls, dogs, pigs, and baggage, attempted to navigate out of the lagoon powered only by a straining 25-horsepower motor. Of the three of us surfing, one was concerned about the babies, one was concerned about the puppies, and one saw the opportunity to catch the best waves of the day.

When the trades come up too strong to surf or the outgoing tidal rip messes with the incoming waves, it's time to fish the flats around London. They may not be the best flats on the island, but they're within walking distance. I've gotten to understand their tides and the movements of the fish. Even when the flats are nearly dry, there are always deeper channels where the bones are hanging out waiting for the tides to flood the flats. It's satisfying to learn on your own as simple a fact as the bonefish will be tailing on a certain flat at four o'clock.

Once, within sight of the docks, I hooked and landed a giant pink bra. A friend nearby yelled a challenge, "Can you still unhook it with one hand?"

From years of trying to hook a milkfish with a fly, I've found that they will, indeed, take a fly—a dry fly dressed to look like bright green *frise* lettuce. If you think bonefish are good fighters, check out those 15-pound gulpers on a glassy day just outside the lagoon.

After surfing one of the other reef passes near Cook Island, I spent a couple of hours fishing for trevally. They were riding in with the tide through a pass. Under the watchful eye of a beautiful Polynesian friend, I was catching one after another. Though she could not understand the concept of catch and release, she took great joy in wading out and unhooking them for me. I did save a couple of fish for *poisson cru* for lunch. Dinner that evening consisted of a huge pile of lobster. We cooked them ourselves, blissful in the knowledge that we had bought the whole pile for 10 cents Australian per pound from the divers, who export only the tails.

The purpose of doing passionate sports like fly fishing or mountain climbing should be to learn and grow and, ultimately, effect some higher personal change. It won't happen on Everest if,

Lone Palm Flat.

The store in London is well stocked this month.

Randall Kaufmann

Shells litter the beaches. Baby hermit crabs often inhabit shells of this type.

Randall Kaufmann

The lagoon entrance and the village of London.

Pulling trevally poppers in the lagoon. Whenever you are moving in the boat, put out a popper. Ten and 12 weights are best. One never knows what might tear into your offering.

before you ever step onto the mountain, there are 28 ladders in place and 6,000 feet of fixed rope, and you have a Sherpa in the front pulling, and one in the back pushing.

Learn all you can from the guide or teacher, but at some point you need to cut loose from the catered experience and, for better or for worse, muddle through on your own.

Yvon Chouinard
Ventura, California
February 1998

First-Time Visitors

Christmas Island is over 1,000 miles from the closest city, Honolulu, Hawaii and about 200 miles from the closest island, Fanning. There is no light pollution to dilute the night. Don't forget to check out the stars! The airplane flies in and out once a week. Potential visitors sometimes wonder if they can handle a week at such a remote location. I, too, thought, "What am I going to do for seven days?"

Time both flies and stands still in remote tropic locations. Suddenly, the week is nearly over and you are already planning your next visit, perhaps for two weeks! Christmas Island is the sort of place you cannot visit just once. You must return again and again. Indeed, many anglers have been there 10 or 20 times, and some have made over 50 trips!

Weather

Because Christmas Island is only about 120 miles north of the equator, air and water temperatures are very consistent. Daytime temperatures average 85 degrees Fahrenheit; nighttime temperatures average 72 degrees; and the humidity is relatively low. The sun sets at about 6 p.m. and rises at about 6 a.m., and the wind blows 10 to 20 miles per hour. Tidal fluctuation is minimal. Rainfall averages 30 inches per year, and most falls as afternoon and evening thunder showers. In other words, the weather and water temperature are the same in January as they are in August, which means bonefishing is *very* predictable.

Fishing

Because the weather is consistent and the flats temperature is ideal for bonefish the year around, *any time* is a good time to fish the island. It is most crowded from November to June, with January through April hosting the most anglers. From July through September, it is practically deserted.

Christmas Island is perfect for the first-time trevally and bone fisherman. The lagoon flats are mostly hardpacked white sand. They are easy to wade, and fish are easy to see. There are no patches of grass and no mangroves to hook your fly, and there are lots of fish.

Besides the lagoon flats, over 100 miles of reef area is available. This area is mostly unknown and offers perhaps the wildest and most exciting trevally and bonefishing. You don't always catch a lot, but the fish are larger and tougher to land in the coral and fast-water environment, and the surroundings require good angling skills.

Experienced anglers can release more bonefish than they can count. Many eager small fish feeding in shallow water or on sand flats keep beginners engrossed. Anglers who prefer to stalk larger singles are not disappointed. Bonefish range in size from one pound to over 10 pounds, but they average two to four pounds. Four- to six-pound fish are common.

Several species of trevally are present, including giant, blue-fin, and golden. They range in size from a few pounds to over 70 pounds. Most run 10 to 40 pounds and are unbelievably aggressive and strong. Many bonefish anglers have become trevally converts at Christmas Island. It is *very* exciting to cast a six-inch popper to a 30-pound trevally in two feet of water and watch it devour your offering in an explosion at the surface! Don't miss the opportunity.

Milkfish are plentiful and are easily seen, especially back in the lagoon. Thinking that they are bonefish, neophyte visitors sometimes cast to them without success. Milkfish have a reputation of being uncatchable, but only because anglers are not offering an imitation of what they eat, which is mostly algae. Experiment! Milkfish are incredibly strong, and there are some big ones at Christmas Island!

Boats are used to gain access to isolated lagoon flats. A

Mary Kaufmann

Randall Kaufmann released this giant trevally at Y-site. Huge trevally often cruise shallow flats, feeding on anything they can catch, including bonefish. Drop-offs and reef areas are the best places to pursue trevally. Look for singles, pairs, and gangs of three or four swimming quickly. Once they target your offering, it is impossible to pull it away from them. Be ready for the big grab!

Giant trevally! These brutes will beat you every time if you let them. Wire leaders, six-inch poppers, and 12-weight rods are the way to go!

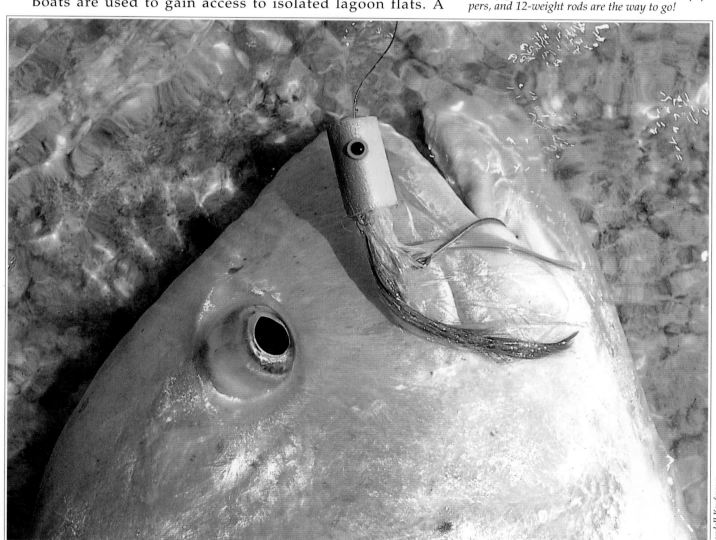

Randall Kaufmann

If I had to pick two colors to fish Christmas Island—and I wouldn't want to do that—it would be tan and yellow, perhaps orange. . .maybe pink. Sparse small flies are usually best, unless you are after the generals. Then, use a large heavy fly. My favorite patterns include the Christmas Island Special (yellow, pearlescent, or orange), Charlies (tan, pink, silver, or yellow), Krystal Flash Charlies (tan, yellow, or yellow/tan), and the George Bush (named after a regular visitor, not the former U.S. president). Others include the JT Special, Chili Pepper, Super Swimming Shrimp, Turd, Clouser Minnow (pink, tan, or fluorescent green), dime-sized crabs (tan or white), and the tan Puff. For deep water, carry some Marabou Shrimp and Christmas Island Specials in various sink rates and assorted crabs that are the size of a quarter.

week's fishing package at Christmas Island includes three days of punt fishing in the lagoon. Trucks carry anglers to other lagoon flats that are accessible on foot. All fishing at Christmas Island is done on foot, so be prepared to do some walking.

My brother, Lance Kaufmann, has been a frequent visitor at Christmas Island. He owns Kaufmanns' Streamborn, Inc., and Kaufmann Fly Fishing Expeditions, Inc. Although he enjoys the consistent climate and excellent fishing opportunities at Christmas Island, especially trevally, he has always wanted to fish the other islands in the area.

Other Islands
By Lance Kaufmann

Over the years every visitor has heard rumors of bonefishing at the "other Christmas islands." Like everyone, I too plotted and schemed how to reach these "secretive" locations. They aren't really secret, just near impossible to reach short of a private yacht. Names frequently heard include Fanning, Washington, and Palmyra islands, all located north and west of Christmas Island. I have seen them from 25,000 feet, and they are remote!

Occasionally, private yachts stop over at Christmas Island and sailors dine at the Captain Cook Hotel. I always inquire as to whether the sailors have noticed any bonefish on their travels throughout the Pacific, but the answer is always the same—"Didn't notice any, but we caught lots of trevally." In the case of bonefish, one must know what to look for and where to look. Nevertheless, bonefish are present at nearly all Pacific islands. Whether they are worth the effort to reach them depends on the stage of your illness. After all, how many and how big can they be, and how many do you need to catch?

Palmyra Island is located about 360 miles northwest of Christmas Island and 960 miles southwest of Honolulu and is the northernmost island in the Line Island Archipelago. It is privately owned and inhabited by one caretaker. From 1940 to 1947, the U.S. Navy constructed a 6,000-foot runway and occupied it. Pilots have recently reported landing there but vegetation is said to encroach upon the runway from time to time. Unlike Christmas Island, Palmyra is lush and has one of the world's last stands of *Pisonia grandis* forest, with trees over 100 feet tall. Most uninhabited South Sea islands have great populations of pelagic birds, and Palmyra is no exception. Next to the Galapagos, Palmyra is said to have the largest colony of red-footed boobies. It is a 2½-day sailboat trip from Honolulu. While fly anglers have reported its remote waters are pristine and offer excellent bonefishing, I know I'm not going there unless the current owners invite me and I can fly. However, when an airplane became available at Christmas Island for trips to Fanning Island, I knew I was going there!

It was rumored that, because it was election year, the president wished to have access to and appear to be interested in the out islands, hence the airplane. Christmas Island anglers were able to charter the twin-engine craft and make the roughly 200-mile journey there and back in a day—a long day!

I enlisted Moana to guide me for the day. Soon a dozen other anglers and I were flying over trackless miles of deep cobalt-blue, wind-swept ocean. After an hour or so, the hazy image of Fanning appeared suspended like a mirage above the ocean. Soon we could make out heavy surf and vegetation along the beach and, finally, the short coral and sand runway.

Fanning Island is remote by any standard, and its inhabitants lead a secluded tropical lifestyle. Housing is on stilts and open air. Visitors are rare, and airplane landings are cause for celebration. We were met by the typical South Pacific welcoming committee—half the village. Everyone was friendly and very inquisitive. I had distributed my usual suitcase of clothing at Christmas Island. Had I known I was coming here, I would have brought more goodies. I did bring five pounds of assorted candies. Needless to say, this was a hit and caused quite a commotion. So, too, was our ice, which fascinated everyone, especially the children. We passed around sodas and upon touching the cold can, the children dropped them! When they tasted the icy cold liquid, they once again were perplexed, having never felt anything cooler than air temperature. Their screams of both surprise and delight brought laughter to our faces and slowed our progress to the fishing. Who cared—this was much more fun!

The only bus transportation on the island was an old Jeep and a tractor with a flatbed trailer. For water transportation, there was an old landing craft and assorted small vintage boats. Moana had a relative on the island who expedited our journey out of the village to the docks and into the fastest and safest boat. We motored to the first flat inside the lagoon and readied our gear. A rising tide sent a river of water through the narrow lagoon entrance and with it swam bonefish—big bonefish. For two hours we hooked (and lost) hefty bones up to 15 pounds! They were rambunctious feeders on the grab and fishing was incredible!

When hooked, the bones ran off the edge of the flat and sawed our leaders on coral, but we did manage to land several prize fish. After the bonefishing slowed and the tide turned out, we positioned ourselves at the lagoon entrance where trevally to 40 pounds were plentiful. They loved our poppers, and the few we cast to tired our

A nice Fanning Island bonefish.

Lance Kaufmann

Christmas Island guide Tyrone, Lance Kaufmann, and a beautiful trevally.

Richard Humphrey

One of the allures of bonefishing is that there is plenty of uncrowded water. Angler works the transition zone between deep and shallow water.

Can't you see them? They are right there!

Randall Kaufmann

Trevally fishing in the back of the lagoon.

Mary Kaufmann

A trevally goes free! A 12-weight rod is best at Christmas Island because you troll large flies in the lagoon and often cast to 40-, 50-, even 60-pound fish!

arms. For once we didn't have to "wait until tomorrow!" Oddly, the anglers who fished at the back of the lagoon had poor success. I attributed our success to Moana, and, on the return flight, I made plans with him to return later in the week, which we did.

I was expecting an instant replay. Like a little piglet rushing to the trough, I couldn't wait to wade out onto my flat. To our frustration a heavy cloud cover appeared, and we could not spot any of the large bonefish that patrolled the flat's edge. We only hooked a few small bonefish while casting blind. Both the tide and weather were against us. We would have to "wait until tomorrow." We packed our rods, tucked our tails between our legs, and headed back to Christmas Island.

Subsequent anglers have been few in number, and they only reported fair success. After the elections, the airplane disappeared into the sunset, and no anglers have visited Fanning Island since. I have again heard rumors of anglers visiting Palmyra. Perhaps I'll reconsider the option. Then there are the Line, Phoenix, Gilbert, and Marshall islands, and the French Frigate Shoals.

Lance Kaufmann
Tigard, Oregon
October 1998

Guides

A standard guide day is about nine hours, and there are usually two anglers per guide. Extra boat days can be purchased, as can longer guide days. I like to hire a private guide, which improves the guide-to-angler ratio and the angling. The extra guide more than repays the added cost within the first hour. You can specify the extra guide you want, but, remember, the best guides get booked early.

Independent guides are also available. One of the advantages of hiring an independent guide is the ability to set your own schedule. If the fishing is expected to be best between the hours of 10 a.m. and 6 p.m., that is your schedule. I sometimes like to start late and stay late. There is something special about South Pacific sunsets, evening trade winds, and being the last back to camp.

Favorite guides include Moana, Tyrone, Palau, Simon, Mario,

Richard Humphrey

English, Tuna, and Tabaki, but other well-trained guides enter the business each year.

The following day's schedule and destinations are set each evening. Good guides make certain you get the best locations, or they take you to their favorite spots. You soon learn which areas provide the type of fishing you enjoy the most.

Recommended Flies

Bonefish: Habitat and water depth determine fly patterns (color and sink rate), and Christmas Island is diverse. Carry a broad selection of flies in assorted sink rates. My favorites include Christmas Island Specials in pearlescent, yellow, pink, and orange; Clouser Minnows in tan-white, pink-white, and chartreuse-white; Marabou Shrimp in tan, pink, yellow, and white; Moana's Chili Pepper and Banana Peel patterns; and assorted crabs.

Trevally: Top picks are six- to eight-inch inshore-offshore poppers in red-yellow, yellow-green, and blue-white. In addition, assorted smaller poppers are great for smaller trevally and miscellaneous species. Lance's Trevally and Crystal Poppers are my current pick. Streakers and Sea Habit Bucktails round out the selection. Offshore anglers need poppers and tandem-hook sailfish flies, the bigger the better.

Richard Humphrey and blue-fin trevally.

Richard Humphrey

Fishing Offshore

Veteran Christmas Island visitors Tim Merrihew and Darrel Mendenhall are the ultimate opportunists. They schedule their daily fishing according to the tides and ocean conditions and target specific species when angling is best. When tides are optimum, they fish the lagoon for bones and trevally. When ocean conditions are good, they fish offshore for yellowfin tuna (and anything else that swims). Sometimes they travel several miles looking for birds and schools of fish breaking the surface. Once tuna are located, everyone hooks 20- to 50-pound fish! These finned rockets literally tear you up. Nothing less than 12-weight outfits and 300 yards of backing, please! If you have "gear," bring it!

Offshore fishing at Christmas Island is not for the uninitiated or poorly geared angler. On my last trip to Christmas Island, one night I noticed that two of our group were not at dinner, which was served two hours after dark. Two hours later, Howell Raines, *The New York Times* editorial page editor and author of *Fly Fishing through the Midlife Crisis,* and his angling partner, Tennant McWilliams, finally arrived back at the hotel. Howell told a story about trolling across the mouth of the lagoon early in the morning. He was fishing his backup salmon-style reel when an 80-pound marlin jumped his fly and took off toward the Gilbert Islands. Howell, his fishing partner, and his guide, Tuna, followed. The ocean was rough, and Tennant began chumming over the side. The marlin continued its progress

Trevally recuperates in the water while angler removes fly. Exert sideways pressure and use a 12-weight to turn and land powerful trevally. Reels should have 200 yards of backing.

Steve DeMoulin and Tyrone relax and let the fish come to them. What is in the cooler, boys?

toward the Gilberts. Every so often they would get the fish in close, but the reel drag was not strong enough to subdue it.

By afternoon, they had no food or water. Everyone was sun-fried, seasick, and exhausted when the plug came out of the boat. They were taking on water, looking for the plug, bailing, and chumming—but Howell hung tightly to his prize. The marlin and Howell were trying out for the movie, *The Old Man and the Sea.*

Land had long since disappeared from the horizon. It was late afternoon. The engine quit. It was an anxious wait while Tuna attempted to restart it. Keep in mind that this was a small skiff bobbing like a matchstick on the open Pacific Ocean. They were dangerously low on gasoline. Finally, in a last-ditch effort to bring the marlin close to the boat, Howell pushed his reel drag beyond its limit. The reel went gunnysack, and both the marlin and sun slowly sank into the sea.

Tuna navigated back to the island by the stars. Howell had a great story for his weekly column in *The New York Times.* I had some good entertainment and a new story about the big one that got away. For Tuna it had been just another day. Tennant could look forward to flats fishing the next day!

Properly prepared anglers can experience the angling thrill of a lifetime offshore. You never know what is going to steal your gear. Wahoo, great trevally, tuna, billfish, and shark are all possibilities. A fly (big ones!), plugs, and bait all work. Pick your gear and poke your boat bow outside the lagoon. You do not usually have to go too far.

The Future

The future can often be foretold by the past. There have been many schemes to modernize (ruin in my opinion) Christmas Island, including building a Japanese missile launching station and luxury hotels. Fortunately, none of these have come to fruition yet! The government has, however, leased offshore fishing to Asian enterprises. It has also encouraged inhabitants of the capital, Tarawa, which is overcrowded, to move to Christmas Island. You can only driftnet the ocean so long and accommodate so many people before the charm of the island, the bird life, and the spectacular offshore, trevally, and bonefish angling is imperiled. Subtle changes have occurred already. Human populations are up, wildlife populations down. If the government does not protect this unique and fragile ecosystem, Christmas Island will be a "remember when." Go while it is still good.

Because of its stable water temperatures and dry weather pattern, anytime is a good time to fish Christmas Island. Fishing is always good. A beautiful bonefish awaits release.

	J	F	M	A	M	J	J	A	S	O	N	D
Bonefish	G-E	G-E	G-E	G-E	G-E	G-E	G-E	G-E	G-E	G-E	G-E	G-E
Trevally	G-E	G-E	G-E	G-E	G-E	G-E	G-E	G-E	G-E	G-E	G-E	G-E
Shark	G-E	G-E	G-E	G-E	G-E	G-E	G-E	G-E	G-E	G-E	G-E	G-E
Offshore	G-E	G-E	G-E	G-E	G-E	G-E	G-E	G-E	G-E	G-E	G-E	G-E
Wind	L-M	L-M	L-M	L-M	L-M	L-M	L-M	L-M	L-M	L-M	L-M	L-M
G=Good　　E=Excellent　　L=Light　　M=Moderate												

Chapter 26

Cuba

Cuba is an 800-mile-long by 50-mile-wide collection of 1,500-odd islands, called "cayos" in Cuba, dominated by the main island. It is the largest landmass in the Caribbean. Located just south of the Tropic of Cancer, 90 miles off Key West, 90 miles south of Andros Island, 90 miles north of Jamaica, and 130 miles east of Mexico's Yucatan peninsula, Cuba is the geographic center of bonefish country.

Seen from the air, its shoreline is a mosaic of beautifully colored water, reefs, cays, sandy beaches, mangroves, and shallow flats crisscrossed with channels. Any bonefisherman who has studied the map or angling history knows that Cuba is bonefishing paradise. Indeed, Cuba is most likely the last bonefish sanctuary in the Caribbean.

Prior to political changes in the 1950s, Cuba was the haunt of the rich and famous, including angler Ernest Hemingway. Resorts situated on beautiful beaches catered to divers, anglers, sailors, dropouts, and sun lovers. It was America's tropical playground. Since then, Cuba has been off limits to Americans, but foreign visitors have rediscovered its charms and fabulous fishing opportunities.

Experiencing the Culture

There is always more to bonefishing than reeling in fish. Perhaps nowhere is this more exemplified than in Cuba. It would be a shame to visit the bonefish flats and not experience the culture, a rich blend of indigenous Arawak natives, Spanish, and

The streets of Havana are a great living car museum. Impressive architecture and the feeling of old Cuba are easily experienced.

Africans, who originally arrived as slaves. African rhythms and ritual dances were blended with Spanish guitars and melodies, which were further developed in the Americas.

Havana has been compared to Cleveland in the 1950s. Learning about Cuban history from the 1500s through the Iron Curtain Eastern Bloc industrial period is fascinating. Great architecture and the feeling of old Cuba are easily experienced.

Visiting old Havana is worthwhile, and Plaza de Armas is the focal point. Evenings can be spent dining and listening to music. View the historical port, wander the narrow streets, reminisce about the freewheeling Hemingway days, and visit his old haunts. Transport yourself back to the glory days of casinos, lavish resorts, Hemingwayesque epic fishing, and the best cigars in the world. Visit El Floridita—birthplace of the daiquiri—and La Bodeguita del Medio—birthplace of the mojito—where great local cuisine is served. To make a killer mojito, combine a half-teaspoon of sugar, juice from half a lime, a sprig of mint (crush the stalk to release the flavor), ice cubes, and 1.5 ounces of Havana Club Light Dry Cuban Rum in a highball glass. Fill with soda and stir. *Salud!*

Walk the Malecon along Havana harbor to the fortress. View the historic Nacional Hotel that has recently been renovated to its original splendor. The famous Tropicana Show is worth the money and a Cuban national treasure. Tour cigar factories, motor through the countryside, or hang out on the beautiful beaches (Varadero,

This is a perfect location to find large bonefish. There is good cover, access to deep water, and plenty of prey. Jon Covich puts the sneak on a trio of tailers wallowing along the edge of the flat. Notice how the flat gradually disappears into ocean.

east of Havana, offers 12 miles of stunning white sand).

In Cuba, everything from health care to infrastructure is in disrepair and in a time warp. Food and medicine are in short supply. Parts and gasoline for the fleet of classic 1950s autos, including Packards and Cadillacs, are scarce. Nonetheless, the streets of Havana are the greatest living car museum in the world.

Although Cuba is a controlled society and there is great poverty, the spirit and life of the Cuban people is inspiring. They make do with what they have. They love music and dancing. People are very friendly, especially toward Americans. The military has been instructed to treat visitors courteously. Some Cubans speak English in Havana and have learned how to make a buck. The most frequently asked question is, "Looking for fine cigars?" Speaking Spanish is a necessity if you travel around the country and makes it far easier to interact with the people and enjoy the culture. It is possible to hire an interpreter. If and when you go, spend some time in Havana and explore the countryside and beaches.

Flora and Fauna

There are about 3,000 plant species endemic to Cuba. The most noticeable are the palm trees, especially the royal palm, *Reistonea regia*, of which there are said to be millions. This is probably an exaggeration, but there are thousands of beautiful palm groves. The rarest palm is the prehistoric cork palm, *Microcycas calocoma*.

The Jardines are a world apart from mainland Cuba. Jon Covich casts for tarpon in a channel patterned in green mosaic.

So far, so good. The hooked fish is following the school (note nervous water) into more open water, leaving a mud trail.

Mangrove roots can rip monofilament like it was kite string.

The release.

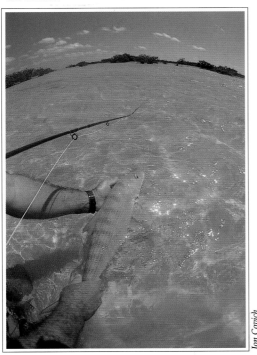

Cuba's most abundant land animals are reptilian, including numerous species of nonpoisonous snakes, lizards, iguanas, turtles, and crocodiles. The bee hummingbird, *Mellisuga helenae*, weighing only two grams and about the size of a grasshopper, is the world's smallest bird.

Weather

The climate is borderline tropical, and temperatures are generally warm and moist. The average humidity is 80 percent. Daytime temperatures seldom reach extremes even during the hottest summer months of July through September. There are two seasons—wet and dry. The wet summer season is mid-May to November. The drier winter season is November through April. The Jardines, off the south coast, enjoy 320 sunny days a year. January and February have five to eight rainy or cloudy days with daytime temperatures between 65 and 80 degrees Fahrenheit. July and August are the hottest months, with daytime temperatures between 75 and 95 degrees Fahrenheit, but fishing remains excellent. There are many sheltered areas to escape the winds.

Fishing Areas

Cienaga Occidental de Zapata, or Zapata National Park, is an extensive area of shallow marsh waters, brackish estuaries, meandering river channels, mangroves, and skinny water flats. This maze of water and ooze encompasses roughly a million acres, 30 by 50 miles along the southern coast. Located 50 air miles and a two-hour drive southeast of Havana, this mostly unexplored and wild area has been compared to Florida's Everglades. Like the Everglades, the marsh supports an incredible biomass of plant, animal, and bird life, including bonefish—lots of them!

At this time only a handful of anglers have cast a fly to these unsophisticated bonefish, which run from two to six pounds. There is also an abundance of tarpon to 40 pounds and barracuda to 15 pounds or so. Permit and snook are also present. The potential fishing area stretches from Bahia de Cochinos (Bay of Pigs) west 50 miles to Cayo Ernst Thalmann and Ensenada de Cazones. Accommodations and guides are available at Playa Larga.

A newly created national park in the Archipelago de los Jardines de la Reina, known as the Queen's Garden Archipelago, has generated the most interest. Since netting and all commercial fishing except lobstering have been banned, both predator and prey species have increased dramatically, and fishing is superb.

Located about 40 miles off the southern coast, midway to the Cayman islands, the Jardines lie scattered across the Caribbean for 140 miles like a broken strand of pearls. The bounty of fishes, fabulous underwater reefs, and varying types of shallow-water flats combine to provide a spectacular visual explosion of beauty and color. Consisting of grass and clear sand flats, mangroves, channels, coral reefs, tropical-colored drop-offs, and deserted beaches, the Queen's Garden is indeed aptly named.

Flats habitat offers a little of everything. Expect grass, coral, hard sand, marl, mud, and muck. Some areas are wadeable, others are not. Brian O'Keefe described some flats as being "suspended." "They were like walking on a mattress. The guides pole these flats,

Baby tarpon are exciting and, when hooked, spend as much time in the air as in the water. A 10-weight rod handles a tarpon this size, but you'll wish you had a 12 weight, especially if a bigger tarpon comes along! Jon Covich shows how to properly handle a tarpon for an above-the-water photo.

but I saw some tails I wanted to sneak up on. Twice I broke through and found myself up to my armpits." Extensive mangroves border most flats. Bonefish are plentiful. Expect singles, doubles, small pods, and big schools numbering in the hundreds. When conditions are right, tailers are everywhere. Most bonefish are two to six pounds. Ten pounders are sometimes caught, and larger fish are present.

Baby tarpon of 10 to 40 pounds are plentiful, with some tarpon to over 100 pounds in the channels and lagoons. Small acrobats can be enticed to a surface popper and provide fantastic sport. The best big tarpon grounds are about a two-hour run from the camp. April through July is the prime time. This is also the best time to find and fish for permit, which range between five and 40 pounds. Mutton snapper are a bonus. Usually scarce at most bonefish locations, these beautiful fish are common and aggressive and run between two and 15 pounds. A 15-pound snapper is nearly unstoppable with bonefish tackle! Be certain you have the proper flies.

In addition, red and gray snapper are plentiful. Jack crevalle and bar jacks are for the taking in the cuts and channels between flats. They readily attack poppers and streamers. Jewfish to 200 pounds inhabit some mangrove areas, and cubera snapper to over 100 pounds can be hooked along the reef. Notice that I said, "Hooked!"

Anglers should be aware that huge barracuda to 30 and 40

Jon and guide, Coki, double release.

No other fishing compares to bonefishing. Both the visuals and the action are unrivaled.

pounds are present. Barracuda this size are terrifying but are a thrill to hook. Don't let them jump in the boat! A long line release is best. Bull, lemon, and gray reef sharks range up to 10 feet and 300 pounds. They are common in the channels and along the edge of deeper flats. Watch for these. In deeper water, anglers can fish for kingfish, wahoo, and amberjack. Sometimes whalesharks and giant manta rays can be seen.

Fishing the remote flats in the Jardines is world class. Visitors continue to be awed by the diversity, exceptional size, and sheer numbers of fish. Prepare. Anglers should be outfitted with 8-, 10-, and 12-weight rods. Now, where do I find those jewfish?

Guides

Guides speak a little English and understand the basics about fly fishing. They are accommodating and personal. Because guiding is a very lucrative position, they strive to improve themselves and are very serious, sometimes too serious. Most anglers are European. The easy-does-it, let's-have-fun-and-enjoy-the-ambiance attitude of American anglers is not yet understood. For five days, Brian tried to get his guide to take him snorkeling: "No time. Many fish to be caught."

John Ecklund once thought the fishing world ended with steelhead. That was before his first bonefishing adventure, which was to Cuba. Now John is trading in his stream cleats for neoprene booties.

Bombshelter Bones
By John Ecklund

I wasn't sure what my parents had heard on the radio, but it must have been important, because my dad began to curse like low rumbling thunder. This kind of cursing was generally reserved for me, a 10-year-old boy, when the baseball went from inside the house to the outside. This time, though, I was in the clear. . .he was cursing the Cubans!

For the last 15 years, I've extracted a meager living from my obsession with Pacific Northwest steelhead. The cold waters of the Grande Ronde have been particularly kind to me, and I could never envision a more spectacular or thrilling fish on the fly than a steelhead. I'd heard all the stories about flats fishing: the blistering runs, awesome rod-busting yanks, and massive fish, but I never really saw myself getting into saltwater flats fishing. That was all about to change when the flight attendant aboard the Russian Yak 45 informed me politely (in Spanish) that we would be landing shortly in Havana, Cuba!

I was in Cuba as a guest of Italians who have a fishing operation 40 miles off the west coast in the Jardines de la Reina (JDR) Islands. The Jardines are home to a few small deer, fox, and iguanas, but the focus was on 100-pound tarpon, nine-pound bonefish, and 30-pound permit.

Other than to bury a pet rabbit, I had never had a shovel in my hands for more than a few minutes. When my dad waved his hands over a marked-out area and informed me that, "We're going to dig her down halfway to China," I was more than just a bit concerned! Summertime in Orange County, California, was for playing ball and swimming, not for digging to China in the sweltering heat.

After several days touring around old Havana, marveling at the beautiful old Spanish buildings, taxiing in 50s vintage classic cars, and drinking countless mojitos in Hemingway haunts, I was ready for some fishing.

After a 45-minute flight, a one-hour car ride, and a five-hour boat ride, we were nearing our home base in the Queen's Garden. The *Tortuga* is a 140-foot, three-story nine-room floating hotel. During the boat ride, Pepe, our Italian host, talked about their fishing program—all the grand slams, 150-pound tarpon, and huge bones. I also heard my first Pepe-ism: "I swear to you, you are going to catch. . ."

On my first day in salt water, I fished the mangroves. Within 10 minutes of going into stealth mode, Pedro was yelling like an auctioneer, "Veinte metros, one o' clock cast, cast, cast, este dia por favor, pronto, pronto!" After what seemed like an eternity, I did three things: I untangled the line from my sandals; I finally spotted the nervous water hiding the school; and I got off a woefully inadequate cast that fell short of the mark, serving only to "shoot 'em in the ass," scattering bonefish in every direction. I had become my own worst client from hell.

Most of the day Pedro was on point like a Brittainy surrounded by quail, yelling, waving his arms, and chain smoking. I met the enemy—it is us. We drank Havana Club Rum and too much beer. For my part, I ditched the sandals and most of the junk dangling from my neck, finally dialed in my cast, and at 4:23 CST (Cuban Standard Time) on May 7 finally hooked an 8 ½-pound asteroid of a bonefish.

The floating Tortuga Lodge is well equipped, complete with a fleet of flats boats with fast motors.

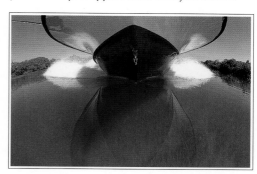

Speed and comfort are only two advantages of a specially designed flats boat. The hull shape deflects water, keeping passengers dry. A fast boat extends your fishing time and reduces travel time.

Guides work very hard at Tortuga Lodge.

Jon Covich

Landing this fish was like a nuclear experience. When the camera went off, I even dared to look directly at the flash. The experience had exceeded all my expectations! At day's end I felt a full range of sensation: emotionally and physically drained, elated with my first fish, and, now that the pressure was off and we were skipping our way back to the *Tortuga*, intoxicated with Cuba—or was it the rum?

After a little over a week of digging we finally finished. When the semi backed up with a load of cinder block, I wasn't a bit concerned; this would be fun. I loved to build things. My brother and I had built tree houses, dug tunnels, and had been nailing and lashing stuff together for years. This had the potential to be the coolest fort on the block. We could hold off the dung-slinging Threadkell twins for weeks!

The bomb shelter project was taking on an almost carnival-like atmosphere. The neighbors were either doing the same thing, making fun, or sucking up. It was a hectic time, building the fort and planning what to do if the Communists took over. I would burn my baseball card collection.

At school, we practice crouching under our desks with a book behind our heads. We were told not to look at the flash of light. Right. . .as if that was our biggest worry! As we put the metal door on its hinges, we got news that the Communists might be backing down.

Day one had somehow turned into day three, and, after the preceeding 30-bonefish day, I was ready for a new challenge. One of the other guests on the *Tortuga* invited me to join him and look for permit. I knew permit were tough and set my expectations accordingly, *muy bajo.* Our interest quickly waned as we spotted bonefish in the eight- to 10-pound range. This style of fishing was more like spring creek fishing, requiring precise fly placement and

line control. Unlike the mangrove areas, we were now fishing over porcelain-white sand with patches of turtle grass. Eels floated by, sharks were on the prowl, barracuda darted here and there, we landed eight- to nine-pound bones, but we saw no permit.

While returning home, our guide, Coki, spotted about a thousand bonefish finning between breaking surf and shore. We anchored the boat and positioned ourselves about 70 feet from the mass of bonefish and cast blindly into them. Coki and I, sharing a rod, would release a bonefish and then pass the rod. It was fun watching my companions catching these rockets. I learned the neat trick of setting the hook and immediately planting the rod butt on your chest, keeping the slack line going where it should go—onto the reel, not around it and the butt of the rod!

That night, over dinner, as we blurted out our incredible story of success, of screaming Tibors and stupid fish, I realized I had committed the ultimate rookie mistake: the first liar doesn't have a chance. I looked over at my buddy, Yasuji Sugai, who was smiling smugly at our story. Two boats had gone after tarpon and had scored in a big way. Four anglers, two dozen tarpon weighing from 30 to 110 pounds boated. _Muy buena suerté._

I spent my last days in the Jardines chasing tarpon. It was one of those "you should have been here last week" deals. The weather changed and a storm rolled in, bringing high clouds and just enough wind to make sight fishing difficult. I've done the rhumba, I've tried the meréngue, but the Bimini Twist took a lot of practice before I felt confident. The tarpon were very skittish. Darting like black ghosts in and out of the mangroves, these pre-storm tarpon were difficult targets. It was particularly interesting that, if we

Because of their colossal size, herculean strength, and astonishing acrobatics, tarpon hook anglers in a big way. Each fish startles your senses, forcing you to clutch the rod and hang on—often forgetting to bow, gawking in bewilderment.

What can you say? This is just another typical flat in bonefish paradise. Imagine spotting, stalking, and casting to six-pound torpedoes in water like this! And the weather—it's perfect.

went too long without a sighting, the guide would rev up the motor and tarpon would come out of the depths.

Eventually, conditions were right, and a group of fish drifted out from the mangroves towards our boat. After two days of cat and mouse, my guide had either given up on me or assumed I knew what I was doing. No words were exchanged as I dropped a size 4/0 Green Tarpon Glo into their path. Pause. A long pull. Pause. Suddenly two fish attacked the fly. A massive surge of adrenalin hit me at the same time the winner of the fly realized it was hooked. One vertical jump, an awesome display of rattling silver armor, and my 30-pound acrobat had cut me loose!

"Well, it's over, son. The Russians have packed up and gone home. I hope these last few weeks have taught you a few lessons." I was confused. Our dad was somewhat of an oddity in Orange County. His hobby was whaling, and he was good at it. . .when my brother or I got out of line, he would whale our butts! It was with a bit of trepidition that I asked him what communism was. "Well, son, communism is when the people have no say in their future, and they just work all the time and never get paid." With an understanding nod, I asked politely if I could have Saturday off from my bomb shelter clean-up chores. He immediately snapped back,

"Hell no, you're working." I had learned a lesson and vowed to run a more democratic family when I grew up.

The drone of the rattly Yak airplane engine brought reality back, and I thought about the hardships and poverty that the Cuban people endure every day, like trading cat meat on the black market or finding something to eat. Eventually, I focused on the vision of the pristine sandy beaches, the pungent smell of mangroves, the seductive aftertaste of an ice-cold mojito, and the lively toe-tapping Afro-Cuban music. This had been a trip of many firsts for me. My feelings for steelheading would certainly never be the same. I would have to scratch some money together and do this again. I wonder how much used spey rods are worth?

John Ecklund
Troy, Oregon
December 1998

Landing a jack crevalle on an oceanside flat.

Brian O'Keefe and Jon Covich decided to travel to Cuba on a combination fishing and photography adventure. I knew that they would return with spectacular images. I wasn't disappointed. They returned with nearly a thousand slides! The photos in this chapter are all from their week-long excursion to the Jardines, as are the other Cuba photos in this book. In the following vignette Jon shares some of his memories.

Bonefishing and the Rhumba
By Jon Covich

"Two permit coming. . .one o'clock. . .long way!" our guide yelled. Brian was in the ready position on the boat bow. He located the fish, made a quick backcast, and put the crab imitation six feet in front of the lead fish. Brian was concentrating. He let the fly settle and did not move it. One permit came within a foot or two and turned. Brian twitched the crab. The permit whirled, veered off, raced back, and unexpectedly devoured the crab! Watching the scene through the lens of my camera, I saw Brian drive the hook home and his rod bend in half.

As Brian cleared his slack line, the big permit burned a path toward open ocean. Our guide, Coki, was patting me on the back, displaying the biggest smile we would see all week, screaming, "Big permit! Big permit!" With the situation somewhat under control, Brian and I were ecstatic. We made the journey to Cuba to photograph the fishing and already on our first day Brian was fast to the biggest permit he had ever hooked.

We began discussing how many photos we would take of this fish—telephoto, fisheye, underwater, etc. and which magazine would be first to scramble for them. It is bad luck to count your photos

Jack crevalle are plentiful in Atlantic and Caribbean waters and are awesome sport. Flats anglers may encounter fish of 25 pounds or more. Large jacks are much like permit—except they eat anything that moves. These trash compactors inhale poppers and streamers. Notice the size of its mouth. Do you think a five-inch popper is too big? Not likely.

Oou-we...a picture perfect bone. Notice the flattened underside and downward shape of its mouth—perfect for swimming and feeding along the bottom. Angler is Jon Covich.

before they are in the can, and, sure enough, at that same moment Brian's line suddenly stopped moving through the water. Coki dove into the water in hopes of freeing the line from whatever held it tight. Too late; coral had cut the backing and both the fly line and permit were lost. Permit are not as easy to come by as fly lines. I have never seen Brian so disappointed over losing a fish.

Perhaps some of his disappointment came from the travel fatigue we felt. Our journey to Cuba's bonefish flats had been customized to get us there as quickly as possible and it was nonstop for 24 hours. Thoughts of communism filled our minds as we cleared customs in Havana. Once we were in our taxi, we were stunned by the reality of Cuba's economy. We sped across the island drinking the last of our Cuban cervézas and watched in amazement as we motored along a freeway empty of vehicles but crowded with pedestrians. It was the widest and longest sidewalk

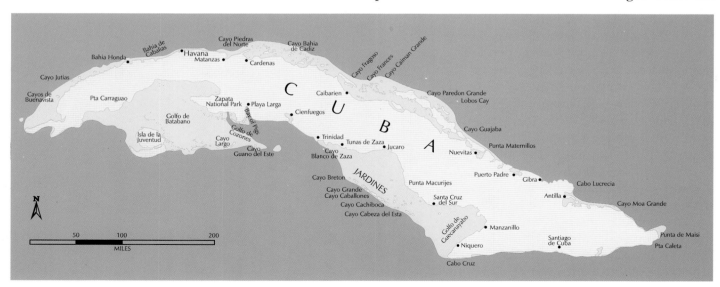

we had ever seen. People were everywhere, on foot and on bicycles, many attempting to flag down the occasional commercial vehicle in hopes of obtaining a ride.

After a five-hour taxi ride we boarded a boat for a five-hour trip across the water to our destination. I remember awakening to the sound of the big boat's diesel engine throttling down, feeling that we were finally in calmer water, beyond the ocean swells that tenderized us most of the night. Looking out the small porthole of our cabin, I saw the barge that was to be our digs bathed in the first light of morning. As we breakfasted with our Italian host, Pepe, he explained the Jardines to us. He had set up his fishing and diving operation in 1993 and could accommodate 35 guests. He had ten guides and seven state-of-the-art flats boats.

It didn't take us long to fall into the routine. Our morning began with a Saturday Night Live-like routine with the kitchen staff. "Bacon, eggs, sir?" they would inquire. "Do you have any fresh fruit?" I would ask. "Two eggs sir?" they would respond. "How about some cereal?" I would ask. "Bacon sir?" they responded. Finally, seeing defeat in my face, they would deliver bacon and eggs every morning.

Our guide, Coki, was the most intense guide I have ever fished with. Guiding in Cuba is a highly coveted and respected position, and they work very hard, are excitable, and expect you to fish nonstop. Coki would start us early each day with a long boat ride to a different location. We would often begin by poling along a crunchy permit flat and then wade a sandy beach, back cove, or lagoon casting to bonefish after bonefish. Then we might zigzag through an interior maze of mangroves only to suddenly stop with our guide pointing at rolling tarpon. Then on to barracuda patrolling the mouths of cuts, snapper tucked into the shade of mangrove roots, jacks cruising the edge of flats. . .we couldn't sample it all.

Bonefishing was phenomenal. It was only occasionally that we would go longer then ten minutes without seeing a fish. Sometimes they would be spooky and have lockjaw as bonefish often do, but we caught them almost at will. They averaged three pounds with some to eight pounds taking the fly. We found great numbers of smaller fish on hard clean flats and experienced casting to larger fish in smaller numbers while wading through mangrove clumps. Sometimes we would stay in the boat as Coki polled over softer flats where all the tails were big.

Like most fishing buddies, we established some traditions on our trip. It became tradition for Brian to catch more fish than I, and for me to get buck fever and blow casts to permit when they were cruising by. But the best of all our routines occurred when we returned to camp each evening. We would be speeding across open water as the sun was glowing orange on the horizon. The water around the boat would shimmer like an oily glow in the suns reflection, and we would be silent thinking of the fish caught, the film burned, and what would await us at the lodge. It hadn't taken the bartender long to know our tastes, and he would be waiting for us with a Cuba Líbre and Piña Colada dockside. We would slurp them down, still standing in the boat with rods in hand, exchanging stories with other anglers also just returned.

There are two separate memories that come to mind when I

It is difficult to lift a bonefish off the bottom, even with a 9-weight rod! Anglers have broken rods trying. Thin, flat water equals spooky fish, and long leaders.

Great habitat.

More great habitat!

Fisheye view of the angler's world.

Jon Covich

Hmmm! Looks good enough to eat! Is this all for me? Don't allow Brian the first cast on the water or at the table! There may not be much left.

Back at camp a Cuba Líbre and Piña Colada were awaiting Brian and Jon's return. They would slurp them down, still standing in the boat with rods in hand, watching the sun set and telling the day's adventures.

reflect on Cuba. I'll think of the day when Coki took us to an oceanside flat where we began the morning casting to permit. Brian was on deck when Coki yelled, "Jacks!" and we scrambled to exchange our rod for another rigged with a steel leader. Fly lines were coiled all over the boat in the first of the day's Cuban fishing drills. Then I was on the bow set for permit when the next yell came, "Tarpon coming!" Again, rods flew about the boat in the exchange, and then I managed a long cast to a school of 15 pounders, success coming with a jump, head shakes, more arching jumps, and finally photos. Afterwards we boated a big mutton snapper, caught more jacks, cast to more permit, and caught bonefish while walking the inside edge of a flat. Brian reflected that he had never seen a mile of beach with such a diversity of species as we had encountered that day. That is what I liked best and what is so special about Cuba, its diversity.

My last thoughts of Cuba have nothing to do with fishing. Our week with Pepe and Coki on the live-aboard barge over, we again made the journey via boat and taxi back to Havana. We decided to take in the show at the world famous Tropicana. It was an amazing spectacle: tall showgirls with long legs and tropical headdresses entertaining a huge, well dressed audience. It was a fitting end to our journey that as the show ended, Brian and I were pulled on stage. There, in front of a sophisticated audience, two short fisherman dressed in flats attire and possessing not an ounce of groove in their bodies, shuffled to a Caribbean rhumba beat as the stage faded to black.

Jon Covich
Bend, Oregon
March 1999

It is only a matter of time before Cuba is once again the haunt of Americans. In the interim, it is illegal for Americans to spend money in Cuba unless you obtain a special license from the U.S. Treasury Department. Those wishing to obtain detailed travel restrictions and exceptions can contact the U.S. Office of Foreign Assets Control, U.S. Department of the Treasury, Washington, D.C. or phone 202-622-2520. Request the Cuban Assets Control regulations.

	J	F	M	A	M	J	J	A	S	O	N	D
Bonefish	G-E	G-E	E	E	E	E	G-E	F-E	F-E	F-E	G-E	G-E
Permit	F-G	F-G	F-E	G-E	G-E	G-E	G-E	G-E	F-E	F-E	F-E	F-G
Tarpon	G	G	G-E	E	E	E	E	G-E	F-G	F-G	F-G	F-G
Snook	F	F	F	F-G	F-G	F-G	F	F	F	F	F	F
Barracuda	G	G	G	G	G	G	G	G	G	G	G	G
Snapper	G	G-E	E	E	E	E	G-E	G-E	G	G	G	G
Jacks	G	G-E	E	E	E	E	G-E	G-E	G	G	G	G
Sharks	G	G	G	G	G	G	G	G	G	G	G	G
P=Poor F=Fair G=Good E=Excellent												

Chapter 27

Florida Keys

The Florida Keys are the only place in the United States where bonefish are found, and they average over five pounds. Eight- to 10-pound fish are an everyday occurrence. Tournament anglers don't usually bother to weigh anything under 10 pounds. You won't hook or land many, but they test your tackle, skill, and patience. When you land a Florida bonefish, you have really accomplished something. Bonefish inhabit Florida Keys waters all year, but cool winter temperatures drive them to deeper, warmer water. Prime time is April through June and September through mid-November.

There are many reasons for fishing the Keys. Everyone speaks English. Guides have safe and comfortable gear. The food and water are always safe, and you have your pick of accommodations. Anglers can continue their Wall Street business, sneak in a round of golf, and relax with a late afternoon massage and a dinner of choice. You don't need a passport, pay departure tax, or have to figure out monopoly money. Nonfishing partners find plenty to do. Anglers can fly to Miami, Marathon, or Key West and rent a car. Accommodations, restaurants, shopping, tennis, dining, and night life are plentiful. Reservations are advised during the tourist season.

Bonefishing in Florida is not what it was in the "good old days," but it is better than it used to be thanks to a ban on commercial netting. Many user groups visit or impact fishing areas on a daily basis. Bonefish are skittish, suspicious, and distrustful of all things unnatural and are not easily duped.

Fishing and exploring the southern tip of Florida is a lifetime endeavor and this is only a tiny fraction of the state! The southern coast of the Everglades, Florida Bay, Biscayne Bay, and the Keys offer more diverse fishing than perhaps any other place. This chapter merely glosses over a tiny fraction of the flats potential.

Geography

The Florida Keys and the flats that surround them are an amazing place. The Keys are surrounded by 4,000 square miles of flats that stretch from Key Biscayne to Key West. They angle south from Miami and turn west toward Key West, the southernmost point in the continental United States. The Keys form a crescent that is about 130 miles long as the seagull flies. There are roughly 500 deserted low-lying keys, of which about 25 are connected by the 200-mile-long highway and a series of bridges.

The western side of the Keys is referred to as the back country. It fronts on the Gulf of Mexico and Florida Bay. The eastern side, or outside, fronts on the Atlantic and the Straits of Florida. Most of the landscape is a series of marshy mangrove isles offset by extensive shallow flats.

A casual glance at the map shows many unnamed and deserted keys scattered across nearly 30 miles of shallow water west from the upper keys to Flamingo on the mainland. Because of the close proximity to the Everglades, which contains a tremendous reservoir of fresh water, the salinity mix changes. About halfway between Islamorada and Flamingo, heading toward the Everglades, there are no bonefish, but tarpon, snook, and redfish are present.

Florida flats, like bonefish flies, come in all sink rates and colors. Some are hard sand, perhaps mixed with grass and coral. Many are soft muck with grass. Others are hard rock or coral—perfect bonefish, permit, and tarpon country.

Weather

The tip of Florida and the Keys are considered semitropical, but, because this area is part of the North American continent, it is subjected to many cold fronts. Cool winter weather patterns usually push flats fish into deeper water from December through March. Hot weather during June through August sometimes drives fish to cooler, deeper water, leaving April, May, June, September, October, and sometimes November as the best months to fish for bonefish. However, anglers intent on visiting Florida during the winter months can always find *something* to fish for, and the weather is much more agreeable than northern Minnesota. Wind can be a problem in the Keys. Prepare yourself for 10- to 20-mph breezes, which can provide some of the best permit fishing.

Poling for tarpon in the back country.

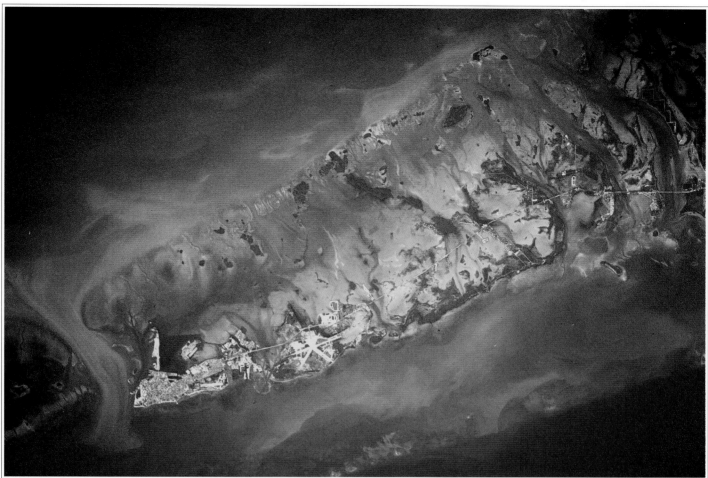

NASA

Roadside Attractions

The Florida Keys begin at mile marker 107 in Key Largo and end at zero in Key West. Mile markers are used as reference points for everything from homes to bonefish flats. It is possible to catch bonefish, permit, tarpon, barracuda, and shark from roadside flats. If you cannot afford a guide or just want to poke around on your own, stop at a local fishing store and ask about the best places and tides. Fishing roadside flats is very dependent on the stage and level of the tides. Some flats are obvious, others are not. Foot access is difficult to find at many. Some areas require you to cross private property. Ask permission before you enter them. Some flats have hard rock bottoms; others are sand, grass, and soft muck. Be careful when fishing alone. Stay clear of soft bottoms! Some hotels have excellent private access to bonefish water.

Briefly, some of the most popular and accessible flats include the two-mile-long beach in the Long Key Recreation Area. Wading can be a little tough in some areas but worth it. Camping is excellent. Little Duck Key offers good flats access on the Atlantic side. Marathon has some excellent flats. Smathers Beach and Bahia Honda State Park offers an extensive sand and grass flat.

There are many places to park an RV or pitch a tent. Everything considered, the Keys are a decent place to go it on your own, but be realistic about the fishing. It is high-tech and difficult even with local knowledge. Remember, weather, water temperature, and tides are the keys to success.

Key West is visible at the lower left. The "back country" and Gulf of Mexico are at the top. The Atlantic Ocean (Straits of Florida) is in the foreground. Following the highway to the right (east-northeast) of the airport are Boca Chica Key, Saddlebunch Keys, and Sugar Loaf Key. Cudjo Key is just above the island (Lois Key) in the right center. Summerland Key is at the right of Cudjo Key. The last barely visible key is Ramrod with Big Torch at the far upper right.

Florida guides have the best equipment (boat, motor, trailer, poling platform, pole, and safety features). Over the past 50 years, they have had the most experience fishing the flats and angling for bonefish, permit, and tarpon. A day in their boat can be very educational.

The angler is standing on the casting platform on the bow. The push pole is secured to the poling platform on the stern. This angler/guide has traded the push pole for the fly rod. Poling and fishing from a boat is a two-person affair.

Doing It Yourself

Many areas are accessible by kayak, canoe, or boat. Consider hiring a guide for a day or two. Level with the guide up front that you are seeking information. Most are glad to help, but it is unrealistic to expect them to take you to their favorite bonefish haunt knowing that you might be there ahead of them tomorrow.

Renting a boat and exploring on your own can be fun, but you should consider what your time and energy are worth and why you are doing what you are doing. Realistically, by the time you rent a boat (or tow your own), gas up, get a pole, dink around looking for a good spot, secure the boat, and get out on foot, a lot of time, money, and energy has been spent. You probably still do not know where you are, where you are going, or what you are doing! You won't have a poling platform or "guide's eyes," and you'll spend more time looking than fishing. In short, why are you there? To save a few bucks or to get a private crash course in the art of bonefishing and some shots at fish? Get a guide if you possibly can. The experts do.

Guides

Fly fishing for bonefish started in 1947 in the Florida Keys and has been on a nonstop, one-way ticket forward ever since. Many bonefish anglers got, or will get, their start in the Keys. Collectively, Florida guides are the most knowledgeable in the world and are among the best in the business. They have the most advanced equipment (boat, motor, trailer, poling platform, pole, safety features, and fly fishing aids) and pride themselves on their knowledge of flora, fauna, and local history. They tie flies, fly fish, and are on the leading edge of the sport. Over the past 50 years this cadre of anglers has had the most experience fishing the flats for bonefish, permit, and tarpon. Many of them developed the knots, flies, tackle, and the presentation, stalking, and casting techniques that most of us take for granted.

The title "Captain" in front of a guide's name means they have been tested and licensed by the U.S. Coast Guard to carry people for hire in their boat. Nowhere else in the fishing world can you find so many dedicated, highly educated, and specialized anglers. Fly fishing for bonefish, permit, tarpon, and whatever else swims is their business.

Captains like to direct the play-by-play from their poling platform. They make certain you see the fish, and they call the shots. It is a matter of pride for them to position the boat perfectly for the best cast. When they say, "drop it," you drop it. That doesn't mean on the next false cast, it means *now*.

The world's best permit guides are in the Florida Keys, and the world's best permit anglers fish with them. Nearly all permit angling strategies, techniques, and flies have been developed here. It is ground zero. If you want to get in the game, grab your 10 weight and fly American Eagle Airlines to Key West. It will be worth it! Permit are year-round residents of Florida, but peak angling time is March through May and October. Fish tip the scales at 50 pounds but average 20 to 25.

If you are in Florida on business or a family vacation, a day or two spent on the water with a veteran Florida fly fishing guide is worth twice the price of admission, even if you don't hook any fish.

The best way to book a Florida guide is to get a recommendation from a friend, booking agent, or local fly fishing store. If the guide is booked, ask for another recommendation. Many of the best guides are booked a year in advance, but cancellations do happen; you might get lucky.

Tarpon

The Florida Keys offer the world's best sight fishing for giant tarpon and the world's best tarpon guides. Tarpon fishing originated here, and it is still the king of Florida sportfish. Florida tarpon commonly run from 75 to over 150 pounds, but a 125 pounder is considered a good one. Early morning and late evening are the best times. Some anglers fish them at night. You may not hook many, but one is all it takes. On a recent visit my brother, Lance, fished for six days without success. The last hour of the last day he jumped a 140 pounder and missed his airplane! Tarpon alter your priorities.

Think big! Giant tarpon require 12-weight rods, floating and/or sinking lines, 300-yard-capacity reels, 80- to 100-pound Bimini Twist shock leaders, and 3/0 tarpon flies set up in a fly stretcher. The best advice I have is to practice casting your 12 weight before you arrive. You won't make a lot of casts, but only a few can tire your arm. Fifty-foot casts on target are usually good enough.

Giant migratory tarpon usually begin showing up in shallow

Captain Tom Rowland, ace tarpon guide, carefully revives and releases a tarpon for Lance Kaufmann.

Florida offers the best sight fishing for giant tarpon and the best tarpon guides. If you can book a few days at prime time with a tarpon specialist, do it!

Bowing to tarpon.

A gill rattler leaps for freedom.

Florida tarpon require rods, reels, and leaders capable of going the distance, which could be miles and hours!

water as it warms in late March or early April. May through early July is peak time. Book accommodations and guides a year in advance.

Anglers wishing to break into the sport should book a few days with a guide and begin researching knots, tackle, and techniques. Read *Fly Fishing in Saltwater* by Lefty Kreh, *The Book of the Tarpon* by A.W. Dimlock, *Practical Fishing Knots II* by Mark Sosin and Lefty Kreh, and *Tarpon Quest* by John Cole. Some excellent instructional videos are also available, including the 3M Scientific Anglers videos by Billy Pate—*The Challenge of Giant Tarpon* and *Fly Rodding for Tarpon.* Master saltwater angler Stu Apte has two excellent videos: *Tarpon Country* and *Saltwater Fly Fishing From A To Z.*

Visit your local fly fishing specialty store and talk with the resident experts. They will be glad to show you flies, demonstrate knots, explain tackle, and play a tarpon video for you.

Tackle, Flies, and Techniques for Bonefish and Permit

Because of the variety of species, the wind, and the range of fly and fish sizes, anglers should be geared for everything. Florida bonefish and permit anglers fish with very similar gear. Nine- and 10-weight rods in conjunction with a floating bonefish taper line, sometimes an intermediate sinking line, are the rule. Clear mono lines are an advantage, especially under clear, calm conditions because the clear line is less easily detected. Therein lies the trade-off: it is also more difficult for you to see it; actually it is impossible. Experienced anglers know how far and where they are casting and where their fly is in relation to fish. Less expert anglers usually rely on their fly line to lead them to the general area of their fly.

Because Florida flies are oversize and heavy, and because bonefish are big and it is usually windy, leaders must have a heavy butt section and tippet. Think of your leader as an extension of your fly line diameter wise. I like a .026 diameter butt section tapered to .015 for casting big bugs to big fish in wind. Fluorocarbon is best, *but do not discard it around waterways! It lasts forever and is dangerous to wildlife!*

Florida flats are often carpeted with luxurious turtle grass. Bonefish feeding on these unkempt lawns can be approached closely, and presentations should usually be made inside a pie-pan-sized area around their face. It helps if the fly is easily visible (big!) and is exciting enough for a bonefish to immediately jump it. Once a fly sinks into or picks up turtle grass, forget it. Neutral buoyancy flies with weed guards are the rule. So are perfect casts.

Permit and bonefish flies are not your normal fare. Expect to tie and fish *big* flies. My longtime friend, Keith Mootry, who lives on Big Pine Key, has always been a maverick tyer. Long ago Keith began incorporating craft fur, wool, and spun deer hair in his odd-ball creations. Today, his style of fly is mainstream, and his bonefish, tarpon, and permit concoctions are the foundation of many of today's best patterns.

Tim Borski is a pirate in the land of misfits—the Florida Keys. Somehow he manages to stay single and engage in his few narrow interests, which include painting, fishing for his favorite subjects, tying innovative flies, and plundering in the fun zone. He recently illustrated Flip Pallot's beautiful book, *Memories, Mangroves and Magic.* Tim has promoted a series of off-the-wall flies that fool Florida's big bones, permit, and tarpon. Such flies have been creat-

ed out of necessity. Wind, tides, habitat, food sources, bigger fish in deeper water, and the gluttony of big bonefish demand "big uglies." I'll let Tim tell it.

Ugly Flies, Friendly Fish
by Tim Borski

A typical early spring breeze in the Florida Keys had been steadily building throughout the morning. At 11 a.m., a stiff wind was herding clouds toward the southwest at a pace fast enough that, looking skyward, you felt obligated to comment. By noon, it had freshened to a point where it had pinned us down. Rowdy, squirrely seas rushing through the bridges had severely limited our options. Many of the deeper edges we had wanted to work were not fishable. The ocean side? Out of the question. There is only so much a 17-foot skiff can deliver in such conditions.

A big tide was being pushed even bigger by the wind, and the water was beginning to "smoke" a bit. Skies were bright, however, and visibility was stellar. In reality, the conditions were a whole lot better than they appeared from a vehicle traveling the Overseas Highway.

Conditions such as we were experiencing are typical enough of the Florida Keys that an angler tends to expect them and fish through them without much thought. It is in these circumstances that a couple of big, hairy bugs tucked away in a remote corner of your fly box will make you smile.

That day we had steadily decreased the length of our leader and increased the size of our flies. We had finally reached the outer limit with an enormous Chernobyl Crab, which resembles an eastern brown bat. Tied on Tiemco 911S 1/0 4XL and fully four inches long, its silhouette could be seen from 10 feet, which was all the precision the wind-blown casts allowed. Tossing so bulky and unwieldy a bug as this is no fun under the best of circumstances. It was O.K. though: under these conditions big fish are often tolerant enough to make you think you know it all. It also helps that all shots were downwind, or nearly so, and close.

Short, choppy, and real ugly.

Tossing a quick 10 weight with a short two-section leader consisting of six feet of 30-pound and three feet of 15-pound mono gets the job done. It's never really stereotypically pretty, but sometimes you just have to get on with your day. This is fishing weather catering toward the slick posed photos that make people ask, "How big?"

By crabbing the skiff bow into the wind, we were able to "skate" along some of the deeper shoulders and edges of a couple of nearby channels. On the second of only four options, we found them. Three fish plainly visible (and enormous) in the bright sun. They were acting exactly as they should: aggressively pushing mud around in 3½ feet of slightly off-color water. They were secure enough to allow a close approach. The first cast, an easy backhand, clomped down loud enough to make me cringe on the poling platform. Fortunately, it was wide right and did not disturb the closest bonefish.

The second cast fell to the water right on her head. She spooked briefly but saw the big bat swoop down toward the turtle grass. Wheeling, she pinned it to the bottom in a plume of bright mud and was off running. And running.

Randall Kaufmann

These Tim Borski flies are effective for Florida bonefish and permit. Top to bottom: Mangrove Critter, Fur Shrimp, Super Swimming Shrimp, Chernobyl Crab, and Slider. A 15.4-pound (pending IFGA world-record) bonefish was fooled with a Borski Slider in April 1999.

The abundant grass in Florida dictates fly selection and presentation strategies.

Ten minutes later, she lay still for a quick, memorable photo. A hurried measurement resulted in 29½ inches to the fork, 20 in girth. The other two fish had looked similar in size. Mission improbable had become mission accomplished, thanks to the large, tasty-appearing morsel.

I finished the day at my vise tying a replacement for the badly-mangled fly. Stuck in the far corner of a battered green fly box with "bonefish" written on it, it will be ready to be dug out when the wind throws a party, the skies are bright, and the casts are as ugly as the fish are friendly.

Tim Borski
Islamorada, Florida
February 1998

Angling Locations

During the proper season you can find tarpon, permit, and bonefish from one end of the Keys to the other, but specific areas offer the most consistent fishing for each species. Bonefishing is best from Key Biscayne to roughly Big Pine Key. Tarpon fishing is best from Islamorada to the Marquesas beyond Key West. Permit fishing is best from the Content Keys to the Marquesas. The area between Marathon and Key West has produced most of the grand slams—permit, bonefish, and tarpon all in the same day.

Fishing in the Keys is usually done from a boat, but many flats

are wadeable. There are some excellent mangrove areas, plus extensive areas of turtle grass mixed with mud and some coral. Some areas have sand flats. Potluck anglers have a chance at many other species, including dorado, snapper, barracuda, jack, king mackerel, yellowfin tuna, and shark.

Florida bonefish are big and strong and always on hyper alert. They are skittish, suspicious, and distrustful of all things. They require you to have skill and cunning if you are to consistently dupe them.

Key Biscayne

Key Biscayne is the paradox of bonefishing. Located within a 30-minute drive of the Miami airport and one of the largest cities in America, Key Biscayne offers fishing for some of the largest bone-fish in America. Most anglers think of seclusion and bonefish as mutual partners. Initially, seclusion may not seem possible in Biscayne Bay, but, indeed, it is. From Stiltsville at the north end of the bay to Caesar's Creek just above Key Largo, flats stretch for about 20 miles. A series of islands form a reef-like barrier at the outer edge of the bay. Places like Elliott Key are mostly unspoiled and are reminiscent of the Bahamas. Much of this area is included in Biscayne National Park.

Bonefishing here is not fast, but the fish are all big, running between five and 10 pounds. Fifteen-pound bonefish have been released here, two on the same day in 1997! The best time to find these finned javalinas seems to be when the wind is blowing 30 mph and you can't see or cast. Tough fishing breeds innovations.

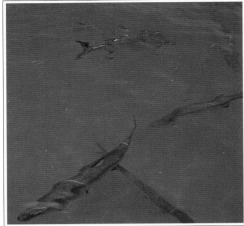

Tarpon! Right under the boat!

None of the bonefish in this country are pushovers. When you hook one, you have accomplished something. This is the most northern consistent bonefishing in America and is easy to reach. Travelers and business people going through Miami should take advantage of a day on the water. Many excellent guides are available.

Islamorada

Islamorada, or "the Purple Isles," was named by the Spanish centuries ago. This is where it all began. This is where the first bonefish was known to be *pursued by boat* across the flats. Preston Pinder poled his boat in search of bonefish for his client, Kentucky Senator William Thompson Martin, in April 1906. Until that day, the accepted method was to fish solo with a live crab from an anchored boat or from shore. It took another 50 years to perfect the method and to incorporate artificial flies into the game. Joe Brooks fished for and hooked tailing bonefish in the area in June 1947.

Islamorada is the name of two keys, Upper and Lower Matecumbe, and is the most popular combined bonefish and tarpon destination in the world. There are dozens of guides, and they are all busy during the prime tarpon season, which is April through mid-July. Islamorada is known for its very big bonefish, and a look at the record book reveals fish over 15 pounds. Many twelve- to thirteen-pound fish are caught each season. This is, in part, a direct result of excellent habitat, great numbers of good anglers, and the skill level of the guides.

Several bonefish tournaments are held here each year that attract many of the best guides and anglers. Bonefish must all be weighed at the marinas. To accomplish this without harm, the bonefish are handled very carefully and put in live wells. When the boats arrive at the dock, the fish are hoisted in a wet sling onto a scale and then placed back in the live well. They are all big—around 10 pounds or better, and they are released offshore in an area known as "downtown" or "bonefish alley." Most of these fish seem to hang around because you seldom cast to any tails that are not attached to eight- or 10-pound fish.

Every angler gets fin fever when tarpon are spotted. After all, they are bigger than you, jump several feet into the air, and bust your tackle.

Captain Tom Rowland

These bones are very much aware of the game, and local anglers fishing the tournaments often use live crab, even though extra points are awarded for fly-caught fish. Obviously, this is high-tech bonefishing at its best. You are, basically, trying to feed a spooky, selective, king-size bonefish a chicken feather and bucktail snack. It is a tough sell. So, if the local experts can't catch them on flies, how can you? You can, but you probably won't. Still, it certainly is exciting seeing the tall tails, casting to the giants, and watching them blow off like a permit. Every once in a while conditions are right and you get lucky.

Marathon

Marathon is strategically located halfway between Islamorada and Key West. As a result, it has become the hub of guide activity. Many guides headquarter here because they can tow their boats to the best fishing areas, which is faster and easier than running through a two-foot chop. Marathon guides might fish Key West one day and Islamorada the next.

Big Pine Key

Big Pine Key is the largest island in the lower keys, extending 12 miles into the Gulf of Mexico and fronting the Atlantic for four miles. Surrounding Big Pine Key is the densest grouping of islands and flats habitat in America. Tarpon, bonefish, and permit can all be found in the maze of islands, channels, flats, and bights. Coupon Bight is the largest and most famous bight. The tiny Key deer call Big Pine Key home. They weigh less than 75 pounds and stand 2½ feet tall. Motorists should drive with caution.

More than one angler has been pulled overboard or lost a fly rod to a surging tarpon. There is no other fish in shallow water comparable to a rampaging tarpon.

	J	F	M	A	M	J	J	A	S	O	N	D
Bonefish	F	F	F-G	F-G	F-E	F-E	F-E	F-E	F-E	F-E	F-G	F
Permit	F	F	F-G	F	F-G	F-E	F-E	F-E	F-G	F-G	F	F
Tarpon	F	F	F-G	F-G	G-E	G-E	G-E	G	F-G	F	F	F
Barracuda	F-G	F-G	F-G	F-G	F-G	F-G	F-G	F-G	F-G	F-G	F-G	F-G
Snapper	F-G	F-G	F-G	F-G	F-G	F-G	F-G	F-G	F-G	F-G	F-G	F-G
Jacks	F-G	F-G	F-G	F-G	F-G	F-G	F-G	F-G	F-G	F-G	F-G	F-G
Shark	G	G	G	G	G-E	G-E	G-E	G-E	G-E	G-E	G	G
Wind	L-H	L-H	L-H	L-M	L-M	L	L	L	L-M	L-M	L-H	L-H

P=Poor F=Fair G=Good E=Excellent
L=Light M=Medium H=High

Key West

This once sleepy subtropical outpost has evolved into the bustling Margaritaville of the U.S. and attracts artists, movie stars, sailors, divers, bikini watchers, authors, rummies, boaters, rock-and-rollers, misfits, and treasure hunters to name but a few. Nobody ever died of boredom in Key West! It also attracts fishermen in search of permit and tarpon. Tarpon anglers are intimately familiar with the banks, basins, and channels between Key West and the Marquesas. The Marquesas Keys are 18 miles west of Key West and are composed of 10 main islands. The inner faces of these islands are mud flats covered by mangrove swamps. Dense weed beds of *Talassia testudinum*, *Dictyota divaricata*, and *Halimeda opuntia trilova* attract shrimp, crabs, baitfish, permit, and tarpon. Permit anglers ply the many reefs, banks, and flats, knowing that this is the best place in the U.S. to hook the phantom and one of the best places to hunt giant tarpon. Good luck!

Imagine being tethered to this wildness, if only for a second!

Richard Humphrey

Chapter 28

Kanton Island

There has been enough publicity about Kanton Island, (shown as Kanton on some maps) situated in the Republic of Kiribati, to put it on the dream list of serious bonefishermen. Located 2,000 miles southwest of Honolulu, 1,100 miles west-southwest of Christmas Island, and 150 miles south of the equator, Kanton is "out there." So is the fishing. Imagine an unpopulated atoll with 28 miles of outside beach flats and 17 miles of sandy inside flats separated by only a few yards of low-lying coral.

It is very much like a miniature Christmas Island except that its trevally, bonefish, and other associated species have never seen a conventional angler or fake shrimp or crab. If it moves and they see it, they eat it—instantly! We observed bonefish colored deep blue-green across their backs riding the waves like surfers. Once inside the surf line, they began a frantic feeding orgy, concerned only about eating as much as fast as they could and keeping from being eaten. Fifty- to 200-pound sharks chased down the first couple of bonefish we hooked and chased us to another location.

The distance between the shore and the reef averages about 100 yards. Nature has crowded many of her most beautiful treasures into this area. Over 250 species of tropical fish and 82 species of coral vie with sponges, giant clams, turtles, and sea birds to represent every color of the spectrum. Trevally (giant, white, blue-fin, and golden), snappers, jack crevalle, and sweetlips also roam this exquisite natural aquarium. Wahoo, yellowfin tuna, barracuda, marlin, sailfish, and who knows what else swim just beyond the surf along the reef drop-off.

It is about 700 miles from American Samoa to Kanton Island, and there is no landing strip along the way. The distance probably does not seem too great if you are traveling on the space shuttle Discovery, *which took this photo, or on a jet aircraft, but it is a long way in a twin engine airplane—four and a half hours, to be exact. Besides traveling by boat, that is currently the only way to get there. Arriving anglers find a narrow land mass encircling a classic South Pacific lagoon that is inhabited by more species of fish than people. Only a handful of bonefish anglers have cast a fly into these secluded waters.*

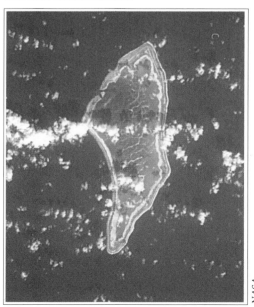

During the 1930s and 40s, Pan American Airlines began using the lagoon as a refueling stop for its island-hopping flights across the Pacific. During World War II, Kanton became a fortified refueling station for Allied aircraft. When modern jets began flying, Pan Am closed the station. Kanton then became a Pacific Missile Range tracking station, operating until the early '70s. Today Kanton is the site of a NOAA meteorological station and home to about 40 people.

At this time the Kiribati government has been unable to provide air service to Kanton Island, so anglers cannot easily reach its fascinating waters. Stay tuned; it may still happen! In the interim you can read about the first two, and only, fly fishing exploratory trips to Kanton.

Kanton Island Luau

Rod Carman of Alaska Sea Coast Adventures contacted me in February 1993 about joining the first exploratory fishing and hotel-site-searching expedition to Kanton Island.

I was ecstatic but, not knowing what to expect or whether to believe what I was told, I packed as I would for any outdoor adventure: tent, sleeping bag, emergency food, and first aid supplies. I kept my gear to the allotted 40 pounds and met Rod at Seattle's SeaTac airport.

After the five-hour trip to Honolulu, we rendezvoused with Rod's partner, George Doubleday II of Geographic Expeditions, architect Mickey Muenig, and Susie Fitzgerald of Frontiers International. After a four-hour layover, we boarded a Hawaiian flight to American Samoa.

In American Samoa, a dark and torrential rain blotted out any signs of life as we boarded our eight-passenger, twin-engine plane for the 4½-hour flight to Kanton. I was soaking wet, and there was lots of condensation inside the plane. I felt a twinge of claustrophobia and immediately returned to the door and the outside air. Naturally, I had reservations about the 700-mile trip across the Pacific Ocean to the only airstrip within hundreds of miles. The

R. Valentine Atkinson

plane was overloaded, and some items had to be left behind. I made certain my stuff stayed on board. I took a seat just as the door closed. The tropical rain was so intense that a truck led the aircraft to the end of the runway.

In half an hour the sky lightened as we flew between beautiful thunderheads that were pink on top and dark gray underneath. The sun eventually reached the ocean 10,000 feet below where whitecaps rode the wind currents. The ocean was desolate and unending. All was well until I had to visit the boy's room about 15 minutes after takeoff. There was, of course, no restroom on the small plane. I knew I should not have drunk three giant glasses of orange juice before takeoff.

After 4½ agonizing hours, the plane touched down. I was the first one off the plane. A saltbush was conveniently located only a few yards from the aircraft, and I provided amusement for the arriving customs officials.

We loaded our gear onto one of only two trucks on the island, which was inhabited by about 40 people. We drove past the 1950s-vintage Pan Am hangers lying flattened on the ground in a pile of rusted steel and twisted sheet metal, long abandoned by the jet age. We reached a moored Korean freighter that was home to a construction crew and was our home for the next few days. Accommodations were on deck. You staked out your territory and defended it against cockroaches and rats. No one in our group had blankets, pads, or sleeping bags except the pilot and myself. He had been here before. We opted to stay on land and battle sand crabs.

Visitors to Kanton, aside from an occasional government or NOAA official, are rare and reason for the locals to celebrate. The islanders invited us to a luau welcome dinner at 6 p.m. Fantastic! I visualized a pit lined with palm fronds and occupied by the village pig. Or blue-fin tuna and great trevally, maybe lobster, with rice, tropical fruit, and dancing. I arrived promptly at 6 p.m. Ninety minutes later only a few people had arrived. Worse, I saw no pig

Kanton and its lagoon have hosted only a handful of anglers. Its bonefish are wild and unsophisticated, as are the many other species that prowl the reef, and the lagoon. If you are fortunate enough to visit, bring plenty of flies and extra everything because you most likely will run out of everything.

Kanton Island bonefish cruise through the breaking surf to feed on the reef flats. They are rambunctious and aggressive and eagerly jump your offering.

pit, the main object of my search, and I had not eaten in 12 hours. By 9 p.m., two families arrived without food, and I knew it was time to cut my losses and get back to my meager emergency rations. I excused myself, begged a ride back to the freighter and my tent, and ate an energy bar. I was exhausted and fell asleep. During the night an intense tropical rainstorm descended on the island. Water poured from the sky, and I heard people on the freighter grumbling and stumbling about in the wet equatorial darkness.

In the morning our party told me about a delightful feast—at 11 p.m. after much hoopla, introductions, and toasts of coconut liquor. It was 1 a.m. before everyone arrived back at the freighter. Imagine being a bit intoxicated and dozing on the open deck of a rat-infest-ed Korean freighter without a blanket or pillow. Add a drenching tropical storm that forced everyone into the 15-foot by 15-foot wheel room with a dozen Samoans and seven Koreans, and you can imagine how lucky I felt.

When it was time for breakfast, I eagerly and hungrily arrived at the table and peeked into the galley. It was like looking into a prehistoric kitchen. Everything was filthy. The cook had a pot of six-month-old rancid coconut oil boiling. He dropped a dozen eggs of questionable origin and age into the bubbling caldron and scooped them out with a dipper, piling them all on a plate. Oil flowed like water as I took a seat at the table. The cook opened a loaf of moldy bread. I surveyed the situation. I was hungry. If everyone else ate, I guess I would too. Rod and Bill arrived but did not appear to be too eager to eat. I made a sandwich out of a couple eggs, took a bite, and walked to the stern of the boat. I looked at the fish swimming below and pitched the moldy, greasy yellow gob overboard. The fish would not touch it! I had made the right decision. It was time for another run on my dwindling supply of emergency rations.

Christmas Island guide Moana T. Kofe displays a sleek Kanton bonefish.

R. Valentine Atkinson

It was, finally, time to sample the fishing, and the day turned out to be incredible! Susie and I found good-sized bonefish for the taking on the reef. Several species of trevally were hooked in the lagoon, wahoo ripped our tackle offshore, and huge sharks ate many of our fish everywhere we went. As we headed back to home base from offshore, the tide changed. Entering the lagoon, we motored for 20 minutes, barely keeping pace with the strong outgoing current. If we had lost power, we would have been swept into a churning rip about a mile offshore, certainly a one-way ticket. If the water had not gotten us, the sharks would have. We finally made it safely across the channel, and I learned a valuable and relatively easy lesson about channel currents and tides.

We had fish for dinner on the freighter—deep fried in egg-battered coconut oil; that was it. Susie had a few emergency rations left. We shared some and laughed about the guarantee the government made to us about accommodations and food. The next, and last, day of our visit, the fishing was again awesome. Because of the stable water temperature, bonefish are always available as are the many other species. Future anglers who visit and cast a fly into these bountiful waters will be fortunate indeed. I cannot wait to return when the camp is built and have fresh water, a shower, and dinner overlooking the lagoon.

The return flight was uneventful. I did not drink any liquid for hours prior to takeoff and was the last on board because I was behind a saltbush readying myself for the return. We toured American Samoa. Everyone should visit. You will never again complain about America.

A year after I visited Kanton Island, another exploratory group assembled. Internationally known photographer R. Valentine Atkinson was shanghaied to document the adventure with fly rod and camera. Valentine's work has appeared in many books, magazines, catalogs, and calendars. He is the author of _Distant Waters, The Greatest Fly Fishing Worldwide, Trout and Salmon,_ and _The Greatest Fly Fishing for Trout and Salmon Worldwide._ He lives in San Francisco. All photos of Kanton Island in this chapter are by Valentine.

The Ghosts of Kanton
by R. Valentine Atkinson

In February 1994, I received a telephone call from Susie Fitzgerald of Frontiers International. She was putting together an exploratory trip to Kanton Island in the South Pacific and asked if I would consider being part of a seven-person team to explore and fish the island to see what we might find.

I've always felt that I was born about 100 years too late. The exciting places in the world have all been discovered and mapped. When an opportunity to visit a remote destination for some high adventure presents itself, I cannot say, "Count me in!" fast enough.

On February 22, five anglers, myself included, gathered in the predawn darkness of the Honolulu Airport to board the weekly 737 jet bound for Christmas Island on its regular schedule. From there we would continue another thousand miles southwest to a tiny speck of land in the middle of nowhere named Kanton Island. Our party included Rick Ruoff, well-known Florida Keys guide; Bill Hunter, industry consultant; world travelers Rod Carman and Bill Wright, anglers and holders of the legal concession to promote and develop the potential fishery for visiting sportsmen; and myself, photographer. We would pick up Moana Kofe, Christmas Island guide extraordinare, and Tek Kaiteie, translator and organizer for the trip, at Christmas Island when we dropped off the dozen or so anglers who had come to fish there.

After we arrived at Christmas Island, united with the whole group, and started loading supplies and equipment on the plane, the local customs agent informed us they had just received a phone call from the Kiribati government. The government would not let our plane take on the extra fuel it needed to reach Kanton because of

The bonefish highway.

On the beach waiting for the cruise ship.

A beautiful mini bone wiser for the experience.

Bonefish flats are truly big sky and big water country. There are no interruptions from horizon to horizon.

R. Valentine Atkinson

unpaid bills. Something had to happen fast. More phone calls were made. Our pilot informed us that air regulations made it imperative we leave within 20 minutes. Suddenly, there was panic in the air. Months of planning ground to a halt. It looked like the adventure would be aborted, all because someone neglected to pay their bills. My stomach was in knots as we waited for a phone call. We watched the minute hand decide our fate. With five minutes left, the phone rang and a voice informed us the bills had been taken care of and we could proceed. The tension was broken; everyone was laughing and talking at once. We scurried on board and took off.

Kanton Island is actually a coral atoll located south of the equator at a latitude of 2'30" south by longitude 172' west. It is in the group of islands known as the Phoenix Islands and is owned by the Republic of Kiribati. The atoll is approximately 30 miles in circumference. A one-lane road encircles the island and is used by a half-dozen pickup trucks owned by maybe three dozen native Kiribati. Most folks ride bicycles and live in thatch-roofed huts. Because Kanton is so close to the equator, days and nights are equally long year-round, and the temperature remains constant: hot with 80 percent humidity. The saving grace is the trade wind.

From the air Kanton is stunning. It has a brilliant aquamarine lagoon in the center surrounded by white sand beaches; it is an oasis of bright colors set in the middle of the deep-blue Pacific Ocean. It is a very surreal scene. Kanton has a good runway left over from World War II days when the island served as a strategically located storage area. Because the island is seldom visited by outsiders today, it is rarely fished. Rumors of 15-pound bonefish and giant trevally danced in our heads like sugarplum fairies.

Every person on the island came out to watch our plane land, a rare occurrence for them. We were greeted warmly and showered with plumaria and hibiscus petals. Grandmothers, old men, little kids, dogs, cats, and birds all showed up. I felt like Captain Cook looking for a bounty of bonefish. We were welcomed to a feast that evening in the local Quonset hut. The meal included many types of fresh fish, crab, the largest lobsters I've ever seen (10 pounds if they were an ounce), and large quantities of coconut wine. Dancing and singing rounded out a wonderful evening.

Feasting and singing with the gracious hosts at Kanton. The arrival of visitors is cause for celebration.

We set up our tent camp in a small grove of tamarisk trees on the windward side of the island because we knew it would be hot and we wanted to take advantage of any possible breeze. We had all packed intelligently (or so we thought) and had tried to bring what we could to make life in camp as comfortable as possible. The most important items, of course, were duffels full of fishing tackle and cases of beer. No one had packed ice, and we were forced to drink warm beer all week. It's amazing how quickly you can get used to it when it's absolutely necessary. We laughed about it.

The nights were filled with camaraderie around the campfire. We dreamed of huge bonefish under stars so bright no flashlight was ever needed. The days were filled with exploring and fishing. We drew maps of the areas that were most productive and kept records of what we caught. We were up having breakfast before the sun. We then split into pairs and headed off in different directions. The lagoon flats were easily wadeable except for a few mucky, soft areas. Most of the flats had white sand or gray marl bottoms. We found singles and large groups of dozens, if not hundreds, of unsuspecting bones, all apparently between two and five pounds. We never saw any large bones on the inside flats.

We caught all species of trevally available, including the most prized of all, the golden trevally. I had never even seen one before. The first one was tailing like a permit. I asked Moana about it, and he got very excited and urged me to cast quickly. The fish took well and put up a spectacular fight. It was indeed very golden in color with darker vertical stripes. Moana told me the golden are never very common and are his favorite gamefish on Christmas Island.

The outside, or oceanside, flats are very different in character from the inside flats. These are rough coral with potholes, often making wading difficult. They have constant wave surges that can throw you off balance. You must stay alert. The reward is the large bones that come in from the deep to feed in the surf line. There are all sorts of new and unusual critters feed-

Inside the lagoon. Chances are good that there are one or more bonefish following the ray.

ing in the coral. We caught mutton snappers, emperor fish (commonly called sweetlips), parrotfish, and black-tipped sharks. We saw giant trevally weighing 50 to 70 pounds swoop in along the breakers and then disappear right in front of our eyes. Our largest bonefish weighed nine pounds. Many large fish were lost to the sharp coral. "Hold 'em or lose 'em," became our battle cry.

One afternoon Bill Hunter and I were exploring a remote part of the lagoon. We had been dropped off by one of the locals in his truck.

R. Valentine Atkinson

Rick Ruoff and golden trevally.

Note: Fish intended for release should be held close to and over the water. Otherwise, if they struggle and fall, and they often do, serious injury is possible.

Bill Hunter and long-nosed sweetlips. Notice the rough and colorful coral reef flat.

R. Valentine Atkinson

Having made arrangements for him to pick us up in two hours for dinner, we hoped to catch a trevally for the grill. Checking our watches and taking a long, last drink of water (thinking this would hold us until we were picked up), we set off. Not taking our water bottles was a terrible mistake. We hadn't fished more than 30 or 40 minutes before we started getting thirsty. The fishing was excellent. For awhile we concentrated on our excitement and forgot about being thirsty. The driver wasn't due back until 5 p.m., and we were miles from camp, too far to walk. All we could think and talk about was water. It was a classic tale of water, water everywhere but not a drop to drink. We decided to quit fishing and walk back to the road. Maybe the driver would come early. By the time we reached the road, we were exhausted and dying of thirst. Bill and I lay down in the shade of a bush where we made jokes that at least they would find our bodies. The happiest moment of the trip wasn't when I caught a 20-pound golden trevally; it was when I saw the truck coming down the road. We were always careful to take plenty of water with us after that.

Another interesting episode happened the last night of our trip. We decided to take the only small boat on the island along with the 25 hp outboard we had brought along and head out to sea through the lagoon entrance. This was a risky venture since we had been warned previously to watch out for strong tidal currents that might sweep a man or boat out into the open ocean never to be found again. Rick and Moana were confident of two things: one, they felt certain there would be yellowfin tuna outside the reef, and, two, Moana could keep the motor running for our return. This was a situation in which we could not afford to make any mistakes.

At 4:30 p.m. the tide was right, and four of us—Rick, Bill, Moana, and myself—pushed off into the mouth of the lagoon. It was an exciting moment. Big waves were rolling in from the ocean. The first task was to punch through to the outside. Within 10 or 15 minutes we had motored beyond the reef and were riding the swells and spotting schools of 20- to 70-pound tuna running and jumping. Rick and Bill began casting frantically as Moana did the thing I was most alarmed about: he shut off the motor, leaving us adrift on the high sea. The light was fading fast, and large fish were showing all around us. Rick had one on only to have it sound and break his 12-weight. Bill connected and fought his fish for 20 minutes before the hook pulled out. It took several attempts before we finally brought a beautiful 40-pound yellowfin tuna on board for dinner. It was almost dark; the moment of truth was at hand. Could Moana start the outboard? This was a very anxious moment for us. It was not even an issue for Moana, who had grown up around boats and motors. The motor roared on the first try, and we were away toward camp confident that future anglers could have great opportunities with large tuna on fly rods.

That evening was our last. As we returned to camp, festivities had already begun. The campfire was going, and the warm beer was flowing. The party carried on until the wee hours of the night. Sometime around 3 a.m., I awoke and noticed that the remainder of our tuna, which we had wrapped in cheesecloth and hung in a tree to keep cool Polynesian style, was glowing like a lantern.

You could have read a newspaper by the light that was radiating off the fish. I had to look twice to believe my eyes. Could this

Miles and miles of untrod ocean flats await anglers at Kanton. Is this beautiful or what?

Oceanside flats just inside the reef are usually rough and demanding places to fish, but the rewards are worth it.

R. Valentine Atkinson

A red bass shows off its beautiful colors and leader-cutting teeth. Such fish are not leader shy.

R. Valentine Atkinson

really be happening? I awakened Bill, and he assured me I wasn't seeing things. Our first thought was that we had been eating fish that had been nuked in World War II. We knew there had been plenty of A-bomb testing in the South Pacific. We checked out the scraps of fish by the fireside. They, too, were emitting a brilliant glow. What could this mean? The next morning we buried the remains of our tuna and broke camp.

Our plane was due around noon. It had been a wonderful experience, and we were all sad to leave. Perhaps the plane would be late or, better yet, not show up at all. No such luck. The 737 touched down right on time. The hospitality of the local Kiribati people was remarkable with their constant desire to please and to do things to help their neighbors. They had showered us with fresh food and drink and helped immensely with practical logistics and ground transportation. We assured them we or other people like us would come again one day soon. It was sad to leave. They gave us more flowers and big hugs and sent us on our way.

We all agreed that the fish weren't necessarily any larger than those at Christmas Island. These fish, however, had never seen an angler or a Crazy Charlie; they were completely unwary. The opportunities for catching large yellowfin tuna on fly rods is a special bonus. The many other types of unusual fish make Kanton Island a unique and very special destination.

When I returned to San Francisco, I made a call to John McCosker of the Steinhart Aquarium. I wanted to ask him about the strange glowing tuna. John laughed and told me this condition is called bioluminescence, a giving off of light from living matter caused by internal oxidation. It can be caused when living organisms start to break down, and, under the right circumstances, it produces light. John added that this very well may be how the phenomenon of ghosts first got started. In graveyards of old, the dead often could not be buried fast enough and would pile up (as during the plagues). As they decomposed, light was given off in the form of an eerie glow, hence, "The Ghosts of Kanton."

R. Valentine Atkinson
San Francisco, California
January 1998

	J	F	M	A	M	J	J	A	S	O	N	D
Bonefish	G-E	G-E	G-E	G-E	G-E	G-E	G-E	G-E	G-E	G-E	G-E	G-E
Trevally	G-E	G-E	G-E	G-E	G-E	G-E	G-E	G-E	G-E	G-E	G-E	G-E
Offshore	G-E	G-E	G-E	G-E	G-E	G-E	G-E	G-E	G-E	G-E	G-E	G-E
Emperor	G-E	G-E	G-E	G-E	G-E	G-E	G-E	G-E	G-E	G-E	G-E	G-E
Shark	G-E	G-E	G-E	G-E	G-E	G-E	G-E	G-E	G-E	G-E	G-E	G-E
Misc.	G-E	G-E	G-E	G-E	G-E	G-E	G-E	G-E	G-E	G-E	G-E	G-E

G=Good   E=Excellent

Los Roques

Wet, metallic bonefish tails were everywhere, glistening like quicksilver in the early morning sun. We hastily spread out from the boat, eager to begin fishing. I flipped my fly to the tallest nearby tail and watched it glide forward, flashing like a signal mirror. When the tail tilted up and the flashing stopped, it was my signal that the fish had the fly. When I set the hook, the fish streaked out of sight, spooking others in its terrified state of confusion. Hollering with excitement, I noticed my companions were also in a state of bonefish excitement and were not concerned about my state.

That morning the fishing was so outrageous that we missed lunch. Eventually, we found ourselves two miles from the boat, which was barely visible as a rusty red speck separating water from sky. We hoped our three guides (actually boat handlers we had picked up on the back streets of El Gran Roque at a cock fight) would bring the boat around and pick us up, but no such luck. This should have tipped us off that there was a problem, but it did not. We continued to cast to unsophisticated bones that had no reason to be suspicious of our offerings. In fact, they actually seemed to prefer them.

When we finally reached the boat, we were exhausted, hungry, and dehydrated. The image of water, beer, and soda sloshing around in an icy cooler seemed like nirvana to us. To our dismay, we discovered that all the beer, soda, and lunch were gone! Our boatmen weren't sleeping; they were passed out in the bottom of the boat surrounded by floating beer cans and wadded-up sandwich wrappers.

We were furious. We practiced our Spanish obscenities and scolded the boys severely. We fired them and took control of the boat.

Arriving at our home base, a houseboat moored on a beautiful key in Los Roques National Park, we found that dinner was not ready, there was no ice, and the toilet was broken. A visit to the toilet now necessitated an armpit-deep wade to shore, which was flat, void of vegetation, and in full view of other moored boats. I'll leave the rest to your imagination. In retrospect, I guess we were expecting too much. How could we demand all the comforts of home *and* world-class bonefishing especially when we were on a budget trip? We got what we paid for.

Most trips to Los Roques are not like this, but travel to Third-World countries on a do-it-yourself basis can have trying, even dangerous, and certainly frustrating, moments. If such scenarios are not for you, book at an established lodge on Grand Roque. Food, lodging,

The underwater world of bonefish is surprisingly colorful and mysterious. The combination grass and sand flats make for prime bonefish habitat and offer excellent wading and sight fishing. Los Roques is famous for its many beautiful and easy-to-wade sand flats, and some extend for a mile or more. Smaller pancake flats are numerous and lie scattered throughout the lagoon. Bonefish are the primary species, but barracuda, mackerel, pompano, tarpon, and snapper are all possibilities.

and water are good, the guides are professional and they speak English.

Any time do-it-yourself anglers are south of the border, a working knowledge of Spanish is very helpful. If you are not fluent, consider carrying a pocket translation dictionary. Veteran travelers also carry pictures of fish to show locals exactly what they want to fish for. Local names vary. Bonefish at Los Roques are called _macabi_ or _raton_—Spanish for rat.

Local boats, called _peñeros,_ are adequate for transportation, but be certain the boatman has plenty of gas—some of the flats are distant. Also be advised that guides (and boatmen) might be scarce when lobster season is at its peak (December to June). If you can find a guide who understands English and fly fishing, you have a much better chance of visiting the premier flats. The best guides are employed by lodges.

When you fly north from the coast of Venezuela and first see the islands of Los Roques, you feel as if you are entering a lost world. Like all bonefish destinations, the vivid colors of ocean meshing with land are first to capture your attention, but you soon imagine what it would be like to foot print the sandy beach and fish the reef below.

Randall Kaufmann

Grand Roque is the largest island in the group and is the location of the only air strip and fishing village. The village itself is Third World; amenities are few. The 500 Spanish-speaking people who call Grand Roque home are mostly lobster fishermen. In the off-season they harvest conch.

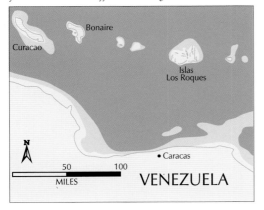

Los Roques is located about 90 miles north of the Venezuela mainland, which forms the northern shore of the South American continent. Caracas is the capitol. La Guaira-Caracas Airport is an easy 3½-hour flight from Miami. From La Guaira, it is a 45-minute flight to Grand Roque, the group of islands collectively known as Islas Los Roques. It encompasses 40 named islands and over 300 keys that are deserted and untrodden. The archipelago's wealth of birds, turtles, lobster, and fish has been legendary for centuries, but lobsters and turtles have long since been over-harvested.

Fishing

Don't think that just because Los Roques lies close to the equator that it is a good destination during December through February. It is not. Los Roques is notorious for bad weather. High winds and high tides make fishing difficult at this time. Spring and early summer are the best. Depending on ocean currents, late summer and fall can bring warm water onto the flats, sending bonefish into deeper, cooler water. *El Niño* is often blamed for this. Normal water temperature during the months of March through June is 80 degrees Fahrenheit, perfect for bonefish. Because tides fluctuate widely, anglers who want to fish to tailers should book during neap tides.

When Los Roques is good, *it is really good*. Three- to five-pound bones with plenty of six to eight pounders, plus some to 10 pounds, make things interesting. The flats and surrounding waters are incredibly rich with every type of sea life imaginable. Anglers wade crystal-clear sand flats, some with beautiful grass beds, but there are also areas of coral and coral reefs. Most flats are about 100 yards long and 30 yards wide, a few extend for miles. Smaller flats are perfect for prospecting the shallows and deeper edges. All fishing is on foot. Nearly all flats are wadeable (some are a little soft) and so beautiful it is difficult to concentrate on fishing. That is the nature of bonefishing—you are immersed in beautiful landscapes that always distract you. Los Roques bonefish have seen few anglers and are easy to approach. A properly presented fly is usually gobbled on sight, no questions asked.

Sharks are rarely a problem, but there are plenty of barracuda. Pompano, or palometa, inhabit the flats and cuts, and some anglers mistake them for permit. You can tell the difference because these fish attack a fly aggressively. In addition, mackerel, large bar jacks, and many species of snapper are easily caught, especially with surface poppers. Tarpon, mostly two to five pounds, some to 50 pounds, are also available. Anglers should be armed with 8-, 9-, and 10-weight rods.

Weather

Daytime air temperatures are in the mid-80s, and evenings are cooled by northeasterly breezes. Bugs are seldom a problem. Expect 80- to 90-degree air temperatures and 15- to 30-mph winds once on the flats. Anglers can escape excessive winds by moving to the leeward side of the many islands that dot the lagoon. When boating from accommodations on Grand Roque to and from the flats, expect a rough ride.

Other Adventures

The northern coast of Venezuela is famous for billfishing, and excellent action can be enjoyed only minutes off the coast. The sport fishing fleet is headquartered at La Guaira. Three hours inland at Tacarigua National Park near Rio Chico there is some wonderful peacock bass and baby tarpon fishing. Laguna Tacarigua is a tarpon nursery 20 miles long and 10 miles wide. Its mangrove-lined channels and river inlets shelter thousands of five to 15 pounders—all eager to pounce on poppers and practice their high jump. At Lake Guri peacock bass may eat your offerings like magpies at your bird feeder. A possible itinerary would be to fish tarpon and bass for four days, billfish for two days, and bonefish for a week. This would provide enough diversity and action for even the most jaded angler.

Venezuela offers visitors much more than fishing. Bold travelers find Venezuela an exciting land rich in natural beauty and cultural contrasts. World famous Aruba is nearby; if you dive or wind surf, passing up an opportunity to visit would be a shame. If you visit, pack your fly rod—there are bonefish. Remote rivers, waterfalls (Angel Falls is the highest in the world), fascinating jungles, and mysterious cloud forests are included in 35 national parks covering nearly 10 per-

Let her rip! When you hit it right at Los Roques, bonefishing is really good!

This beautiful archipelago has hundreds of inside, transition, and pancake flats scattered about its mostly protected, jewel-like lagoon. This is where most anglers fish. The outside flats and reefs remain mostly unfished by bonefish anglers because access can be difficult due to high winds and surf, fast and fluctuating tides, and rough water crossings. There are bonefish and many other species present, if you can get to them!

NASA

Pompano are sometimes confused with permit. Like jacks, they attack flies aggressively.

	J	F	M	A	M	J	J	A	S	O	N	D
Bonefish	P	P-F	P-G	G-E	E	E	E	G-E	F-G	P-F	P	P
Pompano	P	P	F	F-G	G	G	G	F	F	F	P	P
Tarpon	P	P	F	F	F-G	F-G	F-G	F	F	P	P	P
Barracuda	P	F-G	F-G	F-G	F-G	F-G	F-G	F-G	F-G	F-G	F-G	P
Snapper	P	F	F	G	G	G	G	F-G	F	F	P	P
Jacks	P	F	F	G	G	G	G	F-G	F	F	P	P
Shark	P	F-G	F-G	F-G	F-G	F-G	F-G	F-G	F-G	F-G	P	P
Wind	H	H	H	M-H	M	M	M	M	L	L	M	M

P=Poor F=Fair G=Good E=Excellent
L=Light M=Moderate H=Heavy

cent of the country. The largest park, Canaima, inspired Sir Arthur Conan Doyle's book *The Lost World*.

Caracas is a bustling cosmopolitan city of over four million and is a 30- or 40-minute drive from the airport. It is located at an elevation of 3,000 feet and, with an average temperature of 75 degrees Fahrenheit, has a very pleasant climate. Shopping, especially for leather goods, is excellent. Finely crafted shoes are an especially good buy. Take a tracing of any foot you plan to shop for—you'll be a hero. I bought 15 pairs and had to buy a suitcase to carry them home. An adventure in Venezuela can certainly include more than bonefishing, but shoe shopping?

Los Roques offers bonefish up to 10 pounds.

Chapter 30

Seychelles

The first recorded visitors to the Seychelles Islands were from the British East India Company. They landed in 1609. Pirates from the east coast of Africa and the Caribbean followed and used the islands as temporary bases and for provisioning. The infamous pirate Olive "The Buzzard" LeVassuer is believed to have stashed treasure around Bel Omone on Mahe.

The French laid claim to the islands in 1756. They settled with slaves and began cultivating spices, coffee, sugarcane, and sweet potatoes. The British took control after the Napoleonic wars in 1814. The French language and culture remained dominant. Today, three main languages are spoken in the Seychelles—Creole, French, and English. In 1903 the Seychelles became a Crown Colony. They gained independence from the United Kingdom in 1976. Currency is the Seychelles Rupee. Most businesses accept U.S. dollars and there is no advantage to exchanging large sums of money. Seychelles postage stamps are beautiful—they make great gifts.

Modern-day travelers come to the Seychelles to find the ideal tropical paradise. Some find it along granite-fringed powdery white sand beaches, undisturbed coral reefs, and transparent lagoons. Others find it in the seclusion offered at out islands, which are billed as "a thousand miles from anywhere." Others come for the consistent mild and humid weather. Still others come for the lifestyle. There is little crime and a good standard of living (no serious disease or malaria). There are relatively few visitors. The government is considered one of the world's most environmentally conscious and has limited tourist accommodations.

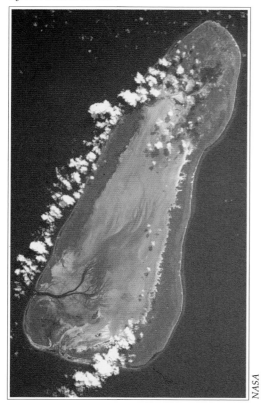

Aldabra, the Galapagos of the Indian Ocean and a world heritage site, is one of the most spectacular island gems in the Seychelles. It is home to 150,000 Aldabran Giant Tortoises, green turtles, Greater Flamingoes, flightless rails, and unique flora. Fishing is not permitted. It is roughly 15 by seven miles in size.

NASA

Because a thousand miles of ocean isolate the islands and because there is a diverse range of habitat, including both granite mountains and coral atolls, many unique and rare species of flora and fauna have evolved. The list of birds, land animals, and sea life is staggering, including bonefish that have never seen an angler. In fact, very few anglers have ever seen a bonefish in the Seychelles, mainly because, until now, no bonefish anglers went there. Located 1,000 miles off the coast of east Africa, 600 miles north of Madagascar, and four degrees south of the equator in the Indian Ocean, the Seychelles are not on the usual bonefish circuit.

Jerry Swanson, travel director for Kaufmann's Fly Fishing Expeditions, Inc., organized and led the first fly fishing tour of the Seychelles in 1998. I'll let Jerry tell the story.

Tall Tails!
by Jerry Swanson

The sun and a light breeze were at my back. Bonefish were moving into the tide—singles, doubles, and triples. They averaged five to six pounds. Opportunities for bonefish were continuous, plus there were shots at trevally, snapper, and emperors. The only unwanted intruders into my surreal world were lemon sharks. They chased my bonefish. The water boiled and the fish argued. I walked toward the stormy horizon, kicking out the runt bonefish under five pounds. The looming curtain of clouds turned a darker shade of gray and approached my position quickly. Powerless to change imminent weather, I continued to fish, as did my companions, who were a mile apart on this unknown flat.

I spotted a thick, solitary bonefish angling up the flat. I positioned myself for a head-on cast and dropped my fly eight feet in front of the wallowing glutton. Twitching the fly, the bonefish slowly accelerated to intercept and eat it. After tasting steel and

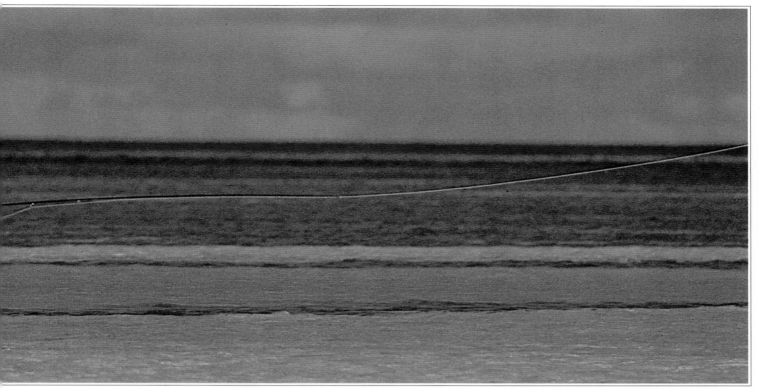

losing its appetite, it raced back from where it came. As the power-ful bonefish extended its distance, the hook pulled free and I gazed anxiously at the ominous sky that was about to devour me. I felt microscopic, alone, as I walked toward my companions.

We converged on an area of exposed gravelly coral and debated the storm, which seemed gigantic. Suddenly, the wind increased dramatically and the rain became torrential. Visibility was only 30 feet. Thunder rumbled, and lightning flashed. We sat exposed, on the highest point for a mile around (by 3"), facing away from the wind and rain with our rods on the ground. Literally inches of rain came down and the water rose around us and began to flow like a freshwater river. Without my rain parka I would have been in a world of hurt! Suddenly, Brian O'Keefe, the fourth member of our group, appeared. "How did you find us?" we asked. He said, "I took a bearing on you just as the storm hit and kept walking."

As the storm abated, I called our boat captain on my VHF radio and let him know our intention to continue fishing. Under a drip-ping sky, we strode off toward a nearby island. From a distance we thought we saw a wrecked fuselage of an airplane, but it turned out to be a navigation buoy. Mother Nature must have been cranky (or very happy) to rip it from its mooring and deposit it in the mid-dle of a shallow flat a mile from deep water.

The island was covered with dense vegetation, including a grove of coconut palms, and was edged with an exquisite sand beach that was alive with crabs. Part of its beauty was the fact that no buildings or inhabitants were present. We reached a beautiful "blue hole," hooked a few bones, surface-busting trevally and moved on. We were drawn irresistibly toward a huge flat of turtle grass and sand. We soon found it was literally infested with big bonefish, many with their tall tails in the air! I rigged up a lightly weighted fly so it would not hang up in the grass. The bonefish

Anglers take a dingy to shore from the mother ship. Once there, miles of exquisite flats teeming with unsophisticated fish await your cast. This is wilderness bonefishing at its absolute best. Angler is Chris Davy.

Swaying coconut palms, a talcum powder beach, ankle-deep bath water, tall tails—and it's all yours!

Every bonefisherman's dream—unexplored territory and aggressive fish.

Many species of snapper are available at South Pacific and Indian Ocean bonefishing locations.

Turtles are unafraid and inquisitive.

were content and unconcerned by our presence. I "lined," spooked, and disrupted several invisible feeders but they did not panic. They seemed to be saying, "Don't bug me, I'm eating!" Big bones were tailing in every direction. Tails, tails, tails as far as I could see. At 4pm the sun broke through shining at a low angle, reflecting golden and metallic off the tails of hundreds of bonefish. I have never seen anything like it. They tailed like contented sheep or cattle grazing in a pasture. I hunted for taller tails and for those fish with the greatest distance between their tail and dorsal fin. Everyone was tied to racing fish.

We were in the middle of a bone fisherman's dream—an exotic unknown location, perfect conditions, and giant tails! I realized that I had landed plenty of fish and did not want to be a pig, but I also did not want to awaken from this dream. Like many bonefish aficionados, I have spent years researching, prospecting and exploring for the mother lode. After years of searching, I exclaimed, "This is it, baby!"

The sun was setting as we piloted our Zodiac through the coral heads back to our 72-foot sailing yacht. We later learned that the wind had been blowing at 50 mph with gusts to 60 mph. We believed it! Our bonefish had a tail wind and seemed to swim at 25 mph with bursts of speed up to 30 mph! Richard Humphrey related that when he reached paradise flat, he was rigged with a size 1/0, five-inch-long baitfish-style fly on 60-lb. shock tippet for trevally and a 10-pound bonefish promptly engulfed it! He knew he wasn't going to chase trevally on this flat! Everyone had a story, but Brian put the afternoon in perspective: He said, "Florida-sized bonefish; Christmas Island numbers!"

The Seychelles fishery is remarkable because it is an extremely rich ecosystem and because people have not degraded it. On a planet with ever increasing human pressure and habitat degradation, the Seychelles is a rare treasure. We had the feeling we were on location with *National Geographic*.

The area we fished is a completely intact saltwater wilderness. The Seychelles government should consider designating it as such. We could walk up to and touch sea turtles! Bonefish paid us little attention, and trevally checked us out for food! If you go, tread lightly, don't be a glutton, and don't tell anybody.

Fishing

The average bonefish is four to six pounds (weighed), with 10-pound fish common. Bonefish that tip the scales at close to 20 pounds have been observed. The bonefish are big, strong, and fat. A 25-inch bonefish weighs eight pounds! During our initial expedition, we only fished flats and adjacent waters but still released 27 different species of fish and saw others! There were several species of trevally, including giant, _Caranx ignobilis;_ blue-fin, _C. melampygus;_ yellow spotted, possibly _C. fulvoguttatus;_ and brassie, _C. papuensis._ Other fish included yellow sweetlips, or spangled emperor, _Lethrinus nebulosus;_ and black spotted emperor, species unknown; green jobfish, _Aprion virescens;_ queenfish, _Scomberoides lysan;_ coronation trout, _Variola louti;_ assorted wrasse, _Cheilinus;_ others known locally only as spotted trunkfish, yellowfin majura, brown hind, picasso fish, grouper; and others unidentifiable, plus a 20-pound milkfish. One angler hooked three milkfish but all three blew him

Seychelles bonefish are big and these gluttonous feeders pounce big flies! Because of these factors, a 9 weight rod is best. Sometimes bonefish grab flies in mid water. Every angler has an amazing story. One group of anglers happened upon a school of surfing bonefish! They were hooking them in the face of five-foot waves! After a few hookups one angler snorkeled and surfed for 20 minutes with the school of hundreds and was blown away.

Bill Erwert unhooks a bonefish without touching or removing it from the water. Slide your hand down the leader and back out the fly. This only works if the fish is not too tired.

Dale Kremer and Jeff Sherman manage a double bonefish hookup. Note the beautiful clear sand flat extends as far as you want to walk.

off on the first run. You need at least a 10 weight. Many of the preceding species were seen tailing in shallow water and are easily approached. Adjacent blue water is rich in tuna, dorado, marlin, etc.

A possible shot at giant bonefish, combined with numerous bonefish to 10 pounds and fish that average half that, plus the myriad species available both inshore and offshore, make the Seychelles one of the top bonefishing destinations in the world.

Recommended Flies

You need lots of flies and some very big ones! Favorites include Borski's shrimps, Marabou Shrimp, and crabs in assorted colors and sink rates. Christmas Island Specials and Clouser Minnows also produced well. The best colors are tan and combinations that include white. A large assortment of Sea Habit Bucktails, Blanton Whistlers, Popovic Candies, and poppers rounds out the selection for trevally, emperor, and other assorted species. If you intend to fish for wahoo, tuna, giant trevally, etc., bring the big stuff and lots of it! Bring wire leaders.

Fishing Conditions

The flats are firm sand and turtle grass, ideal for wading and sight fishing. Edges of flats are sandy drop-offs or coral. Other flats consist of old coral and sand. These are frequented by trevally. Coral flats can be irregular in shape with peninsulas jutting out into the lagoon or the ocean. Coral "bridges" often span lagoons and are great fish habitat but are a danger to navigation. Tides vary from 1½ to 6 feet. This fact is important when considering where

and when to fish. Don't get caught where you don't want to be! Both incoming and outgoing tides fish well.

Getting There

There is excellent air service from the United States and Europe to the Seychelles. Air Seychelles offers direct service from London or Paris. The islands are eleven time zones from the West Coast and eight from the East Coast of the United States. Once you arrive at the Mahe International Airport, I suggest a private charter to your sailing yacht, which takes you to the fishing.

Climate and Seasons

Seasons in the Seychelles are defined by the trade winds. The southeast trades begin blowing in April and continue through November. During the rest of the year, northwest monsoon winds dominate and bring the greatest amount of precipitation. During the time when these winds change is generally the calmest. Temperatures in the Seychelles vary between 75 and 90 degrees Fahrenheit. The best flats fishing is from April through mid-June and from October through November. Because water temperature is ideal all year, bonefish are always present. Unlike the Caribbean, the Seychelles never experience cold fronts, and they are out of the cyclone zone.

Who Should Go

At this time fly fishing is new to the Seychelles and there are no experienced bonefishing guides. Anglers must be able to read flats,

Jerry Swanson laughs as his backing disappears at an alarming rate. Losing a fly line is not the end of the world but the beginning of a great story. Always carry a spare; it is inexpensive insurance.

A baby emperor, also called sweetlips.

spot fish, etc., and be self-sufficient in every aspect of saltwater wilderness fishing, especially safety. It is rewarding to take control of these responsibilities and make it all happen. Extensive pretrip planning and saltwater knowledge is mandatory. If you are not comfortable going it alone, go with someone who is experienced.

Jerry Swanson
Portland, Oregon
June 1998

Boating to Bonefish

If you want to experience some of the world's best bonefishing, you must go where few others have gone. There are two ways to do that—by float plane or by boat. In the case of bonefishing, a boat is usually the only option. Close-in areas reached by day boaters have been explored and are often fished on a weekly basis. Once you get beyond the reach of day trippers, it is pretty much a wilderness experience. To accomplish this, you need to live on the boat.

The advantages of a boat trip are many. You are on the water full time, often moored at the edge of pristine fishing. The sights, sounds, and smells of the flats are always with you. Night views are outrageous. Imagine sleeping where there are no lights, no unnatural sounds, no other people for perhaps 10, maybe 20 miles—complete solitude! Life revolves around your interests, and your schedule.

It is impossible to motor to the flats without making at least one cast along the way. The trouble is you usually hook a fish, and, if you are not careful, you never make it to the flats! Jeff Sherman watches the release.

Anglers who live on boats are perfectly positioned to take advantage of the best tides, the best light for photography, and the best fishing conditions. In fact, you could fish 24 hours a day if you

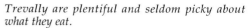
Trevally are plentiful and seldom picky about what they eat.

wished. Just cast your line! You are totally mobile and flexible. You call the shots—casts—and tailor the day to your desires. Sleep in, go snorkeling, have a late brunch, picnic, retire to a deserted isle, take an afternoon nap before fishing the sunset, or cruise to a small island port for dinner. You can even pull up anchor and visit that blank spot on the chart.

Boat trips are perfect for the family. There is something of interest for everyone. Boats usually accommodate four to eight people. Two to four couples are ideal. The sailing yacht that took Jerry to world class bonefishing in the Seychelles was 72 feet long and offered four private double-bed cabins. The group had two beautiful night cruises. Sitting on the bow of the boat after dark was an exciting experience. Jerry related that they seemed to be traveling through both water and stars. It was like a flying dream: too exciting to sleep and too exciting to wake up.

During Jerry's trip through the Seychelles, the group enjoyed fresh fruits, vegetables, and fish every day, plus freshly baked bread for breakfast. This is no small feat in a boat galley, but it shows that the crew went the extra mile and worked very hard.

Boat trippers should investigate boat packages and options carefully. Consider the age, size, stability, communications, safety features, power, and speed of the boat. The boat must have a flats boat or suitable dinghy to get you to the flats. If no flats boat that can be poled is available, be certain the flats are wadeable. Unless you are experienced in flats fishing, a guide should be included in the package. Sleeping quarters are very important, as are bathrooms, showers, the amount of available freshwater, general

Life aboard the sailboat is like you always dreamed it would be, and the bonefishing is better than your dreams!

Trevally!

This green jobfish, Aprion virescens, *attacked a plug behind the sailboat when it was under sail. Can you imagine the conversation onboard? Hmm. . .shall we eat it? Naw. Release it. What is it? Who cares—lets eat it! O.K.—put it on ice. No! Release it. What do you think happened?*

space, generator use, and privacy. The crew must be congenial and service oriented. Be certain you are aware of possible extra charges.

There are many boating possibilities throughout the world of bonefish. Aside from a big adventure in the Indian Ocean or the South Pacific, Belize and the Bahamas offer fantastic inshore cruising for bonefish (and everything else that has a fin). Destinations can be reached within a day, and countless deserted islands await your visit. It is still possible to be the first person to wade a flat and cast for bonefish.

You are probably wondering what the downside is as far as boat trips are concerned. Inquire about the ocean conditions. If you get seasick, don't go! Otherwise, assuming the boat, crew, food, accommodations, and group of anglers are all fishing in the same

	J	F	M	A	M	J	J	A	S	O	N	D
Bonefish	F-G	F-G	F-G	E	E	E	F-E	F-E	F-E	E	E	F-G
Snapper	F-E	F-E	F-E	E	E	E	F-G	F-G	F-G	E	E	F-E
Jacks	F-E	F-E	F-E	E	E	E	F-G	F-G	F-G	E	E	F-E
Trevally	F-E	F-E	F-E	E	E	E	F-G	F-G	F-G	E	E	F-E
Shark	F-E	F-E	F-E	E	E	E	F-G	F-G	F-G	E	E	F-E
Emperor	F-E	F-E	F-E	E	E	E	F-G	F-G	F-G	E	E	F-E
Wind	L-H	L-M	L-M	L-M	L-M	L-M	L-M	L-M	L-M	L-M	L-M	L-H

P=Poor F=Fair G=Good E=Excellent
L=Light M=Medium H=Heavy

If you aren't careful, your dreams disappear with your time.

Chapter 31

Yucatan

The Yucatan Peninsula juts north 200 to 300 miles into the Gulf of Mexico from the Mexico-Central America land mass. It is about 200 miles wide and is bordered by ocean on three sides. Geologically, this area is composed of a giant limestone sponge that sucks water into underground rivers (cenotes) and sinks. Cenotes are popular with swimmers and divers. The entire region is scattered with limestone caves, and most of them are filled with crystal-clear fresh water, a phenomenon found nowhere else in Mexico. The ancient Maya built their villages near these caves and cenotes. When flying over the peninsula, circular ground patterns created by underground water movement are clearly visible.

The east coast is edged with coral reefs, lagoons, mangrove swamps, jungle forests, and offshore islands. Where coral and limestone meet, bizarre shoreline formations result, creating underground caves, springs, and steep-walled underwater canyons. This landscape is unique in the world and has hosted fishermen for centuries.

Cozumel

Cozumel is an island located about 10 miles off the eastern coast of Yucatan. It is easily reached by either ferry or airplane. Ferries leave both Playa del Carmen on the mainland and Cozumel nine times daily, and the crossing takes about 40 minutes. The international airport is a few miles northeast of San Miguel. There is no public transportation on Cozumel, but plenty of taxis are available at reasonable rates.

Almost every international resort and hotel name in the world is represented in Cancun, and they stretch along the Caribbean surf for miles. Most, like the Marriott Casa Magna pictured here, are extravagant structures and decorated with marble, art, flowers, and flowing water.

Average Air Temperatures in Cancún	
January	26°C/78°F
February	26°C/78°F
March	26°C/78°F
April	26°C/78°F
May	26°C/78°F
June	27°C/81°F
July	27°C/81°F
August	27°C/81°F
September	27°C/81°F
October	26°C/78°F
November	26°C/78°F
December	24°C/76°F

Cozumel is especially popular with the scuba and snorkeling community. For the angler, the best flats fishing is in two protected lagoons at the northern end of the island. Monte Cristo and Rio de la Plata offer wade or boat fishing on large flats surrounded by mangroves.

If you are going, pack the fly rod and make the most of fun in the sun and ocean, sip margaritas, and enjoy sunset dining.

Cancun

Cancun rewrote the textbook for the tourist industry. In the late 1960s Cancun was a quiet sand spit bordered on one side by the sparkling Caribbean Sea and the sheltered, wildlife-rich waters of Nichupte Lagoon on the other. The bay and the sea are still there, but native wildlife must now coexist with nonnative wildlife that inhabits opulent hotels, dark cinemas, fast-paced restaurants, all-night discos, and crowded sidewalks. If you desire it, you can probably find it in Cancun.

Cancun is *the* luxury resort destination in Mexico. It attracts romantic honeymooners, jet setters, swinging singles, simple sun seekers, and wannabes from every walk of life. The Yucatan is a popular destination for scuba divers and snorklers who enjoy exploring the blue holes and steep ocean walls. It even attracts a few bonefishermen, who, if they had their way, would be poling the flats of Ascension Bay in a wooden skiff. In the name of compromise, bonefishermen settle for a little bonefishing and a lot of glitter and romantic pampering. It could be worse.

The flats are at least an hour's drive and an hour's boat ride north of (and a world apart from) Cancun. This country is deserted; your closest companions are screaming parrots, hermit crabs, raccoons, caymen, tarpon, snook, permit, and bonefish (mostly one- to three-pound schoolies), all of which are a pleasant diversion from the two-legged specimens that have overrun and exploited Cancun.

There are no established fishing lodges at Cancun or Cozumel. Visitors stay at local hotels and arrange guide service on a daily basis. I suggest you book in advance to ensure that the guide of your choice is available for the days you wish to fish. In a book filled with fishing lodges and camps that cater to fisherman, these destinations are just the opposite. Cancun and Cozumel offer everything for the family with a little flats fishing thrown in for frustrated anglers. I like civilization, but there is a lot of it and I can always go there. I can't always go to the wild places. Book a day of fishing!

Cancun Adventure

Mary and I decided to spend the Christmas holiday in the Yucatan. We divided our time between Cancun and Ascension Bay. We wanted to experience both worlds, the real and the unreal. You decide which is which.

Airline connections to Cancun are excellent, and it is a relatively easy flight from most places in America. After clearing customs and dealing with the typical Mexican hustlers at the airport, we finally gathered our gear, selected a cab, and arrived at the Cancun Marriott Casa Magna. Like dozens of other hotels along the beach,

Angler Craig McCloskey brings a tarpon along-side the boat; guide Sand Flea will release it without taking it out of the water. Isla Holbox.

the Marriott is an extravagant palace constructed of concrete and marble and decorated with art, flowers, and water. Its open court-yard hugs a narrow sand beach.

We did the usual tourist stuff—soaking up the sun, swimming, reading, and planning the next expedition for food. Restaurant fare is excellent and several days should pass before you become bored.

Like most angling tourists, I prefer a boat seat and fly rod to a poolside lounge chair and drink, so I booked a day of fishing. Shortly after the discos closed and the last of the crazies crawled home, Mary and I met our guide in the hotel lobby. It was 4 a.m., o' dark thirty. The quiet drive north took us past every hotel known to the free world. Beyond the hotel strip we continued through dirt and mud streets lined with tiny crowded concrete houses. Some had bars on the windows; some had no windows. There was little doubt that we were in the Third World.

Once we left suburbia behind, we entered the third dimension of Cancun, the quiet sand spit north of town that is a world apart from people and buildings, and their associated noise and pollu-tion. The trip from our hotel to our launch site at Punta Sam took a little over an hour and provided us with an interesting behind-the-scenes perspective of the local culture and economy.

Our boat ride across grass, sand, marl, coral, ocean channels, and mangrove-fringed flats took about 40 minutes. Depending on the season, snook, permit, bonefish, and tarpon are available, but weather conditions limited us to snook and baby tarpon. We poled into quiet mangrove lagoons centuries removed from Cancun and cast to aggressive prehistoric tarpon. They jumped high above the water, shaking their heads, then dashed for the protective cover of red mangrove roots. There was no shortage of fish, and I could see how several friends had previously connect-ed with a super grand slam—a snook, permit, tarpon, and bone-fish all in the same day.

As we ate lunch, I noticed our guide was surveying the sky with a look of concern. An occasional boom of thunder could be heard in the distance, and the sky was turning a serious blue gray. I asked if he thought we should leave. Before I could finish my ques-

The author attempts to keep a baby tarpon away from the shelter of mangrove roots near Cabo Catoche, north of Cancun.

Baby tarpon.

Mary Kaufmann

Mary poses with a bonefish from skinny water in Ascension Bay. Larger specimens can be found in deeper water. Remember to protect yourself from the intense sun.

Randall Kaufmann

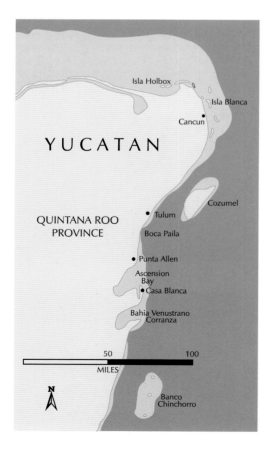

tion, he had the anchor up and the motor running. Something told me he was more than a little concerned.

Within 10 minutes torrential rains driven sideways by 30-knot winds whipped the channel into a blurry frenzy. Visibility was 30 feet, which means zero when you are traveling at 15 mph. Water washed over the boat from every direction, and we became the proverbial toy boat in the bathtub. There was little to do but hope that the motor did not fail, that we did not run into the shallows or hit any floating debris, or that we did not get hit by lightning. Things were not looking good.

Our guide kept us pointed into the gale and negotiated the maze of channels, narrow passages, and obstacles with amazing precision. As we raced through the thick wet air, lightning flashed like a thousand strobe lights and scattered its hot tentacles along the unseen shoreline only 100 yards away. When we reached the dock, the thunder and lightning overtook us with unbelievable fierceness. Electricity crackled through the air, shattering a nearby palm tree, and our wet hair nearly stood on end. Sulfur permeated the liquid air. We could not get into the van and the 20th century fast enough. Happy to be safely in our time machine, we headed for the marble palace, a lounge chair, and a drink.

Weather precluded us from venturing back onto the flats, so we played lounge lizard until it was time to depart for Ascension Bay.

Ascension Bay

It was after dark. Mary and I sat on the edge of the boat dock at Punta Allen on Ascension Bay. An occasional firefly seeking a mate glittered in the dark, but it was the nearly constant barrage of heat lightning that captured our attention. The silent flashes backlit an incredible wall of star-high cumulus clouds. Depending on the intensity of the sky strobes, the clouds were colored creamy white muted shades of green, tangerine, or pearlescent silver. Sometimes the flashes were intense enough to light up the ocean miles out to sea. The light flashes silhouetted boats anchored offshore, and they seemed to float motionless on a gray mirror. In the afterglow of a flash, their red, white, and blue hulls seemed suspended in the thick tropic air.

Above us 10,000 stars and the Milky Way faded in and out of view between bursts of lightning. Below us, smooth ocean water rolled rhythmically ashore, gently tumbling millions of tiny pieces of coral, creating a soothing sound.

Reflecting back on the day, the things Mary and I remembered most were not the fishing (although we released many bonefish and a beautiful permit) but the sights and colors that constantly bombarded our vision. Nowhere else had we seen such a vivid display of unusual and unique colors. They seemed to have spilled from the Creator's palette. Many were mingled in muck and paint-like ooze and took on a primordial character, like those from pterodactyl days.

Ascension Bay is like that; you feel you are a millennia traveler at the dawn of creation, and, in a sense, you are. Everything changes so quickly yet seems so ageless. When I am at Ascension Bay, I feel as if I have been born at the last second of creation.

We made a list of colors in the bay. Some of our favorites included: iced tea, lava, manuka green, peacock blue, sparkling

Randall Kaufmann

Randall Kaufmann

Hundreds of frigate birds, Fregata magnificens, *sometimes roost on Culebra Cay. Common throughout the Caribbean, they are often referred to as man-o'-war birds because they pirate food from all other birds. Their wingspan (seven to eight feet) is greater in proportion to weight (two to three pounds) than that of any other bird, helping them to stay aloft for extended periods. Frigates have sharp eyesight and locate fish at the surface, which they dive upon and catch in their sharply-hooked bill without landing. Because of their sail-like wings, water-absorbing plumage, and short, weak legs, frigates are nearly helpless if they alight on the water. They usually need elevation to take flight. Males are all black with a brilliant red pouch, or gular sac. During courtship, the males inflate the sac, which resembles an inflated balloon. Females are larger, have a white breast, and are without a red sac. Another species,* Fregata minor, *is common throughout the tropical Pacific, Indian, and South Atlantic oceans.*

pearl, mocha chocolate, whipped cream, flamingo, tropic smoke, root beer, pea soup, puke yellow, and others we cannot share with you. On land a half-dozen species of gigantic butterflies soared about us, streaking the blue sky and jungle foliage like flashing rainbows. Ascension Bay is a lepidopterist's paradise and the colors are unique to bonefish habitat.

The Yucatan, especially Ascension Bay, is noted for its many "oh hos," upwellings of crystal-clear subterranean fresh water in the bay. These "springs" often boil to the surface, creating a unique ecosystem. This mix of freshwater and saltwater is a bountiful mesh of nutrients from the past and present that creates the future. Often many species of fish are seen milling about these freshwater fountains. Huge sharks always patrol the bottom. It is not a good place to swim. Once, while snorkeling, we noticed the water seemed to have an oily film and visibility was blurry. After we left the water, we felt slippery, as though we had taken a bath in soft water. We were experiencing halocline, the mixing of fresh and saltwater.

We took time off from fishing to feed iguanas, inspect hundreds of roosting frigate birds on Culebra Cay, and visit a wood stork nursery and a flamingo colony. A manatee scooted out from under our boat as we slowly motored toward a narrow mangrove channel. We were looking for tarpon to complete a grand slam and we finally found them—bolting past our boat.

Sometimes our presence alters the future. As we left the dock and headed for our cabana, we donated blood to several mosquitoes, instantly changing the destiny of ecological, biological, and genetic time. Yes, indeed, it is the dawn of creation, and everyone has a small part to play.

Located about 115 miles south of Cancun and 25 miles south of Boca Paila, Ascension Bay is a vast estuary with many beautiful sand and mud flats and an intricate reef system. Together, the estuary and reef system provide the best bonefish habitat in Mexico. Ascension Bay is the favored place to connect with a grand slam. Until recently, this area was difficult for anglers to reach, but new fishing camps now allow anglers to cast to fish that have never seen an imitation shrimp or a bogus crab.

Some of the area around Boca Paila and all of Ascension Bay and remote Bahia del Espiritu Santo to the south are included in

Randall Kaufmann

The multihued colors of the landscape and water at Ascension Bay are unequaled at any bonefish destination. Add the flora and fauna, and Ascension Bay is simply unbelievable. Monarch-sized butterflies are a spectacular attraction. Their flying colors are certain to enchant you.

Randall Kaufmann

Guide boats, beach, and dock at Punta Allen.

At Iguana Island, we enjoyed the friendly attention of iguanas intent on checking out our lunch.

Randall Kaufmann

the Sian Ka'an Biosphere Preserve. Sian Ka'an is Mayan for "birthplace in the sky." The biosphere is the thin, fragile mantle of the earth that maintains our life and that of all other organisms. It consists of parts of the lithosphere (ground), hydrosphere (water), and atmosphere (air). This 1.5-million-acre preserve encompasses tropical moist forests, mangrove swamps, marshes, and both freshwater and marine ecosystems, including dune-backed beaches and coral reefs, locally known as the Turquoise Coast. The Biosphere promotes the idea of protecting natural ecosystems and at the same time allowing human activities and development of natural resources on an ecologically sound basis.

The Sian Ka'an is a birder's and naturalist's paradise. Nearly 350 species of birds have been identified in the preserve and about two-thirds of those breed there. Many of these are marine and shore species, but 16 raptors; frigates *Fregata magnifiscens* (visit the rookery at Culebra Cay); roseate spoonbill, *Ajaiai ajaja* (try Yaxmogote at Sandali Lagoon); and flamingos, *Phoenicopterus ruber* and *Jabiru mycteria,* call the preserve home.

Over 40 species of reptiles reside here, including the green turtle, *Chelonia mydas;* loggerhead turtle, *Caretta caretta;* hawksbill turtle, *Eretmochelys imbricata;* and leatherback turtle, *Dermochelys coriacea.* Two species of crocodile, *Morelets Crocodylus moreletii* and *American Cacutus,* are also present. Five species of big cats, jaguar, *Panthera onca;* puma, *Felis concolor;* ocelot, *F. pardalis;* margay, *F. wiedii;* and jaguarundi, *F. yagouaroundi,* roam this strange and remote landscape. The big cats are sometimes spotted crossing the road leading to Punta Allen or patrolling a beach. There are also iguana, peccary, manatee, tapir, spider and howler monkeys, white-tailed deer, and anteaters. And there are boas, rattlers, and other snakes you do not want to know about. About 550 terrestrial and 850 aquatic invertebrate species have been observed. Fish are abundant, and over 50 species have been documented. In addition, there are over 20 registered archaeological sites within the preserve with many more yet to be discovered.

I mention all this because Ascension Bay is a fascinating bastion of flora and fauna, and visitors should at least be aware of what exists beyond bonefish, permit, and tarpon. Remote areas of the preserve probably have changed little since before the Spanish arrived in the early 1500s looking for gold and the fountain of youth. Perhaps the fountain of youth is still hidden in the genes of some obscure species of plant or animal.

Currently, there are three lodges located on Ascension Bay, plus two more at Boca Paila. Some fish both waters. Beginning at Cancun, Tulum is 2½ hours south on paved road. Boca Paila is another three-quarters of an hour south on a dirt, sometimes mud, road through the jungle.

A bridge of planks (many missing) leads 45 minutes south of Boca Paila over a sometimes muddy potholed road to Punta Allen. It's one of the most successful lobster fishing villages in Mexico. The road is rough, expect to bottom out or high center. Scout the worst sections. Mud holes can be 50 feet long and just as wide. They look 50 feet deep! Buy damage insurance in Cancun. When you cross the Mexican speed bump—a rope across the sandy road—and see the Cuzan Guest House sign, you have arrived.

Many undiscovered plants await the botanist in the Sian Ka'an Biosphere Preserve. Casual observation should reveal many vividly colored flowers.

The road doesn't go much beyond the Cuzan Guest House sign in Punta Allen.

It takes at least an hour to drive the sandy section of road that ends at Punta Allen. If it is wet or raining, rent pontoons at Tulum. In Mexico, it is advisable not to drive after dark.

Casa Blanca is located at the south side of Ascension Bay. It is reached by boat (about 45 minutes) from Punta Allen, or you can fly to its private air strip 50 minutes from Cancun, which is the recommended way of getting there.

Boca Paila

The term "boca" means mouth in Spanish. The Yucatan has an abundance of bocas, or channels, that lead to open Caribbean waters. Boca Paila is also characterized by flats, mangroves, and a lagoon, and provides perfect access to and from deeper water for all fish species. Anglers using the bocas have ample opportunity to take permit, bonefish, and baby tarpon, so a grand slam is a reasonable expectation for accomplished anglers. Snook, jack crevalle, barracuda, and cubera snapper are an added bonus.

Since the establishment of the Sian Ka'an Preserve in 1986, commercial netting has been banned, and bonefish numbers have increased dramatically. There are enough fish in the preserve to tire the arms of an octopus.

Fishing

This chemically rich environment has helped create plentiful populations of bonefish beginning at Isla Holbox in the north and running south along the east coast in the province of Quintana Roo to the Sian Ka'an Biosphere Reserve. Most bonefishing is accessed through Ascension Bay fishing camps and the resorts of Cancun and Cozumel. More adventurous anglers find their way to Bahia del Espiritu Santo Bay. For those who are interested, Brian O'Keefe reports that Banco Chinchorro is not worth the effort for bonefishermen.

Most bonefish are found in the extensive lagoons and mangrove tidal flats. Sand and mud flats also attract bonefish, and mudding schools might number a thousand or more and create huge muds as they root along the bottom. Some areas are interspersed with turtle grass and occasional coral. Most flats are firm and easy to wade and contain fish during all stages of the tide. Shallow mangrove areas are nurseries and provide juvenile and smaller fish a refuge from large predators that are unable to enter shallow water.

Bonefish run between one and three pounds; five-pound fish are considered big. What bonefish lack in size in the Yucatan, they make up in numbers. They are aggressive and eager to be exercised, providing even novice anglers with good action. However, larger specimens are available. Frank "Mungo" Boyden, an artist-sculptor living in Lincoln City, Oregon, is a frequent visitor to Ascension Bay over the Christmas holiday. Frank searches for larger fish in deeper water and has released bonefish to 10 pounds.

Best flies include the Tan Krystal Flash Charlie, size 6; Clouser Tan/White and Chartreuse/White, size 6; Mini Shrimp Orange, Chartreuse, and Tan, size 8; Mini Puff Tan and Pink/White, sizes 6 and 8; Turd, size 8; Baited Breath, size 8; and Cuzan Special, size 8.

Tarpon are widespread throughout the Yucatan, and there are plenty of baby tarpon to 15 pounds or better. Baby tarpon are found around tidal channels, along secluded mangrove edges, and in lagoons. Migratory tarpon, 40 to 125 pounds, are sometimes

This bridge spans the entrance to Boca Paila Bay, and, while it may cause you to pause, everyone before you has made it. Hopefully you will, too.

Randall Kaufmann

Boca Paila resort fronts the Caribbean and a nice beach.

Randall Kaufmann

Barracuda are hard on gear. Always fish a wire leader and use pliers when releasing them.

Randall Kaufmann

Javier helps Mary Kaufmann pose with a beautiful permit. Ascension Bay is one of the best places to connect with a permit.

found in limited numbers during June and July, mostly in deeper channels, in cuts, and along the beach.

The best tarpon flies in the Yucatan are size 1/0, mostly subdued patterns, including LeMay's Big Eye Tarpon in Orange Grizzly, Furnace Squirrel, and Orange Blue; Borski's Orange Butt; and the Cockroach Deceiver.

Ascension Bay is *the* place to hook permit. They are relatively aggressive and easy to hook. On a recent trip to Ascension Bay, our guide, Javier, spotted a permit of over 30 pounds slowly working along a moderately deep beach. After we chased it for 10 minutes and made a dozen casts, it finally took a crab two feet off the bottom! There are few places where permit are that tolerant and nonchalant. Large numbers of five- to 15-pound schoolies are commonly seen feeding on bay flats, and there are some to 50 pounds. It is common to have several opportunities a day.

At this time, most guides prefer Del Brown's Permit Crab (Merkin) for permit, the bigger and heavier the better. Remember— you must be able to cast it! Another favorite is the Rag Head Crab. The latter doubles as a bonefish getter in smaller sizes. One to two dozen assorted crabs is more than ample for a week. If you lose two to three permit flies per day, you have had a fantastic week. You never know which patterns work best until the week is over. Hopefully, you'll lose your horde of Merkins or Rag Heads in a few days and wish you had more.

One day during our last visit, the wind created rough conditions in the bay so we opted to visit the nearby offshore reef for a little 'cuda fishing. Upon spotting and attacking our long, thin, fluorescent green flies, these slashers went berserk. They spent more time in the air than the water and some would attack again after being released! I recalled Jerry Swanson telling me that he and Dr. Rodney Baine went through three dozen 'cuda flies on their initial trip here. You can always count on barracuda to provide exciting action. The moral is to always carry 'cuda flies and wire leaders.

This is perhaps the best place to score a grand slam: permit, bonefish, and tarpon in a single day. Some anglers like to add snook, which are available at some locales (bring Bendbacks, assorted Deceivers, and Glass Minnows), and cubera snapper. These saltwater thugs can devastate your terminal gear and make your jaw drop. They like a surface commotion, so bring big Lance's Crystal Poppers and wire leaders.

Ed Opler, owner of World's Finest Chocolates, is an angling aficionado and divides his fishing between the tropics and the Wyoming Rockies.

The Bonefish Syndrome
by Ed Opler

I feel smart, smug, and excited as our flight touches down on a beautiful tropical archipelago. Smart because my wife, Pat, and I are exploring a "new" bonefishing destination, which presumably is teaming with undisturbed gigantic fish that are all eager to take our favorite fly patterns. Smug because my trout fishing buddies back in Jackson Hole, Wyoming, are on a daily diet of minus-twenty-degree temperatures and snow on the valley floor approaching five feet! Excited because of the opportunity to share a new fishing experience with Pat in a very beautiful place.

We are met by our host, Vern Briley, after clearing customs. A short drive and a ten-minute boat ride delivers us to our thatched roof, beachside lodge where our hostess, Patrice, greets us and shows us to our own island bungalow. Now the fun begins. Ten years ago I would have been out the door with my fly rod within fifteen minutes of our arrival. Today—finally—I have learned to relax. We walk the pink sand beach and

The author battles a permit as guide, Javier, looks on. It swam off about 150 yards and the tug of war began. Fifteen minutes later the permit was released.

Mary Kaufmann

Baby tarpon are usually located next to mangroves. They can often be observed contemplating attacking the fly. Once hooked, they again may contemplate their situation before beginning their acrobatics. Steve Rewick at Isla Holbox.

swim in a gentle surf of crystal-clear 80-degree Fahrenheit water. Later, on the lodge patio, we enjoy a "specialty of the house" tropical drink while meeting other guests and watching the orange and lavender sunset across the endless palm-studded shoreline to the west.

After a delicious dinner of grilled lobster and homegrown salad, we collapse, dreaming of the bonefish, tarpon, and permit we hope to see during the next six days.

I'm awakened to the sound of the surf, hummingbirds buzzing in the bougainvillea along the walk, and sea gulls screeching and diving on a helpless school of bait fish. We take our pre-breakfast swim and meet our guide for the week.

Eduardo is an expert fishing guide who is totally in tune with his environment. Pat and I ask a million questions about mangroves, tides, birds, and fish. Ten years ago I would have counted bonefish numbers and missed so much of the real beauty and the solitude of these flats.

We caught bonefish, lots of bonefish, including a few big fellows over eight pounds. They performed beyond all possible expectation. These bonefish required hunting both by boat and on foot, wading in places the boat could not follow. One of the great challenges of bonefishing with a fly is hunting and then spotting the fish. Making an accurate and delicate presentation is also required to fool them into taking the fly as an imitation of their food.

When a fly fisher can execute all of these factors, the results are amazing, including a blazing run that can strip 100 or more yards of backing off your reel in a few seconds.

I'm thrilled by a fish that can cause the leader to throw a roostertail of water as it streaks across a foot-deep flat. I just don't ever tire of a bonefish's speed and power. This is what we've come for, and this is what brings us back—an honest-to-goodness great game fish.

One morning a permit takes my orange shrimp pattern and Eduardo says, "He's headed for Cancun." After boating, photographing, and releasing this most challenging quarry, we each quickly catch a bonefish. Suddenly, Eduardo is excited and proposes a plan. We must try for the grand slam. We eat a very early lunch in a shady spot nearby and then head for a distant lagoon where Eduardo had spotted some tarpon earlier in the week. The challenge of the grand slam is to catch a bonefish, permit, and tarpon on a fly in one day of fishing. One doesn't get this opportunity every day.

Eduardo's lagoon is indeed distant. When he finally cuts the motor and picks up his boat pole, there is a notable silence along the shoreline. During the next two hours we each, in turn, catch five or six bonefish but no tarpon. Finally, in a small bay around one more point there is an entire school of tarpon cruising toward us. Quickly, quietly, I pick up the rod with a tarpon fly and leader. Strip line on the bow deck. . .now cast. . .shoot line to the lead fish. . .a beauty. He and the second fish see the fly. Coaxed into a flat-out high-speed rush by the acceleration of the trailing fish, the larger tarpon strikes and almost instantly rockets into the air. After three great slashing jumps, I finally get into some serious hook setting and then the dogfight is on. Eduardo grabs the tired fish by tail and lip. He lifts it for the photo as I jump into three feet of water and then hold the fish a moment longer for more photos. I remove the fly and cradle the fish gently until it regains its composure and swims off to rejoin the school. After handshakes and more photos, we head home to the lodge. Two realizations hit me. First, we accomplished my third grand slam. Second, this day ended our flats fishing adventures until the next winter.

Something was telling me that there was a difference on this trip compared to the many others Pat and I have shared. We discussed this at dinner and realized I had thoroughly relaxed and let myself enjoy the entire trip—the lodge, food, company, weather, and the wonderful environment of these beautiful saltwater flats.

As I fell asleep that evening, I knew that I was deeply hooked, not just by the bonefish as I had been before but by the very special magic of the saltwater flats and the watery shadows of the great game fish that feed on them.

Ed Opler
Jackson, Wyoming
September 1998

Jeff Rose and a nice bonefish from flooded mangroves far back in Ascension Bay.

Nonfishermen

Almost every imaginable tourist activity is available at Cancun and Cozumel. Nonfishermen visiting Ascension Bay can enjoy sunbathing, swimming, snorkeling, bird watching, beachcombing, or just plain relaxing with a good book. If you feel ambitious, take a mystery trip back into time to Tulum, the only Mayan ruins found on the seacoast. Tulum is within a 60- to 90-minute drive of most places on Yucatan's east coast. Coba, another Mayan ruin, is also within reach. If you are driving to and staying at Punta Allen, you should visit ruins on the drive down or back, as you may not wish to make a special trip, especially if the weather is wet. It is advised that you only drive during daylight hours in Mexico.

Swimmers, snorkelers, and divers are never bored in bonefish country.

Language

Most Yucatan guides speak a little English. Some understand most fishing terms, and others can carry on a conservation. All guides should know the English words for bonefish, permit, and other fish commonly encountered. If you speak a little Spanish, it is easy to communicate the essentials. Language, like fishing technique, can be ambiguous and vary from location to location. During a recent visit to the Yucatan, Mary was determined to learn as many words as possible. Our guide, Manuel, was pleased to help and enjoyed the expanded conversation. Just making an effort made our days together much more pleasant. It is a good idea to brush up on your Spanish and perhaps carry a pocket guide. Ralph Cutter publishes a good one.

Health Care

Frank Boyden tells the funniest story of when the Flying Aztec hit his brother, Bradley. They were motoring across Ascension Bay at good speed when, for no apparent reason, Bradley suddenly jumped overboard. The urge had hit him—bam! He left a trail across the boat gunwale as he took to the air.

The water is usually the culprit behind the Aztec Two-Step,

Perched above the turquoise Caribbean, the Mayan ruins at Tulum are worth a stop. Depending on the crowds, figure on spending at least two hours.

Montezuma's Revenge, or worse. Nausea, vomiting, dehydration, fever, and stomach cramps are all symptoms. Believe me, you do not want to get it! I have been sick enough times in the Third World that I consider everything suspect.

To avoid this bacteria, don't drink the water or anything with ice that might be made from unpurified water. Don't put your mouth over the outside of a bottle or can—use a straw. Carry a water filter or purification tablets or drink only purified bottled water, soda, or beer. Brush your teeth with purified water *(agua purificada)*. Be certain bottled water is sealed when you buy it. Eat only cooked foods or peeled fruits and vegetables. Do not buy food from street vendors. *Be wary of eating shellfish.*

Be especially careful in airports, restaurants, and airplanes. Anything and everything you touch can transmit the germ, especially money. Keep your hands clean and away from your mouth. Wash your hands often.

Cancun likes to boast that it is the only city in Mexico that delivers pure water out of every tap, but ask the desk clerk at your hotel to make certain the water is safe. Most resorts that cater to fly fishermen have their own purification systems or obtain clean water from deep aquifers that are safe to drink from.

Concerned visitors should ask their doctor for a suitable drug that kills the germ. If you do not have medicine and you get sick, see a local doctor. As a general rule, vaccination against hepatitis and boosters for standard vaccinations are recommended before travel to Mexico and most other places. Some travelers to Mexico and other foreign countries buy evacuation insurance. At the very least, check with your insurance carrier for out-of-country coverage. Always carry proof of insurance and accident instructions on your person. Health care outside the United States is not like home. If you have a medical emergency and need blood, be certain it is clean blood.

Parting Advice

In Mexico, everything changes. Everything changes before you arrive, and, while you are there, everything changes again.

It's a beautiful day to chase permit, bones, and tarpon. Let's go!

	J	F	M	A	M	J	J	A	S	O	N	D
Bonefish	F-G	F-G	G-E	G-E	G-E	G-E	F-E	F-E	F-E	F-E	F-E	F-G
Permit	F-E	F-E	F-E	G-E	G-E	G-E	G-E	G-E	F-E	F-E	F-E	F-E
Tarpon	F-G	F-G	F-G	F-E	G-E	G-E	G-E	G-E	G-E	G-E	F-G	F-G
Snook	P-F	F	F	F-G	G	G	G	F-G	F	F	F	P-F
Barracuda	F-G	F-G	G	G	G	G	G	G	G	F-G	F-G	F-G
Snapper	P-G	P-G	P-G	F-G	F-G	F-G	F-G	F-G	F-G	F-G	P-G	P-G
Jacks	F-G	F-G	F-G	F-G	F-G	F-G	F-G	F-G	F-G	F-G	F-G	F-G
Shark	F-G	F-G	F-G	F-G	F-G	F-G	F-G	F-G	F-G	F-G	F-G	F-G
Wind	L-H	L-H	L-H	L-H	L-M	L-M	L-M	L-M	L-M	L-M	L-M	L-H

P=Poor F=Fair G=Good E=Excellent
L=Light M=Medium H=Heavy

Chapter 32

Getting into the Sport

If you are in pursuit of your first bonefish, the initial step to a memorable adventure is to select a desirable destination at a productive time. Once this is settled, begin collecting your gear. This can turn into a part-time hobby and provide many pleasurable hours of relaxation and enjoyment. Get the *right* gear, and buy the best you can afford. Proper gear allows you to maximize your angling potential and pleasure. If you tie flies, begin filling your boxes with a good selection of patterns in assorted colors and sink rates. Consider taking your tying gear with you.

If you have a guide, once you are on the water, he will talk you through the cast and hookup and share in the joy of your first bonefish. You will be on a steep learning curve the first few days. As each day unfolds, remember to pause in your search for the next bonefish and closely observe your surroundings. Some of my most memorable days have been those when I caught very few or no bonefish, but I learned something new and observed something beautiful in nature.

Bonefishing is more than hooking fish. It is a tropical odyssey into many worlds. It is a water-colored dream where the edges of the sea, sky, and land are sometimes difficult to define. It is a series of encounters not only with ghostly bonefish but with prehistoric sharks, scurrying crabs, inquisitive sea birds that might land on your rod tip, unafraid iguanas, porpoise, flying fish, darting tropical fish, manatee, and more. Best of all, it is an escape from your day-to-day world. Once you have fished for bonefish, you are changed forever, even haunted, and called back again and again.

It is relatively easy to become a proficient bonefish angler. All you need to do is learn to cast and go bonefishing! Jon Covich, Queen's Garden, Cuba.

Books

Read all you can. Tricks and techniques are hidden in every book and magazine article related to saltwater angling. Books about bonefishing and related subjects include *Fly Fishing for Bonefish* and *Bonefish Fly Patterns* by Dick Brown; *Fly Fishing in Saltwater, Fishing the Flats,* and *Saltwater Fly Patterns* by Lefty Kreh; *Flies for Saltwater* by Dick Stewart and Farrow Allen; *Permit on a Fly* by Jack Samson; *The Book of Tarpon* by A.W. Dimlock; *Tarpon Quest* by John Cole; *West of Key West,* edited by John Cole and Hawk Pollard, and *Fly-Fishing the Flats* by Barry and Cathy Beck.

Magazines

Fly fishing magazines including *American Angler, Flyfishing, Fly Fisherman, Fly Rod & Reel, Fly Fish America, Fly Fishing Quarterly, Gray's Sporting Journal, Flyfishing In Saltwater, Saltwater Sportsman,* and *Saltwater Fly Fishing* often have excellent features pertaining to saltwater angling. Readers can find excellent and timely information in all these and other outdoor publications.

Videos

Videos provide enjoyable and exciting fishing action and offer valuable information. The following are worth a look: Jack Dennis' *Tying and Fishing Saltwater Flies* with Jimmy Nix; *Lefty Kreh's Exciting World of Saltwater Fly Fishing* and *Lefty's Saltwater Fly Tying;*

Scientific Anglers's _Fly Rodding For Tarpon;_ and _The Challenge of Giant Tarpon_ with Billy Pate; Umpqua Feather Merchants' _Pop Flyes_ with Bob Popovics and _Tarpon Country_ and _Saltwater Fly Fishing from A to Z_ with saltwater master Stu Apte. Flip Pallot has several videos available, including _Flats, Bonefish, Tarpon_ and _Sharks and Redfish._ Flip has new titles in the works. _Fly Casting_ and _Essence of Fly Casting II-Advanced Fly Casting,_ both by Mel Krieger, and _Fly Fishing With Lefty Kreh_ are good.

Local Information

Another source of great information can be found at your local fly fishing specialty store. Chances are good that at least one staff member is an experienced bonefish fanatic. Such people can provide a great deal of practical knowledge and may even provide clinics and casting instruction. Stop in and chat about bonefish destinations, tackle, and fly patterns. If you have time, they may show you a video and share a bonefish story or two. If you cannot visit a fly fishing speciality shop, call an expert on the sport, a mail-order house, or a booking agent who specializes in bonefishing.

Internet

The Internet also offers information through guides, lodges, publishers, magazines on line, authors, booking agents, retailers,

Adventuring for bonefish can take you around the globe to interesting cultures, exciting lands and beautiful waters.

Bonefish camp on Anegada, British Virgin Islands.

An Anegada reef bonefish.

individuals, news groups, etc. As with many subjects on the internet, not all information is accurate. Install a fine screen in your filter. Let common sense prevail. If something sounds too good to be true, it probably is. No one is giving anything away. The worn out axiom of "you get what you pay for" is truer today than ever.

Your Best Source

Read all you can, talk to local experts, and view the videos, but there is no substitute for on-the-water experience. If you can, book a group trip through your local dealer or with a reputable international booking agent. Such an experience greatly enhances your progress and enjoyment. The most important step, however, is to book yourself to a good bonefish destination that allows you lots of action. *First-time anglers should visit a location where many fish can be hooked every day.* It is far better to experience 10 small bonefish per day, or even two or three, than none. Bonefish action allows you to practice what you have learned, expand your ideas and knowledge, and develop questions and answers. If the destination allows you to fish for other species, do so.

Kevin Erickson is a travel, tackle, and computer expert and has a degree in Engineering Technology—the application of design into reality—and loves to make things happen. Kevin has outfitted hundreds of anglers and shares his thoughts here on planning an adventure. He specializes in both freshwater and saltwater angling and frequently leads groups to exotic destinations.

Booking A Trip
by Kevin Erickson

How do you best go about selecting a bonefish destination and arranging an angling "trip of a lifetime?" Whether you are going to Christmas Island, the Bahamas, or any of the other wonderful bonefishing destinations around the globe, the simplest, easiest, and most worry-free method is to enlist the services of a long-established and reputable booking agent who specializes in bonefishing. This helps ensure that you get to the best place at the best time with the best gear. When you use an agent, you have everything to gain and nothing to lose. Let's take a detailed look at the benefits of using a booking agent.

Cost: The price you pay is the same whether you book through an agent or directly with a lodge. Agents are paid a commission by the lodge after the trip is arranged. Let the agent track down space availability, guides, accommodations, airfare, and tackle recommendations. Your time is better spent preparing for the exciting trip that awaits you.

Experience: The biggest benefit of a booking agent is the agent's experience with and knowledge about all destinations. Many destinations have more than one lodge to choose from. Which is best? That depends on what you require in terms of accommodations, guides, species, season, and the type and style of fishing you expect to encounter. An agent will discuss your specific needs, desires, and options and make recommendations accordingly.

There are many subtle factors that help determine which lodge is best for you. Possible considerations might include travel time to

Tying and collecting saltwater flies is a mania unto itself.

Bonefishing is not a social sport. Miles of solitude await the flats angler.

and from fishing areas, availability of other species, level of guiding, difficulty of fishing, lodge access, and accommodations. Agents pride themselves on advising you on behind-the-scenes subtleties that can make a considerable difference in your level of enjoyment.

The level of day-to-day fishing at the typical lodge is dependent on many factors: guides, boats, equipment, tides, weather. The list goes on. Booking on your own often becomes a crapshoot. Why roll the dice against the house when you can *be* the house?

Unbiased Opinions and Recommendations: Agents do not usually have a financial stake in the lodges they represent. Therefore, they are not biased against providing honest facts that help you make an objective decision about where and when to fish. It is unlikely that a lodge would recommend that you visit another lodge because of better accommodations or guides but an agent would!

Agents are working as your representative when they book a lodge for you. They earn repeat customers by consistently offering good, honest advice and reliable information—everyone benefits.

An agent may sometimes suggest avoiding a specific destination, refuse to book a trip, or even cancel a pending trip if things aren't right. The agent's reputation is on the line; every recommendation is made carefully and with your best interest in mind.

If a problem arises, an agent has better leverage to seek resolution or even restitution from a lodge than does an individual. The agent is likely to have a long-established rapport with the lodge and the added advantage of volume to back up any claims. Also, a

Sailboarding, windsurfing, diving, beachcombing, sightseeing, snorkling, tennis, and swimming await the nonfishing visitor to bonefish country.

lodge might go out of its way to take especially good care of a client booked by one of its agents. Look at this as an insurance policy.

When agents come upon exciting new destinations, they offer their loyal clients first shot at them. This alone is priceless. A relatively small number of selected anglers are able to get in on the ground floor and experience the absolute best in fishing.

Pretrip Considerations: Many pretrip factors need to be considered for a trip to be successful. Before agents can book space, they must know your arrival and departure dates and the number of anglers. Inform the agent of your budget and your level of angling expertise. Be honest with your agent. First-time bonefishermen with limited casting and angling skills may be directed to a different location from the locations suggested for seasoned experts.

Nonanglers: The most often asked question is, "Where can I take my nonfishing partner?" This depends on the interests of the other person. If relaxing on a quiet beach under a palm tree with a book is ideal, then many angling lodges are perfect. If more diversity is desired, the field narrows. Several lodges in the Bahamas, for example, are well suited for couples or families. Tennis, shopping, beachcombing, sightseeing, snorkeling, and freshwater swimming pools await the nonfishing guest. Other lodges are strictly angling camps. An astute agent might tell a different story than the lodge.

Types of Flats: Some flats are wadeable, others are not. Flats may be grass, coral, sand, or mud. If you have a preference, state it. If you prefer to fish on foot, be certain that is possible. If you are a single paying a double occupancy price, know that you will share a boat, room, and guide with another angler unless you want to pay extra.

Boats: If possible, agents like to book clients to a lodge that offers specialty flats boats with fast, reliable motors that get you to your fishing and back quickly and safely.

Guides: Every lodge has a few ace guides, some very good guides, and a few trainee guides. Obviously, you want the best possible guide. You may not need the best or immediately recognize the difference, but a seasoned guide can be the deciding factor between success and failure. Good agents know the best guides; if they are available, the agent will book them for you.

Accommodations: Each destination has a few "best" cabanas or rooms. They might be preferred because of location, view, ventilation, air conditioning, or any number of other reasons. An enlightened agent knows which units are best.

Lodge Location: Is the lodge close to the fishing? If it takes an hour or more to get to the best water, that's two hours a day of travel time in a boat over sometimes rough water. That significantly cuts into your fishing time—and you'd better bring a good seat cushion!

Meals: Suppose there are two lodges in the same area with all things being equal except that one has a gourmet chef on staff and a reputation for excellent meals. Which would you choose? Probably the same one I would!

Travel Arrangements: What are the best connections to get you to your destination efficiently and comfortably? Perhaps there is a private airstrip that you can charter into, saving time and uncomfortable overland travel. There is a time to save money and a time

Astute booking agents put you in the best place. . .

. . .at the best time. . .

. . .with the best gear.

to save time and maximize comfort. Agents know or can find out the logistics, arrange all transfers, and send you step-by-step travel instructions and a printed itinerary. Guesswork and uncertainty are eliminated.

Tackle Advice: Agents provide a trip list, everything from footgear to fly patterns. If your guide says, "Pick any of those, they all work," it is a good omen for a successful flats trip. Conversely, nothing is more disheartening than going to the time and expense of stocking your fly box only to have your guide pooh-pooh your selection.

A good agent talks you through the hot fly patterns and the best tackle and accessories. Remember—few destinations have flies for sale. Don't short yourself on the most important item, at least from the bonefish's perspective!

Group Trips: Many agents, worldwide outfitters, and local fly fishing establishments offer group trips. This is an excellent way to break into the bonefishing travel scene, especially if you are traveling alone. Sometimes a pretrip question-and-answer slide show that covers tackle, knots, and fly tying is offered. Once on the trip, the trip leader helps facilitate everything from travel to fishing options and may present on-site angling discussions and casting instruction.

Ethics: Agents are in business to make money. The only thing they sell is their time and expertise. They have spent a great deal of time, money, and energy to learn what you need to know. It is unethical to consult an agent seeking detailed information and trip options and then book elsewhere or direct. If your selected agent is truthful, knowledgeable, and helpful, book through him. If not, find another agent.

Timing Is Everything: The seasons and weather are always a factor. Every location has peak times when the best fishing occurs. Your agent will tell you the best time to visit specific destinations.

How can you be certain to nail all this stuff down? You can't, and you often won't even if you book well in advance. Things often do not go according to plan in the tropics. The earlier you book, the better your chances of getting what you want.

The best lodges have a well-deserved reputation for service, attention to detail, knowledgeable guides, first-class accommodations, good gear, and excellent food service. Such lodges have built up a loyal repeat clientele that books the best times and guides year after year. The moral is that the early angler gets the best week, accommodations, and guide. Sometimes late cancellations open up prime space. Your agent can only do so much on short notice. If you want the best of the best, book a year in advance. If you book late, don't expect the beachfront bungalow and Bonefish Charlie to be waiting with his skiff. Be happy with what you get. You will still have a wonderful time.

Good luck! Have fun. Enjoy the fascinating and magical world of bonefishing with a fly!

Kevin Erickson
Tigard, Oregon
January 1999

Each destination has some accommodations and guides that are better than others. It is first come, first served.

Chapter 33

Safety

Safety should always be your foremost concern, especially when visiting remote areas where medical help is often unavailable or hours distant. The chances of illness, accident, and other life-threatening situations are very real possibilities at remote destinations. Look, listen, and think. You are your best protector. No one is going to look after you. You are responsible for your actions.

Many of the following ideas have been mentioned previously, but a refresher course in safety is always a good idea.

Sunshine

Sunshine is intense in the tropics. It can seriously burn your skin or cause heat stroke or even lead to cancer. Cover up. Long-sleeved shirts and long pants, flats gloves, and hats that fully protect the neck and ears are advised. Apply SPF 30 sunblock liberally and often, especially on your face and lips.

Ultraviolet radiation can be many times more intense on the beach and water than on land and is potentially dangerous to your eyes, even when it is cloudy. Always wear polarized glasses that block UV light. Glasses also protect your eyes from errant flies and help you spot fish. Always wear glasses when fishing or casting.

Stay hydrated. Drink plenty of water. Beer and soda do not do it. If you are prone to heat stroke, take proper precautions. Heat stroke is a life-threatening condition. The body becomes heated beyond its ability to cool itself. If you suspect heat stroke, cool down and seek medical help immediately.

When anglers walk across soft flats, they create a trail of mud; watch for aggressive sharks. Be especially careful when releasing bonefish in mud clouds when sharks or barracuda are present. Beware of stingrays (photo below), coral, sharks, etc. as you move across the flat.

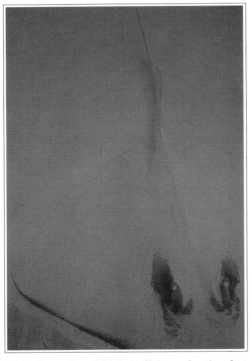

This channel at Bikini Atoll is productive, but rough coral, fast currents, and large sharks make it dangerous. Wade at your own risk!

Food and Drink

Be careful what you eat and drink! Contaminated food and water can cause life-threatening illness. It is advisable to carry a water filter, spare water, and food. Refer to the Yucatan chapter for additional information. Talk to your doctor.

Moving Water

Never underestimate the power of water or overestimate your strength and endurance. All water is potentially dangerous. Moving water, including surf and tides, is the most dangerous! Never turn your back on the surf. Sneaker waves can flatten your face onto coral or worse. Watch for sink holes, sharp coral, drop-offs, etc. Don't wade too deep or get too close to the reef edge.

Tides can and do move quickly, especially in restricted areas. They also rise and fall. Do not get trapped where you do not wish to be. Fast-moving tidal flows can drown you just like a river.

Wading

Watch where you step! Wear footgear that protects you from sharp coral, urchins, stingrays, etc. Shuffle your feet when stingrays are present. Do not wade too close to drop-offs, channels, cuts, etc. When wading soft flats, take small steps, which helps you stay balanced. Avoid wading in extremely soft areas. Soft banks can collapse, and it is possible to sink out of sight in holes covered with muck.

Sharks and barracuda usually want nothing to do with you, but some situations could put you in danger. When you are wading muddy flats where visibility is reduced, sharks may come to investigate. Be alert! Scare them off. When you wade deeper than your waist, especially near cuts, channels, and reefs, you have entered the territory of the big bad boys. When you are in deeper water, your visibility is reduced. Pay attention. If you feel threatened, move.

Tiny particles of coral have a habit of getting between your feet and your footwear. Remove grit at once. Neoprene socks help protect your feet from such grinding. If you still have problems, wear gaiters or neoprene cuffs. Prolonged exposure to salt water inside footwear can soften toenails. Remove your footwear as soon as possible. It doesn't hurt to air and dry your feet from time to time.

Transportation, Accommodations

Any mode of transportation—boats, airplanes, cars, trucks, all terrain vehicles, etc.—is dangerous. Operators, especially outside the United States, may not be properly trained in operation or safety. Equipment may be unsafe or in poor working condition. Accommodations may be unsafe and dangerous for many reasons. If you feel unsafe or threatened, take proper precautions or change your course of action. Don't be afraid to take control of a potentially dangerous situation.

Boating

Each time you step into a boat or travel by boat, you risk serious injury or worse. Always wear a life jacket—it could save your

Jerry Swanson

life. Outside the United States, life jackets may not be available. When you ask guides about them, they shrug and often say, "No use mon, sharks. They eat you anyway!" Ascertain whether or not life jackets are available before your trip. If they are not, bring your own. An inflatable snorkel vest may double as a life jacket in an emergency if it is Coast Guard approved.

Always be careful entering and exiting boats. If you enter a boat over the side, do so carefully and only if the boat is properly counterbalanced. Otherwise, it can tip over. When entering a boat from a pier, dock, or another boat, be careful that the boat does not move away with your feet halfway between the two. You could fall between the two boats or the boat and pier or dock and be crushed.

Never exit the boat to fish unless your guide tells you it is safe to do so. Never enter or exit from a moving boat. When traveling in a boat, keep a firm grip. Help the captain spot potentially dangerous objects, other boats, reefs, shallow areas, etc. Always stay alert. Consider a VHF radio, GPS, and compass. Be responsible for yourself.

Boats are usually the mode of travel in bonefish country. Each time you step into a boat or into any other vehicle or mode of transportation, you risk serious injury or worse. Life jackets are seldom available outside the U.S.

Handling Fish

Some species of fish are dangerous to handle, especially if they have sharp spines, fins, tails, gill plates, or teeth. When you are uncertain, ask your guide how to handle a fish. Have pliers handy and, perhaps, gloves. Barracuda and sharks demand respect regardless of their size and are best released without being handled. Let your guide do it. Sharks and barracuda can chomp off your arm—or worse!

The greatest potential danger from sharks and barracuda comes when you are releasing fish. Predators can be aggressive at this time, sometimes attempting to eat a fish at your feet. Do not put yourself in this potentially dangerous situation, especially in cloudy water. Sharks and barracuda do not know where the bonefish ends and your hand begins. Have a companion help scare off the intruder, or break off the fish, or, better yet, fish someplace else. Everyone loses when predators are conditioned to follow anglers for a meal.

Barracuda and sharks demand respect regardless of their size. It is best to let your guide handle them.

Always have a rain jacket handy and wear protective clothing.

Miscellaneous

Carry rain gear! A balmy 75-degree day can turn into blinding rain and a windstorm. Hypothermia is possible. Know how to recognize, avoid, and treat this condition. In the tropics, 62 degrees feels like 42 degrees You'll wish you had a stocking cap.

When casting, be aware of others, especially your guide. A fly zooming through the air is potentially very dangerous. Smash all barbs. Barbless flies are much easier to remove from yourself and your buddy. I could tell you how Jerry Swanson hooked himself in the tongue or how Gary Thompson drove around Seattle for over two hours looking for someone to remove a barbed fly that was double-hooked through his nose, but I will spare you the details. I can assure you that neither has fished a barbed fly since!

First Aid

Carry first aid supplies and know how to use them. Take a Red Cross first aid and CPR class. Your doctor can prescribe specific

Can you help us out here? We can't seem to locate our position or that school of bonefish on the map.

Do not go where you do not belong or where it is not safe to be. Look, listen, and think!

drugs in case you become ill. Carry these and all medicines with you on the airplane.

If you get coral cuts or abrasions, remove any coral, wash wounds thoroughly, and apply antiseptic immediately. If wounds become infected, get medical help immediately. Blood poisoning is serious!

Biting bugs (no-see-ums, sand flies, mosquitoes, etc.) can be a problem at some locations. I wear socks when tiny ankle biters are about. Repellent is sometimes needed. Tropical itch can be another bother. Carry an anti-itch lotion to treat bites. Cortisone cream relieves symptoms. An ounce of prevention is better than the cure.

Medical Insurance

U.S. medical insurance is not always valid outside the U.S. Supplemental medical insurance with specific out-of-country coverage, including medical evacuation, is advised. Some credit card companies offer foreign coverage. Doctors and hospitals outside the U.S. usually expect immediate cash payment for services. Infectious diseases such as cholera, hepatitus, or malaria may be present. Information on health matters can be obtained from the Center for Disease Control and Prevention on its international traveler's hotline, (404) 332-4559. Internet: http://www.cdc.gov.

Travel Documents

All travelers should carry a photocopy of their passport and credit cards separate from those documents. Know how to cancel credit cards. Carry only those items needed for your trip. Carry a legible copy of prescriptions for any medications, both trade and generic names, and carry 50 percent more of each medication than you need. Separate some in case of loss. If you are carrying syringes or an extensive medicine kit, an official letter from your doctor stating the reason for them is a good idea.

Personal Security

Whether you are in Beverly Hills or the back alleys of Calcutta, be alert and aware of your surroundings. Keep your valuables safe and out of sight. Don't flaunt anything of value. Keep valuables separated. Keep a low profile. Don't wander off after dark in potentially dangerous locales. Most importantly, don't unnecessarily put yourself in a potentially dangerous situation. Useful information on guarding valuables and protecting yourself while traveling abroad is provided in the Department of State pamphlets *A Safe Trip Abroad* and *Tips for Travelers to the Caribbean*. Both are available from the Superintendent of Documents, U.S. Government Printing Office, Washington, D.C. 20402.

Chapter 34

Last Cast!

Saltwater flats are often located at the edges of, or in the middle of, oceans, and oceans are *big*. Because the landscape is flat, space and distance is perceived as vast, almost endless. When remote open spaces are experienced, your insignificance is magnified, actually realized, and a sense of freedom prevails.

Time spent in this unique matrix of land, water, and sky invariably leads you to ponder the eternal questions of how and why and offers a chance to redefine and refresh dreams. It is also a time of discovery. Pretend you are a bonefish, crab, frigate bird, or mangrove. Immerse yourself into another world. There are many more questions than answers.

The next time fishing is too good to be true give yourself a handicap, or better yet, set down the rod. View the world through a camera lens, the eyes of a child, or your own eyes! Your imagination is the limit. Keep an open mind. Everything evolves. Old truths become old wives' tales. Beware of absolute statements—eventually they are absolutely wrong.

Tread lightly. Flats are fragile ecosystems that are easily and often irreparably damaged by man and machine. Realize that you are an unwelcome intruder. Treat everything with respect. "Take only pictures, leave only footprints," is appropriate, but even then, be careful where you place your feet!

Foot traffic can be devastating to corals and other bottom-dwelling organisms. Thousands can be destroyed with every step! Brittle coral that crunches beneath your feet should be avoided. Do not step on sea fans, sea cucumbers, anemones, sponges, stars,

Flats anglers do not want the day to end and they cannot wait until tomorrow. Last cast!

crabs, and other obvious creatures. Walk on sandy areas whenever possible, or fish from the boat.

If the boat prop is disturbing bottom strata and leaving a mud trail, it is probably running in water that is too shallow. Pole the boat to deeper water. Don't anchor on a reef—it is a-l-i-v-e! As a society and species, we must show more understanding and compassion for other life forms. Resources are not unlimited and solely for our consumption, exploitation, and amusement.

Do not leave anything behind that is not immediately consumed by the ecosystem, including monofilament. Monofilament is like a land mine. Any creature that comes in contact with it will most likely be maimed or killed. *This is especially true of fluorocarbon leader material because it does not break down.* Dispose of it properly!

Practice proper fish handling, and do not handle too many. "How was fishing?" is an innocent "how are you?" question, but it invariably invokes a numbers response, and little else. Such responses remind me of the angler who passed onto other flats.

Upon arrival at his final destination, he proclaimed to be a fly fisherman. His guest escorted him to the most beautiful bonefish flat imaginable where he hooked a seven-pound bonefish on the first, second, and third casts. He paused to wonder if he was indeed in the "bad" place. His host appeared and commanded him to "keep fishing."

Anglers go through phases. At first the goal is simply to catch a fish, then the biggest, then lots of big fish, then the smartest fish. Some unfortunate souls have to catch *all* the fish. What comes after you have progressed though the many stages? Nature constantly presents exciting tangents to explore and riddles to solve. You develop a new awareness and begin to understand that fascinating thoughts, ideas, and knowledge come at you from multi levels. Sometimes the best insights and ideas occur as you daydream. Trace the trail of a hermit crab across the sand, ponder wave patterns, smell the wind, or simply watch coral grow. You inevitably come away with a better understanding of nature and yourself.

It is not easy for an angler to skip some of the fishing milestones and get into the real enjoyment of the sport. I was lucky. I learned at an early age that fish may be the focal point, but you don't have to hook a zillion to have a great time or to enhance the learning experience. Quite the contrary. Limiting the catch expands your enjoyment and understanding, and helps you enjoy the true essence of fly fishing.

Whether you are fishing for bonefish or pan fish, ask yourself why you are really there. What is _most_ important? Most anglers realize there is more to fishing than landing fish. Take time to savor the sunrise and contemplate the setting sun. Enjoy and respect the miracle of life.

All bonefish are precious. Treat them with care and respect. Land them quickly, _keep them in the water, and release them safely and unharmed._

Bibliography

Books

_____. *1995 World Record Game Fishes.* Florida: International Game Fish Association, 1995.

_____. *Atlas of the Oceans.* London: Chancellor Press, 1996.

_____. *Scarring of Florida's Seagrasses: Assessment and Management Options.* Florida: Dept. of Environmental Protection, 1995.

_____. *The American Medical Association Encyclopedia of Medicine.* New York: Random House, 1989.

Babson, Stanley M. *Bonefishing.* New York, New York: Winchester Press, 1973.

Baker, Christopher P. *Cuba Handbook.* California: Moon Publications, Inc., 1997.

Barrett, Kirk. *Belize by Kayak: A Guide for Sea Kayaking in Belize.* Iowa: Reef-Link Kayaking, 1994.

Bay, Kenneth E. *Salt Water Flies.* New York: J.B. Lippincott Co., 1972.

Beresky, Andrew E. *Fodor's South America.* New York, New York: Fodor's Travel Publications, Random House, 1991.

Booth, Thomas H. *Adventure Guide to the South Pacific.* New Jersey: Hunter Publishing, Inc., 1988.

Brooks, Joe. *Salt Water Game Fishing.* New York, New York: Harper and Row Publishers, 1968.

Brown, Dick. *Fly Fishing for Bonefish.* New York: Lyons & Burford, 1993.

Carpin, Sarah. *Seychelles.* Illinois: Passport Books, 1997.

Cooke, Tom and Onalee, Skinner, Roland, and Darby, Bryan. *Picturesque Bermuda.* Bermuda: Picturesque, 1996.

Cole, John and Pollard, Hawk. *West of Key West.* Pennsylvania: Stackpole Books, 1996.

Currier, Jeff. *Currier's Quick and Easy Guide to Saltwater Fly Fishing.* Montana: Greycliff Publishing, 1998.

Dimock, A.W. *The Book of the Tarpon.* New Jersey: Meadow Run Press, 1990.

Goodson, Gar. *Fishes of the Atlantic Coast.* California: Stanford University Press, 1985.

_____. *The Many-Splendored Fishes of Hawaii.* California: Stanford University Press, 1985.

Grant, Ern. *Grant's Guide to Fishes.* Australia: E.M. Grant Pty. Limited, 1993.

Hole, Chris. *Exotic Fly-Fishing in the South Seas.* Australia: Kangaroo Press, 1996.

Jones, Tom. *Bahamas & Caribbean Pilot's Aviation Guide.* Georgia: Pilot Publications, Ltd., 1995.

Kaplan, Eugene H. *Southeastern and Caribbean Seashores.* Boston, Massachusetts: Houghton Mifflin Company, 1988.

Kreh, Lefty. *Fly Fishing in Salt Water.* New York: The Lyons Press, 1997.

Kumiski, Captain John A. *Flyrodding Florida Salt.* Florida: Argonaut Publishing, 1995.

Mallan, Chicki. *Belize Handbook.* Chico, California: Moon Publications, 1991.

_____. *Yucatan Handbook.* Chico, California: Moon Publications, 1991.

McClane, A.J. *McClane's Field Guide to Saltwater Fishes of North America.* New York: Holt, Rinehart and Winston, 1978.

McClane, A. J. and Gardner, Keith. *McClane's Game Fish of North America.* New York, New York: Time Books, 1984.

Porter, Darwin. *Frommer's Bermuda and the Bahamas 1991-1992.* New York, New York: Prentice Hall, 1991.

Richards Carl. *Prey.* New York: Lyons & Burford, 1995.

Roberts Jr., George V. *A Fly-Fisher's Guide to Saltwater Naturals and Their Imitation.* Maine: Ragged Mountain Press, 1994.

Samson, Jack. *Permit on a Fly.* Pennsylvania: Stackpole Books, 1996.

_____. *Saltwater Fly Fishing.* Harrisburg, Pennsylvania: Stackpole Books, 1991.

Sargeant, Frank. *The Tarpon Book: A Complete Angler's Guide.* Florida: Larsen's Outdoor Publishing, 1991.

Smith, Martha K. *The Cayman Islands: The Beach & Beyond.* New Jersey: Cuchipanda, Inc., 1996.

Sosin, Mark and Kreh, Lefty. *Fishing the Flats.* Piscataway, New Jersey: Winchester Press, 1983.

Sparano, Vin T. *The American Fisherman's Fresh and Saltwater Guide.* New York, New York: Winchester Press, 1976.

Stanley, David. *Micronesia Handbook.* Chico, California: Moon Publications, 1989.

Swisher, Doug and Richards, Carl. *Backcountry Fly Fishing in Salt Water.* New York: Lyons & Burford, 1995.

Vien, Caroline and Théroux, Alain. *Cancún/Cozumel.* Canada: Ulysses Travel Publications, 1997.

Voss, Gilbert L. *Seashore Life of Florida and the Caribbean.* Miami, Florida; Banyan Books, Inc., 1976.

Waterman, Charles F. *Modern Fresh and Saltwater Fly Fishing.* New York, New York: Winchester Press, 1972.

Wheeler, Tony and Keller, Nancy. *Rarotonga & the Cook Islands.* Australia: Lonely Planet, 1994.

Articles

Anderson, George. "Permit." *Fly Fisherman,* March 1991: 48-52, 61-63, 96.

Babson, Stanley M. "Bonefish!" *Fly Fisherman,* Winter, 1974.

Beck, Barry & Cathy. "Florida Keys on a Budget." *Fly Fish America,* Sept.-Oct. 1996: 12-13, 37.

Bednar, Captain Michael. "Blind-Casting for Bonefish." *American Angler,* Nov.-Dec. 1993: 36-40.

Benchley, Peter. "Swimming with Sharks." *Audubon,* May-June. 1998: 52-57.

Blanton, Dan. "In Pursuit of Permit." *Saltwater Fly Fishing,* July 1992: 32-39, 58-59.

_____. "Permit: Phantom on the Flats." *Fly Fish America,* Sept.-Oct. 1997: 34-36.

_____. "Ripping Lips Off." *Fly Fish America,* Sept.-Oct. 1997: 4-5.

Brown, Dick. "Windy-Day Bonefish Tactics." *Fly Fishing in Salt Waters,* Sept.-Oct. 1997: 76-79.

Carter, Art. "Showboat Bones." *Sporting Classics,* March-April, 1992.

Cole, John N. and Greenberg, Jerry. "The Magic of Mangroves." *Audubon* Mar.-Apr. 1997: 46-52.

Curcione, Nick. "Fishing the Southern California Surf." *Fly Fishing Quarterly,* Winter, 1991.

Emory, Jerry. "Where the Sky was Born." *Wilderness,* Summer 1989: 55-56.

Engle, Ed; Garrison, Becky; Krumm, Bob and Soucie, Gary. "A Special Section: Guided Fly Fishing." *American Angler,* Jan.-Feb. 1998: 41-52.

Fernandez, J.M. "Chico." "The Final Approach." *Saltwater Fly Fishing,* May 1992: 32-37, 59.

_____. "World of the Bonefish." *Fly Fishing Quarterly,* Spring, 1989.

_____. "World of the Bonefish." *Fly Fishing Quarterly,* Spring, 1990.

_____. "World of the Bonefish." *Fly Fishing Quarterly,* Summer, 1990.

_____. "World of the Bonefish." *Fly Fishing Quarterly,* Winter, 1990.

Fong, Michael. "Big Bonefish." *Fly Fisherman,* July, 1991.

Fowler, Sheri. "King Fish." *Texas Monthly,* August 1993: 54-59.

Franklin, Harlan. "Fly Fishing in the Keys." *Fly Fishing in Salt Waters,* Jan.-Feb. 1995: 29-31.

Gerber, Dan. "Permit: The Most Difficult Fish in the World." *Sports Afield,* Sept. 1994: 92-95.

Hand, A.J. "Budget Bonefish." *Flyfishing,* June 1988: 90-91, 43-44.

Hoffman, Spencer. "Fiji Time." *Fly Fishing in Salt Waters,* Jan.-Feb. 1998: 44-47, 50.

Howells, Bob. "The Hyperactive's Caribbean." *Outside,* December 1995: 114-118.

Hunter, Bill. "Kanton Island." *Fly Fishing Saltwater,* June-July 1994: 38-45.

Jaworowski, Ed. "What You Need To Know About Lines." *Fly Fishing in Salt Waters,* Jan.-Feb. 1998: 22-25.

Kreshpane, David G. "Dave's Hermit Crab." *Saltwater Fly Fishing,* Nov.-Dec. 1997: 34-35.

Kumiski, Capt. John A. "Guided Principles." *Saltwater Fly Fishing,* Feb.-Mar. 1997: 20-23, 90.

Leary, Tim. "Gimme Shelter: Hiding from the Sun to Save Your Hide." *Fly Rod & Reel,* Mar.-Apr. 1998: 46-47, 75-76.

Lee, Art. "Bonefish with a Bonus." *Fly Fisherman,* March, 1979.

Lyle, James D. "Tracking Bahamian Bonefish." *Saltwater Fly Fishing,* Sept. 1994: 52-59, 78-79.

Maisey, John G. "The Oldest Bonefish?" *Tropical Fish Hobbyist,* July 1994: 204-206.

Mathews, Craig. "Bonefish Foods." *Fly Fisherman,* February, 1992.

Mazerand, Serge. "Trevally Hunt." *Fly Fishing in Salt Waters,* Sept.-Oct. 1997: 44-45, 47.

Miller, Ron. "Walk and Wade the Florida Keys." *Saltwater Fly Fishing,* Apr.-May 1997: 60-61.

Mitchell, Ed. "Unmasking Unfamiliar Beaches." *Saltwater Fly Fishing,* Summer 1995: 32-35, 74-76.

Moore, Jody. "Florida's Silver Prince." *Fly Fishing in Salt Waters,* Jan.-Feb. 1995: 38-43.

Moser, Don. "Seeking Tarpon." *Sea Frontiers,* Jan.-Feb. 1993: 50-57.

Navarre, Carl. "Bonefishing in the Bahamas." *Fly Fisherman,* Winter, 1979.

_____. "Great Waters: Florida Keys." *Fly Fisherman,* Winter, 1980.

Olch, Jonathan. "Permit Mystique—Angler Madness." *Flyfishing,* Dec. 1993: 66-69.

Oswald, Tony. "Belize, Please." *Flyfishing,* Feb. 1990: 4-5, 22-23.

Profumo, David. "Bones of Contention." *Departures,* Date unknown.

Randolph, John. "Ascension Bay." *Fly Fisherman,* March, 1990.

Ross, Dr. David A. "Fish Senses: Smell and Taste." *Saltwater Fly Fishing,* Nov.-Dec. 1997: 6-9.

Ross, Dr. David A. "Tidal Currents." *Saltwater Fly Fishing,* Spring 1996: 16-19.

Ruoff, Rick. "Los Roques." *Fly Fisherman,* March, 1989.

Rützler, Klaus and Feller, Ilka C. "Caribbean Mangrove Swamps." *Scientific American,* March 1996: 94-99.

Samarri, Fariss. "Helping Urchins May Benefit Coral." *Sea Frontiers,* Winter 1995: 16-17.

Samson, Jack. "Jacks or Better." *Fly Fishing in Salt Waters,* Sept.-Oct. 1997: 42-43, 46.

_____. "Permit Applications." *Saltwater Fly Fishing,* Summer 1996: 40-45.

_____. "Sun, Salt and Singing Reels." *Fly Rod & Reel,* Jan.-Feb. 1998: 56-57, 85-87.

Sharpe, Christina. "The Lower Keys on a Low Budget." *Fly Fishing in Salt Waters,* Jan.-Feb. 1998: 68-71.

Shukman, Henry. "A Slow Boat to Cat Island." *Condé Nast Traveler,* April 1996: 118-121, 154-159.

Smith III, Robblee, Wanless, and Doyle. "Mangroves, Hurricanes and Lightning Strikes." *Bioscience,* Apr. 1994: 50-57.

Sosin, Mark. "The Challenge of Bonefishing. *Fly Fisherman,* January-February, 1979.

Stearns, Bob. "Pre-Trip Trouble-Shooting." *Saltwater Fly Fishing,* Feb.-Mar. 1997: 26-29.

_____. "Introduction to Saltwater." *Fly Fishing Quarterly,* Spring, 1989.

_____. "Saltwater Guide: Part V." *Fly Fishing Quarterly,* Fall, 1990.

Stewart, Doug. "Armed but not dangerous: Is the octopus really the invertebrate intellect of the undersea world?" *National Wildlife,* Feb.-Mar. 1997: 32-40.

Tabory, Lou. "Working the Edge: How to Flyfish the Coast—with No Boat, No Guide and No Second Mortgage." *Outdoor Life,* April 1996: 66-69.

Thornton, Jim. "The Dark Side of the Sun: Summer Bummers." *Men's Journal,* June-July 1998: 147.

Waldie, Scott. "The Ghosts of Christmas." *Sporting Classics,* July-August, 1989.

Waller, Lani. "Belize." *Fly Fisherman,* March 1997: 82-85, 103-107.

Weinstein, Steve. "A Game of Inches." *Fly Fishing in Salt Waters,* Sept.-Oct. 1997: 48-53.

Williams, Ted. "Wild Bonefish, Tarpon and Sex in Venezuela." *Fly Rod & Reel,* Nov.-Dec. 1996: 34-37.

_____. "Dreaming of a White Christmas." *Fly Rod & Reel,* November-December, 1991.

Winsor, Curtin. "Bonefish." *Fly Fisherman,* March, 1989.

Wolverton, Mike. "The Fictitious Phantom." *Flyfishing,* Dec. 1995: 18-19.

Scientific Papers

Broadhead, Gordon C. and Mefford, H.P. "The Migration and Exploitation of the Black Mullet, *Mugil Cephalus L.,* in Florida, as Determined from Tagging During 1949-1953" *Florida Board of Conservation Technical Series.* No. 18 April 1956.

Burger, Gerald E. "Age, Growth, Food Habits and Reproduction of Bonefish, *Albula Vulpes,* in South Florida Waters." Florida Marine Research Publications, St. Petersburg, Florida: Florida Department of Natural Resources. 1974.

Burklew, Mary Ann and Morton, Rose Ann. "The Toxicity of Florida Gulf Puffers." *Toxicon* Vol. 9 1971: 205-210.

Camp, David K. "Stomatopod Crustacea" *Memoirs of the Hourglass Cruises.* Vol. III Part II May 1973.

Carlton, Jedfrey M. "A Guide to Common Florida Salt Marsh and Mangrove Vegetation" *Florida Marine Research Publications.* No. 6, March 1975.

_____ and Moffler, Mark D. "Propagation of Mangroves by Air-layering" *Environmental Conservation.* Vol. 5 No. 2 Summer 1978.

Colton, Douglas Earl. "Movements and Food Habits of the Bonefish, *Albula Vulpes* (Linnaeus) in Bahamian Waters." Florida Institute of Technology. (0473) Volume 43/03-B Of Dissertation Abstracts International, page 614. 76 pages. 1982.

_____ and Alevizon, William S. "Feeding Ecology of Bonefish in Bahamian Waters." Melbourne, Florida: Dept. of Biological Sciences, Florida Institute of Technology. 1983.

Crabtree, Roy E., Snodgrass, Derke and Harnden, Christopher W. "Maturation and Reproductive Seasonality in Bonefish, *Albula vulpes*, from the Waters of the Florida Keys" *Fishery Bulletin.* 1997.

_____. "Maturation and Reproductive Seasonality in Bonefish, *Albula vulpes*, from the Waters of the Florida Keys." *Fishery Bulletin,* 1997.

_____, Cyr, Edward C. and Dean, John M. "Age and Growth of Tarpon, *Megalops atlanticus*, from South Florida Waters" *Fishery Bulletin.* 1995.

_____, Snodgrass, Derke, Harnden, Christopher W. and Stevens, Connie. "Age, Growth, and Mortality of Bonefish, *Albula vulpes*, from the Waters of the Florida Keys" *Fishery Bulletin.* 1996.

_____, Cyr, Bishop, Falkenstein and Dean. "Age and Growth of Tarpon, *Megalops atlanticus*, larvae in the Eastern Gulf of Mexico, with Notes on Relative Abundance and Probable Spawning Areas" *Environmental Biology of Fishes.* Vol. 35 1992: 241-249.

Dufour, Vincent and Galzin, René. "Colonization Patterns of Reef Fish Larvae to the Lagoon at Moorea Island, French Polynesia" *Marine Ecology Progress Series.* Vol. 102 1993: 143-152.

Eldred, Bonnie. "A Report on the Shrimps (*Penaeidae*) Collected from the Tortugas Controlled Area" *Florida Board of Conservation Special Scientific Report.* No. 2 1959.

_____. "Larval Bonefish, *Albula Vulpes* (Linnaeus, 1758), (Albulidae) in Florida and Adjacent Waters" *Florida Board of Conservation Leaflet Series Vol. IV-Immature Vertebrates.* Part 1 (Pisces) No. 3 July 1967.

_____. "Larval Tarpon, *Megalops Atlanticus* Valenciennes, (Megalopidae) in Florida Waters" *Florida Board of Conservation Leaflet Series Vol. IV-Immature Vertebrates.* Part 1 (Pisces) No. 4 August 1967.

_____. "First Record of a Larval Tarpon, *Megalops Atlanticus* Valenciennes, from the Gulf of Mexico" *Florida Board of Conservation Leaflet Series Vol. IV-Immature Vertebrates.* Part 1 (Pisces) No. 7 August 1968.

Engstrom, Norman A. "Depth Limitation of a Tropical Intertidal Xanthid Crab, *Cataleptodius Floridanus,* and a Shallow Water Majid, *Pitho Aculeata:* Results of a Caging Experiment." DeKalb, Illinois: Dept. of Biological Sciences, Northern Illinois University. 1983.

Erdman, D. S. "Notes on Biology of Bonefish and Its Sports Fishery in Puerto Rico." Paper prepared for 5th International Game Fish Conference. Miami, Florida. 1960.

Fitch, John E. "Life History Notes and the Early Development of the Bonefish, *Albula Vulpes* (Linnaeus)." California Division of Fish and Game. 1949.

Florida Marine Fisheries Commission. "Investigations into near-shore and estuarine gamefish distribution and abundance, ecology, life history and population genetics" *Research on Abundance, Distribution and Life History of Tarpon and Bonefish in Florida.*

Futch, Rena Barco and Bruger, Gerard E. "Age, Growth and Reproduction of Red Snapper in Florida Waters" *Florida Sea Grant College Program Report.* No. 17 Nov. 1976.

Futch, Charles R. "The Blue Crab in Florida" *Salt Water Fisheries Leaflet 1.* Oct. 1965.

_____ and Torpey, John M. "The Red Snapper—A Valuable Marine Resource" *Salt Water Fisheries Leaflet 4.* April 1966.

Heemstra, Phillip C. "A Field Key to the Florida Sharks" *Florida Board of Conservation Technical Series.* No. 45 May 1965.

Hildebrand, Samuel F. "Family *Albulidae*" *Fishing of the Western North Atlantic,* pages 132-147. Memoir Sears Foundation. 1963.

Hollister, Gloria. "A Fish Which Grows by Shrinking." *Bulletin of the New York Zoological Society.* May-June, 1936.

Ingle, Hutton and Topp. "Results of the Tagging of Salt Water Fishes in Florida" *Florida Board of Conservation Technical Series.* No. 38 Sept. 1962.

Marshall, Arthur R. "A Survey of the Snook Fishery of Florida, with Studies of the Biology of the Principal Species, *Centropomus undecimalis* (Bloch)" *Florida Board of Conservation Technical Series.* No. 22B March 1958.

Mojica, Raymond Jr., Shenker, Jonathan M., Harnden, Christopher W., and Wagner, Daniel E. "Recruitment of Bonefish, *Albula vulpes*, around Lee Stocking Island, Bahamas" *Fishery Bulletin.* 1995.

Murphy, Michael D. and Taylor, Ronald G. "Reproduction, Growth, and Mortality of Red Drum, Sciaenops ocellatus, in Florida Waters" *Fishery Bulletin.* 1997.

Pfeiler, Edward. "Effect of Salinity on Water and Salt Balance in Metamorphosing Bonefish (*Albula*) Leptocephali" *J. Exp. Mar. Biol. Ecol.* Vol. 82 1984: 183-190.

_____. "Energetics of Metamorphosis in Bonefish (*Albula sp.*) Leptocephali: Role of Keratan Sulfate Glycosaminoglycan." *Fish Physiology and Biochemistry* Vol. 15 No. 4 1996: 359-362.

_____. "Salinity Tolerance of Leptocephalous Larvae and Juveniles of the Bonefish (Albulidae: *Albula*) from the Gulf of California." *J. Exp. Mar. Biol. Ecol.* Vol. 52 1981: 37-45.

_____. "Changes in Water and Salt Content During Metamorphosis of Larval Bonefish (*Albula*)." Bulletin of Marine Science, 34(2) 177-184. 1984.

_____. "Salinity Tolerance of Leptocephalous Larvae and Juveniles of the Bonefish (Albulidae: *Albula)* From the Gulf of California." Guaymas, Sonora, Mexico: Institute Technology de Estudios Superiores de Monterrey. 1981.

_____. "Inshore Migration, Seasonal Distribution and Size of Larval Bonefish, *Albula,* in the Gulf of California." Guaymas, Sonora, Mexico: Institute Technology de Estudios Superiores de Monterrey. 1984.

Pfeiler, Mendoza and Manrique. "Premetamorphic Bonefish (*Albula* sp.) Leptocephali from the Gulf of California with Comments on Life History" *Environmental Biology of Fishes.* Vol. 21 No. 4 1988: 241-249.

_____, Mendoza, Angel, Miguel, and Manrique, Fernando A. "Premetamorphic *(Albula sp.)* Leptocephali from the Gulf of California with Comments on Life History." Guaymas, Sonora, Mexico: Dept. of Biology, University of Puerto Rice. 1988.

Phillips, Ronald C. "Observations on the Ecology and Distribution of the Florida Seagrasses" *Florida Board of Conservation Professional Papers Series.* No. 2 Oct. 1960.

_____. "Notes on the Marine Flora of the Marquesas Keys, Florida" *Journal of the Florida Academy of Sciences.*

Rivas, Luis R. and Warlen, Stanley M. "Systematics and Biology of the Bonefish *Albula Nemoptera* (Fowler)." Pascagoula, Mississippi: Bureau of Commercial Fisheries Exploratory Fishing Base. 1967.

_____. "Systematics and Biology of the Bonefish, *Albula Nemoptera.*" *U.S. Fish and Wildlife Service Fishery Bulletin* Vol. 66 No. 2 May 1967: 251-257.

Robertson, Green and Victor. "Temporal Coupling of Production and Recruitment of Larvae of a Caribbean Reef Fish" *Ecology.* Vol. 69 No. 2 April 1988: 370-381.

Savage, Thomas. "Florida Mangroves: A Review" *Leaflet Series: Vol. VII-Marine Plants.* Sept. 1972.

Shaklee, James G. and Tamaru, Clyde S. "Biochemical and Morphological Evolution of Hawaiian Bonefishes *(Albula)*." Kaneohe, Hawaii: Dept. of Zoology, University of Hawaii. 1981.

Silk, Steve. "Where the Sky is Born" *Houston Chronicle.* 5 July 1992: 2H-5H.

_____. "Yucatan's No-Man's Land" *Hartford Courant.*

Smith, Kenneth N. and Herrnkind, William F. "Predation of Early Juvenile Spiny Lobsters *Panulirus argus* (Latreille): Influence of Size and Shelter" *J. Exp. Mar. Biol. Ecol.* Vol. 157 1992: 3-18.

Springer, Victor G. and McErlean, Andrew J. "Tagging of Great Barracuda, *Sphyraena barracuda* (Walbaum)" *Transactions of the American Fisheries Society.* Vol. 90 No. 4 Oct. 1961.

_____. "Spawning Seasons and Growth of the Code Goby, *Gobiosoma Robustum* (Pisces: Gobiidae), in the Tampa Bay Area" *Tulane Studies in Zoology.* Vol. 9 No. 2 Nov. 1961.

Tangley, Laura. "A New Era for Biosphere Reserves." *Bioscience* Vol. 38 No. 3 March 1988: 148-155.

Thompson, Bruce A. and Deegan, Linda A. _Distribution of Ladyfish (Elops Sayrus) and Bonefish (Albula Vulpes) Leptocephali in Louisiana._ Bulletin of Marine Science. 32(4): 936-939. 1982

Thompson, Ronald W. "Marine Recreational Fishing in the Bahamas—A Case Study" _Proceedings of the 39th Gulf and Caribbean Fisheries Institute._

_____. "Marine Recreational Fishing in the Bahamas—A Case Study" _Proceedings of the 39th Gulf and Caribbean Fisheries Institute._

Thorrold, Shenker, Wishinski, Mojica and Maddox. "Larval Supply of Shorefishes to Nursery Habitats around Lee Stocking Island, Bahamas. I. Small-scale distribution patterns" _Marine Biology._ Vol. 118 1994: 555-566.

Tsukamoto, Y. and Okiyama, M. "Metamorphosis of the Pacific Tarpon, _Megalops Cyprinoides_ (Elopiformes, Megalopidae) with Remarks on Development Patterns in the Elopomorpha" _Bulletin of Marine Science._ Vol. 60 No. 1 1997: 23-36.

Volpe, Alfred V. "Aspects of the Biology of the Common Snook, _Centropomus undecimalis_ (Bloch) of Southwest Florida" _Florida Board of Conservation Technical Series._ No. 31A June 1959.

Warmke, Germaine L. and Erdman, Donald S. "Records of Marine Mollusks Eaten by Bonefish in Puerto Rican Waters." San Juan, Puerto Rico: University of Puerto Rice and Division of Fisheries and Wildlife, Dept. of Agriculture. The Nautilus. April, 1963.

Wheaton, Jennifer Lee. "Observations on the Octocoral Fauna of Southeast Florida's Outer Slope and Fore Reef Zones" _Caribbean Journal of Science._ Vol. 23 No. 2 1987: 306-312.

World Conservation Monitoring Centre. "Descriptions of Natural World Heritage Properties" _http://www.wcmc.org.uk/ protected_areas/data/wh/sianka'a.html._ May 12 1997.

Index